Science for Segregation

CRITICAL AMERICA

General Editors: Richard Delgado and Jean Stefancic

In the Silicon Valley of Dreams:
Environmental Injustice,
Immigrant Workers, and the
High-Tech Global Economy
David N. Pellow and
Lisa Sun-Hee Park

Mixed Race America and the Law:
A Reader
Kevin R. Johnson

Critical Race Feminism:
A Reader, Second Edition
Edited by Adrien Katherine Wing

Murder and the Reasonable Man:
Passion and Fear in the
Criminal Courtroom
Cynthia K. Lee

Success without Victory:
Lost Legal Battles and the
Long Road to Justice in America
Jules Lobel

Greasers and Gringos: Latinos, Law,
and the American Imagination
Steven W. Bender

Saving Our Children
from the First Amendment
Kevin W. Saunders

Elusive Citizenship:
Immigration, Asian Americans,
and the Paradox of Civil Rights
John S. W. Park

Truth, Autonomy, and Speech: Feminist
Theory and the First Amendment
Susan H. Williams

Legal Education and the Reproduction
of Hierarchy: A Polemic against the
System, A Critical Edition
Duncan Kennedy,
with commentaries by Paul Carrington,
Peter Gabel, Angela Harris and
Donna Maeda, and Janet Halley

America's Colony: The Political
and Cultural Conflict between the
United States and Puerto Rico
Pedro A. Malavet

Alienated: Immigrant Rights, the
Constitution, and Equality in America
Victor C. Romero

The Disability Pendulum:
The First Decade of the Americans
with Disabilities Act
Ruth Colker

Lawyers' Ethics and the Pursuit
of Social Justice: A Critical Reader
Edited by Susan D. Carle

Rethinking Commodification:
Cases and Readings in Law and Culture
Edited by Martha M. Ertman
and Joan C. Williams

The Derrick Bell Reader
Edited by Richard Delgado
and Jean Stefancic

Science for Segregation: Race, Law,
and the Case against Brown v. Board
of Education
John P. Jackson Jr.

Science for Segregation

*Race, Law, and the Case against
Brown v. Board of Education*

John P. Jackson Jr.

NEW YORK UNIVERSITY PRESS

New York and London

NEW YORK UNIVERSITY PRESS
New York and London
www.nyupress.org

Library of Congress Cataloging-in-Publication Data
Jackson, John P., 1961–
Science for segregation : race, law, and the case against
Brown v. Board of Education / John P. Jackson Jr.
p. cm.
Includes bibliographical references and index.
ISBN–13: 978–0–8147–4271–6 (cloth : alk. paper)
ISBN–10: 0–8147–4271–8 (cloth : alk. paper)
1. African Americans—Segregation—History—20th century.
2. African Americans—Legal status, laws, etc.—History—
20th century. 3. Racism—United States—History—20th century.
4. Science—Political aspects—United States—History—20th century.
5. Eugenics—United States—History—20th century.
6. Segregation in education—Law and legislation—United States.
7. Brown, Oliver, 1918—Trials, litigation, etc. 8. Topeka (Kan.).
Board of Education—Trials, litigation, etc. 9. United States—Race
relations—History—20th century. I. Title.
E185.61.J145   2005
305.8'00973'09045—dc22   2005007376

New York University Press books are printed on acid-free paper,
and their binding materials are chosen for strength and durability.

Manufactured in the United States of America
10 9 8 7 6 5 4 3 2 1

To my mother, the Rev. Margaret B. Jackson,
my sister Mary J. Fortune, and the memory
of my father, John P. Jackson Sr.

Contents

Acknowledgments

The list is long. Librarians at Florida State University and the University of Colorado–Boulder have been tremendous resources for me, as have the innumerable archivists at the University of North Carolina–Chapel Hill, Duke University, the Hoover Institution for War and Peace at Stanford University, the Stanford University Archives, the Manuscript Division of the Library of Congress, and the National Anthropological Archives at the Smithsonian Institution. The National Science Foundation's Science and Technology Studies Office made much of this archival research possible with a postdoctoral fellowship in the 2000–2001 academic year.

NYU Press has been tremendously supportive of my work. Richard Delgado and Jean Stefancic have been constant sources of encouragement. Ilene Kalish and her assistant Salwa Jabado have been a patient and able editorial team.

I presented portions of this work at a number of academic conferences and the book is better for it. I would like to thank those who shared their thoughts at the History of Science Society meetings in Kansas City (1998) and Vancouver (2000); the Cheiron conferences at Richmond (1997), Ottawa (1999), Portland (2000), and Bloomington (2001); the Rhetoric Society of America meeting in Las Vegas (2002); the National Communication Association meeting in New Orleans (2002). Two workshops I attended were especially helpful for comments and criticisms: Evelynn Hammonds's meeting on race and science at MIT in 2001 and a meeting on the Massive Resistance movement at the Department of American Studies at the University of Sussex in Brighton, United Kingdom. I also need to thank the "underground" historians of science here at the University of Colorado–Boulder: Leland Giovannelli and Susan D. Jones.

A number of people have been researching these people I have dubbed the "segregationist scientists." They have been open about their work, shared their sources with me, and criticized my work when they thought criticism would make it better. This book is much, much better because of Kevin Coogan, Keith Hurt, and Barry Mehler. Every so often a package would arrive from the selfless Kevin Yelvington and would contain materials and information that greatly enriched this final product. Bill Tucker scooped me on all the good quotations from the archives in his books, but I have leaned on them heavily for information and inspiration. Andrew Winston deserves a special mention. Andrew's deep knowledge of right-wing scientists, his generosity in sharing that knowledge, and his absolute integrity have inspired me at every turn.

My deepest thanks go, once again, to my family. My children, Maggie and Jack, are constantly occurring miracles; I can't think of anyone I'd rather spend time with. Any worth in my work or in me owes to my wife, Michele. I cannot conceive of a life without her. Once again, thank you my love.

I was born on "Race and Reason Day," the very day Carleton Putnam stood on the podium in Jackson, Mississippi, and preached his gospel of hate. This book is dedicated to my sister Mary J. Fortune; my mother, Margaret B. Jackson; and the memory of my father, John P. Jackson Sr. Because of them, the home I grew up in was full of love and joy that did not in any way resemble the world I portray in this book.

1

A Scientific Conspiracy

Founded in 1970, the Behavioral Genetics Association (BGA) is dedicated to the "scientific study of the interrelationship of genetic mechanisms and behavior, both human and animal."[1] Like many professional organizations, the BGA has the president of the association address the banquet at the annual meeting. In 1995 the president of the BGA was Florida State University psychologist Glayde Whitney, who had been on the editorial board of the association's journal, *Behavior Genetics,* for a number of years and had an established research program investigating taste preferences in mice. His address, "Twenty-five Years of Behavioral Genetics," started in a typical fashion for such occasions, as Whitney recounted his training at the University of Minnesota and his arrival at Florida State University in 1970, where he established his "mouse lab" and began his lifelong research program. The address soon took a different turn, however, as Whitney began discussing the racial basis of crime. Such an investigation had been hampered, he declared, by the dogma that the environment determined all behavioral traits and by the taboo against scientific research into race. Whitney decried these trends, as he saw them: "The Marxist-Lysenkoist denial of genetics, the emphasis on environmental determinism for all things human . . . [represents an] invasion of left-liberal political sentiment [that] has been so extensive that many of us think that way without realizing it." Whitney's invocation of Lysenkoism was a quick one-two punch for his audience of geneticists. First, it called up the discredited doctrine of the inheritance of acquired characteristics. Often called "Lamarckism" after Jean-Baptiste de Lamarck, one of its eighteenth-century proponents, it claims that changes to the body caused by the environment could be passed down through the generations. Second, it recalled that when Trofim Lysenko, a Stalinist functionary, declared Lamarckism was demanded by Marxist ideology, geneticists who refused to toe this party line were purged.[2] For many in the

West, "Lysenkoism" became a cautionary tale for the dangers of control over the free inquiry of science—science should remain apolitical, or bad science is the result.

Against this leftist tide, Whitney declared that objective scientists should fearlessly investigate racial differences in behavior. As an example, Whitney used crime data from the United Nations to argue, "Like it or not, it is a reasonable scientific hypothesis that some, perhaps much, of the race difference in murder rate is caused by genetic differences in contributory variables such as low intelligence, lack of empathy, aggressive acting out, and impulsive lack of foresight." Whitney ended his address with a call for behavioral geneticists to "do for group differences what we have already accomplished with individual differences."[3]

Many BGA members were appalled by Whitney's address. Beginning in the 1930s, Daniel Kevles has argued, "students of human heredity insisted that human genetic investigations had to be emancipated from the biases that had colored mainline-eugenic research—notably the attentiveness to vague and often prejudiced behavioral categories." After World War II and the overt eugenic racism of the Nazi regime, geneticists in general, and human geneticists in particular, had struggled to guard their growing discipline from accusations of racism. BGA member Nicholas Martin spoke for many of his fellow geneticists following Whitney's address: "To have all this blown in one evening by one insensitive person is galling, to say the least."[4]

The official minutes of the business meeting noted that Whitney had "shared his feelings about ethnic differences." The Executive Committee also made explicit that "the Association has no official spokesman and the presidential address does not represent official policy of the association." For some, this disavowal of Whitney's speech was not enough, and there were calls for his resignation. Two members resigned from the BGA Executive Committee in protest, including the incoming president, Pierre Roubertoux. A compromise was eventually reached where Whitney would not be asked to resign but would not attend next year's meeting and would not identify himself with the BGA when he wrote on racial differences.[5]

In 1998, in his next published piece on racial differences, however, Whitney was listed as the "Past President of the Behavioral Genetics Association," and unlike his presidential address, the piece brought him some national notoriety. The piece was the introduction to the autobiography of David Duke, the American Nazi and Klansman. The major theme of Whitney's presidential address, that racial differences were real and that scientific investigation into them was being smothered, was reemphasized in this introduction but with a new element: the Jewish conspiracy to control academia. "From personal experience in academia," he wrote, "it is sometimes hard to believe that Jews constitute only 2% or 3% of the general population. Individuals of Jewish ancestry are vastly overrepresented in the ranks of highly successful scientists." When these Jews organized, danger was afoot, for "[o]rganized Jewry . . . dogmatically attempts to keep the general population from awareness of the findings of modern science."[6]

As Whitney came under increasing criticism, Florida State University, like the BGA, anxiously distanced itself from his views. The university was quick to defend his freedom to write and speak as he saw fit, without agreeing with his conclusions. Robert J. Contreras, his departmental chair, made it clear that "Glayde's views are his alone and do not represent my views or those of the department."[7]

While Whitney's brief national fame quickly faded, he continued to write on racial difference and the smothering of scientific research. Whitney's most extensive critique of Jewish control over racial research was given in 2000 at the Thirteenth Annual Conference of the Institute for Historical Review (IHR), where he claimed:

> Even though common knowledge among academics, the suppression of knowledge about Jewish involvement in issues linking genetics, race, psychology is being actively pursued. In many countries "politically incorrect" discussion of these topics can get you fired, while worldwide the B'nai B'rith and allied pressure groups are pushing to criminalize any mention of race differences.[8]

It was no accident that Whitney made these claims at this venue. The IHR was dedicated to "historical research" that purported to show the Nazi genocide of Jews was a myth created by worldwide Jewish conspiracy to extort money. The parallels between the IHR's conspiracies about the fabrication of history and Whitney's conspiracies about the taboo on racial research were the result of a commonly shared anti-Semitic worldview. For example, Whitney pointed to the early-twentieth-century rise of cultural anthropology that signaled "the shift from legitimate science to ideological pap under the direction of the Jewish immigrant Franz Boas." Boas as the chief villain of racial science was a theme in other writings by members of the IHR.[9]

While he had saved his depreciation of Jewish control over scientific research for David Duke and the IHR, the basic thrust of Whitney's argument about the taboo on racial research and the reality of racial differences in crime appeared in pieces he authored long before. In a 1990 article, Whitney had surveyed the history of behavioral genetics, noting that the decline in hereditarian thinking owed in large part to political rather than scientific reasons. After the Nazi regime, Whitney noted, "considerations of genetic bases of individual and group differences in human and animal behavior tended to be received with an assortment of responses that ranged from impolite to insensitive to outrageous violations of taboo. Even today it is not unusual for the epithet 'Nazi' to be hurled at any public discussant of behavior genetics." In a 1995 article in the *Encyclopedia of Bioethics,* Whitney explained the decline of hereditarian thought in a similar fashion and argued that it was time to abandon environmental explanations for human behavior. "The theory of a flat Earth at the center of the universe would not have gotten us to the moon," he wrote, "and environmental determinist theories of human behavior have not yet solved most of our social problems." Writing specifically about race and crime, Whitney declared in 1990 that "[i]nclusion of a racial dimension in developmental studies obviously could be productive for criminology. Ignoring or denying the possible genetic bases of racial differences in criminal behavior has not made the differences go away."[10]

The Whitney episode represents a number of tensions in postwar American scientific discourse. There is a tension between Whitney's claim of the reality of racial differences and his claim that scientific research into racial differences has been taboo—how do scientists know if this reality if the research is smothered? There is a similar tension between mainstream scientists' toleration of claims of racial differences in staid scientific prose and their attempts to distance themselves and their professional organizations from those claims when baldly stated. These tensions and the arguments that give rise to them have a documented history in the United States. Since the 1920s a small number of scientists have lent their names and the mantle of scientific objectivity to the political cause of the American racialist right wing. The focus of this book is to explore the symbiotic relationship between racist ideology and science by examining the origins of these arguments in the fight to preserve racial segregation in the 1950s and 1960s. My central argument is that science provides racist ideology with important rhetorical tools that allow the perpetuation of racist claims that would otherwise not be tolerated in public discourse. At the same time, the use of science, or rather speaking in a scientific mode, gives us insight into the nature of science.

Massive Resistance and Racism

The three great racist regimes were Germany during the Nazi era (1933–1945), South Africa during apartheid (1948–1980), and the American South before 1965. It was in these three regimes that, as George Fredrickson has argued, "white supremacy attained its fullest ideological and institutional development."[11] In the American South, whites articulated their defense of the racist regime most fully in two historical periods. The first was between 1830 and 1865, when the threat of slave uprising and a militant abolitionist movement required the white South to elaborate the "proslavery argument" against threats to the established order. The second was in the wake of *Brown v. Board of Education,* when the burgeoning civil rights movement required a similarly elaborate defense of the "southern way of life" that segregation represented.

The proslavery argument has received a lot of historical attention, but despite the importance of the massive resistance movement, scholars have paid little attention to the articulated ideology of the segregationists. Historian David L. Chappell wrote, "Historians have on the whole ignored the ideas of the segregationists of the 1950s and 1960s. They assume, apparently, that racism—which historians have studied from every conceivable angle—is enough to explain how and why people fought to preserve a racist institution in a specific time and place."[12] Chappell argued that the segregationist cause ultimately failed, at least in part, because they had no coherent intellectual agenda. Writing on what he calls "The Divided Mind of Southern Segregationists," Chappell states that there were at least two distinct groups of southern segregationists. The first group centered their demands on constitutional and legal arguments. For these writers, among them Senators Richard Russell of Georgia and Harry F. Byrd of Virginia, the U.S. Constitution laid out a specific division of powers between the state and federal governments. This division of powers was violated by the U.S. Supreme Court in its 1954 *Brown* decision and again in 1957 when President Dwight D. Eisenhower sent in paratroopers to enforce the desegregation of Central High School in Little Rock, Arkansas. "After 1957," writes Chappell, "the federal executive was helping the courts usurp the powers reserved to the states. According to this interpretation, it was not merely a state's right, but an American's duty, to resist [desegregation]."[13]

In Chappell's second group were racial purists who believed that states' rights were a diversion from the real issue, which was the threat of racial intermarriage. The archetypal example of this second group was segregationist writer Carleton Putnam—a key figure in this book. Time and time again, Putnam warned that the South was wasting its time with the call to defend "states' rights" and should instead call forth the true danger: miscegenation. Putnam laid out his case clearly in a speech before the Citizens' Council of Jackson, Mississippi, in 1961:

> The issue here is *not* equality of opportunity. The issue here is *not* the democratic way of life. The issue here is that school integration is social integration, that social integration always and everywhere, has and does lead to intermarriage in the long run and that intermarriage, under our population ratios in the South, will destroy our society.[14]

Putnam believed that science had proven the truth of his contention regarding the dangers of miscegenation and was the most outspoken publicist for a small group of scientists who provided him with his scientific armamentarium. Yet Putnam's racism, based as it was on the notion that the races were clearly divided by immutable differences, was not the only argument science could provide to the South. It was possible to defend segregation scientifically without resorting to biological racism of this sort. When it came time directly to assault the *Brown* decision, segregationist lawyers abandoned Putnam's biological argument in favor of an argument that did not turn on essential biological differences between the races but that held it was sociologically and psychologically beneficial for the races to attend separate schools. That the segregationists could so easily abandon an essentialist argument about race gives us insight into the flexibility and adaptability of racial ideology.

Recent writers on the history of racial ideology in Western thought and society agree that racism is a recent phenomenon, quite different from forms of subjection and oppression that existed before the late eighteenth century. Audrey Smedley provides a convenient listing of the traditional relevant elements of racial ideology that distinguishes it from "mere" ethnocentrism: first, humans can be classified into discrete biological groups; second, these groups can be arranged hierarchically; third, physical characteristics of human beings are indications of their inner mental and spiritual qualities; fourth, these qualities are inherited; fifth, and finally, these racial groupings are fixed and cannot be transcended.[15]

One puzzle this has left for historians is that racial oppression, or what certainly looks like racial oppression, has existed in times and places when there was no coherent concept of a race to support it. The most telling example is the racialized slavery that developed through the Atlantic slave system in the Americas. Europeans developed the racialized slavery that typified the American South without a firm concept of Africans as racially "other."[16] One historian who has addressed this dilemma is George Fredrickson. Fredrickson notes that the South African regime that founded apartheid did so because of cultural rather than biological differences. Fredrickson concludes that our conceptualization of the ideology of racism needs to be reformulated in light of the different ideological justifications for racial oppression. "If the term racism is to apply," Fredrickson argues, "its association with the specific form of biological determinism that justified slavery and segregation in the nineteenth and twentieth centuries must be regarded as fortuitous rather than essential." In his most recent book, Fredrickson noted correctly that "deterministic cultural particularism can do the work of biological racism quite effectively."[17]

Science and Objectivity

The actors at the center of this book were scientists, and as such, they had a unique voice in American society. One way the objectivity of science could aid the segregationist cause was by providing appeals to the natural order of the world. Scientific arguments could be persuasive in the public forum because "science" had, and has, a unique cultural authority in American society.

In a public dispute in the postwar United States, science is a powerful weapon. As Gordon Mitchell has argued, "Advocates who can claim successfully the mantle of objectivity tend to gain the upper hand in public disputes by virtue of their ability to exploit the ethos of scientific research and tie their arguments to favorable cultural practices about the scientific practice."[18] At the center of this conception of objectivity is the idea that a scientific text does not represent the perspective of the author but is rather an unmediated account of how the world "really" is. This notion of objectivity, called "the view from nowhere" by Thomas Nagel or the "god trick" by Donna Haraway, allows scientists to present their arguments without acknowledging scientists' own agency in their creation.[19]

David Hollinger has cast the notion of scientific objectivity in terms of personae. He argues that modernity has two hallmarks: In the *strategy of artifice,* people respond to the modern condition by creating resources artistically, as a novelist or painter might. The *strategy of reference,* by contrast, looks to the logical analysis of the world provided by science; instead of creating something new, it seeks to discover what is already there. Hollinger argues that these two strategies can be represented by the personae of "Artificer" versus "Knower." The Artificer embraces such terms as "making, generative, contriving, myth-constructing," while the Knower embraces "finding, referential, demystifying." The Knower persona presented itself as the discoverer of a truth that existed in nature rather than a truth created by artistic endeavor.[20]

The Knower persona was, itself, a creation of the scientific enterprise and grew out of the increasingly social nature of scientific investigation in the nineteenth century. Lorraine Daston has called the "view from nowhere" "aperspectival objectivity" that aims at "eliminating individual . . . idiosyncrasies."[21] One way scientists present themselves as aperspectival is through a specific form of writing that "focus[es] attention away from people and toward things."[22] Scientific prose is designed to give the impression that it is not the author who is making the argument but nature; hence to dispute science is foolishly and futilely to dispute nature.

The appeal to nature as a justification for racism was, as Michael L. Blakely argued, "endemic, untested, and marginal compared to other justifications [for racial inequity] throughout much of European history" and did not come to the fore until the rise of science.[23] When science proclaimed the biological basis of our social relations, the result was to undercut attempts at social reform. Immaculada de Melo-Martin argues that both critics and supporters of biological determinism in human affairs agree that "if biological determinism were correct, then we would be exempt from critically analyzing and maybe transforming our social practices and institutions."[24] We cannot possibly change the present order because it is nature's order.

When Glayde Whitney invoked the dangers of leftist-Lysenkoist doctrines, he was, perhaps unknowingly, recreating the scientific–political battles in the early twentieth century between neo-Lamarckians and the new Mendelian/Weissmanian proponents of "hard heredity," which declared that acquired characteristics could not be inherited. Often lost in the history of these battles was that those who believed the doctrine of hard heredity did so for both scientific and political reasons. As Robert Proctor has argued, those attracted to the notion of a heredity immune from environmental changes

> were attracted to the conservative implications of this idea. Those objecting [to Lamarckian ideas of heredity] did so (in part) out of fears for the political implications conceived to flow from a doctrine that suggested a high degree of plasticity in the genetic or "racial" structure of life.[25]

What was not made explicit in Whitney's address was that *both* sides in the debate over the nature of heredity had a political stake; it was not just the Stalinist purges of apostate geneticists but also the horrors of race hygiene under Hitler. Whitney's speech can then serve as a model for most of the figures I will address in this book: they refused to recognize that *their* science was imbued with their values and ideology. While using the club of "a science dictated by social wishes" against their political and scientific opponents, they did not acknowledge their own social and political stances toward purportedly scientific evidence.

Conspiracy Argument in Science

The scientists who spoke out in favor of segregation were a tiny minority compared to the "liberal orthodoxy" that reigned in the scientific academy in the 1950s and early 1960s. One reason the National Association for the Advancement of Colored People Legal Defense and Education Fund (NAACP-LDEF) could call upon social scientists to serve as expert witnesses in *Brown v. Board of Education* was that most working social scientists in psychology, sociology, and anthropology had rejected the scientific racism of the prewar era. Most American social scientists believed that segregation was harmful to the psychological development of schoolchildren and that there were no fundamental differences in intelligence between the races. Indeed, many scientists were rejecting the entire notion of race as a scientific concept.[26] Despite Glayde Whitney's protestations to the contrary, since the 1930s there has been very little scientific evidence for innate behavioral differences between races, even in IQ or intelligence. Indeed, the concepts of "race" and "IQ" are often argued to be scientifically valueless. And yet frequent, well-publicized studies, such as Arthur Jensen's "How Much Can We Boost IQ and Scholastic Achievement?" in 1969, Richard Herrnstein and Charles Murray's *The Bell Curve* in 1994, and, indeed, Glayde Whitney's address in 1995, continue to draw the nation's attention back to the matter of innate differences between the "white" and "black" races.[27] In his recent history of racism in psychology, Graham Richards claims, "The interesting question is no longer which side is correct [on the race/IQ issue] but why the issue resists closure despite the demonstrable incoherence" of the case for differences in race and IQ.[28]

I will answer Richards's question by arguing that for the past five decades, scientists who claim there are racial differences in IQ consistently have held that scientific truth was and is being muzzled by a conspiracy of powerful, shadowy figures who control the public airings of academic discourse. But, because of the unique cultural position of science in American society, scientists could use their minority status to their rhetorical advantage in the face of overwhelming rejection of their arguments by mainstream scientists and their organizations. While the public dispute over segregation is over—no one in public life calls for a return to legally enforced racial segregation—the dispute over the nature of the scientific inquiry into racial differences remains a live issue. J. Philippe Rushton, currently one of the more outspoken proponents of this view, claims that contemporary scientists are forbidden "even daring to look through the genetic analog of Galileo's telescope."[29] Invoking Galileo, as Rushton does, is drawing on the Galileo legend as "scientific folklore," to borrow Thomas Lessl's phrase.[30] In particular, the Galileo legend is a cautionary tale that science, viewed as the search for the unvarnished truth, cannot be controlled by the superstition of the church. Peter Weingart argues, "The legacy of Galileo comes in two related but distinguishable parts: as the (ultimately futile) suppression of scientific 'truth' through church and/or state, and as the (equally unsuccessful) support of 'false' science (i.e. pseudo-science) and thus abuse of the authority of science."[31] The conspiracy rhetoric invoked by racial researchers for five decades uses both sides of the Galileo legend.

In part, the consistency of this rhetoric is explained by the tight organizational structure of this particular scientific community. Often funded by the Pioneer Fund, a philanthropic organization founded in 1937 to support scientific research into human differences, this small coterie of scientists often write and publish in the somewhat obscure journal *Mankind Quarterly*. Since 1960, *Mankind Quarterly* and the scholars associated with it have held forth against what they view as the political domination of the scientific enterprise by liberals, Communists, and Jews.[32]

The legend of Galileo is mirrored in the institutionalization of science in the postwar United States and the prevalence of the metaphor of science as a "free market." Uskali Maki writes that, "The belief that there is—or should be—a market, or something like a market, within science, seems to be increasingly popular among philosophers, sociologists, and other students of science."[33] Like Galileo, who should have been free from the dogmatism of the church, science should be free from all external controls. Such was the message of Vannevar Bush in *Science the Endless Frontier,* widely viewed as the template for the organization of the scientific community in the postwar United States.[34] David Hollinger writes:

> Bush was merely codifying two popular beliefs that dominated American discourse about science and society in the 1920s and 1930s. First, knowledge advances the most quickly and surely when its pursuers are liberated from social influences of any kind. Second, society's welfare ultimately depends upon advances in scientific knowledge. . . . Individual investigators were best left to do as they wished, for the truth controlled the outcome of inquiry in much the same way that Adam Smith's "invisible hand" controlled the outcome of entrepreneurial activities.[35]

This view of science as a free marketplace of ideas was put forth in order to free science from external controls, which, it was argued, belonged to the domain of "political questions." According to this view, only scientists themselves could truly understand which questions to investigate and which answers would lead to the truth, which, presumably, would be socially useful.[36]

The creation of this public image of science as a free market is an example what Thomas Gieryn refers to as "boundary work." According to Gieryn, such work "construct[s] a rhetorical boundary between science and some less authoritative residual non-science."[37] By demarcating "real" science from its pretenders, Gieryn argues, scientists create the cultural space they need to exercise epistemic authority.

> When credibility is publicly contested, putatively factual explanations or predictions about nature do not move naked from lab or scientific journal into courtrooms, boardrooms, newsrooms, or living rooms. Rather they are clothed in sometimes elaborate *representations* of science— compelling arguments for why science is uniquely best as a provider of trustworthy knowledge, and compelling narrations for why my science (but not theirs) is bona fide.[38]

These public disputes over what "counts" as trustworthy science are influenced by the notion of aperspectival objectivity. Science reveals the truth about nature because it speaks with no one's voice. But the Knower, like all personae, is a constructed identity—even the most dedicated believer in scientism knows that scientific articles do not write themselves. However, the objective ideal nonetheless relies on forms of social relations in which scientists are isolated from the larger, social environment. It is this isolation that produces knowledge. David Hollinger wrote, "The presumption has remained that the crucial dynamism in [knowledge's] wondrous advance was human energy, distinctly organized. Whatever might be the ontological status of truth itself, knowledge of it was inseparable from the human activity of truthseeking." [39] This social organization required that science be an autonomous field of activity, free from social and political concerns. The architects of postwar U.S. science policy freed science from many institutional controls by contrasting the failures of science in totalitarian regimes with its triumphs in democratic ones. Steve Fuller points to Harvard's James B. Conant as one architect of the public image of science after World War II:

> Conant sold the public value of "basic research" . . . by providing contrasting explanations for the success of the atomic bomb project and the failures of Lysenkoism in Russia and eugenics in Nazi Germany. The atomic bomb was built because the relevant aspects of atomic physics were already known. This knowledge was the natural outgrowth of the physics research agenda, not agenda of some governmental planning board. . . . By contrast, the Russians and Germans wanted science on demand to suit their ideological goals. This resulted not only in political failure, but also in the perversion of science.[40]

This view of science is an argument by disassociation, whereby "real" science results from a scientific community that is free from outside control and "false" science results from one that is constrained by political or social norms.[41] Researchers who maintain that science has demonstrated racial differences in intelligence have used this disassociation. *Their* science is the one threatened by political outsiders who should have no place in science.

The scientific defenses of segregation, and other controversies around the existence of innate racial differences, are examples of "expulsion debates," which Gieryn defines as "a contest between rival authorities, each of whom claims to be scientific. All sides seek to legitimate their claims about natural reality as scientifically made and vetted inside the authoritative cultural space, while drawing up a map to put discrepant claims and claimants outside (or at least on the margins)."[42] In a manner similar to Conant and Bush, race/IQ researchers charge that the attacks on racial research are motivated by ideological, rather than scientific, reasons. Conspiracy rhetoric is well suited to create a rhetorical boundary around the race/IQ researchers' "good science" and the "bad science" of their critics.

Just as scientists' boundary work is a disassociation that separates real science from pretend science, conspiracy rhetoric is a disassociation that aims to separate social reality from its appearance.[43] In the political sphere, conspiracy rhetoric flourishes during time of social stress when those who perceive themselves as powerless begin to posit the "real" explanation for society's ills as a conspiracy of a powerful group who is ultimately responsible. As David Zarefsky writes, "It is alarming to think that a secret cabal is afoot, but some stability is provided by the belief that one knows what is going on, can make sense of difficult and complex phenomena, and hence can be on one's guard."[44]

In conspiracy rhetoric, however, "normal modes of appeal are vitiated."[45] Conspiracies are committed in secret, by powerful figures. Moreover, counterinstances can always be "reinterpreted as the work of clever conspirators to conceal their true intentions"; thus, concludes Zarefsky, "[s]ince the argument can neither be proved or disproved, who 'wins' will likely depend upon who shoulders the burden of proof."[46]

In the debate over the reality of racial differences, those who endorsed scientifically proven racial differences seized presumption and pushed the burden of proof onto their opponents by offering two arguments. First, they maintained that science has proven the existence of these racial differences. In other words, the status quo (which by definition enjoys presumption) lies with those who argue for racial differences. Hence it is the burden of racial egalitarians to establish a case for racial equality. Second, those who argue for racial inequality argue that scientific research is smothered by a conspiracy to stop racial research. Obviously these two claims are in tension: if race research is stifled, how can we know that science has proven racial differences? However, because both claims are offered in the context of a conspiracy, both are used to prove the existence of the conspiracy—hence the conspiracy argument is "self-sealing."

Segregationist scientists depended on the public image of science as free inquiry. The conspiracy claim gained persuasive power because the notion of an ideologically controlled science was anathema to how science was widely perceived in U.S. culture. It was not necessarily government that was controlling racial research, however. Identification of those responsible for the conspiracy depended on who was making the argument and where they were making it: Jews, Communists, liberals, cultural anthropologists, and "politically correct" professors have all been fingered as those responsible for silencing the objective science of racial research. All these claims gain coherence from their ability to link to widespread beliefs about the autonomy of science from social influences.

Although segregationist scientists differed on a number of points, a central point of their agenda was to debunk the "equalitarian dogma" of modern anthropology. Glayde Whitney was hardly the first to criticize modern anthropology and Franz Boas in particular; such criticisms date back at least to the early part of the twentieth century, when Boas first rose to prominence. According to the segregationist line in the 1950s, Franz Boas and his students, the "equalitarians," had substituted their political and religious belief in racial equality for hard scientific evidence when they proclaimed the races equal. The equalitarians had infiltrated the scientific establishment and, through political pressure, had successfully suppressed the truth about racial differences in a host of disciplines. In control of hiring and tenure decisions of all major universities and the publication boards of major scientific publishers, the equalitarians quickly and severely punished any "objective" scientists who dared reveal that the races were fundamentally unequal. In this way, the equalitarians perpetuated what segregationist and psychologist Henry E. Garrett described as "the scientific hoax of the century."[47]

According to the segregationist scientists, in the *Brown* school desegregation case the equalitarians succeeded in writing their scientific hoax into constitutional law. In *Brown* the Supreme Court had found that segregation psychologically damaged schoolchildren, citing the work of Kenneth B. Clark and other social scientists who had worked with the NAACP-LDEF. After *Brown,* segregationist scientists took to print arguing that Clark and his colleagues had misled the Court about racial differences, and they eventually went to court themselves, serving as expert witnesses at trials directly aimed at a reversal of *Brown* on the basis of their scientific testimony.

If they spoke in the voice of science, the segregationist scientists' forum was the courtroom, which further complicates how they framed their arguments. Historians have noted that one of the struggles social scientists have had in American culture is the difficulty in getting people to replace their "common sense" about the social world with "expert knowledge" as provided by social scientists. This problem was particularly acute in a court of law when scientists would be called as expert witnesses to provide testimony on race relations. Courts consistently refused to substitute scientific understanding of race for "common sense" understandings.[48]

The segregationist scientists were then in a unique rhetorical position. Just as they were in the scientific minority, they were in the popular majority—especially in the American South. In their testimony, segregationist scientists were providing scientific evidence that *supported* common-sense notions of race in the American South. Most white Southerners assumed that African Americans were not as smart, industrious, or trustworthy as white Americans.

The objectivity of these institutions was particularly important for upper-class defenders of segregation. In his study of the Citizens' Councils, Neil McMillen noted that many white Southerners had an obsession with respectability. Many wanted to defy integration but also wanted to distance themselves from the violence and destructiveness of the Ku Klux Klan and other militant branches of the massive resistance movement.[49] Litigation offered one road to respectability, as violence and threats were put aside in favor of reasoned discourse within an accepted legal forum. Layered over the respectability offered by the courts was the respect garnered by science. Science, viewed as a value-neutral, apolitical institution, could transform highly emotional issues of human differences into one of objective reality, immune from moral criticism. Hence the prospect of embracing both the neutrality of science and the neutrality of law offered segregationists a unique opportunity to claim the mantle of objective truth. The court system provided the perfect venue for segregationist scientists because it allowed them to take advantage of their minority status within the scientific community. Segregationist scientists knew that their views did not reflect those of the vast majority of their scientific colleagues; indeed, several professional scientific associations drew up formal resolutions of condemnation of segregationist science. However, as the segregationist scientists were fond of saying, scientific truths were not decided by majority vote but rather by the cogency of scientific arguments. As the antimajoritarian branch of government, segregationist scientists believed, the court system provided perfect venue for them to put forth their case and let the court decide if the evidence was sound and the conclusions worthy. The segregationist scientists felt that judges, as experts in sifting evidence and discovering truth, would prove that segregation was scientifically justified. I hope to explore in some depth how the twin facets of the "objectivity" of the law and the "objectivity" of science were melded in these cases.

Organization of the Book

The second chapter traces the origins of the conspiracy rhetoric in the professionalization of Boasian anthropology and its opposition by racial anthropologists, most notably New Yorker Madison Grant. Grant despised Boas as a Jewish leftist who was polluting the science of anthropology. A key figure here was Virginian Earnest Sevier Cox, who was a close associate of Grant. Unlike Grant, Cox was concerned with "the Negro Question" and, far more than Grant, saw the racial problems of the United States through the lens of the black/white binary. Cox also lived three decades longer than Grant, becoming a central figure in the racist underground in the postwar United States.

Chapter 3 explores the origins and ideology of that racist underground, which came up into the sunlight in the late 1950s. I trace the origins of different groups of activists who eventually joined together by 1959. First were the heirs to the anti-Semitic worldview of Madison Grant and associated with the "Northern League" a Nordicist group organized by British writer Roger Pearson and American political activist Willis Carto. The Northern League members published a series of interlocking publications such as *Truth Seeker, Northern World,* and *Western Destiny*. In these publications, Northern Leaguers held forth against the

Jewish domination of the Western world and championed the Nordic as the true representative of the white race.

Chapter 4 examines a second group concerned about the Boasian conspiracy. This group was composed of an older generation of southern scientists who had grown up under segregation. These men were born in the late nineteenth century or the first two decades of the twentieth century. A good example of this group was psychologist Henry E. Garrett, one of three scientists who testified in favor of segregation during the *Brown* litigation. Garrett was on the faculty of Columbia University for decades before retiring in 1956 and assuming a position in his home state at the University of Virginia. Also in this group was anatomist Wesley C. George, who had been on the faculty of the University of North Carolina Medical School since 1919. For this group, having grown up in the South during the height of Jim Crow, the dismantling of segregation represented the dismantling of their culture. They were fully prepared to use their scientific expertise to defend the old order.

In chapter 5, I look at how these two groups came together in a formal organization. They were joined by a number of what I have chosen to call the "idiosyncratic conservatives." Ernst van den Haag, psychoanalyst and social philosopher, was one of the earliest critics of the use of social science in *Brown*. A. James Gregor, who was closely associated with members of the Northern League, published widely within the social science literature criticizing *Brown*, published psychological studies with psychologists R. Travis Osborne and Stanley Porteus, and wrote highly theoretical articles on racial thought. These writers rejected the notion that African Americans were biologically inferior to white Americans and instead based their arguments for segregation on notions of group identity. These disparate groups came together in their own professional organization, the International Society for the Advancement of Ethnology and Eugenics (IAAEE), founded in Washington, DC, in 1959. The expressed function of the IAAEE was objectively to investigate racial differences and to publicize their findings.

The IAAEE provided an organizational basis for the scientific attack on *Brown*, which is explored in chapter 6. The district court in the first of these cases, *Stell*, found segregation constitutional, justified on the basis of the inferiority of African Americans. The *Stell* decision was overruled by the court of appeals. The subsequent cases were forced to follow the rule laid down by the appeals court and the cases were denied a hearing by the U.S. Supreme Court. The court cases died with a whimper after the passage of the 1964 Civil Rights Act, which permanently ended *de jure* segregation in the American South.

In chapter 7, I look at how the mainstream scientific community struggled with the segregationist scientist attack. The mainstream scientific community needed respond to the segregationist appropriation of science when asked to do so by educational groups who were being bombarded with segregationist propaganda. Additionally, the scientific community struggled with notions of what it meant to be an objective scientist and the relationship between the production of scientific knowledge and the role of the scientist in the larger society.

In the final chapter I explore how the issues raised by the IAAEE proved enduring. The mainstream scientific community reacted to the activities of the IAAEE and struggled to take back the authority of science from what they viewed as the segregationists' abuses of science. Despite a number of official condemnations of the conspiracy charges, within a few years William Shockley and Arthur Jensen would put forth the position that there were significant heritable differences in IQ separating the races and that racial research was being smothered by political liberals. Of course, given the changes in political climate, no one argued on the basis of these arguments that the country should return to legally enforced segregation. Nonetheless, the conspiracy argument remains.

2

Racial Science and the Anti-Nordic Conspiracy

Few scholars have addressed how scientific arguments, as developed by the racial anthropologists of the early twentieth century, were enrolled to support racial segregation in the American South. There is good reason for this: by the early twentieth century, Jim Crow and the disenfranchisement of African Americans were firmly in place; indeed, Rayford Logan declared the late nineteenth and early twentieth centuries the "nadir" for African Americans in this country.[1] This racial regime, which grew out of the post–Civil War "redemption" of the white South in the late nineteenth century, had no real need of scientific justification. In his study of scientific racism of the nineteenth century, John S. Haller argued that "the subject of race inferiority was beyond critical reach in the late nineteenth century." Racism, argued Eric Foner, became a vicious circle as disenfranchisement of black Americans, itself the product of racism, gave birth to more racism, as "the emergence of blacks as a disenfranchised class of dependent laborers greatly facilitated racism's further spread."[2] Science, while certainly proclaiming white supremacy, was not a necessary component of the creation and maintenance of the legal system of Jim Crow. As David Bishop argued regarding the legal underpinnings of the *Plessy* case, "who needed Charles Darwin" when common sense spoke so clearly on the subject of black inferiority?[3]

Given the entrenchment of racism and legalized discrimination in the American South, there was little need or room for the scientific improvement of the racial order. In his study of eugenic sterilization in the Deep South, Edward Larson noted that most of these sterilization programs were targeted at poor whites rather than at African Americans. "So long as southern Whites did not expect African Americans to contribute substantially to the intellectual progress of civilization," Larson argued, "the need for eugenic improvement of Blacks lost urgency."[4] Yet some organizations sought to bring the science of eugenics to bear on the South's situation, most notably in Virginia. These efforts would lay the groundwork for the postwar scientific defense of racial segregation, especially in the years following *Brown.*

Eugenic Doctrines

Between 1900 and 1945, nearly every modernizing society had some form of eugenics movement. Recent work on the history of eugenics movements underscores how diverse the ideologies and policies were that went under that name. Frank Dikötter argued, "Eugenics was not so much a clear set of scientific principles as a 'modern way' of talking about social problems in biologizing terms."[5] As such, the language of eugenics could be as easily adopted by leftists as by those on the right.

Early histories of the eugenics movement too often distanced the "real" science of genetics from the "pseudo-science" of eugenics, but beginning in the 1970s, two different threads of research opened up the history of eugenics to different interpretations. The first thread internationalized the history of eugenics, bringing the story outside the German, British, and American contexts. In many countries, eugenics was confined to what we might think of as prenatal care, focusing on the "future generations" carried by pregnant women. In other countries, particularly those where Lamarckian doctrines still were scientifically respectable, eugenics focused as much on environmental improvement as it did on selective breeding.[6]

The second thread of research captured the complexity of eugenic thought even within the Anglo-American and German contexts. For example, in the United States and Britain, leftists proclaimed their adherence to eugenic doctrines as much as those on the political right.[7] The key work was Daniel Kevles's *In the Name of Eugenics,* which contrasted "mainline" eugenicists—the traditional racist eugenics tradition—with "anti-mainline" eugenicists and "reform" eugenicists, who opposed what they saw as the naive racism of the mainliners.[8]

Of particular interest is the close social and ideological alliance between American and German Nazi eugenicists. Stefan Kühl has shown that Nazi eugenicists admired the American lead in sterilization laws and other eugenics measures. Kühl argues that the closest admirers of Nazi

Germany were those he dubbed "racial anthropologists," such as Madison Grant, Lothrop Stoddard, and Clarence G. Campbell, whose "belief in Nordic supremacy was combined with a strong anti-Semitic bias. Racial anthropologists were more explicit than mainline eugenicists in voicing support both for eugenic racism in Nazi Germany . . . as well as for racism directed specifically at ethnic and religious minorities."[9]

The racial anthropologists, who were centered in New York City, had an emissary in the South: Earnest Sevier Cox. This chapter traces how Cox brought Madison Grant's scientific ideas to Virginia in order to ensure a white America. In so doing, I show that an important thread of Grant's argument survived the attack on his thought brought by World War II: the conspiracy against Nordic science.

Nordicism and the Anti-Nordic Conspiracy

Broadly speaking, Nordicism (which could also be called Teutonism, Anglo-Saxonism, or Aryanism) was the doctrine that northern Europeans were superior to other races. The ancient Roman historian Tacitus (ca. 55–120), expressed admiration for the Teutonic tribes who lived north of what Tacitus considered a decadent Rome. In England, the doctrine began in the sixteenth century when the break with the Roman Catholic Church brought increased scholarly attention to the history of the Anglo-Saxon church and, by extension, other Anglo-Saxon traditions. From the sixteenth and into the early nineteenth century, English scholars extended these studies of Anglo-Saxon traditions by arguing that English common law and parliamentary democracy were, in fact, ancient Anglo-Saxon traditions rather than recent innovations.[10]

Many antebellum writers in the United States trumpeted the superiority of the Teutons, and many took Tacitus's writings as proof that democracy as a form of government was actually an ancient practice that began in the woods of ancient Germany. These writers used this theory of the "Teutonic origin" of democracy as proof against conservative critics who argued that democracy was an inherently unstable form of government. Not so, these writers argued; democracy originated in these German tribes with their primitive parliaments and proto-representative government. According to this line of argument, the Teutonic tribes of Angles and Saxons brought this heritage to England and then across the Atlantic to the United States. Hence, democracy was in some sense part of the racial heritage of the Germanic people who settled in the United States. In the late nineteenth century, the "Teutonic origins of democracy" theory became racialized and the justification for democracy became minimal. In the 1880s, during a lecture tour of the United States, writer Edward A. Freeman argued that there were three homes of the Teutonic race: the United States, England, and Germany. These nations, Freeman argued, should put their differences behind them, for they could surely rule the world. The division between superior Anglo-Saxons and inferior Celts, as well as other lower races, was succinctly stated by Freeman: "The best remedy for whatever is amiss in America would be if every Irishman killed a Negro and be hanged for it."[11]

Anthropologist William Z. Ripley had divided Europeans into Teutonic, Alpine, and Mediterranean races in 1899, solidifying a division of Europeans into different races based on head form. An "important guarantee that the head form is primarily the expression of racial differences alone lies in its immunity from all disturbance from physical environment," he wrote; "the colour of the hair and eyes, and stature especially, are open to modification by local circumstances; so that racial peculiarities are often obscured or entirely reversed by them."[12]

The most common racial division of European races was based on the cephalic index, a measure of head shape. The superior Nordics were doliocephalic, or oval-headed, and the inferior Mediterranean and Alpine races were brachycephalic, or round-headed. Head shape was a good indicator of true racial essences for anthropologists because it was relatively immune from environmental differences. As Darwin had shown scientists, the shape of an organism's body was subject to environmental pressures that selected for certain traits. Head shape, by contrast, was not under such selection pressures and therefore was believed to be a good indicator of ancient differences between races.

For Nordic writers in the late nineteenth century, while Darwin and physical anthropology provided the evidence for the existence of racial differences, world history provided the evidence for the truth of Nordic superiority. Race, not nation or political alliances, was the basis of social order. The appeal to history had a long lineage in Nordicist thought. Comte Joseph-Arthur de Gobineau's (1816–1882) *Essay on the Inequality of the Races*, published in four volumes between 1853 and 1855, took the racial basis of civilization as its central theme. Gobineau affirmed the widely accepted division of the races into white, black, and yellow and introduced the idea that civilization itself was based on race. What Gobineau called the Aryan race was the only one capable of creative thought and building civilization. The downfall of the great civilizations of the past, such as Egypt or Greece, owed to the commingling of Aryan blood with that of the lesser races. Houston Stewart Chamberlain (1855–1927), in *Foundations of the Nineteenth Century,* argued that all great historical figures were, on close examination, Aryan. For example, Marco Polo, Copernicus, Galileo, and especially Jesus Christ were Aryans in Chamberlain's account.[13]

Both Gobineau and Chamberlain discussed how the great Teutonic race was bound by German blood and shared the same racial soul. While Chamberlain accepted all the anthropological evidence for the existence of the Teutonic/Aryan/Nordic race, for him the reality of race really turned on a spiritual sharing of the "race-soul." Hence, the importance Chamberlain placed on the supposed Aryan heritage of Christ can be understood as an embrace of a mystical racism that had a spiritual, not materialistic, core.

The most famous Nordicist writer in the United States in the early twentieth century was New Yorker Madison Grant (1865–1937). Trained as an attorney, the wealthy Grant had no need to practice his profession in order to make money and could therefore indulge his passion for natural history. Like his close friend Theodore Roosevelt, Grant was very active in the nascent conservationist movement. He was a great organizer of causes for the environment and was an active member of the Save the Redwoods League and the president of the Bronx Parkway Commission that created the Bronx Zoo. Grant was instrumental in saving the American bison from extinction, as well as whales, pronghorn antelope, and bald eagles. He was a key figure in preserving pristine wilderness for future generations to enjoy. Just as he wanted to preserve the environment, Grant wanted to preserve the race; for him, these were two sides of the same coin.[14]

Grant's racial *magnum opus* was published in 1916 as *The Passing of the Great Race or the Racial Basis of European History.* Grant celebrated the Nordic stock that made up the original population of the British colonies but was in danger of being swamped by the inferior races in what he called the "survival of the unfit."[15] Grant declared, "Speaking English, wearing good clothes, and going to school does not transform a Negro into a white man." Immigration was a similar threat: "We shall have a similar experience with the Polish Jew," Grant warned, "whose dwarf stature, peculiar mentality, and ruthless concentration on self-interest are being engrafted upon the stock of the nation."[16] The danger, Grant warned, was allowing more than one race in the same geographical area under the belief that the "melting pot" would erase racial differences. "Whether we like to admit it or not," Grant reasoned, "the result of the mixture of two races, in the long run, gives us a race reverting to the more ancient, generalized and lower type. The cross between a white man and an Indian is an Indian . . . and the cross between any of the three European races and Jew is a Jew."[17] The solution, Grant declared was simple: man "can breed from the best, or he can eliminate the worst by segregation or sterilization." Grant believed that it would be very difficult to increase breeding of the best types, but "under existing condition the most practical and hopeful method of race improvement is through the elimination of the least desirable elements in the nation by depriving them of the power to contribute to future generations."[18]

Grant had two targets in *Passing*. One was recent immigrants from southern and eastern Europe, especially Jews, whom he thought were racially inferior. African Americans were not racially troubling for Grant because they were consigned to the cultural backwater of the South rather than the streets of his beloved New York. Moreover, the white South had African Americans under firm control with disenfranchisement and segregation. What was needed, Grant believed, was for the North to emulate the racial policies of the South and keep as Nordic as the South was white. Grant was pleased by the passage of the Immigration Restriction Act in 1924, which sharply curtailed immigration from inferior racial stocks.[19]

Grant's second target was the "sentimentalists" who held the "fatuous belief in the power of environment . . . to alter heredity."[20] Even as Grant published *Passing*, his entire scientific program was under attack from Franz Boas in the field of anthropology. Many reviewers, even while agreeing with much of Grant's position, argued that he did not adequately prove that racial differences were immune from environmental amelioration.[21]

Boas (1858–1942) was everything Madison Grant was not. Grant was a proud "native American" from old stock, Boas a German Jewish immigrant. In 1881, Boas received a Ph.D. in physics, with a minor in geography, after studying at the universities of Heidelberg, Bonn, and Kiel. He traveled to Baffinland in the Arctic Circle in 1883, a trip that convinced him that cultural relativism, or the belief that the only way to study a foreign culture was to put aside one's old cultural preconceptions, had to be the guiding principle of the anthropological method. The Inuit of the Arctic thus should not be considered savages, as they had their own culture that had served them quite well in their environment.

In 1887, Boas came to the United States. He obtained a professorship at Columbia University, where he spent his career until his death in 1942. At Columbia, Boas trained an entire generation of anthropologists, who quickly revolutionized the field. A central tenet of Boas and his students was that culture was the proper object of study for anthropologists. Race was, at best, a biological category that was unrelated to cultural achievement. Moreover, Boasians had significant doubts as to the stability of race as a type, since racial markers could change over the space of a generation.[22]

Jonathan Spiro has noted that the conflict between Boas and Grant existed on three levels. First, they split intellectually on the reality of race and racial differences. Second, they split ideologically, with Grant representing cultural purity and Boas championing a pluralistic egalitarianism. Third, they split professionally, with Grant representing the nineteenth-century gentleman naturalist and Boas representing the newer generation of professional scientists with academic credentials and affiliations.[23]

By the time Grant published *Passing* in 1916, Boas and his followers were winning the battle over the shape of American anthropology. Boasians (as his students and those who agreed with his views were sometimes called) were in the majority in the American Anthropological Association, and articles trumpeting Nordic supremacy were not welcome in the pages of the *American Anthropologist*. This is not to say that biological determinism vanished from the American anthropological scene. As Elazar Barkan noted, "The congenial relations between racists and anti-racists, and the cooperation between supporters of rigid racial typology and cultural relativist blurred the classification of scientists into precise categories."[24] Barkan's nuanced view is undoubtedly correct, as scientists moved easily from camp to camp, depending on the needs of the moment. However, Madison Grant's perceptions of the situation were much different. For Grant, the rise of the Boasians, many of whom were, like Boas, Jewish, served to "confirm me in the belief that you must have at the head of any anthropological work a member of the North European race, who has no bias in favor of helots or mongrels."[25] Grant's solution was to found the Galton Society in 1918. Named after Frances Galton, Charles Darwin's cousin who had coined the term *eugenics*, and based at the American Museum of Natural History, which was directed by Grant's friend, Nordicist Harry Fairfield Osborn, the Galton Society was entirely underwritten by Grant and his friends. The membership would be racially pure, old-stock Americans whose politics were in line with Grant's.[26]

There were enough racially pure scientists for the Galton Society to boast a roster that included any number of first-rate scientists. This included most leaders of the mainline American eugenics movement: Harry H. Laughlin, Raymond Pearl, Paul Popenoe, Clarence G. Campbell, Lothrop Stoddard, Carl C. Brigham, Robert Yerkes, and Charles Davenport. Corresponding members included anthropo-sociologist Vacher de Lapouge of France and physical anthropologist Arthur Keith. Jonathan Spiro noted that the members were "respected and accomplished scientists, and most held positions at Harvard, Yale, Princeton, Columbia, or the American Museum of Natural History," although not all of them were strict Nordicists.[27] For a time in the 1920s, the program of Grant and the other Galtonians was ascendant, though always defending itself against the hated Boasians. While the main scientific activity was taking place in northeastern cities, in the American South, a mirror image of Grant's battle was taking place in Virginia.

Earnest Sevier Cox and White America

For Grant and his fellow Nordicists in 1920s New York, the racial problem the United States faced was coming in from southern and eastern Europe. By contrast, white Southerners were convinced that the racial problem of the United States was the Negro, their racist ideology in some ways mirroring the Nordicist beliefs of Grant and his disciples in the American North. In his analysis of race relations in the American South, Joel Williamson noted three strands of white southern thought concerning the Negro at the end of the nineteenth and beginning of the twentieth century. Liberals believed that all the evidence concerning the Negro's potential was not yet in. Conservatives believed that the Negro was an inferior being, eternally resigned to the lower rungs of southern society. The Conservative solution to race relations was segregation—keep a place for the Negro, but a place under firm white control. Radicals believed that the Negro had no place in American society and needed to be completely eliminated. One of the standard-bearers for Radical thought in the early twentieth century was Cox's mentor, Mississippi senator James K. Vardaman, who argued that the best solution to the Negro menace was to

repatriate them back to Africa and abandoned that ideal solution only reluctantly. Vardaman's fellow Radical, Earnest Sevier Cox, never gave up
the idea of repatriation, holding on to the idea until his death in 1965.
"The attainment of White America," he concluded, "is not possible save
by removing the Africans and excluding the Asiatics."[28]

Joel Williamson argued that by the early twentieth century, the Conservatives had won the battle over southern race relations. Radicals had
preached that the two races could never live in harmony, even under a system of rigorous segregation that guaranteed white supremacy. After
1915, Williamson noted, the Radicals "warned of the race war to come.
Most alarming to them was the apathy of uncommitted youth, and the
tendency of those to lose sight of the black menace." Unfortunately for
the Radicals, their voices were increasingly marginalized. "They continued to preach a race war, but nobody came," concluded Williamson; the
Conservatives had won, and the Negro was fixed on the lower rungs of
society, guaranteed a subservient place, but a place nonetheless.[29]

Recent historical writing has begun to question whether the Negro
question was settled in the early twentieth century in the minds of most
white Southerners or was still in doubt. In his analysis of the racial politics of Virginia, J. Douglas Smith pointed to "an ideological fissure in elite
ranks between advocates of genteel paternalism and those who favored
rigid extremism. Supporters of both courses of action were certain that
they knew best how to manage and perpetuate white supremacy."[30] The
key extremists were found in the Anglo-Saxon Clubs, whose chief propa-
gandist, Earnest Sevier Cox, shared the basic suppositions of Grant and
Stoddard: inferior races could not create civilization, and the United
States was in decline owing to the dangers of interbreeding with racial inferiors. Cox, like Grant and Stoddard, was politically active, putting his
writing in the service of society. Unlike his colleagues, however, Cox was
a Southerner whose writing focused exclusively on the danger of "the
Negro," a subject that Grant did not address until the 1930s.[31]

Born in Tennessee in 1880, Cox was a Methodist preacher as a young
man. After attending Vanderbilt University but not receiving a degree,
Cox attended the University of Chicago in 1906, pursuing graduate studies in sociology. At Chicago, Cox focused on the "Negro question," arguing in a series of papers that African Americans were, as a race, inferior to whites, their brutality held in check only by white governance.
Writing to his sister in 1906 regarding the Atlanta race riot, wherein
white mobs attacked and killed Atlanta's African American population,

Cox declared his eagerness to join in the violence, noting that the only true solution was to return the "black savage to his native jungle."[32]

While at Chicago, Cox took a course from Frederick Starr, who had just returned from a tour of Africa. With Starr's encouragement, Cox set off on his own tour of that continent in 1910. By 1914, Cox had returned from Africa and had set off for a tour of South America. Holding himself out to be an "ethnological expert," Cox claimed he was preparing to write a book on interracial contacts. Upon his return to the United States, Cox worked on his manuscript while working for Mississippi senator James K. Vardaman, who read a portion of Cox's in-progress manuscript into the *Congressional Record*.[33]

After a brief stint of military service during World War I, Cox settled in Richmond, Virginia, where he sold real estate to support his writing. Despite having completed his manuscript and receiving some encouragement from Madison Grant, Cox was unable to find a publisher. Finally, Cox paid for the printing of *White America* himself.[34] The book was a crude retelling of Grant's *The Passing of the Great Race*, and the similarities are not accidental: as Jonathan Spiro, Grant's biographer, made clear, Grant tutored Cox in the findings of modern biology and eugenics, guiding the "half-educated" Cox's manuscript toward coherence.[35]

Cox made his starting assumptions clear by declaring in the first chapter, "Scientific research has done much toward establishing the following propositions":

1. The white race has founded all civilizations.
2. The white race remaining white has not lost civilization.
3. The white race become a hybrid has not retained civilization.[36]

Cox argued that only those who did not really live with the Negro could believe in racial equality. "The teachings of the whites who live apart from the negro have placed great emphasis upon environment, rather than upon race and heredity," Cox wrote, "whilst those whites who live in daily contact with the colored races are agreed that there is a difference between the white and colored which cannot be bridged by present environment." Cox placed his work firmly in the latest scientific thinking by couching his calls for racial purity in the language of eugenics. "A race devoid of creative genius is an unfit type," he declared, "and is a matter of concern for the eugenist. Those who seek to maintain the white race in its purity within the United States are in harmony with the ideals of eugenics."[37]

It was history rather than the growing science of eugenics, however, that served as evidence for Cox's claims. The bulk of *White America* is a review of civilizations that have perished because of race mixing. Cox argued that Egypt, India, China, Mexico, and Peru had all perished because of miscegenation. "The intensity of civilization," Cox concluded, "is in inverse ratio to the numerical proportion of the negro in the populations of the various cultural centers."[38]

Cox's aims were precisely the same as those of Houston Stewart Chamberlain, Comte Arthur de Gobineau, and Madison Grant: to show that race was the driving force behind all historical development and that this racial history should guide social action.[39]

As a Radical, Cox favored outright exclusion of the Negro over segregation. Segregation, he argued, led to "mongrelizing the nation." He criticized white Southerners who continually made a place for the inferior race. Such an attitude, Cox claimed, was a danger to civilization, as it led to miscegenation. He blamed the white South's greed and demand for cheap labor that led to the paradoxical position of "the historical South, in proclaiming the Negro a racial danger and yet clinging to him as an economic asset."[40] The only true solution to the menace of the Negro was complete separation through the physical removal of Negroes from the country.

The reception of Cox's masterwork was indicative of the split in the scientific community of the 1920s. Boas's student Melville Herskovits found the book "fallacious in its assumptions, incompetent in its handling, and loose in its logic."[41] Sociologist Guy Johnson found that "there is no doubt that Cox is a student for he has collected a great amount of historical material. . . . But there is plenty of doubt as to his being a *scientific* student. His logic . . . is faulty at every step."[42] Grant, however, heaped praise on Cox's book, which is not too surprising given that the book was written under his close supervision. Charles Davenport called Cox's mission to deport all African Americans one of vital importance of the country. These views were echoed by Lothrop Stoddard, E. A. Ross, and William McDougall.[43]

Buoyed by such praise, the negative views may not have bothered Cox too much. Additionally, as he was not primarily a scientist but a man of action. Cox had social action as his primary goal rather than winning over academic converts.

Cox, Eugenics, and Black Repatriation

Cox worked tirelessly toward the goal of black repatriation to Africa. Chief among Cox's allies in Virginia were John Powell, a concert pianist who had used his celebrity to preach the Nordicism of Cox and Grant; Walter A. Plecker, the state registrar of the Bureau of Vital Statistics, who was seemingly unable to write an article without citing Cox's *White America*; and Louise Burleigh, Powell's fiancée.[44] All these individuals were active in founding and maintaining the Anglo-Saxon Clubs of America (ASCOA), a breakaway group from the Ku Klux Klan. ASCOA's stated policies were identical to those outlined by Cox in *White America*: strict racial separation, immigration restriction, and repatriation of blacks back to Africa. ASCOA maintained an upper-class demeanor, eschewing violence and threats of violence in favor of preaching eugenic doctrines and lobbying for the enactment of those doctrines into law. From its founding in 1922, ASCOA grew to thirty-six active posts in 1925, though it declined quickly thereafter. Before it dissolved, however, ASCOA enjoyed one triumph: Virginia's Racial Integrity Act, which Cox proclaimed "the most perfected expression of the white ideal since the institution of caste in India, some four thousand years ago."[45]

Miscegenation had been illegal in Virginia since the nineteenth century. An 1853 law required that birth certificates record the race of every child born in the state. A 1910 law defined a "colored person" as anyone "having one-sixteenth or more Negro blood." While such a definition may have satisfied most Virginians, it did not satisfy the ASCOA. Inspired by Madison Grant, who had pointed out the dangers of such a lax definition at a meeting of the Galton Society, Cox and his allies realized that the danger of miscegenation and the swamping of the white race by inferior types required a much more strict definition of "colored person." Through fervent lobbying by Powell and others associated with the ASCOA, the Virginia legislature passed the Virginia Racial Integrity Act in 1924, and it remained on the books until ruled unconstitutional by the U.S. Supreme Court in 1967.[46]

The Racial Integrity Act was remarkable for several reasons. First, the act was the strictest in the nation. Cox summarized the provisions of the law, "which defines a white person as a person having no trace whatsoever of the blood of a colored race, with the exception that persons whose blood composition is that of the white race and one-sixteenth or less of the North American Indian are deemed to be white, and makes illegal the marriage of white persons with those not white." The act put the burden of proof not on the state but on the individual, who needed to use tax records, census returns, and military records to prove racial purity.[47]

The second remarkable aspect of the act was that it was the first miscegenation act in the nation passed on a eugenics basis. As Richard Sherman argued, the act "was not the product of a great popular ground swell" but of a few individuals who believed that stricter laws were a scientific necessity. This was a break with most nineteenth-century miscegenation statutes, which did not need the backing of science in order to appeal to a majority of southern whites.[48]

Miscegenation statutes, like many other segregation statutes, were often motivated by the cult of white womanhood. Central to the concept was the white woman as in need of protection from the world, especially from the sexually degenerate black male.

The image of the predatory black male violating the purity and sanctity of the white woman was the driving force behind much of the South's racism. Joel Williamson wrote, "Above all else, it was this threat that thrust deeply into the psychic core of the South, searing the white soul, marking the character of the Southern mind radically and leaving it crippled and hobbled in matters of race long after the mark itself was lost from sight." In the legal realm, the responsibility of carriers to provide safe transport, specifically for white women, led to the first laws requiring segregated railway coaches.[49]

Such a view of white womanhood was not part of Cox's worldview. Indeed, one of his central arguments was that part of the Negro problem owed to the systematic disempowerment of white women. He celebrated, for example, women's recent enfranchisement, arguing that the result would be stricter miscegenation laws. "We do not believe that, if Southern women had possessed the privilege of suffrage, either concubinage or the more irregular sex relations between white men and Negro women would have been overlooked by white politicians."[50]

Instead of gendered notions of separate spheres for men and women, Cox and his associates traded on the eugenic notions of the racial basis of civilization and the deleterious effects of racial amalgamation that were then very much in vogue. It was not until the early twentieth century that race mixing transcended the moral dimension and became a problem of "race suicide." As Gary Nash has argued, the early twentieth century was when whites began to "indulge in a fetish of genealogy, and invent a comforting history of Anglo-Saxonism," all supported by "an outpouring of purportedly scientific research." In her study of miscegenation lawsuits in Alabama, Julie Novkov noted that the science of eugenics provided new arguments at the beginning of the twentieth century for courts to enforce segregation statutes.[51]

The Racial Integrity Act, with its requirements that an individual produce family records proving "no trace" of colored blood in the name of Anglo-Saxon supremacy, must be read as a new rationale against miscegenation. As Barbara Bair wrote, Cox and his associates "shifted from . . . an emphasis on imperiled white womanhood and used in its place a eugenics framework of degeneration, notions of cycles of civilization, and what they saw as the devolution of the species."[52]

The strict requirements of the act were not aimed so much at people who were obviously black or white—the 1910 law could easily be used to prevent such a marriage—but at those marginal people who could "pass" as white. It was through these mixed-blood individuals that the race would be corrupted, and with it civilization. Walter Plecker wrote that the law was needed not for the Negro, whose cheap labor the South valued, but because of the "mixed breeds," who were a "menace" and "the greatest problem and most destructive force which confronts the white race and American civilization."[53]

The 1924 act proved to be the high point for the ASCOA coalition. Further efforts to tighten the racial purity laws in 1926—for example, efforts to outlaw "illicit carnal communication" between people of different races and requests that the U.S. Congress appropriate funds for black repatriation—met with failure.[54]

Cox, however, was far from finished. During the fight for the Racial Integrity Act, Plecker, who had been in contact with a member of the Universal Negro Improvement Association (UNIA), brought that organization to Cox's attention. The UNIA was founded in 1914 by Marcus Garvey, a Jamaican publicist and organizer. Garvey came to the United States in 1915 to meet with one of his heroes, Booker T. Washington. Like Washington, Garvey preached racial self-help with a focus on economic advancement rather than civil or political rights. Garvey's UNIA was dedicated to black self-help, including building a black economy that would eventually fund the creation of a homeland for African Americans in Africa. Like Edward Blyden and other black nationalist leaders, Garvey did not believe that salvation could come from white society. As Garvey's organization grew in popularity in the 1920s, he came under increasing attack from W. E. B. Du Bois, the NAACP, and other racial progressives who were fighting for integration and political and civil rights for African Americans.[55]

By the time Garvey and Cox began corresponding, Garvey was imprisoned for mail fraud for financial improprieties surrounding his steamship line. Garvey viewed his imprisonment as a political act instigated by those within the civil rights movement who opposed his focus on racial pride. He had turned to white supremacists in part because he sought political allies against racial moderates such as the NAACP and other "mulattoes" whom he despised.[56]

He, his wife Amy Jacques Garvey, and Cox corresponded regularly, with Cox offering his support to Garvey's repatriation until Cox's death in 1965. Cox dedicated a short pamphlet, *Let My People Go,* to Garvey, and Garvey advertised *White America* in the pages of UNIA publications.[57]

Cox's relationship with Garvey and the UNIA was severely circumscribed, however. While both shared an interest in black reparation to Africa, for Garvey's movement repatriation was not necessarily the driving force for the membership. In his study of Garveyite membership, Emory Tolbert found that the UNIA was an important alternative to the middle-class NAACP for many members, but few even acknowledged that the "migration of all blacks back to Africa was . . . the explicit or implicit goal of the UNIA."[58] While Garvey advocated that African Americans establish a new geographic homeland in Africa, the core of his philosophy was built on an idea of racial separatism and self-help in order to achieve that goal. Black self-reliance was as important as the goal of an African homeland.[59] Cox, by contrast, cared little about black self-reliance as long as blacks were removed from the United States.

With Garvey's expulsion from the United States in 1927, his organization collapsed. At the dawn of the 1930s, however, Cox soon found those who claimed to be the heir to Garvey's dreams—black nationalists who called for a return of their people to Africa. Unlike Garvey, however, these nationalists were less interested in creating the black economy necessary to support voluntary repatriation and turned instead to federal funding for such efforts. For Garvey, going cap-in-hand like this to the white Congress would have been unthinkable; for those who claimed his mantle, and for Cox, it was the only logical course of action.

In addition to the remnants of Garvey's organization, Cox soon found another ally for the cause: Wickliffe Draper. Draper, like Grant, came from an established New England family. Also like Grant, Draper had a love of big-game hunting and the manly outdoor life as well as eugenics and racial preservation. Unlike Grant, Draper had no wish to be in the center of the action by heading up organizations and societies or by taking pen in hand to educate the American public. Indeed, Draper had every wish to remain out of the public eye as much as possible.[60] However, the wealthy Draper found a way to combine his wealth, his concern about racial amalgamation, and his reclusiveness by funding scientific projects he thought would demonstrate white superiority and the dangers of racial mixing. His most ambitious project in the 1920s was sponsoring Charles Davenport's studies on the mixing of races in Jamaica, which purported to show that white/black mating yielded individuals with disharmonious physical characteristics. Davenport's study was poorly received by the scientific community, who were beginning to retreat from the racial essentialism that informed how Davenport defined "race," as well as his methods for discovering disharmonious crosses between them.[61]

Draper was frustrated that his money was so poorly used by Davenport and went looking for better ways to show the public the dangers of racial intermingling. His search led him to Cox, who had been asked to speak at a meeting of the Eugenics Research Association in New York in 1936. Cox and Draper met that year, and soon after Draper bought one thousand copies of *White America* for distribution to influential individuals who could aid Cox in his quest for black repatriation. Draper's money proved to be well spent, for Cox and his allies found a sponsor for their repatriation efforts: Senator Theodore G. Bilbo of Mississippi, who had received a copy of the book and vowed to make Cox's dream a reality.[62]

As the 1930s drew to a close, Bilbo sponsored the Greater Liberia Bill, which called for monies to be dedicated to supporting voluntary black repatriation to Africa. Bilbo, an extreme racist even by the standards of the time, cared even less than Cox about black self-reliance. Many black nationalists who supported the bill were deeply suspicious of the overtly racist Bilbo; Cox was the pivotal figure in holding the fragile alliance together during the debates over the Bilbo's proposal. It was a short-lived effort, however; with the invasion of Poland by the Nazis in 1939, the meager support for Bilbo's effort vanished.[63]

The outbreak of war in Europe, and especially the American engagement after Pearl Harbor, meant more for Cox and his allies than the abandonment of the Greater Liberia Bill. World War II mobilized the country against an enemy with an explicitly racist agenda, which meant that those who espoused explicit racist ideas were under attack in a way they had never been before. The change in national attitude precipitated by the fight against the Nazis was only an added bit of ammunition in the fight against scientific racism.

Riding against the tide stood Grant and his coterie, who admired the Nazi race policies. In 1935 eugenicist Clarence G. Campbell and Cox's patron Wickliffe Draper attended a eugenics conference in Nazi Germany, where Campbell sang praises to Adolf Hitler.[64] However, Draper and Campbell were increasingly outside acceptable scientific opinion on racial matters. Nordicism and the scientific belief in white supremacy were already on the ropes in the 1930s. One of the exemplars of the battle was the racial interpretation of the new technology of intelligence testing. The rapid rise and decline of the racial interpretation of testing set the stage for the conspiratorial version of history offered by Grant regarding racial science.

Intelligence Testing and Race in the 1920s

The racial interpretation of intelligence tests in the wake of the U.S. Army's Alpha and Beta Tests during World War I is well known.[65] The tests consistently found differences in scores among different racial groups of people. Psychologist Carl Brigham popularized the army test results in his widely read *Study of American Intelligence.* Brigham found that only the Nordic race from northern Europe performed adequately on intelligence tests. Eastern and southern Europeans (the Alpine and Mediterranean races) were sub par, and "Negroes" fared even worse. Brigham recommended that immigration among Alpine and Mediterranean races be sharply curtailed and that segregation and miscegenation statutes be strictly enforced. As Graham Richards recently noted, Brigham's work was "explicitly Nordicist and Negrophobic."[66]

Less well known than the racist uses of intelligence tests are the critiques of these racial interpretations mounted by African American social scientists during the 1920s. In a series of writings, often appearing in the official organ of the NAACP, *The Crisis,* or that of the National Urban League, *Opportunity,* African American scholars attacked racial interpretations of intelligence test results. Historian W. B. Thomas noted that these scholars "(1) assailed the causal validity of prevailing hereditarian studies; (2) pointed out methodological errors and abuses in the assumptions and administration of mental tests; and (3) developed alternative data bases by administering the tests themselves."[67]

Among these African American scholars was the young Horace Mann Bond. Born in 1904 to upper-class, college-educated African American parents, Bond was a precocious learner. He received his college degree from Lincoln University at age nineteen. He entered graduate school at the University of Chicago, where he studied under Robert Park in sociology briefly before switching to the school of education. At Chicago, Bond would take two or three quarters of classes and then work for a year or two to earn tuition for further study, finally receiving his doctorate in 1936.[68]

Like many African Americans, Bond grew up reading *The Crisis,* edited by W. E. B. Du Bois, and in 1924, in his first published article, Bond joined the ranks of its authors. Bond warned of the dangers posed by what he took as the misuse of intelligence tests by those who were predisposed to think that Negroes were inferior in intelligence. The nineteen-year-old Bond took Carl Brigham to task for positing a racial explanation for differences in intelligence test scores. Bond pointed out that test scores for northern Negroes were higher than those for southern Negroes and noted that "a perusal of those nationalities whom [Brigham] classifies as inferior will be found to have a close correlation existing between the sums of money expended for education and their relatively low standing. . . . The time has passed," Bond wrote, "for opposing these false ideas with silence; every student of Negro blood ought to comprise himself into an agent whose sole purpose is the contravention of such half-truths."[69]

In a second article published that same year, Bond took aim at the claims made by Brigham, Terman, and others regarding the army tests. "It is on the basis of these tests," Bond wrote, "that the Nordic races have been granted the heaven sent mental superiority over Southern Europeans which entitles them to entry into this country; [and] that . . . justifies the policy of segregation in the public schools." But, he continued, the test's proponents seemed to run into a dilemma. According to the racial hypothesis of intelligence, "the representatives of such communities as Georgia and South Carolina, with the purest racial stock of the so-called Nordic branch now existent in America, would be superior to any other section [of the country]." But the results for those states showed "the medial score of White soldiers from the states of Mississippi, Kentucky, Arkansas, and Georgia, averaged . . . the mental age of a twelve and a half year old child." Bond asked, "Are the exponents of intelligence tests as discriminators of racial differences prepared to assert that the white population of Arkansas is inherently and racially inferior to the whites of another section of the country?"[70]

The critiques of African American scholars were not definitive, primarily because they were limited to low-prestige institutions and activist periodicals. However, their thrust was taken up and extended by white scholars such as Thomas Russell Garth and Otto Klineberg, both products of Columbia University and one (Klineberg) a student of Franz Boas.[71] In his study of the career of Thomas Garth, historian Graham Richards argued a close examination of Garth's career shows:

> At the heart of the demise of race psychology lay what looks suspiciously like a good old-fashioned "internal" failure. . . . The empirical research was inconclusive, the opposition's arguments were more powerful, and the new paradigms more interesting and productive. Failure to admit this was irrational. Those unable to accept the message were thus victims of a cognitive quasi-psychopathology and became marginalized within the discipline.[72]

Beyond seemingly intractable problems of test design, the impossibility of equalizing environments, and confusion about both the meaning of the scores themselves and "race" as a scientific category, hereditarian views of group differences in IQ scores were largely abandoned in the face of changes in social climate. Revulsion against the explicitly racist Nazi regime made scientific claims of racial superiority suspect in the minds of many mainstream social scientists. Not, however, for Madison Grant and others at the Galton Society.[73]

From Mainstream to Margin: Decline of the Galtonians

Despite the impressive roster of scientists who assembled for the Galton Society's monthly meetings, which it held beginning in 1918 and continuing into the 1930s, the society produced very little scientifically. The monthly meetings allowed Grant to give an address on the dangers facing the Nordic but did not spark new scientific research. The secretary of the society, William K. Gregory, asked Charles Davenport, "Which of us so far has taken up any new line of research or has modified his old methods, as a result of attending these meetings?"[74]

While the Galtonians clung to their old methods and interpretations, the Boasians were revolutionizing the study of anthropology, just as Klineberg and Garth had in race psychology. The culture concept was quickly supplanting the older racial studies as an explanation for group differences. Moreover, Boas's students were firmly in control of both university anthropology departments as well as the discipline's journals. The Nordicism of the Galton Society and hereditarian interpretations of group differences in general were supplanted by new cultural interpretations. Grant explained the rejection of his racial science as an "anti-Nordic conspiracy," to which Henry Fairfield Osborn replied, "There is undoubtedly a conspiracy of the Radicals against the whole Nordic and racial theory."[75]

By the 1930s, the Galton Society was in disarray. Its driving force, Madison Grant, was seen by many as out of touch with both the new egalitarian sciences as well as the political climate of the Great Depression. Grant's second book on the race problem, *Conquest of a Continent,* was seen as anachronistic by many reviewers in the 1930s. "Substitute Aryan for Nordic," noted reviewer William Macdonald in the *New York Times,* "and a good deal of Mr. Grant's argument would lend itself without much difficulty to the support of some recent pronouncements and proceedings in Germany."[76] "By the early 1930s," historian Mathew Pratt Guterl wrote, "only the far right maintained an abiding interest in the calling cards of authoritarian antidemocracy: racial eugenics, forced sterilization, and state control of the gene pool."[77]

Many supporters of the Jim Crow system of the American South, however, did not recognize the similarities between the authoritarian racial regime of the Nazis and the authoritarian racial regime of Dixie. Throughout the 1930s, southern newspapers were nearly unanimous in their condemnation of Nazi racism, seemingly unaware that their racial attitudes toward African Americans were eerily similar to the Nazi's attitudes toward the Jews. As a consequence, as social scientists brought their talents to bear against race prejudice by pointing out that the Nazi doctrines of race supremacy had no basis in modern science, and that a necessary part of the war effort was to unify the country through the elimination of race prejudice, many Southerners read these as attacks against Jim Crow and the southern way of life—which, of course, they were.[78]

Races of Mankind and the Jews

In October 1943, the Public Affairs Committee, Inc., published a small pamphlet entitled *Races of Mankind,* authored by Boasian anthropologists Ruth Benedict and Gene Weltfish, both of Columbia University. Benedict and Weltfish claimed they wrote *Races of Mankind* to aid the war effort. "Most Americans are confident," they wrote, "that, whatever our origins, we shall be able to pull together to a final victory. Hitler, though, has always believed we were wrong. . . . He has believed especially that America was a no man's land, where peoples of all origins were ready to fall to fighting among themselves. He believes this is a front on which we are doomed to lose the battle. It is certainly no less important in this war than the Production Front and the Inflation Front."[79]

Benedict and Weltfish devoted the bulk of *Races of Mankind* to debunking Hitler's racial notions. According to Benedict and Weltfish, there were no reliable indicators of "race" at all. Moreover, there were no reliable indicators that one "race" was, in any way, innately superior to another. They pointed to the results of the army tests of intelligence during World War I and argued that the Negroes in northern states outscored southern whites, but that this was no indicator of innate racial difference; rather, it indicated greater expenditures on education in northern states. Moreover, civilization, contrary to Nordic doctrines, was not the product of race. "There were great Negro states in Africa when Europe was a sparsely settled forest. Negroes made iron tools and wove fine cloth for their clothing when fair-skinned Europeans wore skins and knew nothing of iron."[80]

Within a few months, controversy began to swirl around *Races of Mankind.* The army had purchased fifty thousand copies to distribute in orientation courses. U.S. Representative Andrew J. May of Kentucky blocked the distribution of the book through the House Military Committee. In particular, May was outraged by the claims of northern black intelligence scores when compared to southern whites. "It won't be distributed by the Army," May declared. "We intend to keep an eye open and see that this book does not go out to our soldiers through War Department channels. If it does, somebody is going to have to do plenty of explaining." The United Service Organizations (USO) also dropped the circulation of the pamphlet, for similar reasons. One of the sponsors of the pamphlet, Harold S. Sloan of the Alfred Sloan Foundation, defended the pamphlet by noting, "It seems a pity that the Military Affairs Committee of the house sees fit to withhold from our armed forces the simple fact of science that completely refute the enemy's contention of a super race."[81]

For Gene Weltfish, the controversy over *Races of Mankind* would prove the beginning of a controversial career. As an untenured member of Columbia's faculty, Weltfish was a radical feminist and belonged to a number of leftist political groups that were deemed subversive after World War II. Columbia stood by her in the early 1950s when she took the Fifth Amendment before the congressional committee who had asked her if she were a member of the Communist Party, but it refused to renew her annual contract in 1952 after she publicly proclaimed that she could prove the United States had used germ warfare during the Korean War. In 1953, Roy Cohn, Joe McCarthy's counsel, would offer the fact that *Races of Mankind* was found in State Department libraries as evidence of Communist infiltration of the government.[82]

For the racist Right, however, Communism was the least of the problems with *Races of Mankind*. The real problem was the Jews. In the midst of the controversy during World War II, Senator Bilbo sent a copy of the pamphlet to Cox, asking him to review it. In his review, Cox quickly noted the university affiliations of the authors: "The Department of Anthropology of Columbia University was brought into considerable prominence by the late Professor Franz Boas, a Jew . . . who labored long and with great energy to break down the American concepts of race and promote general miscegenation. There is nothing of moment in the pamphlet that is not found in the prolific works of Dr. Boas, and I assume the authors to be his disciples."[83]

Cox was not concerned, as Representative May was, with the psychometric data of intelligence tests. For Cox, the real issue was the racial ancestry of past civilizations. Cox declared that Egypt was a white civilization that fell because of racial intermingling. Moreover, the great civilizations of western Europe were the product of "one particular race of Europe, the Teuton race, descendants of which as Anglo-Saxons and allied racial stocks Dr. Boas found well established in the United States and proposed that they should be mixed with the Negro."[84]

Cox proclaimed that the science represented by *Races of Mankind* was, in fact, part of a Jewish conspiracy led by Franz Boas to sap the strength of the Nordic United States. Rejecting Benedict and Weltfish's claim that there was no Jewish race, Cox pointed to the Jewish domination of non-Jewish states. "The Jew," Cox wrote, "always a minority, could not dominate all nations by physical force. He entered these nations not in armed array but by process of infiltration. . . . It is absolutely certain that the Jew in his domination of nations had to have aid from non-Jews. . . . The technique of using 'Gentile Fronts" to promote Jewish scheme must be an old one."[85]

The technique that the Jews had used throughout the ages, Cox declared, was just the technique that Boas used to destroy the racial basis of the United States. "The colonial stock had established this nation and given to it laws and institutions on such a broad base of freedom that Dr. Boas, as a newly arrived immigrant, had liberty to propose the complete abolition of the stock that had established the nation," Cox wrote. While he felt he had sufficient evidence to show that Boas was bent on the destruction of a racially pure United States, Cox was hesitant to claim that Benedict and Weltfish were actually part of the scheme, "for though the authors are from the schoolhouse of Professor Boas they may feel that they are advancing his schemes wholly uninfluenced by his personality."[86]

Bilbo used the core of Cox's critique in his 1947 book *Take Your Choice: Separation or Mongrelization.* Cox's critique became a large section of chapter 10, "Astounding Revelations to White America." Bilbo stripped the overt anti-Semitism of Cox's review while keeping the conspiracy claim central:

> Where is the true, straight-thinking, decent white American man or woman who can read of the dreams of objectives of Professor Boas without being nauseated? But we cannot dismiss his teachings with a shrug of the shoulders regardless of how much we would like to turn away from them in disgust. As Professor and Dean of Anthropology and Ethnology of Columbia University, this immigrant from Germany—totally un-American to the last—literally pried open Pandora's box. Through the tens of thousands of students who came under his influence and teachings and accepted them, he scattered his evil, disastrous, and racial suicidal preachments and his insane and corrupt doctrines of miscegenation, amalgamation, intermarriage, and mongrelization throughout this broad land. Carefully and deliberately he sowed the seeds for the undermining of both the white and Negro races in this Nation.[87]

Bilbo died in 1947, the same year *Take Your Choice* was published, and it is probably the last statement of Radical southern racial ideology published by a major political figure in the United States. However, Earnest

Sevier Cox lived for another two decades. Cox never surrendered the dream of a white America and would continue to publish, aided by generous grants from Wickliffe Draper.[88] He also continued correspond with others who shared his vision of black repatriation and a racially pure United States. For this group surrounding Cox, the doctrines of Nordicism remained a guide to their view of the world. The Jew, often in the form of Boas and his students, remained as the chief villain who was blocking the implementation of Nordic doctrines. Madison Grant's view of the world, and of Boas, lived on in the racist underground of the American right wing in the postwar United States. The belief in the Boasian conspiracy would be kept alive by the underground to emerge once again in the polarized racial politics in the American South in the 1950s, following *Brown v. Board of Education.*

3

Radical Right Underground

Cox was the link between the racialist thought of the 1920s and the racialist thought of the 1950s. In 1951, Earnest Sevier Cox published *Teutonic Unity*. Like *White America*, the book was self-published. Unlike *White America*, Cox did not offer *Teutonic Unity* for sale but distributed it at his own expense to government officials as well as historians "in the nations of the Teutonic broodland and in the several nations formed during the Teutonic migrations."[1] One person who received the books was Dr. Johann von Leers, an expatriate Nazi living in Argentina. "I have participated in the ideological indoctrination of Hitler's bodyguard SS, to which I belonged," wrote von Leers to Cox, "and now I find with surprise that more or less all what was the central idea of our thinking and indoctrination I find again the book of an American writer." von Leers offered to translate Cox's book into German so it could be read in that country, for "neither the Russian rule in the East nor the Jewish democracy backed by the Church in Western Germany have a future."[2]

von Leers had worked directly under Joseph Goebbels editing the anti-Semitic *Wille und Weg* and writing twenty-seven books criticizing the Jews. After the war, he had escaped to Argentina and continued to publish *Der Weg*, which remained faithful to the most anti-Semitic aspects of Nazi ideology. Soon after this he immigrated to Egypt, converted to Islam, and continued to churn out anti-Semitic propaganda for Gamal Nasser. In the words of historian Kurt Tauber, von Leers was "[i]n the very front rank of those for whom the catastrophe of 1945 and the unspeakable vulgarity and savagery of the Hitler regime held absolutely no lesson at all."[3] The same might be said about the figures I discuss in this chapter, many of whom followed the racial ideology of Nazi regime rather closely.

Two things about *Teutonic Unity* impressed von Leers. First were Cox's familiar Nordicist arguments that the basis of all civilization was

Nordic (or, in Cox's term, Teutonic). Cox decried the "fratricidal wars" of the twentieth century that pitted Teuton against Teuton and called for peace among Teutons and an alliance with the Slavs of the East. "Each should recognize that in their Nordic blood they have ancient blood ties, the one with the other," he wrote, and advised that an alliance would guarantee that "for . . . the present time nor in any predictable future will these great races be endangered, save one from the other."[4]

The second praiseworthy aspect of Cox's work, according to von Leers, was Cox's argument concerning Christianity. Cox argued that Christianity was a "Judaic religion" and basically intolerant of other faiths, especially the Nordic pagan faiths. This meant, for Cox, that Christianity, like Judaism and Islam, was a "gangster religion." Cox firmly rejected the notion that the Nordic pagans needed Christianity as a basis for a moral code. "Nor will we debase our own race in the eyes of posterity nor give to mankind a belief that Saxons knew not a distinction between right and wrong until they had been brought under Jewish religious instruction. For this reason alone we would reject the Ten Commandments as a code."[5] Additionally, because it rejected any empirical finding that conflicted with the Bible, Christianity was responsible for halting scientific knowledge and progress "as science began to question the validity of much that had been proclaimed as knowledge revealed by God to the Jews."[6]

Teutonic Unity and its favorable reception by von Leers indicated the continuity in Cox's ideological beliefs across the great divide of the Second World War. Cox's call for Negro repatriation continued after the war as well, despite the death of Theodore Bilbo, the congressional sponsor for repatriation. In 1949, to Cox's surprise, he found a repatriation bill had been introduced by Senator William Langer of North Dakota. Throughout the 1950s, Cox would work with Langer and a number of black nationalist groups to pass a repatriation bill.[7]

What had changed after the war was Cox's standing as the elder statesman of the racialist right wing in the United States. The greater lights of the 1920s, Madison Grant and Lothrop Stoddard, had passed away before the end of the war, leaving Cox as the most prominent surviving American Nordicist from the twenties. As such, he became a revered figure for a new generation of racialist right-wing figures who shared his views regarding race and the Nordic basis of civilization.

Northern League

Cox's status was evidenced by his honored position in the Northern League. Founded in 1957 in Calcutta by British Army officer Roger Pearson, the Northern League was an organization dedicated to building "Pan Nordic friendship."[8] Pearson, who would eventually earn an anthropology doctorate from the University of London in 1969, was convinced that Darwin had shown the necessity and value of racial struggle. In this, he took his lead from Sir Arthur Keith (1866–1955), a renowned British anthropologist who had been one of the two corresponding members of Grant's Galton Society. Trained as an anatomist, Keith would himself train Harvard's Earnest Hooten, who was Boas's main sparring partner in the academic anthropological community, as well as Ashley Montagu, the heir to Boas's title as equalitarian villain to scientific racists.[9]

In 1916, Keith gave a public lecture wherein he announced his theory that race prejudice, far from being a learned trait that could be unlearned and therefore avoided, was, in fact, an innate instinct responsible for the very act of natural selection. As Keith later recalled, he began with the common idea that "to make evolution an effective process there must be a machinery of group isolation." Keith argued that Darwin conceived of geographical boundaries such as mountains, deserts, and seas to serve as this mechanism for group isolation. However, people could transverse these barriers, which led Keith to his search for "machinery which would keep groups or communities permanently apart and so isolated." The search for this mechanism led him to observe that racial and ethnic friction was endemic all over the globe. "Human nature itself provided the means of isolation of which I was in search," Keith proclaimed. "Inborn human nature as a factor in securing isolation," thus leading to speciation and evolutionary change, meant that an inborn racial prejudice was unavoidable and, indeed, a key mechanism for the evolution of the human species.[10]

Keith developed his idea that racial prejudice and nationalism were the driving forces behind human evolution through two world wars. World War I was the cataclysmic event that inspired Keith's idea that war could be mechanism for evolution, as the weak were culled and tribal, national, and racial barriers were erected to prevent intermingling of races. World War II, Keith maintained, merely proved his ideas correct. "The German Fuehrer . . . is an evolutionist; he has consciously sought to make the practice of Germany conform to the theory of evolution." When critics accused Keith of being an apologist for German atrocities, Keith waved the accusation aside as sentimentalism in the face of nature's brutal ways. "The process of evolution has been at work from the beginning of time," he explained; "all that Darwin did was to draw the attention of humanity to its existence." As a simple messenger, Keith could not accept responsibility for revealing nature's brutal truths, just like Darwin: "Were I to give a vivid account of a criminal trial that should not lay me open to the charge of being in complicity with the criminal.[11]

In 1958, Pearson announced his allegiance to what he took to be Keith's views in an article he published in *The European,* which in turn was published by British fascist Oswald Mosley. While Mosley had intended *The European* to serve as a forum for debating his ideas in public, in practice it attracted only contributors who had some sympathy to fascism and debated the type of fascism that Europe should implement. In Mosley's journal, Pearson praised the theories of Keith, noting that "many will see [Keith's observations] as a defence of Hitlerite philosophy." Pearson decried modern civilization's foolish attempt to overcome tribal and racial prejudices, for when "the pattern of genes is lost . . . the work of evolution is destroyed." The lower species lived on "instead of meeting the natural death which competition, instead of assimilation, would have brought it." Pearson declared that, with the influx of inferior types into Britain, "another evolutionary experiment is on its way to an untimely end." Such a view would become a staple of much of the writing produced by members of the Northern League.[12]

In the 1950s, the Northern League produced two publications: *Northern World* and *The Northlander.* As these publications made clear, Pearson's organization was dedicated to a pure Nordic science; the first issue of *The Northlander* announced new works by Nazi Nordicist Hans F. K. Guenther, and the third offered a fawning portrait of Houston Stewart Chamberlain. The League defined its aims as preserving the "biological and cultural" heritage of the Nordic while destroying the "leveling forces of Communistic and Cosmopolitan theory." Pearson contributed articles on Arthur Keith as well as recommending a policy of "Pan-Nordicism," which, he argued, could be viewed as the Nordic's "splendid patriotic duty." What was needed was for "a totalitarian state, with conscious purpose and central control . . . to embark upon a thorough-going policy of genetic change for its population. . . . [T]here is surely little doubt that it could soon outstrip rival nations."[13]

So fervently did Cox believe in the aims of the Northern League that he became a member. This was unusual for Cox, as he normally shunned membership in any organization that was not dedicated solely to repatriation of the American Negro. Roger Pearson, however, assured Cox that "I am entirely with you on your efforts to obtain Federal aid to American Negroes who wish to return to Africa." Conversely, Cox shared with Pearson the desire to foster Nordic friendship across national boundaries, as he advocated in *Teutonic Unity.* Cox suggested to Pearson that the League sponsor a "ceremony . . . at the battle site in the Teutoberger Forest where Herman's defeat of the Romans prevented the mongrelization of Germany."[14]

As it developed, the League did indeed meet in the Teutoberger Forest, as Cox suggested. Cox and Pearson had labored mightily to have Hans F. K. Guenther give a speech at the meeting but also worked hard to ensure that Guenther's presence was not widely known. Cox himself was an honored speaker at the meeting, although he was ill and needed to have his speech read for him.[15]

The Northern League was a clearinghouse of sorts for a number of disparate racialist organizations and publications in the United States. Not only was it linked to Cox's efforts for repatriation, but it also united Cox to political activist Willis Carto and a number of ideologues clustered around a small publication called *Truth Seeker.* All these individuals shared a belief in racial inequality, Nordic supremacy, and the Jewish control over racial discourse.[16]

Willis Carto, Aldrich Blake, and Political Action

In 1954, Cox received a letter from Willis Carto (b. 1926), a political activist who wrote to express his admiration for Cox's writings, especially Cox's review of *Races of Mankind,* because, as Carto explained, "the theory and science of race . . . becomes of staggering importance in this day of racial contact."[17] Racial science was a concern of Carto, who had written an "open letter" to the Regents of the University of California under his pseudonym of "E. L. Anderson, Ph.D." Carto warned of the deliberate suppression of racial science while "equalitarianism," which was "the idiot-child of the Russian tin-god Lysenko," was living on "at the expense of society."[18] For the remaining decade of his life, Cox would remain in close contact with Carto, who was dedicating his time to building the racialist right wing of American politics. By the time he contacted Cox, Carto was deeply involved in conservative political groups, including the anti-internationalist group the Congress of Freedom, but was working most closely with a political activist, Aldrich Blake.[19]

Aldrich Blake came to national prominence in the 1920s when he was the executive counselor for Oklahoma governor J. C. Walton. The colorful and unorthodox Walton had run for governor on an "antiestablishment" platform and was elected governor in 1922. Upon election, Walton immediately caused controversy through political patronage appointments and financial improprieties that seemed designed to enrich the governor personally. In August 1923, when local Klansmen began beating and flogging those in Tulsa whom they suspected of being lawbreakers, Walton declared martial law. While Walton did succeed in sentencing Klansmen to prison for rioting—the first governor in the nation to succeed in legal action against the Klan—his actions provided ammunition for his political opponents, and the legislature impeached him in November 1923.[20]

While Walton lost the governorship, at least in part because of his stand against the Klan, his chief aide in the fight, Aldrich Blake, used the national prominence of the Tulsa riot to become prominent on the lecture circuit. Blake told his story in a lecture titled "The Ku Klux Kraze: A Trip through the Klavern." In Detroit, at one stop on his tour, Blake was greeted by five thousand Klansmen, who had to be dispersed by local police using tear gas.[21]

For Blake, the problem with the Klan was not necessarily that their goals were incorrect; it was that their antidemocratic ways prevented the achievement of those goals. According to Blake, the Klan proclaimed itself to be for law and order, "one-hundred percent Americanism," Protestantism, and white supremacy, but the Klan's methods were inadequate to these tasks. For example, on immigration, one of the important issues of the day, Blake argued that keeping foreigners out led to the decline of Athens and Sparta, while letting them in led to the decline of Rome. The key, then, was to regulate how much foreign blood came into country. "Does it require a hood and gown and secret signs to solve a profound scientific problem of this kind?" Blake sneered. "That there ought to be a careful regulation of immigration, the people of all races will admit, but shall we leave this to the students of race eugenics or to goblins and cyclops and titans and wizards?"[22]

The Klan's methods were similarly inadequate for ensuring white supremacy. Blake argued that the Klan was actually counterproductive in its fight to "make the south a white man's country. Does the Klan imagine that those negroes could mysteriously disappear into the air or into the bowels of the earth?" In fact, Blake argued, the southern Negro migrated north in response to the Klan's terror, making the Negro problem a national one rather than one that was confined to the South. "Is it best for white civilization to confine the negro in the south, where he is more happy than anywhere else, or shall we support the Klan terror, send the negro on a joy ride around the country?"[23]

The Negro's "joy ride" would become Blake's major concern after World War II. He was not alone. The effect of the Great Migration of African Americans out of the American South and into northern cities, which had begun after World War I and accelerated during World War II, caused, in Thomas Sugrue's words, "a profound transformation in the politics, urban geography, and economies of dozens of large northern industrial cities. . . . Urban whites . . . redefine[d] urban politics in starkly racial terms." One critical facet of the urban white reaction to the influx of African Americans into their neighborhoods was to set the issue in terms of "freedom of choice." The issue turned on the notion that the government should not interfere with a private citizen's freedom to discriminate, even on racial grounds, in employees, rental agreements, or even the sale of a private home.[24]

Blake became an eloquent defender of this kind of freedom of choice, and his writings demonstrated how the libertarian ideals of private property and contract could combine with the more conspiratorial rhetoric of the racist Right. His most extensive presentation of his racial views was in his 1950 novel, *My Kind! My Country!* The novel is set in a mythical town in the United States, New Holland. It tells the story of Martha Wilder, a woman from one of the most established families in town, and her husband, Jim. The novel consists of a series of set pieces wherein the characters put forth various viewpoints on "the race problem" in the years surrounding World War II. It also provides a clear view of the themes of racial politics of the 1950s: many of those who call for civil rights are naive and misled by social science; civil rights agitators are Communists and agents of the Soviet Union; Jews are not trustworthy or truly loyal to the United States; those who oppose civil rights do not hate racial minorities but merely recognize that people prefer to associate with those of their own race.

At the opening of the book, Europe is already embroiled in World War II, but America has not yet joined the fight. Jim, an accomplished novelist, is beginning a new book on the race problem that he titles *Assignment Utopia*. Jim is portrayed as a well-meaning but naive person who has read too much "brotherhood of man" propaganda. Martha Wilder is upset by her husband's new work, but not as upset as by her discovery that a Negro girl, Susie, has enrolled in the same school as her youngest daughter, Alice. As the story develops, we discover that Susie is the granddaughter of Sam Ford, a trusted family servant. Sam explains that he wants a good education for his girl, but he does not want to offend Martha. "Mebbe 'twould be best if we sent Susie back to the school she's been in. We sure don't want to 'barrass our white folk friends, specially you, Miss Martha."[25] Susie's racial crisis is averted when Martha works with "Grandma Weinberg," a good Jewish matriarch of the community, to build a private school for the Negroes of New Holland to replace the inadequate public one. But, as Grandma Weinberg explains to Martha, there is no good solution to the ongoing race problem: "You can't solve the race problem any more than you can keep the human body free from aches. A good osteopath can soothe a muscle but he can't prevent other muscles from getting sore. I fear that America, our country, is in for a lot of sore muscles."[26]

Martha becomes determined to save her town from the encroachments of African Americans who threaten to move into white neighborhoods. To her dismay, they are assisted by her husband, who has nothing but sympathy for the Negro cause. Jim goes so far as to insist on taking the family vacation at Grand Lake, the Jewish resort, rather than Pine Manor, the traditional family vacation spot, which is restricted against Jews. At Grand Lake, Jim meets Max Abrams, a rich Jewish Hollywood producer, who entices Jim to write *Assignment Utopia* for the screen. Abrams assures Jim that "*[t]he United States will be in the war before the year is out. The attack will come from the Orient. The whole world will be aflame. It's going to be a long war. . . . Our confidential reports are seldom wrong.*"[27] As Jim becomes more and more involved with Jewish Hollywood, Martha resolves to write her own book, defending the right of those who wish to choose their neighbors and employees even, or perhaps especially, on a racial basis. The question of racial equality is secondary to the fundamental issue of racial separation. Martha declares at one point that the matter of racial equality is beside the point; there is a natural racial aversion, regardless of whether or not that aversion has a grounding in real racial differences or not. "So far as whites, blacks, and yellows are concerned," she declares, "I think that color keeps them apart more than anything else."[28]

Perhaps the most interesting ally Martha has is Willard Jones, a character obviously based on Gerald L. K. Smith, whom Blake had supported at one time. Morton Green, Martha's closest ally in town in fighting the Civil Rights Ordinance, explains that Jones believes all Jews are Communists and that "Jones has a big following, but his people are extremists. We want their help without an open alliance."[29]

When Martha goes to meet Jones, she finds him a calm and dispassionate person who is merely concerned with minority control over majority rights. "Economically the Jew is the most dangerous of our minority groups," explains Jones. "His dollar is the only army and navy he has. Already he controls much of American business and industry without owning it. He may not own a single share of stock in a bank but he controls certain aspects of its policy through his huge deposits. He may not own a newspaper, but as an advertiser he can influence it in many ways."[30]

Allied against her fight to maintain the racial integrity of her hometown is her husband, Jim, who has been taken in by the "sociologists," who were "too much on the sentimental side, inclined to do what they thought was good";[31] "Negro Anderson," a rich black man with a white wife; and Jake Bernstein, the editor of a radical Jewish newspaper, *The Call*, which is constantly agitating for "civil rights." Anderson and Bernstein are publicly working hard for a Fair Employment Practices Act while privately hoping that their proposed bill fails because, in reality, they are both Communist agents who think that they can use the discrimination issue to their advantage. If the Fair Employment Practices Act fails, explains Bernstein, "[t]he *Call* will spend the time agitating. God, how the niggers and Jews will holler when they get beat. We'll make Commies or fellow travelers out of all of 'em. They'll come through with dough and they'll all be reading the *Call*!"[32]

Eventually, the two Russian agents, Anderson and Bernstein, engineer a race riot by planting an African American soldier in a white-owned restaurant. When the soldier is refused service, a minor scuffle breaks out that soon spreads throughout the town, aided by rumors spread by the Communists in the black community that a white police officer has killed a black man and, in the white community, that a black man has raped a white woman. The riot results in thirty-eight people dead in the town and hundreds injured. However, the riot also provides the solution to the racial problems that the community faces. Phil Ford, a Negro leader in the community, delivers the memorial service for the slain Negroes. Portrayed throughout the book as a brilliant mulatto who graduated first in his class at UCLA, Ford calls for the creation of a separate state for African Americans, called Negroland. Because racial friction is inevitable, Phil Ford announces, the only solution to the country's racial problems is the complete separation of the races into different political entities, which solves the problem of northern migration of Negroes and the southern problem of segregation in one fell swoop.

Immediately after the funeral, Martha returns home to her husband to break a piece of awful news to him: because of his quixotic views regarding racial equality, their own children have made dreadful mistakes. Their son, David, has chosen to marry an Orthodox Jewish girl who despises Negroes; their other son, Harry, has chosen to marry a Japanese girl who despises Jews; and their precious daughter is in love with the mulatto Phil Ford. In a sudden flash, Jim realizes the error of his ways: "A new social brew, composed of Jew, Gentile, white, black, and yellow, about to take over the Wilder tent, a conglomeration of blood strains, skin textures, unfamiliar habits and customs, different ideologies, and deeply imbedded human likes and dislikes which would soon supplant the Emory and Wilder family roots!" He had been "duped by two subversive rascals! Victim of rash sentimentalism! . . . Taken in by Max Abrams!"[33] With Jim's realization of the error of his ways, the Wilders manage to save their family and then their community. Anderson and Bernstein are arrested by the FBI when Anderson's white wife turns state's evidence against them. The book closes in 1975, as Martha Wilder enjoys her eightieth birthday on the same day that Phil Ford is inaugurated as the first president of Negroland in the former state of Mississippi.

In the book's introduction, Blake claimed that these characters did not speak for him, but he did note that the complete separation of blacks into their own state "reflects, in the opinion of the author, *the most powerful inner yearnings and hope of both the white and black races in America.* I am sure that the majority of both groups would like to see the race problem resolved in Phil Ford's way, if it could be brought about by some inspired miracle of statecraft."[34] Blake's solution of a separate state, however, would not work for American Jews. As Dr. Huxley explains to Martha, "The American Jew wants to create a separate nation within another nation, providing himself with a double alliance—two flags—one, that of the United States, the other that of Israel. Thus, he will be able to continue to prosper where he now lives, and at the same time satisfy his racial pride by the formation of a new Jewish Nation."[35]

Blake's novel contained the essential message of his, and Carto's, political activities in the early 1950s. For Blake, the battle for civil rights was not against the South's Jim Crow laws (which were almost never mentioned in his writing) but in northern cities where civil rights commissions were attempting to pass antidiscrimination laws in housing, public accommodations, and employment. In 1953, Blake wrote, "It may surprise you to know that there are now one or more state laws covering 139 different phases of the so-called civil rights problem in America." Just as in his fictional account, the minority agitation of the NAACP, the Anti-Defamation League, and the Communist Party was to blame for these antidiscrimination laws. According to Blake, these organizations used the same tactics of intimidation and subversion as the Klan had in the 1920s. "I have no list of the personnel of the hidden minority Gestapo, no sensational exposure of its conspiratorial activities to make," Blake declared. "I need none. For the Gestapo's strategy and methods are an open book."[36]

In 1952, Blake joined forces with California state senator Jack B. Tenney, who had been the chairman of the anti-Communist Fact-Finding Committee on Un-American Activities for the state, to form America PLUS—P for Property, L for Liberty, U for Unity, and S for Strength. Blake and Tenney worked to ensure that the property rights of home owners could be maintained in the face of encroachment by racial minorities. Among other things, America PLUS called for a constitutional amendment restoring the rights of property owners to enforce restrictive covenants preventing the sale of homes to racial minorities.[37]

America PLUS was changing in 1954 as Blake and Carto changed the name of the organization to Liberty and Property, a political organization dedicated to fighting the activities of the "minority Gestapo" against which Blake had been writing. Blake provided the ideological agenda and Carto the organizational work. As the name indicated, the organization embraced a libertarian idea of property rights, including the right to protect the disposition of one's private property in a racially discriminatory manner. Blake proposed a "Second Bill of Rights" that forbade the federal income tax and wage and price controls, as well as membership in the United Nations. It also guaranteed right-to-work laws and the right of landlords and owners of places of public accommodation to dispose of their property as they saw fit. Carto proclaimed that Blake's "new approach to the problems faced by the forces of liberty and property" was "both original and startling."[38]

Despite the accolades Carto gave Blake, within months Blake had withdrawn from Liberty and Property, ostensibly for health reasons, leaving Carto in control of the organization.[39] Carto immediately set to work remaking the organization more along his lines. In 1955 he used his contacts to create, with Cox's blessing, the Joint Council on Repatriation (JCR), an odd mix of black nationalists and white racists working together for moving African Americans back to Africa. The need for such an organization, explained Carto, was that "the revolutionists have seen to it that only a few Americans are concerned about the inevitable niggerfication of America. And present-day academic trends are, if anything, even better designed to keep racial truths from the attention of the growing generations."[40] The JCR did little to repatriate anyone anywhere and existed only on paper, and perhaps to give Carto another avenue to search for funds.

Carto was more serious about uniting the disparate branches of the American right wing. Writing to Blake, he noted that "rightwing activity in America shows definite signs of growth. Indeed, if things continue on the upgrade, the enemy has much to worry about."[41] Carto also began publishing *Right,* a monthly newsmagazine that pushed his agenda. In November 1955, *Right* announced that "Liberty and Property has recently soft-pedaled its political program in order to concentrate on its objective of attempting to bring all patriotic groups a little closer together." Race and the science of race would remain a central preoccupation of Carto throughout his career. Writing in 1957 under his pseudonym "E. L. Anderson, Ph.D.," Carto declared, "Most of the books on this vitally important subject [of the science of race] have been suppressed by the Anti-Defamation League Gestapo and related subversive groups."[42]

Carto also attempted to bring Cox into the movement. In 1956, as part of this unification effort, Carto wrote to Cox to ask if Cox was "in correspondence with Robert Kuttner, of the University of Connecticut? If not, you should be. Definitely." In a later letter, Carto explained that Kuttner "is a real brain. A very, extremely valuable man for our side, and a racist to his toes."[43] Carto's introduction of Cox into the world of the Robert Kuttner also introduced Cox to another outpost of the Northern League. Kuttner was an associate editor of the journal *Truth Seeker,* which historian Frank P. Mintz declared to be the forum for "the most extreme racist sentiments ventilated in postwar America," and which Willis Carto declared as full of "wonderful work."[44]

Charles Smith and Truth Seeker

Truth Seeker was founded in 1873 as a forum for free thought and atheism. It was part of what Jennifer Michael Hecht has called "evangelical atheism," led by people who were convinced that they had an obligation not just privately to doubt God's existence but to convince others to abandon their religious beliefs.[45] Between 1937 and 1964 it was edited by Charles Lee Smith. The son of a Methodist minister, Smith had been converted to free thought by reading Thomas Jefferson's writings. In the 1920s, Smith became a distributor and writer for the Truth Seeker and was arrested several times by New York authorities for doing so. He founded the American Association for the Advancement of Atheism (4A) in 1925, which enjoyed a small amount of notoriety for its aggressive stance toward religious leaders. 4A sponsored a series of lectures, the Ingersoll Forum, in New York City, where speakers would discuss science and religion or debate well-known ministers. In addition to his activities in New York, Smith was arrested for blasphemy in 1928 while distributing pamphlets in Arkansas promoting atheism and criticizing the state's antievolution laws. The charges against him were eventually dropped, but not until a long series of court appeals and a hunger strike by Smith. In 1931, Truth Seeker editor George E. MacDonald wrote that Smith was "a man with no sense that enables him to detect defeat. He has lectured and been hissed, debated and lost the decision, taken the aggressive and been repulsed, agitated and landed in jail, talked Atheism and been convicted of blasphemy, attempted the enlightenment of a prophet of God and been fined for his pains."[46]

While it was not apparent from the first fifteen years of his editorship, Smith was the heir to a particular brand of Darwinism that combined atheism with racism. In this he followed ideas first expressed by a French writer, Vacher de Lapouge (1854–1936), who, along with Arthur Keith, had been a corresponding member of the Galton Society. Lapouge and Nordicists who followed him, most notably Hans F. K. Guenther, founded a science he called anthroposociology. An outspoken atheist, Lapouge had no patience for Chamberlain's and Gobineau's emphasis on a "race-soul." Anthroposociology was completely materialist and rejected any and all appeals to any sort of quasi-religious mysticism. For Lapouge, the science spoke for itself and had no need for any other concepts, and certainly not for any religious or moral ideas. He called for the elimination of all moral sentiment that would stand in the way of a massive breeding program that would eliminate racial inferiors. In his writings, Lapouge warned that sentimentality, especially religious faith, blocked the necessary social reforms for the elimination of racial inferiors through selective breeding. Like Ernst Haeckel in Germany, Lapouge rejected all religion and all morality and called for a strict breeding program that left no room for environmental improvements. For Lapouge, the only solution to the racial crisis would be the elimination of the inferior races.[47]

Like Lapouge, Smith believed that atheism and racism were flip sides of the same coin. By far the most outspoken of *Truth Seeker*'s writers, Smith was a Nordicist of enough repute to have been a featured speaker in the Teutoberger Forest along with Cox.[48] Smith left a very complete record of his particular ideology in *Sensism: The Philosophy of the West,* a sprawling, sixteen-hundred-page work he published in 1956.[49] Shot through with neologisms and often shy of coherence, *Sensism* proclaimed that the spiritual realm had no meaning other than in people's minds, and that sense data were the only source of meaning for human activity.[50]

Of more significance for Smith's philosophy were his criticisms of the concept of equality. Smith argued that Christianity's doctrine of spiritual equality was not rational. In the present political climate, obvious physical differences were swept away in favor of easy "brotherhood of man" slogans. This was a danger to clear thinking and racial self-preservation, Smith argued, because "[t]his religion conditions its accepters against self-protection" by denying the justice of racial and ethnic discrimination.[51] Smith argued that communism and Christianity were both committed to equality and therefore equally dangerous. "The Christian Gospel and the Marxian message is equalism," Smith declared. "With the decline of faith in the Bible . . . it was inevitable that equalism . . . would be expressed in the form of Communism."[52]

The result was that religion and communism blocked the biological advancement of the human species. Social progress toward equality was destroying the biological basis of civilization. "Social progress is racial debasement," according to Smith. "If universal amalgamation occurs, if the White race disappears, it may never reappear. . . . The Jew-led equalists are marching to world-wide conquest."[53] By contrast, those who were rational "would not save a human being so defective as to have no physical potentialities of intellectual or moral achievement."[54]

When he brought his ideas to the pages of his journal, Smith trimmed the turgid prose of *Sensism* and laid bare his underlying anti-Semitism. For Smith, as for Cox, Christianity was a "Jewized" religion that taught the brotherhood of man, an "equalizing" doctrine that prohibited clear thinking about race. For example, Smith rejected the notion that racial segregation as practiced in the American South was the answer to racial problems, for "seepage of blood through social barriers is inevitable. . . . The final remedy is not segregation but gradual reduction, leading to virtual elimination, which Christians, from fear of everlasting pain, dare not practice."[55]

Clearly, Smith argued, all lives were not equal, and some lives, notably those of Negroes, were not worth living. The most logical solution to the country's problems was "legalizing and subsidizing abortion to prevent the birth of a mulatto or a Negro." Blinded by the "Jew-led Love mongers," Smith wrote, Americans "simply cannot discriminate; having lost the use of their senses in judging others, they obey words absolutely. . . . They are Jewized." Of particular concern for Smith were "certain professors at some of our universities" who taught the "propaganda" that "Nordics and Negroes are equal in mental and moral qualities." Smith declared, "Whoever coldly considers the race problem must conclude that the preservation of the white race requires a reduction of the percentage of Negroes," and he demanded that "each state should establish a race commission to supervise racially therapeutic birth control and abortion."[56]

Under Smith's editorship, *Truth Seeker* lost a significant portion of its readership, as few atheists were willing to follow Smith, who subtitled the magazine "The Journal for Reasoners and Racists" and renamed the Ingersoll Forum the "Racist Forum." The Racist Forum's speakers included not only the stable of *Truth Seeker* writers but also political activists from the neo-Nazi underground such as James Madole, the leader of the National Renaissance Party.

Formed in 1949 by Frederick Charles Weiss, an admirer of Nazi Germany who was closely allied with von Leers's group of expatriate Nazis in Argentina, the National Renaissance Party (NRP) was the first postwar neo-Nazi organization in the United States.[57] Madole was, in many ways, a front man for Weiss but was responsible for much of the writing that appeared in the *National Renaissance Bulletin,* which was funded in part by *Truth Seeker.* Madole himself was praised by George Lincoln Rockwell, the leader of the American Nazi Party, as a "brilliant theorist" who produced an "excellent newsletter."[58]

The NRP enjoyed the dubious honor of being investigated by the House Committee on Un-American Activities. The committee outlined the avowed program of the NRP, which included the elimination of any parliamentary system, destroying Jewish power, and the complete subservience of the individual to the needs of racial nationalism. The committee concluded that "the program and propaganda of the National Renaissance Party is virtually borrowed wholesale from the Fascist and Nazi dictators."[59]

Madole argued that the NRP was "erected on the solid immutable laws of Nature which have governed the universe throughout eternity." Racial inequality and the natural racial struggle for survival were being drowned out by "the man-made doctrines of liberal democracy, socialism and communism," all of which were "invariably promoted by Jewish intellectuals." Madole pointed out that "many of the world's leading scientists, historians and philosophers have opposed the doctrine of racial equality but have been buried in a blanket of silence by our Jewish-controlled publishing industry, press, cinema, and television networks."[60] After Madole's appearance at the Racist Forum was covered by the *New York Daily News,* the owners of the venue canceled future reservations for Smith's group. Smith claimed that "Jewish pressure . . . blocked the Racist Forum." His associate editor, Robert Kuttner, agreed and argued, "Our Jewish enemies love to paint themselves a glorious red, white, and blue, but it is notable that they are the ones who speak constantly of censorship and thought-control."[61]

Byram Campbell

While Madole was more outspoken than most writers for the *Truth Seeker,* the same arguments about the dangers posed by organized religion to racial purity were echoed by *Truth Seeker* writers. For example, Byram Campbell, described by the Northern League as "America's leading authority on the psychology of communists and collectivists," was an important writer for *Truth Seeker.*[62]

In 1952, Campbell offered one of the first extended explanations for the widespread racial egalitarianism found in the social sciences in *Amer-*

ican Race Theorists, a critique of Gunnar Myrdal, Alfred Kroeber, and other scientists who had argued that the races were equal in abilities and intelligence. Campbell dubbed these scientists "equalitarians." Rather than facing up to the fact that the races were inherently different in genetic potential, the equalitarians invented wild suppositions to try to explain the shortcomings of the "Negro." This blindness to the reality of racial differences would be easy to ignore, Campbell believed, except that the equalitarian viewpoint seemed ascendant in the country. Of particular importance was the widespread acceptance of equalitarianism in the sciences. Campbell concluded, "Equalitarians have prostituted the sciences of biology, eugenics, and genetics to their own ends. . . . They have all but completely captured anthropology. They invent history."[63] From their secure posts in the academy, the equalitarians were spreading their propaganda in "popular literature, the press, radio, school, and church," as well as controlling "the production of moving pictures."[64]

While recognizing the limitation of methods employed by Madison Grant, Campbell found greater fault with Grant's opponents than with the great man himself. "Franz Boas," wrote Campbell, "was particularly offended by claims of race superiority, and probably had a great deal to do with starting the reaction against Grant's position which ended in the avalanche of mud throwing, personal abuse, smearing and belittling of Grant that was later witnessed." In this way, Boas and his Jewish followers within anthropology had "a profound effect on our anthropologists, and through them, on our country."[65]

According to Campbell, the equalitarians were skilled at winning converts not because of the soundness of their scientific case but because they played upon the misguided sympathies of "idealists and the emotionally unstable."[66] Of particular importance in the equalitarian movement were "Jewish propagandists" and Communists who believed that race equality "ties in with their theme of social equality."[67]

In his writings for the Northern League, Campbell declared himself as allied with Gobineau and that the "Nordic ideal" was "symbol of protest against the prodigious efforts of zealots for human oneness to make us into a mongrelized and nondescript group of mulattoes."[68]

Like Smith, Campbell set out his own personal philosophy (although he was mercifully concise compared to his mentor) in a book, which Campbell dedicated to Willis Carto. Campbell argued "there is no doubt" that Arthur Keith was right about race prejudice being "implanted in us by nature to help prevent divergent races from crossing."[69]

Such admiration for Keith was echoed by another important writer for *Truth Seeker,* Robert E. Kuttner—whom Carto had recommended to Cox.

Robert Kuttner

Kuttner was an associate editor of *Truth Seeker* from 1951 until 1965, when Charles Smith died and the editorship changed hands. When he began writing for Smith, Kuttner was a graduate student in biochemistry at the University of Connecticut and embraced scientific racism (a term he used to describe his own position) in a series of *Truth Seeker* articles in the late 1950s. Three interrelated ideas underpinned most of Kuttner's writings: Nordicism, a conspiracy argument about the scientific establishment, and biopolitics.

Kuttner, like Campbell and Smith, was an unabashed Nordicist. "In recent times Gobineau, Chamberlain, Nietzsche, Wagner, Bismarck, and Hitler have added to the Nordic's insight of his own destiny." Kuttner called for a similar reawakening in his own time. "The Nordic," he wrote,

> is our best hope. If he cannot be aroused to fight for Europe and the White Race, then no other group can either, and disaster is inevitable. . . . [T]he Nordicist doctrine, whatever the follies committed in its name, stands today as one of the chief bulwarks of civilization, of European civilization. If the races of Europe wish to survive as creative, unmixed, biological configurations, they had better promote a greater awareness of Nordicism in the sleeping Nordics.[70]

In a series of articles that Kuttner originally delivered at the Ingersoll Forum, Kuttner compared Iceland, the pure Nordic country, with Haiti, the black-controlled Caribbean island. Since Toussaint L'Overture's revolution against the French at the end of the eighteenth century, Haiti had been a favorite target of white racial ideologues when they pointed to the dangers of black control of society; Lothrop Stoddard, for example, wrote his Ph.D. dissertation on the topic.[71] Despite living in harsh Arctic conditions, Kuttner argued, the Nordics of Iceland had produced Nobel prize–winning scientists and had the world's oldest parliamentary democracy. By contrast, Haitians lived in on a lush, rich island full of natural resources and had produced nothing except political turmoil. "If it is not race," Kuttner asked rhetorically, "what is it that makes the Ivory of Iceland a credit to human achievement and the Ebony of Haiti the shame of the Caribbean?"[72] The Northern League's house publication, *Northern World,* provided Kuttner with a forum for his historical writings that purported to show, as Chamberlain had, that all ancient civilizations were Nordic in origin.[73]

As a scientist in training, a particular problem for Kuttner was not only that most postwar scientists rejected Nordicism; most rejected any proof for racial differences. According to Kuttner, in the modern sciences

> we have the curious phenomenon of anthropology professors teaching that the subjects of their specialty (races) do not exist. . . . Laughter would result if a doctor told us diseases do not exist or if a nuclear physicist claimed atoms were a myth. Yet no one laughs while physical anthropology vanishes from the lecture rooms in the corrosive solvent of social propaganda.[74]

Kuttner took aim at the postwar notion that race was a "myth." He claimed he would "document part of that conspiracy that churns science and society into a maelstrom—the conspiracy against a free people's right to know the truth about race."[75]

Particular targets for Kuttner were the UN Educational, Scientific, and Cultural Organization (UNESCO) Statements on Race, the first of which was issued in 1950 and the second in 1951. The UNESCO statements were drafted in response to the racial genocide perpetuated by the Nazis during World War II. Although many geneticists and physical anthropologists hoped to salvage the term in a nonracist manner, there was a strong consensus that "race," at least as traditionally defined, was a scientifically suspect concept. There was no evidence that there were differences in intelligence between the races, though some held out the possibility that scientific evidence could still make such differences known. The primary author of the 1950 statement was Ashley Montagu, who was on record as opposing any scientific concept of race. The 1950 statement was controversial not so much for its statement on the mythology of the race concept but for its claim that "[b]iological studies lend support to the ethic of universal brotherhood; for man is born with drives toward cooperation, and unless these drives are satisfied, men and nations alike fall ill."[76]

Kuttner believed that this drive for universal brotherhood was an idea that could originate only from "men closely linked with that mongrel parliament—the United Nations."[77] Rather than offer vague generalities about Jews and propaganda, as Campbell and Smith were wont to do regarding equalitarian science, Kuttner's critique of the UNESCO statement indicated that he was well acquainted with the authors and the arguments they offered. Like mainstream scientific writers, he objected to the constitution of the panel of experts that had favored sociologists and cultural anthropologists over physical anthropologists and geneticists. Like mainstream writers, Kuttner particularly objected to Montagu's claim for a feeling of "universal brotherhood," which Kuttner declared "the ravings of lunatics."[78]

To begin with, Kuttner argued against the notion that official statements on any scientific issues by scientific organizations decided any scientific truths whatsoever. "Equalists are . . . prone to act in concert. Issuing manifestos is a way of life for them," Kuttner declared, whereas "[a]ll the racist can display are the eternal truths of nature," which means that "[s]cientists with racist convictions usually speak as individuals."[79] Kuttner was opposed to the notion that "anthropology deals with cut and dried universal opinions which can be doled out with easy conscience as the chemically pure truth."[80]

Kuttner claimed that the authors of the UNESCO statements were either "long on the record as equalist propagandists" or "delegates of races or ethnic groups who could be counted on to know which ideology buttered their toast."[81] Like Madison Grant, who believed that the true scientist needed to be racially and politically pure, Kuttner distrusted all those on the UNESCO panel who were not from a Nordic country. Delegates from Mexico and Brazil should have been rejected because these were countries "where mixing with Negroes and Indians are almost an approved social pattern." Humayn Kabir of India and E. Franklin Frazier, the Howard University sociologist, should have been rejected because they "represented the colored races," and "how else could these men deliberate on race but to oppose the entire concept out of understandable personal motives?"[82]

Kuttner declared that world history proved the Negro's inability to build and create civilization. Pointing to the great Nordic figures of the past, and the complete absence of Negro geniuses that could be ranked alongside them, it was understandable that whenever white civilization came into contact with Negroes, whites found Negroes racially inferior.

"In science one does not multiply causes," Kuttner concluded. "It is easier to believe that the Negro does not rank with the white race than to believe that every society that has contact with him has judged him unfairly."[83] The focus on world history as the key to understanding race led Kuttner to lay out his scientific political philosophy in a series of articles under the rubric of "biopolitics."

Kuttner first worked out his ideas on biopolitics in a work with Eustace Mullins (b. 1923). Mullins was a frequent speaker for the National Renaissance Party and received a prominent mention in the House Committee on Un-American Affairs report. The committee reprinted Mullins's essay for the *National Renaissance Bulletin* that praised Adolf Hitler for uncovering the menace of the Jews to Aryans. "Either the Aryan or the Jew must yield in the world struggle," Mullins concluded. "The goal of our National Renaissance Party becomes clear."[84]

The NRP was only one of many connections Mullins had to the racist Right. He was also responsible for resurrecting the Jewish banking conspiracy for American audiences with his analysis of the Federal Reserve system as part of a plan to put the monetary system into the hands of international Jewish bankers. In a 1956 press release, Mullins listed his organizational affiliations as including the National Renaissance Party, executive directorship of the Aryan League of America, and the National Association for the Advancement of White People. He also claimed to have worked for the American Petroleum Institute, which, he claimed, had hired him to "offset the very favorable pro-Israel press and Jewish bloc in Congress by presenting the Arab case through Mullins propaganda."[85]

Another of Mullins's pet projects was the Institute for Biopolitics, which seemed to consist of him and Kuttner. The institute issued a booklet titled the *Biopolitics of Organic Materialism,* dedicated to Morley Roberts (1858–1942), a British novelist and writer who developed his ideas about evolution and race prejudice in conjunction with Arthur Keith and is often credited with coining the term *biopolitics.* In his autobiography, Keith wrote of Roberts that "it is hard to say how much I borrowed from him and how much he borrowed from me."[86]

In 1937, Roberts put forth a comprehensive treatise that he claimed united biology and sociology into "biopolitics." Taking Herbert Spencer's *The Social Organism* as his model, Roberts attempted to extend the organic society metaphor into every aspect of society, just as Spencer had. While Roberts did not discuss race in any great length, his discussion of "status" harmonized nicely with the ideology of *Truth Seeker* writers. Roberts argued that caste and status differences were necessary for a healthy society, just as differentiation of cells was necessary for a healthy organism. Like Smith, who argued that social progress was actually retrogression, Roberts argued that the democratic urge that occasionally overtook societies and led to the de-differentiation of status was "obviously a retrograde step" that led "to the conclusion that democratic 'progress' is retrogression." Moreover, social enforcement of equality was tyranny; "the equalitarian and totalitarian states may not in the end be distinguishable," Roberts concluded.[87]

Kuttner and Mullins also reprinted a few pages of Roberts's argument when he wrote of the Jews as a "fully and completely differentiated . . . race, wandering as 'foreign bodies' of peculiar, inalterable, and easily recognized characteristics among comparatively undifferentiated nations." They titled these passages "The Jews: Homo Parasiticus."[88]

The Institute for Biopolitics used *Truth Seeker* as its outlet for publication, with most of its work eventually appearing in the journal's pages.[89] In his contributions to *The Biopolitics of Organic Materialism,* Mullins declared that the world's geographic barriers were no longer barriers to racial friction, leaving the "Whiteman" with a stark choice: kill or be killed. "The animal-like existence of the colored world is a mockery of human potentialities," he wrote. "Western man will either terminate that existence or he himself will be swallowed up by it." After all, Mullins argued, "[w]hen a Negro rapes a white woman, he is only expressing the dumb futility of his existence. This aggression is a dumb appeal for his extermination." To carry out this program of extermination, Mullins argued, it was necessary to implement the biopolitical order in which Europeans must give "unquestioning obedience to the leaders" who would improve them by "making ever-greater demands of them, and by accelerating the selective agencies which advance them." Mullins's dreams of racial extermination surpassed those witnessed during World War II. "The Whiteman's effort to protect his genes on an international level," he concluded, "[w]ill be the most vigorous physical manifestation the world has even [*sic*] known."[90]

Compared with Mullins's frank calls for genocide, Kuttner's contributions to the institute seemed rather pale. Like Mullins, Kuttner maintained that "[b]iopolitics emphasizes the importance of race. It is grounded on the basic truth that every man is part of a biological kingdom, his race, to which he owes his primary loyalty."[91]

Kuttner argued that Marx was essentially correct in viewing conflict as endemic to society, but wrong in viewing conflict as that which exists between classes. Relying on Keith's idea that race prejudice was an important driving force behind evolutionary change in humans, Kuttner argued that the fundamental nature of human conflict was racial, not class-based, in nature. "Long before money created classes, evolutionary natural selection created races. It follows that the true history of the world is genetic and not financial."[92] Hence, "[t]he biopolitical system is expressed in racial nationalism. Implicit in the thought of this school is a social order based on racial distinction."[93] Part and parcel of racial nationalism was the ability to judge cultures and peoples as inferior. "Cultures that fail are inferior," Kuttner concluded; "this is the judgment of nature which biopolitics heartily seconds."[94]

Association for the Preservation of the Freedom of Choice

By the end of his life, Madison Grant had won the battle to keep the hated immigrant Jew out of his beloved New York City only to realize that the city was being threatened by the massive immigration of African Americans escaping the rural South. Aldrich Blake, the founding ideologue of Carto's Liberty and Property, was concerned about the Great Migration, which had only intensified after World War II. It was this concern for the racial integrity of New York City that first led to a formal organization of scientists and academicians who wanted to fight against the equalitarian orthodoxy that had prevailed in race relations since World War II.

For many northern cities, the influx of black immigrants lead to a severe housing shortage, and one response northern cities and states had to this crisis in housing was pass "open housing" laws that made racial discrimination by landlords and realtors illegal. It was against these laws that Aldrich Blake had fought. The city of New York became the first in the nation to pass an ordinance that prevented discrimination in private rental housing, the Sharkey-Isaacs-Brown ordinance, which was signed into law on December 31, 1957.[95]

The ordinance stirred opposition, for example, many realtors were opposed to the restrictions the ordinance created for them. For those New Yorkers associated with *Truth Seeker*, the open housing ordinance was a call to arms, and they joined with others who believed that the ordinance was an assault on cherished American freedoms. In February 1958, they announced the formation of the Association for the Preservation of Freedom of Choice (APFC). APFC executive secretary A. James Gregor outlined the danger: "the Sharkey-Isaacs-Brown Compulsory Housing Integration Law," he wrote, was "the most dramatic attack . . . on freedom of choice in New York City. The bill outlaws the right of a landlord to choose his tenants, as well as the right of a developer to choose his buyers of private homes."[96]

The legal case against open housing was wrapped in the rhetoric of democracy: the very name of the organization was meant to defend the "freedom of choice" in social relations. The central component of the APFC's case was the value of racial and ethnic differences; indeed, the first paragraph of the constitution of the APFC read as if it were penned by a twenty-first-century scholar of multiculturalism:

> American society today is a multicultural society, composed of numerous racial, religious, cultural, and ethnic groups. Not only has the immigration of such groups contributed to American culture, but the continuation of such subcultural patterns and groups makes a continuing contribution both to the development of the individual members of the groups and to society as a whole, and the very diversity of these groups is a substantial benefit to American society. The maintenance of the above groups and their continuing development is a value which both the individual members thereof, and a democratic society as a whole, has an interest in preserving.[97]

The call for "freedom of association" became a staple of conservative argument in the 1960s and 1970s. It was consistent with the fight against communism and the call for a free-market and minimalist state. However, the APFC also demonstrates, as Eric Foner has argued, that during the early 1960s, "libertarians proved amazingly indifferent to the denial of blacks' economic and educational opportunities."[98] The lead attorney for the APFC, Alfred Avins, argued that antidiscrimination legislation was an incredible infringement of freedom. "Compared to this," he wrote, "Prohibition was the quintessence of farsighted statesmanship."[99] Avins held:

> This uncoerced individual right to choose to associate or decline to associate based on ethnic grounds is basic to a free society, and its denial threatens not only the rights and proper privileges of the individual, but

menaces the institutions and foundations of a free society, and tends to the creation of a totalitarian society devoid of the right of the individual to freely choose whom he shall associate with.[100]

According to Avins, free choice of association was not only a formal right but also a rational choice in the face of ethnic differences. Concluded Avins, "Since ethnic differences are beneficial, their perpetuation is likewise a rational value. But subcultural groups cannot perpetuate those differences in the face of the general tendency to amalgamate and lose them unless these different heritages are institutionalized and instilled into both children and adults alike through numerous reinforcing techniques."[101]

When it came time to enact their program to preserve racially pure neighborhoods in New York City, the APFC was a singularly ineffective organization. The APFC faced a significant legal hurdle immediately, when Judge Irwin Shapiro found they were a "hate group" and denied them the privilege of incorporation. Shapiro found, "While individuals, as such . . . may freely indulge in their prejudices and bigotries . . . their purposes and intended practices should not be sanctioned by receiving the imprimatur of this court."[102] At issue was not the right of the membership to associate but rather their right to incorporate and enjoy the attendant privileges. Avins did not give up easily, however, and he finally won the right to incorporate in 1961.[103]

By 1961, the open housing ordinance was three years old and the APFC's chance to fight it had long passed; in fact, as I show in the next chapter, many of the scientists associated with the organization had moved on. However, the APFC still provided Avins with an avenue to fight legal battles against civil rights. The association filed a suit to stop the election of Edward K. Dudley as president of the Borough of Manhattan and Abe Beame as city controller. Their suit charged that these nominations for office were discriminatory, as Dudley was nominated because he was a Negro and Beame because he was Jewish; thus their nominations were acts "of discrimination against persons of other races who might otherwise have been considered for such designation."[104] The courts viewed these complaints with little sympathy, and the action was rapidly dismissed.[105]

Such quixotic lawsuits soon became Avins's stock-in-trade. Throughout the 1960s he would attack the Voting Rights Act of 1965 for "diluting" the votes of white voters, sue the student editors of the *Rutgers Law Review* for refusing to publish his article attacking *Brown v. Board of Ed-*

ucation, and sue for the firing of the Columbia Board of Trustees for "political discrimination" against conservative faculty members.[106]

While the legal efforts of the APFC came to very little, the organization had more lasting effects on their second avowed purpose, which was, as Gregor wrote, to "break the log-jam of free scientific inquiry by making the anti-integrationist position once again respectable." The APFC despaired that in the academic world, the antiracist position that arose in the wake of the crimes of World War II had produced a "reaction almost as perverted as the so called 'scientific' foundation upon which these crimes were perpetrated."[107] This battle for the scientific case against integration would soon be joined in earnest in the American South, as the scientists associated with the APFC joined forces with Southerners in the massive resistance movement to desegregation. By 1961, when APFC was incorporated, most of the figures involved were actively involved with the fight to maintain racial segregation in the American South. The "natural, human, and civil" right to associate with whomever one chose apparently did not extend south of the Mason-Dixon line, as APFC officers took to the stand in a series of court cases designed to overturn *Brown v. Board of Education* and maintain racial segregation in southern schools. Alfred Avins went on to join the staff of Senator Strom Thurmond. In his writings after 1961, Avins argued that "freedom of association" did not mean that southern schoolchildren should be integrated or interracial marriage legalized.[108] Apparently, racial purity was more important than freedom.

4

The South and the
Scientific Backlash to *Brown*

The fulminations against modern scientific arguments for racial equality were not confined to the extremist fringes of the neo-Nazi movements in New York City. Just as southern congressmen objected to Benedict and Weltfish's *Races of Mankind,* white Southerners objected to any science that purported to prove white and black racial equality.

Many of the white southern objections to the findings of modern science would be refuted by African American scholars and other mainstream scientists, who pointed to the nearly overwhelming rejection of scientific claims of white superiority by a consensus of scientific opinion. It was this consensus that made conspiracy claims central to segregationist scientists: it was the explanatory mechanism for them simultaneously to claim the findings of science and the virtue of being in the minority of scientific opinion.

To this extent, white Southerners shared a common rhetorical trope with their neo-Nazi counterparts at *Truth Seeker.* Unlike Kuttner or Smith, however, white Southerners were much less likely to point to a Jewish conspiracy, instead choosing to focus on the dangers of Communism or "liberalism" generally. Just as Senator Bilbo kept the conspiracy launched by Boas while eliminating the anti-Semitic aspects of Cox's critique, white Southerners would seldom directly accuse the Jews of masterminding the suppression of scientific truth. Also, given the black/white binary that defined southern politics, Southerners would be much less likely to speak of the Nordic, instead focusing on whites in general. The issues of the equalitarian conspiracy were first brought to southern audiences in reaction to the racial liberalism fostered by World War II.

The Cult of Equality

One of the most complete statements of the southern position on racial science was *The Cult of Equality,* published in 1945, immediately after World War II, by Louisiana writer Stuart Omer Landry. Landry had been involved in the early-twentieth-century debates over the impending "race suicide" as many pointed to the alarming drop in birthrates among upper-class whites. The changed atmosphere in race relations and the changing scientific consensus about white supremacy were a cause of some alarm for him, and he attempted to rehabilitate prewar ideas about race. In many ways, Landry's book set the template for much of the segregation-ist use of scientific evidence by combining the equalitarian conspiracy with traditional southern justifications for segregation.[1]

First, Landry argued there was a movement of "equalitarians" that strove to undo all that white civilization had accomplished. He called this movement the "cult of equality," and it preached that all people were equal mentally, physically, and culturally. As the "equalitarians" grew in power, they threatened the very existence of the white race.

Second, Landry gave special scrutiny to equalitarian scientists. Point-ing to the Weltfish and Benedict fiasco of 1943, Landry explained that many scientists were helping the equalitarian movement "by advancing theories that are more or less unproved." Racial intermingling would lead to the destruction of the white race, which was the only race capable of building civilization. Race mixing was therefore dangerous; "although many biologists say this would make no difference, common sense tells us that it would be a biological mistake."[2] This use of "common sense" to trump the findings of modern science was used widely in the subsequent debates over the maintenance of segregation.

Third, Landry maintained that "real" science had clearly proven the races were not equal in abilities. Landry examined the common argument of the Boasians that racial differences were really cultural differences and found it wanting. History and the theory of evolution, Landry declared, proved that "race comes before culture, and a high form of civilization is the result of efforts of an energetic, aggressive and inventive people."[3] Landry specifically criticized the work of "equalitarians" Alfred Kroeber, Melville Herskovits, Robert Redfield, Otto Klineberg, and John Dollard —all of whom had taken public stands in favor of racial equality. In their stead, he embraced the work of Lothrop Stoddard and Charles Daven-port, as well as Carl Brigham's 1923 book on American intelligence. This work was based on reality, as opposed to that of the equalitarians, who had perverted science to their equalist ends.

Finally, the irony, Landry argued, was that the darker races had already been freed by their white benefactors. Landry, like many white Southerners, was especially mystified by demands by southern African Americans for equality, since they believed that the Negro should be perfectly happy under segregation. "The Negroes of the United States," Landry explained, "already have their freedom. Yet in the country that has offered the race its greatest opportunity, some of its leaders complain of the oppression they endure."[4] This argument was certainly not invented by Landry and was a key theme in segregationist discourse: since Negroes already enjoyed substantive equality with the white man, their poor performance on IQ tests and their "social pathology" must owe to a genetic difference between the races.

If they noticed it at all, scholarly reviewers largely dismissed Landry's "tattered battery of arguments to justify the past and present racial order." In a second edition, Landry noted the lack of reviews and interpreted it to mean that he had hit is mark. "Because the subject is so controversial," he noted, "the press has practically ignored the book. . . . No magazine or newspaper would dare print articles expressing such ideas [as found in *The Cult of Equality*]."[5]

That his book was ignored, and that this was proof of its truth, underscores an important point about how conspiracy rhetoric operates. Conspiracies are committed in secret, by powerful figures. Any event can be interpreted as part of a conspiracy to hide the truth; even counterinstances could be "reinterpreted as the work of clever conspirators to conceal their true intentions," as rhetorician David Zarefsky argued. In this way, Zarefsky claimed, conspiracy rhetoric becomes "self-sealing" because any piece of evidence can be interpreted as to the truth of the conspiracy claim—even if that evidence appears to directly contradict the existence of a conspiracy. In the battle over the scientific reality of race, segregationist scientists would argue that if they were ignored, it was because the equalitarians wanted to cover up the truth. Conversely, if the scientific community denied their scientific arguments, segregationist scientists declared this, too, was proof of a conspiracy, since their arguments were consistently rejected.[6]

Landry's argument was essentially the same as those of the *Truth Seeker* regarding science and racial equality, but Landry was not interested in unmasking the Jews, as Northern League members were apt to do. Rather, Landry saw the cult of equality as inspired by Communist dogma, which was equalist to the core. He also was critical of the Soviet Union for the "ugly spectre of anti-Semitism" and the treatment of Jews who fled from the Germans only to die at the hands of the Soviets.[7]

Landry's claims about the equalitarian conspiracy would be given new life in 1954 when the U.S. Supreme Court declared school segregation unconstitutional. *Brown v. Board of Education* would polarize southern politics, and the equalitarian conspiracy would be brought forth as a weapon against the Supreme Court's call for racial integration.[8]

Brown *and the Polarization of Southern Politics*

While the *Brown* decision's impact on the desegregation of southern public schools would need a decade of civil rights agitation and legislative action by Congress in the form of the Civil Rights Act of 1964, the symbolic impact on white Southerners was almost immediate. The White South quickly declared that desegregation posed a threat to the "southern way of life" and vowed to block any attempts at racial intermingling through policies of "massive resistance." Constitutional historian Michael Klarman has written that "*Brown* temporarily destroyed southern racial moderation," as all white southern politicians moved "several notches to the right on racial issues."[9] One example of the political times was the "Southern Manifesto," which was signed by nearly every southern congressman and senator. The manifesto declared that "outside agitators are threatening immediate and revolutionary changes in our public school systems. If done, this is certain to destroy the system of public education in some of the States."[10]

Historian David Goldfield has underscored the importance of "respectable resistance." Like Earnest Sevier Cox's Anglo-Saxon Clubs of the 1920s, many advocates of massive resistance portrayed themselves "as advocating preferable alternatives to race war."[11] On the local level, the Citizens' Councils were only the most famous and largest of several respectable resistance organizations that sprang up throughout the South, holding themselves out as the alternative to the violence of quasi-military organizations such as the Ku Klux Klan. Like Aldrich Blake in the 1920s, these organizations did not disagree with the Klan's goals of white supremacy but rather with the method of violence and intimidation. These organizations would fight for the cause through reasoned discourse, legal battles, and the scientific truths of white supremacy.[12] Fundamental to the respectable resisters were the perceived flaws in the *Brown* decision itself.

Brown *and the Social Scientific Wedge*

The *Brown* court cited social-scientific evidence in its finding that segregation was psychologically damaging. In 1954 the U.S. Supreme Court ruled that racial segregation in public elementary and secondary schools was a violation of the equal protection clause of the Fourteenth Amendment of the U.S. Constitution. Chief Justice Earl Warren noted, "To separate [colored schoolchildren] from others of similar age and qualifications solely because of their race generates a feeling of inferiority as to their status in the community that may affect their hearts and minds in a way unlikely ever to be undone. . . . Whatever may have been the extent of the psychological knowledge at the time of *Plessy v. Ferguson,* this finding is amply supported by modern authority." Here, in the eleventh footnote of the opinion, the Court cited a number of psychological works to support its claim.[13]

The citation of social-scientific evidence in *Brown* was the result of a decades-long campaign by the NAACP-LDEF to erode the separate-but-equal doctrine that had been enshrined in American constitutional law in the 1896 case of *Plessy v. Ferguson.* The NAACP's strategy, according to constitutional historian Mark Tushnet, was to transform unfavorable case precedent into favorable case precedent by "pointing out anomalies in doctrine and identifying the inevitable failure of society's efforts to explain why unjust doctrines nonetheless were acceptable."[14]

The actual citation of social science in *Brown* was controversial even for defenders of the decision. New York University professor of jurisprudence Edmond Cahn expressed concern that the opinion rested on the "flimsy foundation" of social science rather than on solid legal reasoning. Cahn believed that in this case, social scientists had overstepped the bounds of proper science into the realm of advocacy. Given the undeveloped state of social psychology, Cahn saw danger for the law. It was imperative, argued Cahn, for judges to "learn where objective science ends and advocacy begins. At present, it is still possible for the social psychologist to hoodwink a judge who is not over wise."[15]

For white Southerners, the citation of social-scientific evidence was a triple affront. First, many white Southerners resented any federal intru-

sion whatsoever into their local affairs, especially regarding race relations. As Michael Klarman argued, even southern moderates on the race
issue objected to federal intervention into southern politics, which was "a
cause that resonated deeply in a southern political consciousness for
which the Civil War and Reconstruction remained seminal events."[16] Second, many followed Cahn and objected to what they perceived as a violation of the due process of the law by substituting social science for court
precedent. Georgia's Charles Bloch, an attorney closely allied with segregationist senator Richard Russell, asked rhetorically, "Are established judicial precedents to be swept aside at the whim of those nine [justices]?
Are established rules of law to be supplanted by rules of philosophy and
psychology?"[17] Finally, many white Southerners believed that the "socialistic" social science cited in *Brown* was produced by Communists or
Communist sympathizers and therefore not to be trusted.

In 1955, Mississippi senator James O. Eastland brought many of these
themes together on the floor of Congress in what he claimed was the result
of a complete investigation into the scientists who had worked with the
NAACP in the *Brown* litigation. Eastland argued that many of these social
scientists were deeply involved in the Communist conspiracy for world
domination. He spoke for many white Southerners when he declared that
the citation of social-scientific material was "the final indication as to the
degree that the Court has been 'brainwashed' by pressure groups and is
willing to sacrifice the people, the Constitution, and established law to
communistic and socialistic dogma and principles." Eastland's charges
were quickly and widely distributed by the Citizens' Councils.[18]

Eastland's lead was picked up by southern politicians such as former
Supreme Court Justice James Byrnes of South Carolina, who declared:

> Loyal Americans . . . should be outraged that the Supreme Court would
> reverse the law of the land upon no authority other than some books
> written by a group of psychologists about whose qualifications we know
> little and about whose loyalty to the United States there is grave doubt.[19]

Judge Leander Perez, the segregationist political boss of the Mississippi
Delta in Louisiana, in his testimony against a proposed civil rights bill in
1959 claimed that by using social science material,

> [t]he US Supreme Court [in] . . . its May 17, 1954 decision . . . played
> "footsie" with the Constitution by adopting the type of trash appended

to the National Association for the Advancement of Colored People brief as authority on psychology, sociology, and anthropology to replace provisions of the Constitution which have been consistently interpreted and adhered since 1868.[20]

Despite the proclamations that social science was not to be trusted and could not serve as the basis for political or constitutional decisions, the white South soon came to approve at least one form of scientific evidence: intelligence testing. White people and black people differed in mental abilities; this was proven by their performance on intelligence tests. These differences were immutable and did not owe to socioeconomic conditions. Nothing the white South said about intelligence tests in the 1950s had not been given a full hearing in the 1920s, yet these tests would be the first rallying cry for the scientific argument in favor of segregation. Intelligence differences meant that school segregation could not be accomplished without destroying the school system, as it was impossible to design a curriculum that would be appropriate for both groups. These views were given a very public hearing in 1956 during a congressional "investigation" of conditions in Washington, D.C.'s newly desegregated public schools. These hearings foreshadowed the coming battle over the legitimacy of racial science on the desegregation issue in the decade between *Brown* and the Civil Rights Act of 1964.

The Battle of Washington, D.C.

The nation's capital, Washington, D.C., long had segregated schools. A 1948 study, popularly known as the "Strayer Report" after its director, George D. Strayer, and commissioned by the appropriation committees of the House and Senate, documented wide disparities between the facilities available for each race. For example, the report found that "[c]lasses are in general much larger in the colored schools than in the white. . . . Classes in most of the colored schools visited are entirely too large." A popular pamphlet prepared by social scientists Louis Wirth, Donald Young, Charles Dollard, E. Franklin Frazier, and others summarized the issues by baldly stating, "Segregation by its nature implies a superior-inferior relationship. The services provided by the dominant group are always superior to those accorded the group segregated."[21]

In the wake of the *Brown* decision, President Dwight D. Eisenhower declared that desegregation in Washington, D.C., would begin immediately, setting an example for the rest of the nation. On May 25, 1954, ten days after the Supreme Court's decision, the District of Columbia's Board of Education issued a "Declaration of Policy" that maintained, "No pupil of the public schools shall be favored or discriminated against in any matter or . . . by reason of race or color."[22]

In 1956, the House Committee on the District of Columbia conducted a series of hearings into public school conditions in the District. Known as the Davis Hearings and led by Georgia representative John C. Davis and Mississippi's John Bell Williams, the series indicated that the committee was not interested in hearing about the underfunded school system for African American children. Rather, Davis explained that they were investigating "juvenile delinquency and alleged and reported low standards in the District public school system."[23]

Throughout the hearings, Davis and Williams, joined by Chief Counsel William Gerber, closely cross-examined witnesses regarding the low test scores of African American students. For the segregationists, the test scores of the two groups could not be explained by the poor schooling provided to African American children in Washington's segregated schools. The difference was due to innate and immutable differences between the two races' ability to learn.

A typical exchange was that between Williams and a white principal of a District high school, Hugh Stewart Smith. Smith had maintained in his testimony that the poor performance of African American children owed to their relatively poor socioeconomic status. Williams pushed Smith to admit that white children also came from poor backgrounds:

> *Mr. Williams*: Do you notice a difference in the white children's rate of achievement coming from those same neighborhoods, with the same economic status as their colored neighbors?
> *Mr. Smith*: Yes.
> *Mr. Williams*: Then, on the basis of that, could you say that environment and economic status are not the sole contributing factors to that condition?
> *Mr. Smith*: Yes sir.
> *Mr. Williams*: That there is actually a physical difference, perhaps between the two children, on the average, of course, other than the color of the pigment of the skin?

Mr. Smith: I don't know Mr. Williams. I can't answer that one. That is too much for me.[24]

The result of this intelligence gap between white and African American children, according to Davis, Williams, and Gerber, was generally a lowering of standards for white children in the District, a great increase in discipline problems within the schools, and white families leaving the District altogether. As Chief Counsel Gerber concluded, "You cannot mix oil and water, can you?"[25]

The committee's report quickly became a rallying point for the segregationist cause. An abbreviated report by Davis and Williams with a list of findings and recommendations was quickly picked up by the Citizens' Councils. In Washington, D.C., Floyd Fleming of the local Citizens' Council warned that desegregation had led to white flight and an impossible teaching situation in integrated schools, due to "the wide disparity in mental ability to learn and educational achievement between the white and negro students." Concluded Fleming, "[I]ntermarriage . . . is what integration in the schools leads to and as that comes to pass, the white race becomes a mongrelized race and history records that the breeding is downward instead of upward."[26]

The Citizens' Councils' headquarters in Mississippi issued a twenty-page summary of the hearings, noting that the results of the IQ tests administered in the District schools demonstrated that "the white elementary students had an average IQ rating of 105, which was above the national average. The Negro elementary students had an average of 87, or 13 percentile below the national average." The Citizens' Councils' pamphlet also included the recommendation of Davis, Williams, and the two other southern representatives on the subcommittee that "racially separate public schools be re-established for the education of white and Negro pupils in the District of Columbia."[27]

"A Diabolical Conglomeration of Meaningless and Unintelligible Nonsense"

All the fuss over the desegregation in the Washington, D.C., school district sounded familiar to African American educator Horace Mann Bond. In 1924, when he first waged the battle against the racial interpretation of IQ tests, he was a young graduate student. Three decades later, he was

an experienced college president who was deeply committed to integration, as well as to quality schooling for African Americans. He had
worked with the NAACP on the *Brown* litigation, providing them with
historical evidence on education during the Reconstruction era in the
American South.[28] The Davis Hearings came to Bond's attention in November 1956. In a letter to Clarence Mitchell of the Washington, D.C.,
bureau of the NAACP, Bond mused that it might be possible to get
"[c]omparative standings in these tests for white high schools in Memphis, Mr. Gerber's home; and, perhaps from other sections of the South.
I believe such data would show that the Negro high schools in Washington had an attainment . . . not very different from that of Memphis white
high school students."[29]

Bond asked his friends in Memphis for information about test scores
as well as on Counsel William Gerber, who had conducted much of the
Davis Hearings.[30] Bond also investigated how segregationist groups
throughout the South were circulating the Davis Hearings. In a speech a
few years later, he recounted how he discovered that

> Congressman Davis . . . had 50,000 copies [of the hearings] printed;
> such a number, of course, was not intended for the District of Columbia,
> or even for his own Fifth Georgia Congressional District. They were in-
> tended for distribution throughout the United States . . . and the White
> Citizens Councils of the South became its more enthusiastic circulator.[31]

Within a few months of the release of the hearings, Bond had completed
his response, "A Study of the Intelligence of Congressmen Who Signed
the Southern Manifesto as Measured by I.Q. Tests Administered by the
Army to Them and to Their Constituents, and by the American Council
on Education Psychological Examinations as Administered to, and Reported by, Their Colleges."

Bond claimed his study followed "the methods, major premises, and
research techniques of these distinguished and forthright exponents of the
science of psychometry [Representative Davis and Counsel Gerber]." In
other words, no environmental explanations for deficiencies in IQ scores
or scores on achievement tests were to be allowed when

> [r]eviewing the published scores of the colleges attended by such of these
> gentlemen as did attend college, so that we my apply, to an evaluation of
> *their* "intelligence" the same criteria . . . that has been the main prop of

Congressman Davis and Counsel Gerber in analyzing the implications of "integration" in the District of Columbia public schools, by race.[32]

In analysis, Bond found that Davis "attended a college where the median score on a highly praised 'Psychological Examination' located that college in a position inferior to 94% of American colleges."[33] Davis was not alone, however, as Bond meticulously reproduced the standings of colleges attended by each signer of the Southern Manifesto. With a few exceptions (those attending Vanderbilt, Duke, Mercer, or Emory), the colleges performed woefully on American Council of Education exams.

Chief Counsel Gerber fared little better. Bond well remembered the debates of the 1920s when white skin was not a guarantee of racial purity. Hearkening back to the racial categories used by Carl Brigham and Madison Grant, Bond noted that Gerber had "migrated from a country—Russia—where draftees born in that country made such low scores on Army tests, as to lead our Congress, in 1924, to adopt immigration quotas designed to keep further immigration from that country, out of America, as far as possible."[34]

Yet Bond had further use of the army tests beyond skewering the chief counsel, for he extended his analysis to an examination of the army scores of the white populations of segregationist states. His conclusion was that "[i]n terms of "IQ test scores," the typical senator and congressman who signed the Southern Manifesto may be described as

  a. A man whose voting constituency is in the lower 20% of mental ability, of American Whites, so far as that mental ability is shown by Army "IQ test scores."

  b. A man, most of whose constituency fall (again, according to William Gerber's highly regarded "IQ test scores") in the "dull, normal," "Moron" category.

  c. A man who attended a college where the median (middle) score of the students, places that college in the lowest ten percent of median scores made by American colleges throughout the Nation.[35]

Policy recommendations logically flowed from his findings, and they echoed the policy recommendations that Davis and Williams had for African Americans. Bond recommended that congressional committee assignments be made on the basis of IQ scores, not seniority. This plan, Bond admitted, would have the effect of denying congressional leadership to southern senators and representatives, but he noted that the country would undoubtedly be better off to have the "slow learners in a group together, where they could . . . have remedial attention to make up for their basic deficiencies." Bond concluded that "in making these recommendations, we believe we have been entirely faithful to the principles, techniques, and procedures, by which Congressman James C. Davis, and Chief Counsel William Gerber" addressed black/white school achievements in their hearings.[36]

The NAACP released Bond's "study" on December 19, 1956. Press requests for copies soon outstripped the supply as the wire agencies picked up the story. "Southerners Branded 'Moron' by NAACP," screamed the headline of the United Press story. Representative Davis refused to "dignify" Bond's report with a comment. Representative John Bell Williams declared Bond's report "a diabolical conglomeration of meaningless and unintelligible nonsense quoting an alleged educator apparently unknown outside pressure group circles." Bond merely replied that he was "highly enough regarded by Mississippi educational authorities to be invited to serve as an 'expert' by them during their Study of Higher Education conducted in Mississippi in 1945."[37]

Bond referred to the study as his "foolishness" but clearly believed that he had made his point, given "the enraged reaction to my little joke, as represented by the bitter anonymous letters I have been receiving."[38] Still, the central argument made by Representative Davis, that differences in IQ scores justified racial segregation, would become staple of segregationist science for a decade. One of the key proponents of the IQ argument would be Villanova psychologist Frank C. J. McGurk.

U.S. News and World Report

Even before he received his Ph.D. in 1951, Frank C. J. McGurk (1910–1995) was investigating racial differences in performance on intelligence tests. In a 1943 publication on data he had collected while working at a children's clinic in Richmond, Virginia, McGurk analyzed the performance of Negro and white children on several standard tests of mental ability. What was remarkable about this article is that it clearly outlined, and apparently agreed with, the standard objections to racial interpretations of intelligence tests, objections that McGurk would wave away in the 1950s as irrelevant to his use of intelligence tests.

McGurk's 1943 article was a recommendation against the use of intelligence tests in clinical practice, since "using established norms, a great many Negro children were scoring in either the borderline or feebleminded range."[39] The problem, McGurk argued, was that the norms were established using white children and were probably not applicable to Negro children, who should have tests normed to a lower standard. Using separate norms for the Negro recognized that there was a fundamental difference in the lived experience of whites and Negroes.

McGurk remained agnostic as to the cause of the differences in test scores. Without citing Klineberg by name, McGurk apparently accepted the central argument of Klineberg's pioneering work. McGurk noted that there was evidence to indicate that "racial differences tend to disappear in the northern states, where segregation is less stringent, and where each race has the same or approximate school equipment, teaching methods, etc." McGurk also noted that racial differences decreased depending on the length of the stay in the North. Finally, he noted a variety of cultural factors, most of which were tied specifically to the segregated life of Richmond Negroes, that justified different tests for them:

> If the Negroes of the South are to be segregated, if they are to be deprived, if they are to be slovenly because of lack of opportunity, teaching and ambition, and if their lives are to be lived in such totally different surroundings, with different chances than their white brothers, they then should be judged according to the standards which are common to their life.[40]

In his writings on race and intelligence testing in the 1950s, McGurk would abandon this nuanced view of the effect of culture on test performance in favor of a claim that Negroes and whites who had equivalent socioeconomic status shared the same lived experiences. McGurk completed his Ph.D. at Catholic University in 1951 and published two articles out of it. His research attempted to match white and black subjects in terms of socioeconomic status and then investigate their performance on "cultural" and "noncultural" test questions. Taking aim at Klineberg's research, McGurk claimed that his data showed "the test superiority of high socio-economic status over the Negro of low socio-economic status is associated more with a superior performance on the non-cultural questions than on the cultural questions." Nor, according to McGurk's findings, did the difference in performance between white and black subjects decrease when he controlled for socioeconomic status.[41]

In 1955, McGurk had achieved enough notoriety for his writings on race to begin receiving mail from Senator Eastland, who was leading Mississippi's fight against the *Brown* decision. McGurk complained to a sympathetic correspondent that "the dominant philosophy in race difference theory is social determinism. . . . I think that it is time that the biological side of the picture were made known."[42] Toward this end, McGurk assembled his case and submitted it to the prestigious *Journal of Heredity*. The rejection of his paper by a biological journal that he probably thought would be sympathetic to his argument undoubtedly bothered McGurk. Soon after this time, he would begin complaining of being persecuted for speaking the truth about race. Ironically, he was given a much wider forum for his views after being rejected by the *Journal of Heredity*: the newsmagazine *U.S. News and World Report*. The resulting controversy around McGurk's piece underscored the difficulties segregationists would have in using intelligence tests as evidence for segregation.[43]

"If we in America are going to make any sense out of the Supreme Court's desegregation decision," wrote McGurk in *U.S. News and World Report* in 1956, "we are going to have to be more factual about race differences, and much less emotional." To avoid emotion, McGurk pointed to data that he claimed proved "there is ample evidence that there are psychological differences between Negroes and whites," that the differences have not decreased over the course of two generations, and that "these differences were not the result of differences in social and economic opportunities, and they will not disappear as the social and economic opportunities of Negroes and whites are equalized."[44]

To prove his claim, McGurk began with the army tests of 1918 and pointed to the gap in scores between Negroes and whites. Since that time, he maintained, "[t]o say that the socio-economic status of the Negro has risen at a faster rate than the white's is not an exaggeration." If it were true that equalizing economic and social opportunities affected test scores, then the vast gains made by Negroes since World War I should have done much to close that gap. McGurk noted that there were 140 studies published in the psychological literature that addressed the question, but "only six presented enough material to permit us to compare the World War I performance of Negroes and whites with latter-day performance." McGurk emphasized that these six were "not a selection of studies intended to emphasize a point of view. They are the *only* existing studies that relate to the problem."[45]

Despite only closely examining six studies, McGurk stated strongly that it had been "demonstrated over and over" that "Negroes as a group do not possess as much [capacity for education] as whites as a group." The clear implication for McGurk was that "a fruitful approach to racial equality cannot follow the lines of social and economic manipulation," because "there is something more important, more basic, to the race problem than differences in external opportunity."[46]

Both the Right and Left of the political spectrum recognized that McGurk's piece was not ivory-tower research but had political implications. Willis Carto's journal, *Right,* crowed about "Frank C.J. McGurk's stupendous article on Negro inferiority" that *"pulls the rug from under the integrationists. . . .* So called 'extremists' have been saying these thing for years." Bernard Hennessy, writing in the liberal *New Republic,* noted that the scientific question of genetic differences in intelligence were immaterial to the question of equal treatment under the law. "In a political democracy," he concluded, "the root concept of equality is: equal protection of the laws and equality of public services. It has never demanded that all should be equal in ability."[47] Such a stance would eventually be met by segregationists, who pointed to the *Brown* decision's quotation of social science as proof that science *was* relevant to questions about school desegregation.

On the scientific front, the mainstream psychological community immediately leaped to criticize McGurk's apparent apology for segregation. Many of the social scientists who had worked with the NAACP on the *Brown* litigation wrote a response that was published in *U.S. News and World Report* a few weeks after McGurk's piece. They quoted the brief they had written for the Supreme Court in *Brown* that had argued that the "consensus among experts who have studied this question as objectively and scientifically as is at present possible" found no innate differences in intelligence between the races. In any case, they argued, in every study, including those used by McGurk, there was overlap between the scores of both racial groups. This meant average differences between the races were irrelevant to the segregation issue, since there would be white and black children in every IQ range. In an extensive critique, Ashley Montagu criticized the very idea that intelligence tests could provide any sort of guide to capacity for education, that the United States provided equality of opportunity for American Negroes, and that any test was ever culturally neutral as McGurk's own test purported to be.[48]

A much more extensive analysis of McGurk's article was published by the Chicago Urban League, which noted with alarm that McGurk's article was being used as "a scientific prop in . . . arguments against Supreme Court decisions on integration in our schools."[49] The Urban League commissioned a number of responses to McGurk's paper and circulated the resulting document to a number of libraries and social action agencies. The League's report underscored why McGurk's piece was published in a popular venue rather than a refereed journal. There were a number of interrelated problems, according to the authors of the Urban League report.

First, and most fundamental, McGurk's report, like all other psychological studies of race differences in intelligence, relied on a commonsense definition of race. Because all these studies relied on social definitions of race, the only comparisons they could make were between groups that were socially defined as racially different. But as Willard Kerr asked in the Urban League report, "Genetically, what is a Negro? There is more here than a strong suspicion that Dr. McGurk does not know." Kerr explained that modern genetics defined "race" only be a relative frequency of genes within a population. This definition did not include the broad categories that McGurk and other psychologists used when they compared Negro and white IQ scores. "[W]hite and Negro genes have intermixed substantially . . . through almost all the geographical areas of North Africa and southern Europe." Hence the McGurk's inference that the difference in IQ scores could be explained genetically was scientifically unsupportable.[50]

Second, many authors pointed out McGurk's collapsing of all cultural differences into a simple measure of socioeconomic status. Kerr proclaimed this a "uniquely materialistic assumption—and he writes exactly like a Marxist rather than a psychologist," because while the material standard of blacks may have increased more quickly than that of whites, this should not be equated with cultural background. Peter Jacobsohn pointed out that "the American Negro is always held inferior in some respects to even the lowliest American white," which "influences attitudes, values, behavior patterns and aspirations" and makes "a valid matching of the races . . . impossible, no matter how much the material circumstances of their members may resemble each other."[51]

Howard Hale Long, a pioneering African American psychologist, raised a related point in a review of McGurk's article. In the last article he published before his death in 1957, Long mocked McGurk's claim that Negroes had made any significant socioeconomic advancement between

1937 and 1951, the years McGurk selected for his study. Obviously, Long argued, the "rate" of increase in socioeconomic status, which McGurk relied upon, was a useless measure. "If the reader has five hundred dollars and adds one dollar, the increase is five-tenths of one percent (.5%)," Long wrote; "if the writer has one dollar and adds one more, he has increased his holding by one hundred percent (100%)." Such comparisons, Long concluded, were obviously useless, as was McGurk's claim that "two generations" had passed between 1937 and 1951. Long pointed to Department of Labor statistics that showed little, if any, evidence of significant Negro advancement on white employment, incomes, or other indicators of socioeconomic status.[52]

The largest problem with McGurk's analysis was its selective use of evidence, which was a bone of contention for all commentators. This particular issue was most fully fleshed out by an exchange of articles in the *Harvard Educational Review* in 1958. William M. McCord of Stanford and Nicholas Demerath of Harvard examined the studies McGurk quoted and found that, in nearly every case, the authors of the studies did not argue that the environment had been equalized for whites and blacks. McCord and Demerath argued that McGurk could omit these caveats only if he was guilty of "conscious biasing of the evidence."[53] McGurk's own study, they argued, was not standardized and did not attempt to measure the cultural or emotional motivations of the subjects. Most important, McGurk simply ignored a number of studies that contradicted his findings, particularly the findings of Otto Klineberg, whose work was often taken as the definitive work in the field.

McGurk's response to McCord and Demerath showed both the weaknesses of his scientific case and the rhetorical strategy of deferring to "nature" rather than "interpretations" of nature. McGurk pointed out that the studies he used had argued that socioeconomic status was equal for both groups, but he did not address that he ignored the cultural and emotional factors that McCord and Demarath had indicated were crucial to test performance and that McGurk himself had recognized in his 1943 article. As for ignoring Klineberg's work, McGurk argued that "I was concerned only with the data that had been published between 1937 and 1950."[54] He did not justify this range of years on any scientific grounds, but it did serve to eliminate Klineberg's work from his sample.

Of more interest than McGurk's rather weak attempt to defend his choice of studies was his rhetorical tactic that he was not speaking as an interpreter of data but that the data spoke for themselves. As he did in his original article, McGurk argued that the six studies were the only ones in which the data were clear enough to address the question regarding the educability of the Negro. Despite the authors' of the studies claim that the data should not be interpreted to mean Negro inferiority, McGurk maintained that these opinions should not be taken seriously, as the facts clearly demonstrated the unvarnished truth. "I do not believe that opinions, no matter how authoritative," he concluded, "have any place of value in a situation where facts are available. The available facts indicate without question that the social and economic manipulations of the past 35 years have not changed the psychological test score relationship between Negroes and whites."[55]

McGurk would repeat the claim that the scientist was not concerned with value judgments in an article on academic freedom, a subject in which he considered himself something of an expert. In private correspondence, McGurk complained that after his *U.S. News and World Report* article, "Villanova has censored me stiffly. I may not write without their specific approval."[56] Unhappy with this situation, McGurk was actively searching for a new position at the end of the 1950s, one where he would be free to pursue his interest in racial studies.

McGurk's account of experiences at Villanova may well have been accurate. In many southern universities, race relations had been a controversial topic. However, the far more likely situation in the South was for liberals on the race issue to face harassment. Those academics who spoke out in favor of integration in the years after *Brown* came under fire from both the segregationist political establishment and from the House Un-American Activities Committee, who often suspected integrationists of Communist tendencies.[57]

At a private, Catholic university such as Villanova, it is possible that McGurk came under administration pressure to avoid racial topics. However, if he was under pressure, as he claimed in his private correspondence, his public pronouncements gave no indication that his employers or his professional association were lax in protecting his right to research and write as he saw fit. His professional organization, the American Psychological Association, gave him a forum to share his experiences, where he claimed that Villanova supported him during the controversy caused his article.[58] Moreover, Villanova gave him an opportunity to present his case for academic freedom publicly, in a *Villanova Law Review* symposium on the interaction of social scientists in the legal process. McGurk argued that "social scientists should play a role in guiding legal processes," but the role should not be that of the "propagandistic social reformer." Such a role was a real danger given the subtle and not-so-subtle pressures put on academics to avoid controversial topics. McGurk pointed to pressures not only from universities but also from academic journals to toe the proper political line in social-scientific writings. The result was "there has been created an impression of solidarity of liberal opinion which has very effectively reduced the role which capable scientists of all disciplines could play" in the legal processes. McGurk advised that a special panel be formed, with liberal and "regular" members, as a way to check the liberal bias of academia that was prevalent. Apparently, he thought no checks were needed to check possible conservative biases.[59]

McGurk was the first psychologist to claim that science had decided the segregation issue. More influential and outspoken than McGurk, however, was Wesley Critz George, who argued that biology, not psychology, provided the evidence against the integrationists.

Wesley Critz George, North Carolina's Patriot

Wesley Critz George (1888–1982) was a professor of anatomy at the University of North Carolina School of Medicine. Even before the *Brown* decision, George was an opponent of attempts at race mixing. In 1933, he advised the president of the University of North Carolina against the relaxation of informal quotas on the number of Jewish students at the medical school. Treating all people the same, regardless of race, George advised, was "out of harmony with the realities of nature. There are few things in nature more fundamental and inescapable than racial solidarity and racial antagonisms, whether we observe jay birds and thrushes or the races of men."[60]

George's views, however, were increasingly out of step with sociological views on race relations. Right on his own campus, to George's amazement, he found purported scientists who disagreed with his view that racial friction was nature's way. The villain in this case was Howard Odum in the Sociology department. Odum was trained as a sociologist by Franklin Giddings at Columbia University. His doctoral dissertation in 1910 had embraced a hard version of scientific racism, and he had argued that racial differences were immutable and whites were definitely superior. In the 1920s he built the Department of Sociology at the University of North Carolina nearly single-handedly, founded the *Journal of Social Forces,* and established a number of other important institutions.

He had also softened his views about white supremacy, declaring himself agnostic on the issue. He became a "southern moderate" who was unwilling to embrace either white supremacy or any challenge to segregation. Believing that integration could not be forced on an unwilling South, Odum did little to challenge the existing social order. While he had shaken off the white supremacy taught by his mentor, Franklin Giddings, Odum never abandoned Giddings's Sumnerian teaching that folkways changed slowly, if at all. By the 1940s, Odum had founded the Southern Research Council (SRC) as an institution to conduct sociological investigations into southern folkways and was embroiled in political battles regarding integrating it. Odum opposed all attempts to integrate the SRC, hardly an indication of his racial radicalism.[61]

Despite the fact that Odum did not challenge the segregationist order, his soft stand on white supremacy did not sit well with George. In 1944, George fired off a letter of concern to Odum about the latter's creeping liberalism and failure to teach about white supremacy. "You are a breeder of fine cattle, and know something about genetics," wrote George. "And yet according to newspaper accounts and local reports you are promoting public policies the ultimate results of which would be to do to the white race in America the sort of thing that would be done to your Jersey herd if the state were to require you to incorporate into your herd the sorriest scrub bull in North Carolina."[62]

Odum, ever the conciliatory voice, allowed George to lecture to his class on the dangers of race mixing to the genetic basis of white civilization in the South. Like the writers for the *Truth Seeker,* George argued in his lecture to Odum's class that religious leaders were responsible for teaching "brotherhood of man" propaganda. Unlike *Truth Seeker* writers, who rejected religion outright, George argued for a true religious understanding that "God made the races different and first segregated them," and there was no reason to abandon "God's original policy of segregation." George argued that heredity was far more important than environment in determining behavior, as common sense clearly demonstrated: there were genetic differences in the behavior of dogs, cats, cattle, hogs, and so forth. This metaphor to agricultural breeding reflected not only the history of eugenics, which grew out of studies of agricultural breeding, but also the prevalence of agriculture in the American South, where eugenicists were fond of such metaphors. George argued that "you can teach things to cows and dogs and cats and hogs, but the fundamental racial and individual qualities are there in the fertilized eggs from which they came. The leopard cannot change his spots nor can the Ethiopian change his skin or his genetic constitution." This was the immutable truth of nature, despite the fact that the "public is being bombarded more or less persistently with the suggestion . . . that the races are all equal and the only real difference between the white man and the negro is the color of their skin."[63]

George repeated the same message about how scientific truths were at odds with political propaganda in his presidential address before the North Carolina Academy of Science in 1952. Applying the Cold War rhetoric of a Communist conspiracy, George pointed to the Lysenkoism of the Soviet Union, where "the knowledge and theories about heredity that have been established during the past 50 years have been denied." The danger was not, unfortunately, limited to the totalitarian regime of the Soviets. George warned of those "who would defy the truth and subvert the intellect of our people in order to gain their objectives." These conspirators were gaining ground by taking advantage of those with "good hearts and frail intellects," who were "deceived by the smooth language of humanitarianism into support of and evangelism for theories" that simply were not true—chiefly, the declaration that there were no genetic differences between individuals. Repeating some of the same arguments he gave in his lecture to Odum's class, George objected to confusing democracy's call for equality before the law with genetic equality.[64]

In his 1952 address, George pointed to so-called committees of experts who issued declarations regarding scientific truths—a clear dig at the UNESCO statements. The findings of these experts was then taught in "re-education" workshops in schools and churches. "The real purpose," George declared, "is to indoctrinate people, somewhat clandestinely, with the particular ideologies of those directing the re-education." Such a process was abetted by "controlling or influencing the distribution of information," such as giving "favorable press to party-line books" and ignoring "or giving unfavorable press to opposition books."[65]

Ten years after his lecture to Odum's class, the *Brown* decision made all of George's nightmares a reality. Three days after the *Brown* decision, George had fired off a letter to his governor, William B. Umstead. "The end result of integrating the races in the educational and social spheres," George wrote, "would be to promote the amalgamation of the races. This must not be allowed to happen. Although the maintenance of our public

school system is desirable it is not so vital as the maintenance of the protoplasmic integrity of the white race, upon which our civilization depends."[66]

In 1954, George was not a young man, but he soon launched himself
into a flurry of activity designed to "maintain the protoplasmic integrity
of the white race." By the summer of 1955, George was the head of the
Patriots of North Carolina, one of several white supremacist organizations that sprang to life in the wake of *Brown*. A respected scientist and
president of the North Carolina Academy of Science, George was only
one of several distinguished members; Patriot ranks included three ex-
speakers of the North Carolina House of Representatives, a Democratic
National Committee member, and a state senator. In 1956 the Patriots
were instrumental in defeating two North Carolina Congress members
who had refused to sign the Southern Manifesto. Like the ASCOA in
1920s, however, the Patriots could not maintain the momentum that
launched the organization, and by 1958 the Patriots were effectively dis-
banded.[67]

One of the shortest-lived massive resistance organizations, the Patriots
had limited impact on the political landscape. However, the ideology the
group represented is of more interest. In his classic study of the massive
resistance movement, political scientist Francis Wilhoit offered a typology of its leaders. There were "opportunists" who joined the movement
simply because it was the politically expedient move in racially and politically polarized times. There were the "traditionalists," who simply
supported segregation because it was the status quo and they did not like
rapid social change. Finally, there were the "zealots," who were true be-
lievers in white supremacy and "acted from a blazing certitude of their
own virtue and of the total depravity of their opponents." Among the
zealots, Wilhoit listed the Ku Klux Klan, the paramilitary National States
Rights Party, and the North Carolina Patriots. Despite their upper-class
membership and their intellectual sophistication, the Patriots were on the
extreme fringe of racist beliefs, and George was their leading ideologue.[68]

The collapse of the Patriots did not mean the collapse of George's fight
to maintain racial segregation. In a series of writings and lectures, most
of which simply repeated the themes he had developed before *Brown,* he
argued for the scientific validity of white supremacy and the dangers of
miscegenation. He published the lecture he had given for Odum's class,
and it was distributed by segregationist groups looking for scientific support.[69] In a speech he made at Dartmouth College, he laid out essentially

the same arguments that Earnest Sevier Cox had in *White America*: social mixing would lead to racial mixing and eventually result in the United States becoming a "Negroid" nation. The white race was responsible for all civilization, and blacks had been the beneficiary of white largesse when they were brought to America; race mixing would be a disaster, as evidenced by the mongrel nations of South America. Unlike Cox, George was a segregationist who believed that segregation was necessary unless the nation was willing "to sacrifice our children on the altar of integration."[70]

George's activities brought him to the attention of a wide circle of racial writers. Mississippi senator James O. Eastland believed that George's Dartmouth speech was "brilliant and penetrating" and thought that segregationists should "marshal behind us the maximum amount of valid scientific opinion," because "it is all on our side" even if "many of those in the Northern universities are afraid to speak the truth." Georgia attorney general Eugene Cook believed that George's address was "a definite contribution to peace and tranquility and continued progress of the two races" and arranged to have the speech widely distributed. What these segregationists recognized was that George could speak with authority on what one sympathetic correspondent noted was "the sand foundations of the neo-socializers who see racial consciousness as a 'scientific' error, a moral sin, and to be legislated out of its evolutionary pace."[71]

George's segregationist activities also brought him to the attention of Wickliffe Draper, who had been Cox's patron for repatriation and underwrote the distribution of *White America*. Draper was interested in giving money to organizations that would use science to oppose the *Brown* decision and ensure that America would remain white. In 1955, George suggested that Draper contact Frank McGurk and British geneticist R. Ruggles Gates, who would be sympathetic to Draper's cause. George tried to dissuade Draper from funding further studies in racial differences, since "many editors and publishers today, even of scientific journals, shy away from publishing anything that is not party line." Beside, George explained, "[t]here is already enough knowledge available to show the folly of [the *Brown*] decision. Our problem is to get that knowledge presented in impressive form and disseminated to the public to counteract the sophistry of the integrationists." This advice was apparently in line with Draper's ideas on the subject; he eventually funded the distribution of George's speeches. This was the first step in the creation of a network of scientists and other "respectable" Southerners who would be funded by Draper to fight integration.[72] The event that would give this network its most effective spokesman would be the crisis at Central High in Little Rock, Arkansas, which would teach southern politicians that integration would be enforced at the point of federal bayonets, but that massive resistance had very real payoffs at the ballot box.

5

Organizing Massive Resistance and Organizing Science

In September 1957, Arkansas governor Orval Faubus ordered the National Guard to prevent the integration of Central High School in Little Rock. The escalating racial crisis in Little Rock, with white students taunting the "Little Rock Nine"—the nine African American students attempting to attend Central High—and Faubus's refusal to comply with the integration order of the court convinced President Eisenhower, who had been indifferent to integration, that this was a matter of insurrection rather than race relations. As a military man, Eisenhower knew the value of overwhelming force and ordered the 101st Airborne Division into Little Rock to enforce the federal court order for integration.[1]

The white South was enraged at the sight of federal bayonets enforcing what they viewed as the "Second Reconstruction." Michael Klarman argued, "By manufacturing a racial crisis that in turn led to a confrontation with the federal military, Faubus transformed himself into a nearly invincible state politician as well as something of a regional folk hero."[2] The Northern League writers also took note of the events in Little Rock. Byram Campbell penned an open letter to President Eisenhower where he warned of Chief Justice Earl Warren's reliance on Swedish sociologist Gunnar Myrdal, "a socialist," in footnote eleven of the *Brown* opinion. Campbell warned of the "vast propaganda build-up inspired by our left-wing elements" that has "simply assumed there is some moral worth in integration." The Northern League's official southern publication, *The Virginian,* noted that white Americans would not long tolerate federal troops "herding white children through the streets like cattle." It concluded, "The big question is: how many white Americans will the federal government slaughter in order to enforce its mongrelization edict?"[3]

The crisis of Little Rock would also launch the segregationist career of Carleton Putnam (1904–1998), whom historian Adam Nossiter dubbed the "high priest of respectable white supremacy" and David Southern called "the Madison Grant of the 1960s."[4] Southern's appellation for Putnam was exactly on the mark. Putnam took as his bellwethers Madison Grant, Lothrop Stoddard, Earnest Sevier Cox, and Omer Stuart Landry. Like these writers, Putnam was convinced of white supremacy and the Boasian conspiracy to smother the truth about racial differences.[5] It was Putnam who would move the conspiracy claim into wider circulation and force the scientific community to take a stand defending anthropology as a science. In so doing, Putnam transformed the scientific question of racial differences into a battle about the public authority of anthropology. Putnam was the leading segregationist to directly challenge anthropologists as to the basis of their scientific conclusions and the nature of their "control" over the scientific study of race. The result was that the mainstream scientific community, especially anthropologists, underwent an intense self-examination about the nature of their discipline in relation to society.

Carleton Putnam and the Equalitarian Dogma

The scion of an established New England family, Carleton Putnam was educated at Princeton and Columbia Law School in the 1920s. In 1933, Putnam established his own airline, building it into a successful business. After World War II, he merged his airline with others, forming Delta Airlines. Having made his fortune, Putnam stayed on the board of Delta but increasingly turned the reins over to others and began a second career as a biographer of Theodore Roosevelt. The first of a projected four-volume Roosevelt biography appeared in 1958 to positive reviews.[6]

The first volume of the biography would prove to be the last, as Putnam abandoned the project to take on what he saw as a much more important one: the protection of white civilization. In the wake of the events following Little Rock, Putnam penned an "Open Letter to President Eisenhower" making the case for continued school segregation in the South. Putnam sent the letter to several southern newspapers, which published it enthusiastically, typically with an introduction like that of the *Richmond Times-Dispatch,* which editorialized: "Unlike many of his fellow-citizens in the North, [Putnam] understands and appreciates the problems with which the South has been confronted, was a result of the staggering series of Supreme Court edicts."[7]

Putnam's letter echoed themes that had long been prevalent in the South. "Social status has to be earned," wrote Putnam, and the "Negro" simply lacked what was required to earn the white man's status. "Any man with two eyes in his head," Putnam wrote, "can observe a Negro settlement in the Congo, can study the pure-blooded African in his native habitat as he exists when left on his own resources, can compare this settlement with London or Paris, and can draw his own conclusions regarding relative levels of character and intelligence—or that combination of character and intelligence which is civilization."[8]

Putnam's letter was a great success in the South, and soon a Putnam Letters Committee was formed to collect donations to sponsor reprinting the letter in northern newspapers. Putnam's letter eventually appeared as a paid advertisement in several large newspapers such as the *New York Times* throughout 1959, as well as being distributed by the Citizens' Councils in pamphlet form. Further contributions led to the creation of a National Putnam Letters Committee, which printed and distributed Putnam's writings defending segregation.[9]

While Southerners reacted gleefully to Putnam, other reactions to his letter's appearance in the *New York Times* were equally enthusiastic in their condemnation. A letter to the editor pointed out that "Mr. Putnam makes the point that social status has to be earned. But this is just what is prevented by racially segregated education," as Negroes were perpetually routed to inferior schools where they could not learn. A more lengthy response by Fawn Brodie took exception to Putnam's claim, which he had borrowed from Cox, that Abraham Lincoln declared during the Lincoln-Douglas debates that he did not favor Negro social equality. Brodie pointed to Lincoln's actions at the beginning of Reconstruction to try to bring the newly freed Negroes exactly that.[10]

By March 1959, two months after his letter had appeared in the *New York Times,* Putnam struck again with a letter to Attorney General William Rogers. There, Putnam declared that the sources in footnote eleven of the *Brown* decision appeared "to form the foundation of the decision." These sources reflected "a point of view rooted in what I may call modern equalitarian anthropology—a school which holds that all races are currently equal in their capacity for culture, and that existing inequalities of status are due solely to inequalities of opportunity." Putnam claimed, "Two generations of Americans have been victimized by a pseudo-scientific hoax in this field [of anthropology and] that this hoax is part of an equalitarian propaganda typical of the left-wing overdrift of our times." Like the first, Putnam's second letter was widely reprinted, making Putnam a well-known opponent of integration efforts.[11]

For Putnam, the question became why the simple truth about the racial inferiority of African Americans was so widely denied. The answer seemed to be that modern anthropologists hid racial truths from the American people. He took it upon himself to educate policy makers and scientists about the reality and importance of race. His tool for so doing was the pen, and he began a correspondence campaign to inform important people of the dangers of equalitarian anthropology. As he noted to a sympathetic reader, in words that could have been written by Madison Grant himself: "I happen to be financially independent. . . . I happen likewise to be in a position to hit hard, and if I can be sure a core of sound anthropologists behind me I'll keep striking my mark further and further out—and gladly."[12]

Putnam wanted to influence those who held the reins of power in society, but his efforts on that front met with minimal success. Eisenhower's staff was not impressed with Putnam's efforts, merely filing his letters away—one with a cover note that explained, "Anyone in his right might wouldn't write the President a letter like this."[13] Similarly, Putnam's letters to Justice Felix Frankfurter must have frustrated both men. Putnam wanted Frankfurter to consider the possibility that the *Brown* case rested on a scientific mistake, and Frankfurter could not, by virtue of his position on the U.S. Supreme Court, make any comments on Putnam's material. By contrast, Frankfurter admired Theodore Roosevelt deeply and constantly answered Putnam's tirades against *Brown* by pleading for more books on Roosevelt: "When, oh when, am I going to have your next volume on T.R.?"[14]

The NAACP received several letters demanding that the organization take a stand against Putnam's public tirades against egalitarian science. Roy Wilkins explained to P. L. Prattis, the influential editor of the *Pittsburgh Courier,* that the organization did not want to issue an official answer, since to do so might "revive interest in it on the part of those who may have forgotten about it." However, John A. Morsell, Wilkins's assistant, prepared a packet of materials for NAACP branches that wished to answer Putnam's positions themselves.[15]

Morsell, in preparing his response to Putnam, fell into a correspondence with Putnam in which the two men made their positions, and the distance between them, abundantly clear. Morsell's position was that current science had declared questions of race differences to be fundamentally undecidable because "no student has ever been able (or is ever likely to be able) to control enough of the conditioning factors to make genuinely scientific comparison possible." He argued that "there is virtually complete agreement, among contemporary psychologists, geneticists, and anthropologists that the available data, taken as a whole and carefully assessed for scientific rigor do not sustain a thesis of biological racial inferiority. Neither do they conclusively disprove it. . . . The literature on this is unusually compelling."[16]

In his subsequent writings, Putnam would openly acknowledge his debt to those who answered his letters, as they helped him sharpen his arguments against the equalitarian dogma. In his response to Morsell, Putnam sounded much like Cox and Theodore Bilbo when he managed to explain that Boas was not a "true" American, while not explicitly naming him as a Jew:

> The Boas school was initiated and advanced by non-Negro minority pressure groups after the "new immigration" of the 1880s as a deliberate self-serving device, aided by others whose hearts were softer than their heads were clear, and it is now being used by radical whites in the integration fight more to entrench the theory than to help the Negro. It has no basis in sound science. Its ideology is wholly alien to original American concepts.[17]

As for Morsell's argument that the scientific study of race differences was fundamentally impossible, Putnam granted that anthropology was "not an exact science"; however, when Morsell argued "that the inferiority of the Negro race cannot be either proved or disproved," he misunderstood how policy was made. "In the management of human affairs," Putnam explained, "all law and all practical judgments are based on a balance of probabilities," and "not only does the evidence on the racial inferiority of the Negro meet the requirements of the civil law, it meets those of the criminal law. Observation and experience confirm it 'beyond all reasonable doubt.'"[18] Despite his declarations that the real battle was a scientific one, Putnam consistently would defer to the evidence of history and the historical case that the Negro had never built a civilization. As he declared in his original letter to Eisenhower, the evidence was obvious to any who would simply open their eyes to look. For Putnam, then, science and its complexities could never really trump the evidence that common sense provided. This would be especially evident when he attempted to communicate directly with the scientific community. For while he would never let modern science explain away the obvious truth of white supremacy, Putnam was also determined to convince contemporary scientists that Madison Grant had been right a generation before.

The Two Carletons

Just as he was trying to convince policy makers that they had been brainwashed by modern anthropology, Putnam took it upon himself to re-educate the American anthropological community about the reality and importance of race. Putnam began a long correspondence with a number of anthropologists, arguing with their findings and attempting to discover why they made the absurd claims they did about racial equality. On January 5, 1959, the same day that Putnam's letter to Eisenhower appeared in the *New York Times,* Putnam composed a letter to Harvard anthropologist Clyde Kluckhohn. Putnam drilled Kluckhohn with a number of questions about his book *Mirror for Man,* in which the anthropologist argued against innate racial differences. Putnam argued that Kluckhohn claimed that "culture supersed[ed] the concept of race," but "[n]owhere do you deal with what seems to me an obvious fact, namely, that culture is, in the majority of cases, a product of race." Putnam wrote, "I am left with the conviction that Madison Grant and Lothrop Stoddard, with all the limitations of anthropological technique to which their generation was subject, nevertheless thought more clearly and came closer to the truth than the followers of Boas. . . . I begin to suspect that anthropology in the last half-century has been drafted to serve the demi-Goddess of Equalitarianism instead of the Goddess of Truth."[19]

Putnam was undeterred by the fact that few anthropologists answered his letters. In July 1959, Putnam began circulating drafts to "a selected list of those whom I know to be interested in the racial integration of southern schools." The recipients included a number of anthropologists as well as political leaders. In thirty-four single-spaced pages, Putnam put forth his proposition that anthropologists' control over racial discourse extended far beyond the scientific realm. "There is a strong clique of equalitarian anthropologists under the hypnosis of the Boas school," Putnam explained, "which . . . has captured important chairs in many leading northern and western universities. This clique, aided by equalitarians in government, the press, entertainment, and other fields, has dominated public opinion in these areas and have made it almost impossible for those who disagree with it to hold jobs."[20]

Among the scientists who received this material was University of Pennsylvania anthropologist Carleton S. Coon, who was, in fact, Putnam's cousin. Coon had been trained as a physical anthropologist at Harvard under Earnest A. Hooton in the 1920s. Harvard was the "intellectual antithesis to the Columbia school [of cultural anthropologists led by Franz Boas], focusing on the definition and study of race instead of its demise."[21] Throughout Coon's life, much of his work focused on identifying morphological characteristics as a means to classify humans, both living and dead, into clearly identifiable races. Carleton Coon had spent much of his professional career fighting what he viewed as a battle with Boasian cultural anthropology over the entire concept of race. For example, in his 1954 book, *The Story of Man,* Coon had warned against "academic debunkers and soft-peddlers who operate inside anthropology itself. Basing their ideas on the concept of the universal brotherhood of man, certain writers, who are mostly social anthropologists, consider it immoral to study race, and produce book after book exposing it as a 'myth.' Their argument is that because the study of race once gave ammunition to racial fascists, who misused it, we should pretend that races do not exist. . . . These writers are not physical anthropologists, but the public does not know the difference."[22]

Coon was deeply suspicious of cultural anthropology and Boas's followers, especially Ashley Montagu, whom he liked to refer to as "Ehrenberg," which was Montagu's birth name. He also believed that congressional investigations into Communist influences on university education showed the dire influences they had on anthropological education, particularly the testimony of Bella Dodd, a former Communist who had taught at Columbia for a number of years.[23] Writing to a former student, Coon declared that "somebody should do two things: 1) Investigate the communist influence on American anthropology via Bella Dodd, Boas and the Boasinines . . . 2) Find out why Ashley [Montagu] changed his father's name retroactively in Who's Who whether or not he has ever carried a card."[24]

As he did in all his mailings, when he wrote to Coon, Putnam asked for advice on improving his materials as well as "your opinion on the extraordinary situation I find among anthropologists, many of whom seem to be actually intimidated by the equalitarian trend. Yet this matter is no longer an academic argument. It has become a desperate issue of public policy" Coon's response was to invite Putnam to his home to discuss the matter as well as to see some antiques that had once belonged to their mutual ancestor, Revolutionary War general Israel Putnam.[25]

Throughout 1960, Coon and Putnam communicated frequently through telephone conversations, visits, and a voluminous correspondence. The men shared a deep suspicion of cultural anthropology, especially of Boas and his students. This mutual mistrust of Boasian anthropology translated into a working relationship as Coon helped the segregationist sharpen his arguments against cultural anthropology. This was consistent with Coon's concept of the role of a professor in society. He wrote to Putnam, "The role of the professor is a responsible one, like that of a minister, doctor, or lawyer. As he is in charge of teaching he should strive for the truth and not engage in movements nor join pressure groups. He is free to publish what he likes as long as he remains non-partisan. Anything that he has published can be quoted by anyone interested. Professors . . . should not be on anyone's side, but should give their advice, if they wish, to both or any number of sides."[26]

Coon and Putnam exchanged ideas throughout 1960 as Putnam prepared his book. To offer two examples: first, Coon warned Putnam away from questionable sources. For example, Putnam's admiration for Madison Grant, Coon warned, was a mistake because of Grant's Nordicism. In his 1939 book, *Races of Europe,* Coon used the term *Nordic* as a scientific term but criticized *Nordicism,* which he defined as "the misuse of racial terminology for political purposes, based on the unproved assumption that Nordics are superior in mental and moral attributes to members of other races." To Putnam, Coon wrote: "To most minds [Grant] evokes fascism and racism of a Hitlerian variety and to quote him would only reduce the number of persons who would continue reading after seeing him." However, Coon thought that Lothrop Stoddard was "a bird of brighter feather," although "he was later discredited as a racist and died in obscurity." Putnam could "do worse than to mention the success and accuracy of his predictions" in *The Rising Tide of Color.* In the end, however, Coon warned Putnam away from these popular writers and instead pointed his cousin to recent works by Garrett Hardin, Georges A. Heuse, and J. Millot, all of which are "little known in this country and authoritative." All this material was included in Putnam's final product.[27]

Second, Coon supplied Putnam with an anonymous source that the scientific community was rejecting its equalitarian ways. However, while Coon was always willing to help Putnam, he was also anxious that Putnam not identify him by name. Putnam noted that he was going to quote from various sources but asked Coon for quotations from his own writings because "you are in *Who's Who* and [the readers] can see your record and standing." Coon attempted to steer Putnam away from his own work. "No one," wrote Coon, "is more Whos Whoey than Alfred Kroeber [and] he does not believe in racial equality in intellect, and that has been in print for many years and no one has challenged him."[28]

Coon's unwillingness to become directly involved was exemplified when Putnam wanted to quote from their correspondence. Coon had written to Putnam, "The tide is turning. Heredity is coming back into fashion, but not through anthropologists. It is the zoologists, the animal behavior men, who are doing it, and the anthropologists are beginning to learn from them." Putnam quoted this paragraph in a subsequent draft, without using Coon's name. Coon was uncomfortable with this maneuver. He wrote, "What bothers me is the quote without identification. Anybody who tried would know who it was in a minute, by my style alone."

Putnam pleaded with Coon to use the quotation from Coon's letter, for it directly dealt with the "main pivot" of the "key question" in the book: "whether the white man and the Negro are equal in their capacity to adapt to Western civilization. . . . The remarks in your letter about heredity illuminate this issue." Putnam offered to disguise the quotation and refer simply to a "distinguished scientist, younger than I am," and Coon eventually relented to the use of the quotation.[29]

In March 1961, Putnam wrote to Coon that "*Race and Reason* is now off the press and on its way to the bindery." There was very little in Putnam's argument that had not been said before in the white South: African Americans were incapable of self-governance, civilization was racial in nature, and social intermingling (such as school desegregation) would lead to racial intermarriage, which would lead to the destruction of the white southern civilization. "I must ask the Northern integrationist," Putnam demanded, "by what authority he claims the right to gamble with the white civilization of the South, against the will of its people, while he personally sits with his children in all white schools."[30]

The authority Putnam found was Franz Boas, and the vast influence Boas and his students had in American society was "the hidden issue" that Putnam would uncover. He claimed have learned the "facts about

Franz Boas himself—his minority group background . . . his association with Columbia in 1896 . . . the names of his students—Herskovits, Klineberg, Ashley Montagu."[31] The "minority group background" of Boas—the fact that Boas was Jewish—was central to Putnam's argument and indicates his admiration of Madison Grant. Like Grant, Putnam believed that the Jews who came to the United States after 1880 "were not readily assimilated" and had no record for "maintaining stable, free societies" and therefore set out to prove that "*all* races were equal in adaptability to our white civilization."[32]

When Putnam turned to the anthropological writing produced by Boas and his students, which he claimed he had approached with "impartial mind," he was stunned: "page by page my amazement grew. Here was clever and insidious propaganda posing in the name of science, fruitless efforts at proof of unprovable theories. . . . I went on to Herskovits and others until the pattern began to repeat itself, the slippery techniques in evading the main issues, the prolix diversions, the sound without the substance. Was it possible that a whole generation of Americans had been taken in by such writing as this?"[33]

Alas, Putnam concluded, too few scientists were willing to step forward and pronounce the truth about racial differences. Putnam claimed that he had exchanged letters with dozens of "Ivy League professors" and noted that they were "paying the immemorial price for their own deceit, they had hypnotized others so long they were now the victims of their own trance." Putnam concluded, "Either from their silences or their comments, I had sensed the thinking of Kluckhohn and Handlin of Harvard, Murdock of Yale, Herskovits of Northwestern, [and] dozens of others."[34]

The book was aggressively promoted by the Putnam National Letters Committee, probably underwritten by Draper, which created a mailing list for Putnam's writings. "We have been functioning for less than a year," committee director Mark German wrote in August 1961, "but can say that were are definitely on our way. Our mailing list grows and grows." A few months later, German kept the equalitarian conspiracy central even while he noted the tremendous success the book was enjoying despite the fact that "most Northern review journals and many Northern bookstores, affected by the same influences that attempted to stifle the letters, will give the book the silent and under-the-counter treatment, or subject it to name-calling."[35]

Coon provided important behind-the-scenes help for *Race and Reason*, but the book also sported a very public introduction from scientists

R. Ruggles Gates, Henry E. Garrett, Robert Gayre, and Wesley C. George. These scientists declared that "there is a logic and common sense in these pages; there is also inescapable scientific validity."[36] For while many scientists had simply ignored Putnam's letters, a number of others were sympathetic to him and, unlike Coon, willing to ally themselves publicly to him.

International Association for the Advancement of Ethnology and Eugenics

The New York Association for the Preservation for the Freedom of Choice (APFC) had been stymied in their attempt to incorporate and fight New York City's open housing ordinances. Not to be deterred, the same group of individuals incorporated the International Association for the Advancement of Ethnology and Eugenics (IAAEE) in Washington, D.C., in April 1959. Unlike the APFC, which had declared its political goal of free choice in combination with its scientific one of encouraging racial research, the IAAEE had no stated political goal. Those invited to join the IAAEE were courted to join a scientific society dedicated to "encouraging research in the various fields of race science," for "the climate of opinion at many American colleges and universities during the past thirty years has been unalterably opposed to free and open discussion of race, racial differences, and race relations."[37] Among those who attended the first meeting of the IAAEE were Robert Kuttner and Donald Swan, both of whom were associated with the *Truth Seeker,* as well as the segregationists Carleton Putnam and Frank C. J. McGurk and psychologist Henry Garrett. Also in attendance were A. James Gregor, who had been the organizer for the APFC, and Alfred Avins, who was the legal mind behind both organizations. This meeting of the IAAEE was the first time that the neo-Nazi underground in New York joined forces with the segregationist establishment of the South.[38]

The first meeting of the IAAEE was held in February 1960 the home of Charles Tansill (1890–1964), a historian who had retired from Georgetown two years before. At one time Tansill had been a respected diplomatic historian, but in his writings on World War II, he was notorious for his criticisms of Franklin Roosevelt. He had spent 1935 in Nazi Germany and upon his return to the United States became such an active supporter of the regime that he was dismissed from his post at American University.

In his writing on the origins of World War II, Tansill argued that the United States and Britain, rather than Hitler, were responsible for the invasion of Poland. Tansill's writings would eventually be adopted by the Holocaust denial movement, who would look upon him as one of the founders of their own brand of historical "revisionism."[39]

Tansill was also an outspoken opponent of integration. He argued that since the Fourteenth Amendment was illegally ratified, the *Brown* decision could not have applied it to the states. He advised Virginia governor Albertis Harrison to claim, "There is no 14th Amendment, and then tell the Federal courts to go to hell. They have really been there since July, 1868."[40]

Tansill became the host for the first meetings of the IAAEE probably because of his close friendship with H. Keith Thompson (b. 1920). As a young man, Thompson had been a believer in the goals and views of the Third Reich and had been active in the German/American Bund in the 1930s. After World War II, Thompson became a registered agent in the United States for the Socialist Reich Party in West Germany, which saw itself as the successor to Hitler's own Nazi party. Thompson was a tireless supporter of Hitler's regime and worked to help Nazis fleeing capture from the victorious Allies and to free those who had been captured. Well connected in the neo-Nazi underground, Thompson counted among his friends those in the National Renaissance Party, which was also closely allied with the *Truth Seeker*. Thompson was a common touch point for the scientists who made up the IAAEE, the neo-Nazi underground, and the proto-Holocaust denial of Tansill. When the IAAEE began publishing their scientific attacks on racial equality, it was Thompson who would arrange for the printing.[41]

Donald A. Swan: Guenther's Champion

Much younger than most of the figures in the IAAEE, Donald A. Swan (1935–1981) did not have an advanced degree but did serve as the corresponding secretary and helped with daily operations of the organization. Indeed, it is doubtful that the organization could have succeeded without his tireless efforts to keep people connected. William H. Tucker found Swan to be "the most important single person behind the scenes in the IAAEE and the legal attempts to overturn *Brown*."[42]

Very early in his life, Swan became involved with the racist underground of New York City. Swan was a brilliant child, completing high school at fifteen and getting a degree from Queens College, where he attempted to organize a Nordic group for undergraduates. The same year he graduated, 1954, the nineteen-year-old Swan read an article by H. Keith Thompson for a tabloid newspaper in which Thompson declared himself "An American Fascist." Swan quickly followed suit, declaring himself an American fascist. Swan entered graduate school at Columbia but was eventually expelled for stealing books from the university library.[43]

While his academic career foundered, Swan's status in the racist Right flowered. Perhaps first brought to Thompson's attention by Swan's declaration of his fascism, Swan was soon assisting Thompson in giving aid to imprisoned Nazis. One project was a letter-writing campaign Thompson organized to for Admiral Karl Doenitz, Hitler's legal successor to the leadership of the Third Reich. Doenitz had served a ten-year sentence after being convicted of war crimes at Nuremburg. Thompson was gathering from Americans letters of appreciation for Doenitz, as well as letters condemning the war crimes trial. According to Thompson, Doenitz's sentence was the result of the "vindictiveness of the slimy minority which runs the Western World today."[44] For this project, Thompson solicited letters from Robert Kuttner and Donald Swan. In Swan's letter he told Doenitz:

> Although you have been judged guilty by the court of world jewry, history will render the verdict of—"hero and martyr in a great and noble cause." Adolf Hitler, will be judged by future generations, as the man who brought about the spiritual regeneration of a defeated and divided Germany in 1933, and who vainly and prematurely tried to unite Europe, and to awaken the Western world to the dangers of Asiatic Bolshevism.[45]

By the late 1950s, Swan was contributing to *Truth Seeker* and speaking at the Racist Forum under the pseudonym Thor Swenson. His contributions to *Truth Seeker* were academic in tone and quite unlike most of the fulminating contributors. In a series of articles all titled "Inherited Natures of Negroes and Whites Compared," "Swenson" laid out the case for biological differences between the races. His careful writing, complete with footnotes—a rarity for *Truth Seeker*'s pages—relied on IQ studies of the early twentieth century and the Nazi anthropologists Erwin Baur, Eugen Fischer, and Fritz Lenz.[46] Swan was also the most outspoken defender of Hans F. K. Guenther, whom he described as "one of the world's foremost authorities in the field of raciology." As an avid book collector, Swan showed a close familiarity with all of Guenther's works.[47]

A. James Gregor: Among the Nordicists

The final person at the core of the IAAEE was A. James Gregor, who had been the organizing secretary for the earlier APFC. A superficial glance at Gregor's *vita* in 1959 would appear to place him firmly in the same camp as Swan and Kuttner: he had published a number of articles in Oswald Mosley's fascist periodical, *The European,* and had spoken at *Truth Seeker*'s Racist Forum. Such a glance, however, would obscure some very important differences between Gregor's views and those of the Northern League.[48]

A. James Gregor (b. 1929) had been born Anthony Gimigliono. In the late 1950s he was a graduate student at Columbia University in social and political philosophy. His dissertation, which he would complete in 1961, was a study of Fascist philosopher Giovanni Gentile.[49] Gregor's two most important influences on his racial thought were demographer Corrado Gini and sociologist Ludwig Gumplowicz. Gini, who would also become a member of the IAAEE, was a key figure in the first "fusion of eugenics, demography and fascism," serving on the constitutional council in the mid-1920s, encouraging Mussolini's strong pronatalist policies.[50]

There were important differences between how Gini conceptualized racial science and how the Nazis conceptualized it; however, one thing they shared was the metaphor of the state as an organism, which had the implication of subverting individual rights to the needs of the state. Gini argued that society was "a true and distinct organism of a rank superior to the individuals who compose it." The view of the state having its own agency meant that the state had to see to its own survival and the survival of future generations, "sacrificing, wherever necessary, the interests of the individual and operating in opposition to the will of the present generation."[51]

Ludwig Gumplowicz (1838–1909) was one of the first to offer a full-blown sociological theory of race and racial conflict. For Gumplowicz, it was a mistake to view race as a biological entity. Race was more properly understood as a sociological phenomenon. People have a natural tendency to form groups, Gumplowicz argued, and these groups have a natural tendency to come into conflict over natural resources. "Race," on this view, is nothing more than a group of individuals who may have formed in a variety of ways: there was not biological necessity in the concept of race but rather a series of contingently formed groups who have faced off against one another. Such a view was reflected in early American sociology as well, particularly in Franklin Giddings's concept of "consciousness of kind," which he defined as when "any being, whether high or low in the scale of life, recognizes another conscious being as of like kind with itself."[52] For this view, which Gregor would make his own, it was the natural tendency to form groups that was the key to race, rather than any biological traits that particular groups possessed.

An implication of this sociological view of race is that Gregor was a critic of Nordicism and the crude biological determinism of Kuttner and Swan, despite his close association with them. For Gregor, the biological reality of racial differences was not the central point he wished to make in his racial writings; rather, it was how the social reality of race factored into political, social, and class conflicts. For example, in his earliest publication on race, Gregor argued that both Communists and northern capitalists were urging for Negro equality. Capitalists hoped to use Negro migration into northern cities to break the power of labor unions, while the Communists planned to use the Negro as "shock troops to be sacrificed in the revolutionary violence against the system."[53]

Gregor's first attack on Nordicism appeared in *The European,* where Gregor targeted Guenther's work. He admitted that Guenther had enjoyed a brief vogue in Nazi Germany in the early 1930s; however, Gregor argued that "Günther was purchased at too high a price," since a strict adherence to his teachings would have eliminated the vast majority of the German population from Nordic purity, including some important party leaders. By 1935, Gregor claimed, Nazi theoreticians had rejected Nordicism and opted for a more realistic view of race: "Everywhere the talk was no longer of fixed and immutable races but of races in formation, the components for which arise out of the crucible of the past." A few years later Gregor repeated his criticisms of Nordicism in an article for *Phylon,* the journal that had been founded by W. E. B. Du Bois. Here his target was specifically Northern League writers, mentioning the writings of his colleague Robert Kuttner by name and taking aim at Northern League outlets such as *Northern World, The Virginian,* and *Truth Seeker.*[54]

Gregor argued that race prejudice was naturally occurring and that it was the basis for a rational social order. To build a case for race prejudice, Gregor had to confront a series of arguments that seemingly had ended the debate about race and race prejudice in the larger scientific community. The social-scientific consensus in the postwar United States was that race prejudice was a learned behavior and that it could be undone by social action set on eradicating it. This was the fundamental starting point for the social scientists who were involved with the NAACP in *Brown v. Board of Education,* for example.[55] Gregor met modern social science on its own turf, offering subtle and sophisticated versions of previously discredited doctrines about racial attitudes.

Gregor argued that there was a natural group preference that caused spontaneous and inevitable segregation of groups within society. "What passes as 'race prejudice,'" he wrote, "is actually but a single variety of a whole class of related responses rooted in normal human behavior" that centered on the need for group identification.[56] In making this argument, Gregor was firmly rooted in mainstream social-scientific thinking about prejudice. Gordon Allport, whose 1954 study, *The Nature of Prejudice,* set the tone for at least two decades of psychological research on race prejudice, argued along similar lines, titling one chapter "The Normality of Prejudgment" and asserting that the formation of in-groups was a natural phenomenon and was often accompanied by the rejection of out-groups.[57]

However, writers in the 1940s and 1950s who argued that the tendency toward group formation meant that race prejudice was a natural and normal part of society had little success. In the 1940s, sociologist Gustav Ichheiser maintained that there was a "universal" tendency to reject those physically different from oneself, making effective integration impossible. In response, Louis Wirth countered that race prejudice was hardly "universal" because Ichheiser did not seem to understand that "certain physical characteristics are defined as socially significant. Others are not. One might ask, for example, why blond-haired persons do not react especially differently to brunets or to red-haired people than they do to their own kind."[58] It was because of this seemingly arbitrary nature of group preferences that race prejudice could not be an "instinctual" trait humans possessed.

Gregor had several answers to the "arbitrariness argument." First, he attempted to make an empirical case for the existence of racial preferences, pointing to the long history of intergroup hostility. "Hostile aggregates which regularly make contact," Gregor wrote, "generally share the same physical features, distinguishing themselves through special cultural traits (speech, religions, modes of dress and ornamentation)." An examination of the historical record, Gregor concluded, showed that "preference for one's kind is a generic social fact."

Further, Gregor accepted the contingent and arbitrary nature of group associations. The tendency to form groups was the essential social truth, and it can indeed manifest itself in a variety social forms. Race prejudice, argued Gregor, "as an object specific response, is but one variety of response in a more comprehensive pattern identified in the literature as ethnocentrism."[59] It was not that any specific form of race prejudice was a necessary and inherent feature of our social order; it was that there was an inherent drive for the formation of groups. An analogy was that of language acquisition: "While no one would contend that language is 'inherited,'" wrote Gregor, "few would deny that the capacity to learn a language is genetically determined, i.e., is 'innate.'"[60] Because the drive to form in-groups and out-groups was an innate part of human psychology, societies necessarily were divided, and in the United States, the form of division was racial. Gregor concluded, "Discriminatory practices and preferential treatment are almost universal concomitants of the contact of two widely different races" that cannot "be eliminated by education, by legislation or by time itself."[61]

Gregor's position (which was very similar to that of Ernest van den Haag, another IAAEE writer) that discrimination was an ineluctable part of social life cut to the heart of the social-scientific underpinning of *Brown,* indeed far more than the racial essentialist arguments of the Nordicists and the Southerners. At the heart of the social-scientific case presented to the Court in *Brown* was the idea that racial discrimination was a contingent fact of society. Racially discriminatory actions by whites were indeed part of their psychological makeup, but those actions themselves contributed to racially prejudiced attitudes. The social scientists in *Brown* argued that segregation laws were not just reflections of racial attitudes but were also a source of those attitudes. Since segregation contributed to racist attitudes, by eliminating segregation, the Court could stop one source of racism. The social scientists in *Brown* certainly recognized that to be human was to belong to social groups, but they attempted to distinguish between healthy group identification and unhealthy group prejudice. Legalized segregation, they argued, was a sign of group formation but an unhealthy one, since it was predicated on the identification of the out-group as socially inferior. Since the identification of the out-group as inferior was enforced by law, the law then was partly responsible for racial formation and the identification of Negroes as inferior. A change in the law would be a step toward ameliorating an unhealthy social situation.[62]

In their response, Gregor and later van den Haag flattened out the distinctions made by the social scientists in *Brown*. They did not distinguish between healthy and unhealthy forms of group demarcation; they did not see the law as contributing to group prejudice, only as a reflection of a naturally occurring prejudice; finally, they did not see the law as a possible source to break down naturally occurring group prejudice. As social conservatives who questioned the power of government to change the social landscape, Gregor and van den Haag simply declared that governmental power was useless against racial prejudice, which arose spontaneously rather than as an outgrowth of government power itself.

IAAEE: Rounding Out the Cast

While the real work of the IAAEE would be conducted primarily by Swan, Kuttner, and Gregor, other scientists were also members. Wesley Critz George and Frank C. J. McGurk were quickly brought on board, as well as Corrado Gini. Another addition was psychologist Charles Josey (1893–1975), the chair of the Psychology Department at Butler University in Indianapolis, whose views on race had not changed substantially since the 1920s. In his 1923 *Race and National Solidarity,* Josey made clear his belief that "the white races dominate mankind. They are the rulers *par excellence*. In the white man the evolutionary process seems to have reached the highest point. He is its culminating achievement." As such, the white man had the evolutionary obligation to impose his will on the colored race, and yet he had been shirking his responsibility. "In the most important of all matters—race domination—we wish to do nothing while the non-rational forces take from us our position of world domination."[63]

Even in the heyday of racial nationalism, the reviewers were stunned by Josey's frank calls for racial war. Malcolm Willey believed the book to be "sociologically immoral." A. B. Wolfe suspected that Josey could be "perpetuating a hoax upon his readers" because his book was "the most unblushing and brutal appeal for the cultivation and extension of the white race that we have seen. He outdoes Madison Grant and Lothrop Stoddard."[64]

Decades later, Robert Kuttner praised Josey in the pages of *Truth Seeker* for noting that while democracy and Christian charity "may be good in moderate doses, too much or too free an application can be lethal to our society." In his writings for the IAAEE, Josey continued to trumpet the virtues of racial antagonism and the natural advantages of racial prejudice.[65]

Scientists of higher profile would be willing to lend their name to the IAAEE as well. Most notable were psychologist Henry E. Garrett (1894–1973), geneticist R. Ruggles Gates (1882–1962), and cytogeneticist C. D. Darlington (1903–1981). Not all these individuals participated to the same extent, and not all for the same reasons.

Henry Garrett was a key figure in the IAAEE. A native of Virginia, Garrett received his Ph.D. in psychology from Columbia University in 1923 and then continued there, becoming the head of the psychology faculty in 1941 until his retirement in 1955. As one of the first to bring statistical methods to psychology, Garrett was prominent in the field, becoming APA president in 1946 and a fellow of the AAAS. In 1955 he returned to his native Virginia and took a courtesy appointment at the University of Virginia's Department of Education.[66]

By the time he helped form the IAAEE, Henry A. Garrett's "racial prejudices" were "something of a legend," according to John Morsell of the NAACP. In the trials that led up to the *Brown* decision, Garrett had been the only social scientist of any repute to testify in favor of segregation. In 1956, Willis Carto's *Right* praised Garrett for being willing to tell the truth about racial differences even though it "would offend the powerful ADL [Anti-Defamation League] and the NAACP, both of which have a vested interest in upholding the racial equality lie so as to bring on eventual mongrelization and degeneration of the races."[67]

As a member of Columbia's faculty, Garrett had spent his career in the center of the equalitarian conspiracy. He was there during Boas's reign in the Anthropology Department and was a member of the same faculty as Otto Klineberg, the psychologist who had been trained by Boas and whose pathbreaking work in the 1930s had helped undermine the case for racial differences in intelligence. While Garrett and Klineberg had remained on civil terms in the years before World War II, immediately after the war, when Garrett's favored views regarding racial differences were in full retreat in the scientific literature, the relationship soured as Garrett began criticizing the environmentalist interpretation of the result in IQ scores.[60]

In the years after the war, Garrett was not content to battle in the scientific journals; he took action against the equalitarian trend. Garrett went so far as to warn the Federal Bureau of Investigation of the dangerous doctrines taught by Klineberg. An FBI security report noted that "Professor Garrett stated that [Klineberg] believes in and advocates many Communistic theories," among them the doctrine that "there are no basic differences in the races of mankind," which was "the same theory advocated by the psychologists, anthropologists and scientists in Communist Russia." Garrett pointed out to the FBI that Klineberg had "read and approved" of Weltfish and Benedict's *Races of Mankind* pamphlet that had caused such a stir during the war. Garrett tempered his criticisms to the FBI by noting that Klineberg was "not as Communistically inclined as others in the field of environmental psychology."[69]

In contrast to Garrett, who was a central figure for much of the IAAEE's existence, R. Ruggles Gates's involvement was cut short by his death in 1962. Gates's position on race had been firmly established by the 1920s and remained unchanged until his death in 1962. In 1923, Gates claimed that "the negro in the United States, through interbreeding chiefly with the lowest strata of whites, is already producing a visible effect on the colour and features, and surely also on the mentality of those elements. Unless this process is checked, the ultimate result would appear inevitably to be a gradual incorporation of these more primitive elements in the whole population."[70]

Such views were, as we have seen, commonplaces in the 1920s, but Gates took the position a step further by maintaining that the races of were actually separate species. Species did not exist as biological realities for Gates, except as mere placeholders for taxonomic purposes. Thus, he advised that biologists consider different races as different species, since "[t]he fact that all the races of mankind are fertile with each other is no longer a sufficient reason for classing them as one species." Second, Gates held firmly to the racist line of argument he had begun in the 1920s. Writing after World War II, Gates maintained his view that the races were separate species. "The evidence is clear," he argued, "that the primary so-called races of living man have arisen independently from different ancestral species in different continents at different times." Like Earnest Sevier Cox, Gates would not be swayed by the enormous social changes of World War II or by the rejection of scientific racism that had begun in the 1930s, and he continued the arguments he began in the 1920s into the 1960s.[71]

A final notable name to grace the IAAEE roster was British cytogenecist C. D. Darlington. In 1932, Darlington became the first scientist to describe chromosome behavior during cell division and wrote what became the standard work on cytology. He was also one of the most outspoken scientists to condemn Lysenkoism in the USSR. Even at a time when British and American geneticists were tempering their criticism of Lysenko, primarily to protect Soviet geneticists who did not toe Lysenko's line on the inheritance of acquired characteristics, Darlington wrote visceral condemnations of the doctrine. After 1948, when Lysenko's doctrines became part of official party doctrine, Anglo-American scientists finally rushed to condemn the totalitarian control of science, only to find Darlington waiting for them.

Darlington, together with Oxford zoologist John R. Baker and chemist Michael Polanyi, formed the Society for Freedom in Science (SFS) to condemn any political or governmental control over scientific research. The SFS was clear in its call that science needed to be completely unfettered from political ideology, and was clearly designed to counter the dangers of Lysenkoism in the USSR—dangers that seemed all too real in Great Britain as leftist scientists called for scientific planning of society and social planning of science. SFS members came to it with different perspectives, however. Polanyi had fled from the Nazis and was a liberal democrat. Baker and Darlington, by contrast, were political conservatives, both convinced that among the dangers of science allying itself with the political Left was that the Left was bent on denying the scientific truth of the inequality of the races.[72] Darlington, therefore, believed in the IAAEE's positions on both the scientific truth of racial inequality and the threat posed by leftist science.

Even with the notable scientists gracing their roster, the IAAEE had its failures, the most notable of which was Carleton S. Coon. Coon was well known to IAAEE scientists. He and Corrado Gini corresponded regularly about the existence of the Abominable Snowman, in which Coon apparently believed. He and Gates also corresponded regularly, having become close while Gates was a visiting faculty member at Harvard during Coon's tenure there after World War II. With Coon, Gates found a sympathetic ear for his concerns that "[t]he 'all men are equal' propagandists are at it again." Coon also knew Frank C. J. McGurk, who would soon join the IAAEE, and wrote how he was concerned about "poor Prof.

McGurk who lives near me in my winter residence in Devon, PA. He has been persecuted for his [*U.S. News*] article to such an extent that it has affected his health."[73]

Given his well-publicized views on the reality of race, his views of Boas, and his scientific standing, it was natural that Coon would be courted by the IAAEE. In fact, he was invited to join twice: first in January 1960, when Garrett suggested he be on the executive board, and again in October 1962, when the death of R. Ruggles Gates opened a position on the board. Coon declined both times, explaining that although he was "very glad to get your monographs and also your magazine . . . to accept membership on your board would be the kiss of death, here in the so-called land of the free and home of the brave."[74] Coon was also invited twice to contribute to a volume IAAEE writers were assembling to answer UNESCO's 1950 *Statement on Race,* because "a number of academicians connected with the Association believe that the UNESCO publications present too one-sided a view of the subject." Coon declined this offer as well, noting that he was under contract with Knopf to produce his new book on race and was reserving time for that project, although he believed the list of names assembled for the IAAEE volume was a "most distinguished one."[75] So, while Coon was sympathetic to the aims of the IAAEE, he was hesitant to become directly involved with the organization.

The IAAEE and Publicity

In 1960, Donald Swan described two goals for the IAAEE: first, to sponsor a book "designed to counter the UNESCO book *The Race Question in Modern Science,*" and second, "the preparation and distribution of articles and reviews to various professional journals."[76] The book would be delayed for a number of years, but the distribution of materials by IAAEE authors would soon be a going concern. Within two years, the IAAEE mailing list would include sixteen thousand people. This list would include 70 percent of the membership of the American Sociological Association, 85 percent of the membership of the American Anthropological Association, 95 percent of the membership of the American Association of Physical Anthropologists, 90 percent of the membership of the Genetics Society of America, and other professional organizations. Also on the mailing list were southern state school superintendents and congressmen.[77]

Mailings of articles and pamphlets on such a scale was possible because the IAAEE was underwritten by Wickliffe Draper, Cox's old patron. Draper's agenda was not, according to William Tucker, "to finance studies that would demonstrate white, northern European genetic superiority but to support projects that would use this presumptive fact as a point of departure and encourage policies to prevent the contamination of this superior group by inferior races, especially blacks."[78] Draper had funded a number of segregationist efforts in the five years between *Brown* and the founding of the IAAEE, including those of Wesley Critz George and Henry Garrett. Through his attorney, Harry F. Weyher, Draper would fund the distribution of IAAEE materials while simultaneously channeling substantial resources into other organizations dedicated to preserving segregation.[79]

Because of Draper's largesse, within a very short time the publications of the IAAEE would appear in the mailboxes of many scientists who were interested in the study of race and race relations. Moreover, because of the indefatigable Carleton Putnam, who would be the point man for the scientific case for segregation, the mainstream scientific community would soon be debating how to respond to the IAAEE. Few in the mainstream scientific community were apt to think that the IAAEE positions should be debated on their scientific merits, however. Most of the views put forth by the IAAEE had been rejected as fruitless scientific avenues decades before. Perhaps no other publication associated with the IAAEE exemplified the debates to come than the "bible" for the IAAEE psychometricians: *The Testing of Negro Intelligence*, a massive book of intelligence test results compiled by Audrey Shuey, a doctoral student of Garrett while he was at Columbia.

Audrey Shuey and The Testing of Negro Intelligence

In 1958 the chair of the Psychology Department at Randolph-Macon Women's College in Lynchburg, Virginia, Audrey Shuey, published *The Testing of Negro Intelligence*, a compilation of several hundred studies that compared intelligence test results of whites and African Americans. According to Shuey's conclusion, these studies showed a "remarkable consistency" that pointed to "the presence of some native differences between Negroes and whites as determined by intelligence tests."[80] Shuey argued that the gap in intelligence test scores persisted across time and geographic areas; hence it could not be attributed to environmental influence. This was the position advanced by Garrett, Shuey's doctoral adviser at Columbia, who had provided an introduction to her book.

Like Frank McGurk, who had always insisted that it was his data, not his interpretations of those data, that proved the necessity of racial segregation, Shuey attempted to distinguish her presentation of the test "results" from the author's mere "interpretations" of these results. Following Garrett and McGurk, Shuey claimed that the mass of data proved there were racial differences in intelligence and that attempts to explain away these differences were unscientific "interpretations" of what the facts clearly demonstrated. For example, Shuey quoted approvingly Carl Brigham's 1923 conclusions that found Negro children to be inferior to Anglo-Saxon children in intelligence but waved away his famous 1930 recantation of the significance of his own findings.[81]

Once again, intelligence tests could provide ammunition for the segregationist cause. The Northern League newspaper, *The Virginian,* praised Shuey's study as "objective and scientific" while noting that the book would probably not be given the "Madison Avenue type of promotion and build-up which would have been accorded her had she written a book in favor of race mixing." Carleton Putnam, though no great fan of IQ tests, argued that "Shuey's material belonged in the record" for the *Brown* decision and would have led the Supreme Court to uphold racial segregation. Willis Carto's journal, *Right,* editorialized that Shuey's book was merely common sense for honest people but that it would be "nothing short of revolutionary for the White-hating Zionist Zealots and scientific prostitutes in our universities and those who write, censor, and review our books and encyclopedias."[82]

The issues surrounding Shuey's book were illustrated by the stinging critique offered by Horace Mann Bond. As with the school integration situation in Washington, D.C., Bond was presented once again with the argument he believed he had refuted in 1924. He noted that the book had been distributed free of charge throughout the South and that the Citizens' Councils had been active distributors. Eventually he discovered that the distribution of Shuey's book was bankrolled by Wickliffe Draper's Pioneer Fund, a philanthropic organization that was dedicated to funding scientific research aimed to prove white superiority. He considered the entire affair "as striking an example of academic skullduggery, aimed at propagandizing the cause of Negro inferiority that, I think, has ever transpired in these United States."[83]

Bond reviewed Shuey's book, noting that many an author of the studies she reported would not be able to "recognize his own brain-child after it has undergone the deft, assiduous surgery of [Shuey's] excisions" and that her tactic of presenting the "results" independent of the "interpretations" resulted in "this reviewer" and other "Negro students . . . [being] made . . . to appear as heralds of their own native inferiority." Bond argued that in 178 of 288 studies, African Americans tested in a geographical area were compared to national norms rather than to white norms in the same geographical area. "Many of these instances," Bond wrote, "were in the South, and the studies were carried on by Negroes who, manifestly, would have found it impossible to test white subjects in the same neighborhood."[84]

Bond closed his review by asking if Shuey's "results . . . may be applied to other material reported by her, but not discussed in her text." Once again, Bond pointed to the poor scores of white Southerners compared to white Northerners and asked if it was true that "Southern white persons are the descendents of the degenerated portion of the American Anglo-Saxon heritage. . . . Her own 'results' . . . inevitably lead to the conclusion that there are 'some native differences' between Northern and Southern whites. . . . Dr. Shuey, is it true what they say about Dixie?"[85]

Despite the critiques of Shuey's use of IQ tests, critiques that were decades old, these tests would form a central argument in the scientific case for segregation. However, they were not the only scientific arguments segregationists had available. Indeed, for certain segregationists, notably Carleton Putnam and Wesley Critz George, psychological tests were not as effective in proving white supremacy as biological arguments that pointed to anatomical differences between white people's brains and black people's brains.

6

The Attack on *Brown*

For the decade following *Brown,* the white South tried every mechanism, legal and illegal, to resist desegregation. The IAAEE provided a formal organization of scientists that could crystallize the white South's scientific arguments for segregation. Eventually, the scientists of the IAAEE would appear in the courtroom arguing that since *Brown* was decided on scientific evidence, they could provide the court with more firm science upon which to base a more realistic decision. The path to the courtroom, however, was not a straightforward one. Indeed, preparing a case for the court would split the IAAEE down the middle, with hardline segregationists insisting that the case had to be about the biological differences between the races and more sophisticated voices insisting that biology was, at best, tangential to the issues before the court. Before they got to the courtroom, however, further groundwork needed to be laid and the ammunition needed to be prepared. The most visible organizer was the indefatigable Carleton Putnam.

Reaction to Race and Reason

Race and Reason was enormously popular in the South. Putnam also received plaudits from one of those whose work inspired *Race and Reason,* Earnest Sevier Cox, who lavished praise on Putnam for recognizing that the problems facing the country were racial "rather than . . . political, economic, or religious." Cox concluded, "It is a godsend to our race and nation when men like you . . . approach our race problem from the angle of race. We will win this struggle and the white race will not be eliminated from the nation it produced."[1]

The man who would revitalize the Ku Klux Klan in the 1970s, David Duke, described *Race and Reason* as the "book that would change my life." In his autobiography, Duke claims that as a boy he was a racial egalitarian until "*Race and Reason* made me realize another legitimate scientific viewpoint existed." Duke was not the only Southerner to be enamored of the book. Stuart B. Campbell, a Virginia attorney, reviewed it for the *ABA Journal* and concluded that the book's central message, that *Brown* would lead to "mixing the superior with the inferior," leaving "only the less desirable mixed progeny to continue, thus weakening or destroying the American civilization," was a welcome antidote to the commonly heard "half truths, propagandized history [and] pseudo science."[2]

Carleton Putnam was tailor-made for the Citizens' Councils, which looking for a way to attract Northerners to their cause, as many segregationist leaders believed this would be the key to their success. Carleton Putnam, a self-proclaimed "Yankee" and a businessman rather than a politician, was widely seen as someone who could rally the North to the cause of segregation. He wrote elegantly and, at least by comparison to many segregationists, dispassionately. Moreover, his focus on science gave his work a learned air. With these factors in mind, Governor Ross Barnett of Mississippi declared October 26, 1961, as "Race and Reason Day" in Mississippi. Putnam gave a speech in Jackson, Mississippi, that day and won praise from Barnett and U.S. Representative John Bell Williams.[3]

At the podium, Putnam regaled his audience with the story of the Boasian corruption of American ideals. He proclaimed that he could not actually name names when it came to Boas's victims "because there is risk of persecution." Putnam urged the southern politician to stop focusing on states rights and start focusing on science because it should be so obvious to all who would look with an unbiased—or unBoasian—eye that Negroes could not possibly adapt to modern civilization. The Southerners were guilty of letting the North focus on the sins of the white man when, clearly, the white man had done nothing except help the Negro for centuries. In his stirring finale, Putnam offered what he would be telling the nation had he a few moments on national television:

> Do you mean to tell me we're holding this race back! I say to you we've done more for this race in two centuries than they've done for themselves since the beginning of the world! If they hadn't been brought over here as slaves to white men, they would have been slaves to other Negroes and many of them would have died in Africa as human sacrifices! You nation of sheep! Have you no minds of your own? Can't you see

through this hoax? How much longer must *we* be offered up on *your* gullibility?[4]

The Citizens' Councils dedicated an entire issue of their official journal to the events on "Race and Reason Day," announcing in a breathless editorial: "This is perhaps the most significant and the most important publication ever to bear the imprint of the Citizens' Council movement." Mississippi was not alone in its admiration for Putnam's work. Earlier in 1961, the State Board of Education of Louisiana made the book official reading for high school students because "[t]here is increasing evidence that the sciences of biology and anthropology are being distorted and perverted to serve the purposes of certain pressure groups whose aims are inimical to the customs, mores, and traditions of this Nation." A few months after "Race and Reason Day," Virginia would follow Louisiana's lead and make Putnam's book part of its high school curriculum.[5]

Despite these accolades for his work, soon after these events Putnam wanted to shift focus away from his work and toward what he thought was an even more powerful argument for segregation: Wesley Critz George's *The Biology of the Race Problem*. Putnam wrote to Harry Weyher, the attorney for Wickliffe Draper who was underwriting much of this activity, that "every effort must be made to lead the educated public to read the George report. The focus must shift to it from *Race and Reason*."[6] What excited Putnam about George's work was George's "discovery" that the brains of black people were significantly different from those of white people. This, thought Putnam, was indisputable proof that African Americans could not adapt to white civilization.

Origins of The Biology of the Race Problem

Mississippi led the way in the race to the right on racial issues in the 1950s, but Alabama was not far behind. In 1956, invoking an obscure anti-Klan law, Alabama attorney general John Patterson effectively dismantled the state's NAACP branches by requiring the organization to hand over the names of every member of the organization, something the NAACP certainly was not going to do in those dangerous times. In 1958, Patterson, ironically enough with the help of the Ku Klux Klan, ran to the right of George Wallace—in Wallace's own word, "out-niggered" him— to win the governor's office.[7]

In early 1961, Governor Patterson wanted to commission a study that could be used as scientific evidence in a court case defending segregation. The obvious choice was Wesley Critz George, who had won his segregationist spurs with the North Carolina Patriots and was an active member of the IAAEE, giving him a veneer of scientific respectability. Patterson's special counsel on matters relating to desegregation, Ralph Smith, met with George, who recounted the meeting to Garrett:

> Up until now, Alabama has escaped integration, but it is anticipated that in time they will be the object of frontal attack. They want to be prepared to meet that attack in the courts. They hope to base their case not only on legal precedent but on scientific evidence that will withstand the attacks of lawyers and other scientists.[8]

Smith, explained George, was asking for a report that laid out the scientific basis for continued segregation in the American South. Garrett was enthusiastic about the project. He wrote, "There are certainly grounds for asking for a re-hearing. The Warren Court cited 8 'experts' in the 1954 decision. . . . Of these 8, 4 were left wing Jews . . . and 2 were Negroes. . . . On such expert evidence hung the fate of 50,000,000 people."[9]

Perhaps realizing that Alabama's offer was too good to pass up, George agreed to undertake the project for Patterson. George wrote to Smith that his report "should be written in a format and style adapted to the most convenient and effective use of lawyers in making their case and in resisting the attacks of other lawyers and scientists." Smith agreed to pay George's summer salary to enable him to write the report, a sum of $3,000.[10]

When the announcement of the arrangement was made public, there was little doubt about what the final report would look like. Ralph Smith told the press that "scientific data support the contention that the white race, intellectually, is superior to the Negro, and that is the point we are making with this study," to which NAACP director Roy Wilkins slyly responded, "Is Governor Patterson confessing, through the initiation of this study that for all these decades the segregation policy of the state of Alabama has been based on guesswork?" *Newsweek* noted the irony of Patterson spending $3,000 of Alabama taxpayers' money the same week that Public Affairs Press was publishing its one-millionth copy of Weltfish and Benedict's *Races of Mankind*.[11]

In the face of this rather bemused response from the national press, which George probably put down to the equalitarian conspiracy, George pressed on. By the time he was commissioned to write the report, he had already published what was, in essence, a working outline in a short article for *The Cross and the Flag,* an anti-Semitic newspaper published by Gerald L. K. Smith, who had been the model for the racist rabble-rouser Willard Jones in Aldrich Blake's *My Kind! My Country!* In his article, George laid out the essential arguments that he would expand into his report: that the scientific case for racial equality was made by "men of evil design" and that the scientific truth of racial inequality was firmly established. The proof, George said, was in the research of Dr. Bennett Bean, who had published "the most important study" of the Negro brain structure. George supplemented Bean's study with that of J. C. Carothers, who had been working in African hospitals for the World Health Organization. These two authors would underpin George's report for Alabama.[12]

George's final report was titled *The Biology of the Race Problem,* but it was often called the "George Report." George conducted no original research, relying on arguments he had made in his speeches since *Brown.* His technique for the George Report was to cull quotations from other sources to support his position that racial amalgamation would be a disaster. Central to his argument was that those sociological and psychological traits that George attributed to black people—for example high crime rates and low IQ scores—owed to deficiencies in brain structure rather than to any social cause. In some ways this was a retrogressive move, hearkening back to nineteenth-century craniometry—the measure of skulls and head shapes as a way to rank the races. Many historians have noted that with the advent of intelligence testing in the early twentieth century, the new technology quickly supplanted the weights and measures of the earlier century.[13] In many ways, then, the arguments that would ensue with the publication of the George Report would simply repeat the arguments about craniometry during the end of the nineteenth century. Yet, in a significant way, the controversy over George's work reversed the earlier debate. One reason that intelligence tests replaced craniometry was that the tests' advocates argued they were a *direct* measure of intelligence and thus should be preferred over a measurement of a skull or brain, which required an inference that related head size to intelligence. In other words, craniometric measurements could prove Negroes inferior in intelligence only by finding that they had smaller brains and then arguing that a smaller brain indicated less intelligence. IQ testers could make do without that inference and claim that they were directly measuring intelligence: since Negroes consistently scored below whites, they were less intelligent. By the 1960s, when George was writing, psychologists had effectively undercut the argument that intelligence tests were measuring innate differences in intelligence. The irony in the George Report was that George returned to the older science in order to argue against these environmental interpretations of the gap in IQ scores between whites and Negroes.

In his report, George rehearsed the now-familiar tirade against Boas and his students. He also appended a list of those he claimed were "Boasians," which included a number of people who had minimal contact with Boas such as psychologist Isidor Chein, geneticist Theodosius Dobzhansky, and sociologist Howard Odum, George's old sparring partner from the 1940s.[14]

After a brief lesson in Mendel's laws and a second on "disharmonious" crosses in dogs, George got to the heart of his argument: racial differences in brain structure. George made three basic claims about race and brains. First, George argued that, on average, white people's brains were one hundred grams heavier than black people's brains, even when corrected for physical stature. For this argument, George relied on the studies conducted by Robert Bennett Bean and Franklin P. Mall, which were reported in 1906 and 1909.[15]

George's second argument was that whites and black differed significantly in terms of the sulcification of the frontal lobes of the brain. George again relied on the dated studies of Bean and Mall, who reported that blacks had less sulcification than whites. He also relied on a third study, from C. J. Connolly, professor of physical anthropology at Catholic University, who obtained similar results in a study published in 1950. George then quoted three researchers—Ward C. Halstead, Wilder Penfield, and Theodore Rasmussen—who argued that the frontal lobes were responsible for higher thought and "the portion of the brain most essential to biological intelligence."[16] Since the brains of blacks were less sulcified than those of whites, George argued, this could explain why they were so socially stunted.

Third, and finally, George raised the researches of F. W. Vint at a colonial hospital in Kenya, who had found 14 percent less thickness in the supragranular layer of Negro brains in his examinations. Vint's claims were supplemented by the views of J. C. Carothers, who argued that there were significant behavioral differences between the races that must have a biological basis in the differences in the frontal lobes of the brain. The implication of less gray matter for blacks was clear for George. African Americans were physically unable to assume the responsibilities of white civilization. To allow social intermingling between the two races could only result in inbreeding that would inevitably destroy the country.

George based his entire argument concerning the differential structure of brains on these few studies. Most of the works George relied on had less than distinguished pedigrees, and George's use of these studies did not add any luster to them. Robert Bean's 1905 study, which was dated even in 1961, was enmeshed in political questions from its publication. Bean was a Virginia physician who examined the brains of blacks and whites. He found that white brains had significantly more highly developed frontal lobes than those of blacks. This, Bean argued, was the cause of Negro indolence and incapacity for higher thought, which, as a Virginian at the turn of the century, was obvious to him. Not restricted to medical journals, Bean took to the popular presses to argue that his research showed the folly of enfranchising Negro voters, as they obviously lacked the capacity for forethought necessary to be trusted with such a responsibility.

Franklin Mall, whose study was also used by George, had been Bean's mentor in medical school. Mall distrusted Bean's conclusions regarding the differences between white and black brains and repeated the experiment. The significant difference between the methodologies was that Mall did not know beforehand if a given brain had come from a white or a Negro. Mall found no significant differences in brain structures between white and Negro brains. Once the possibility for prejudgment had been removed, so had the racial differences. Although not reported by George, Bean's arguments had also been thoroughly refuted by anatomist Burt G. Wilder, who had repeated Bean's experiment in 1909 with a much larger sample size and found no significant differences.[17]

Mall's refutation of Bean was seen as decisive because it removed possible biases from the procedure. Both Mall and Wilder argued that Bean was a racist who had discovered just what he had wanted to discover: proof of Negro inferiority. Curiously, George took Mall's blind procedure as a criticism of his conclusions. George argued that Mall's study was flawed precisely because "*Mall did not look for racial averages and frequencies* but for exclusive features that might serve as bases for classification."[18] Only by knowing the race of the body the brain had been in, by this logic, could one discover the races differed in brain structures.

That this procedure resulted in begging the question of racial differences, George did not acknowledge.

The idea that the investigator was finding in the scientific data exactly what he wanted to applied with equal force to the other main sources for George's conclusions. These studies came from pathologist F. W. Vint and the South African psychiatrist J. C. Carothers, both of whom were based in Kenya. In the 1930s, Vint was one of the first colonial medical practitioners to attempt to find a physiological basis for African inferiority by dissection and measuring the brains of Africans after they had died in the hospital where he had worked. Although enthusiastically received by South African medical researchers, Vint's work suffered from methodological problems that would be underscored for George by a most unexpected source: Robert E. Kuttner.[19]

The second colonial source for George was a series of works published in the late 1940s and into the 1950s by J. C. Carothers. Carothers argued that Africans were remarkably like lobotomized white people and hypothesized that the African frontal lobes of the brain must be unconnected from the rest of the brain, just as lobotomized patients' were. He later dropped this theory and argued that, while there must be some underlying physiological differences between white and black brains, medical science at present did not know what they were. Carothers undertook no dissections of African brains and his theories where entirely speculative, although, as Graham Richards notes, "[t]he old Deep South slaveowners would have sympathized deeply" with his view of Africans.[20]

George borrowed from the colonial physicians Vint and Carothers liberally in order to fix firmly the existence of racial differences in the brain. For the origins of these racial differences he turned to Carleton Coon. At the same time that George was working on *The Biology of the Race Problem*, Coon was working on the culmination of his career: *The Origin of Races*. Coon's theory in that book would be that *Homo sapiens* evolved from *Homo erectus* not once but five separate times. He wrote in the book's introduction, "My thesis is, in essence that at the beginning of our record, over half a million years ago, man was a single species, *Homo Erectus*, perhaps already divided into five geographic races or subspecies. *Homo Erectus* then evolved into *Homo Sapiens* not once but five times, as each subspecies, living in its own territory, passed a critical threshold from a more brutal to a more *sapient* state."[21] According to George, this meant that racial differences were older than humankind itself and thus not merely skin deep. "It would be strange indeed if," he wrote, "during those thousands of years, the different racial groups, in their different areas, had not accumulated different pools of genes and varied racial characters, with all that we have seen this to mean in the fields of intelligence and behavior."[22]

One problem George faced by relying on Coon was that Coon's book was not yet released. However, Putnam had obtained some of Coon's material and supplied it to George. George's citation of Coon's material, then, was actually of a pamphlet titled "Evolution and Race: New Evidence," which was Carleton Putnam's report on the second edition of Carleton Coon's *The Story of Man*. Putnam pulled select quotations from Coon's book that foreshadowed the arguments Coon would be making in his yet-to-be-released *The Origin of Races*. According to Putnam, this new evidence uncovered by Coon showed that "the Negro is 200,000 years behind the White race on the ladder of evolution." As for most things written by Putnam, he had mailed it to scientists and policy makers with a cover letter wherein Putnam invoked Coon's prestige in the scientific community: "When . . . the president of the American Association of Physical Anthropologists, a magna cum laude graduate of Harvard and a native of New England, states that recent discoveries indicate that the Negro is 200,000 years behind the White race on the ladder of evolution, this ends the integration argument."[23]

It was no accident that George relied on Putnam for Coon's material. Just as the Northerner Madison Grant had guided the Southerner Earnest Sevier Cox through the writing of *White America* forty years earlier, Putnam helped George with *The Biology of the Race Problem*. It was Putnam who had the document vetted by the experts: IAAEE executive secretary Donald Swan ("Thor Swenson"), Harry Weyher (Wickliffe Draper's attorney) and Carleton Coon. Putnam himself had gone over the report with George "paragraph by paragraph." It was also Putnam who arranged for Weyher and William Simmons, the leader of the Citizens' Councils, to publicize and distribute the work widely.[24]

Anatomy offered something to George and Putnam that was not offered by IQ tests: an unalterable difference between black and white that could not attributed to environmental differences. In this way, all the arguments about discrimination and prejudice could be swept away by pointing to the physical difference in the brains of both races, differences that could explain not only intelligence differences but differences in crime, morality, and "level of civilization." The differences between black and white were biological and therefore immutable, giving Putnam and

George what they thought was the ultimate weapon against the equalitarians. Upon its release, the report was gleefully received in the South. The architect of the Citizens' Councils, William J. Simmons, declared that George's "major scientific report has shattered the equalitarian myth!"[25]

Even while Putnam and George were declaring that they had the ultimate argument against the integrationists, an alternative stream of research was developing within the IAAEE. This one came from A. James Gregor, who rejected essential biological notions of race.

Natural Race Prejudice and Psychological Damage

The natural inferiority of Negroes to whites was the most well known of the segregationist arguments. However, the argument that segregation was merely the natural order of the world was also a very popular appeal. Such "natural" racial segregation was used by white Southerners as a way to explain to the benighted Northerner that segregation laws were merely reflections of people's natural dispositions. Preacher Byron M. Wilkinson put forth a commonly made claim that segregation was divine in origin. The only time the human race was fully integrated, the Reverend Wilkinson claimed, was "at the Tower of Babel," where "Satan was nearer to a complete victory in that day than he ever has been since. . . . God, Himself, had to come down and deal directly with the situation. Segregation was born at Babel and our God was the creator of it."[26]

Georgia attorney general Eugene Cook made the point explicit in his testimony before the U.S. House of Representatives Judiciary Committee in 1957:

> I say without fear of contradiction that numerically speaking there is in New York a greater state of segregation . . . as strong or stronger than we have even in Georgia. . . . I bring that up . . . to point out this one basic fundamental proposition. Why do you have that situation in New York without any laws? It goes to the very basic fundamental proposition, that the people wanted it that way. And they voluntarily did what we in Georgia have given legal sanction to.[27]

This argument for spontaneous segregation meshed well with Gregor's claim that racial prejudice was an almost innate trait of the human species. Given that there was a natural tendency for the formation of in-

groups, in American society it was natural for there to be racial separation between black and whites. For Gregor, it was not only to be expected
that whites would shun interracial contact, it was completely rational.
Gregor pointed to sociological studies of African Americans who suffered
from "significant social and psychological disabilities." Gregor argued,
"Whatever the ultimate causes of reduced academic performance and the
high incidence of venereal disease, immorality and delinquency among
Negroes as a group, those differences do exist"; hence the desire for all-
white neighborhoods was a rational and healthy response by whites to
calls for integration.[28]

In an article written with other social scientists who worked within the
Association for the Preservation of Freedom of Choice (APFC), Gregor
concluded:

> The deterioration of the standards of local schools, the increased inci-
> dence of delinquency and crime, greater public health hazards, regular
> exposure to a group which, because of conditions prevailing in its sub-
> culture, is characterized by lax sexual morality, broken homes and mini-
> mal academic aspirations, would seem to provide, in general, sufficient
> rational motive for white flight.[29]

By 1960, Gregor and the New York group had joined forces with the
Southerners to form the IAAEE and were ready and willing to abandon
their previous commitment to "free association" to fight for the maintenance of school segregation in the South. Gregor would soon develop
a series of arguments that segregation was not only the rational choice
for white parents but was, in fact, psychologically beneficial to school-
age children. Nor were these arguments designed merely for academic
consumption. In July 1961, Gregor and Swan made a two-week tour
of the South in order to, in Swan's words, "meet Southern state educational officials in order to discuss a comprehensive educational program in the field of race and race relations." It may be just a coincidence, but it is striking that the only southern state with a central purchasing authority, Louisiana, was the same state that adopted *Race and
Reason* as a high school text immediately after Swan and Gregor's
visit.[30]

The scientists of the IAAEE were ready for their assault on *Brown*. The
George Report specifically was designed to defend segregation in a court
of law. It arrived just as such a case was ready for litigation. Swan and

Gregor had made their tour and were making contacts with school authorities throughout the South. The moment was nearly at hand.

The Road to Reversal

Carleton Putnam had never envisioned his writing as a strictly academic exercise. In a February 1962 speech before the district attorneys for the state of Louisiana, Putnam laid out his general strategy. After thanking the state for adopting *Race and Reason* as a textbook in their high schools, Putnam explained that his writing was part of a "two-pronged" attack on *Brown*. Because *Brown* had clearly turned on science, in order to reverse *Brown*, segregationists had to do two things: "On the one hand the climate of public opinion must be changed, on the other the change must be crystallized in specific legal action."[31]

The general contours of the legal attack were easy enough: if *Brown* turned on a "finding of fact" rather than a "finding of law," then white southern leaders believed they could show *Brown*'s facts to be wrong. Georgia attorney and arch-critic of *Brown*, Charles Bloch, wrote, "It can be shown that in our society of 1959 . . . these findings and factual conclusions [in *Brown*] are erroneous and have no place."[32] To mount an attack on *Brown*, therefore, all that needed to be done was to return to the courtroom with what Southerners believed to be more objective social scientists to show that the factual basis upon which the case rested was in error, thus overturning it and preserving segregation. The question remained as to how, exactly, to get such a reconsideration of *Brown*. John Graves, an attorney and admirer of Putnam, wrote to him that "*procedure* is the hard guts of the law," and it was not necessarily a straightforward enterprise to design a case in which "valid anthropology could be marshaled and the tripe of Myrdal and Boas refuted." Herbert Sanborn, a Vanderbilt psychologist and IAAEE member wrote that "R. Carter Pittman of Dalton, Georgia might be the one to organize the legal matters."[33]

As things would develop, Pittman would lead the legal charge against *Brown*, and he was a logical candidate for the job. A Georgia attorney and the first president of the States' Rights Council there, Pittman was an early and vocal critic of the *Brown* decision. A few months after the decision, Pittman began a long campaign against what he called the Communist system of thought control that he dubbed "cybernetics." It was by this thought control that "sociological doctors . . . practiced fraud upon the judges to victimize a helpless people." Pittman maintained the social science was brought to the Supreme Court through conspiratorial means rather than through established legal procedures; it was brought "as gossip, in whispers and undertones in the secret chambers of the judges." Pittman's reasoning seemed to be that because social science was not direct testimony from the parties under dispute, it was "hearsay and gossip. No court this side of Moscow admits such evidence." Betraying that he had not read the testimony of the *Brown* cases or the briefs submitted to the Supreme Court, Pittman claimed that the states had not been given an opportunity to examine the social science or cross-examined social-scientific experts, for "[a]n 'opportunity to meet' Myrdal with a pointed cross-examination would have withered him in a few minutes."[34]

Besides his claim that the social science evidence cited in the footnote to *Brown* was "illegal, unsworn, and hearsay evidence received by [the Supreme Court] in secret," Pittman took a stand on the concept of equality that sounded very much like that of Charles Smith of *Truth Seeker*. Like Smith, Pittman argued that the concept of equality was inimical to freedom. In a series of articles, Pittman attempted to prove the word *equality* did not appear in the Constitution, the Bill of Rights, or the Bible. While it did appear in the Declaration of Independence, Pittman explained that away as meaning only equal in freedom, not that all people were equal. The concept of equality, however, was the centerpiece of "*Das Kapital* which is the Bible of communism. All communist front organizations in American propagate the doctrine that all men are equal. It has been written into sociology text books and is being taught in practically all the schools and colleges of America." Most terrifying, Pittman concluded, "[t]he Supreme Court of the United States has been thoroughly brain washed with" the doctrine of equality.[35]

With a point of view that was so close to that of the Northern League, at least regarding equalitarian brainwashing and white, if not Nordic, supremacy, it was natural that Pittman would join Willis Carto's Liberty Lobby, the successor organization to Liberty and Property. Formed in 1957, the Liberty Lobby was Carto's attempt to move into the Republican Party and remake it as the party of racial purity. Segregationists were among the first on Carto's board of directors, and they played an active role in maintaining the organization's base. For example, John Bell Williams, who had shared the stage with Carleton Putnam on "Race and Reason Day," was the guest of honor at the Liberty

Lobby's Third Annual Political Action Banquet in 1962. Pittman was on the Board of Policy by 1961. Pittman would be the attorney who would bring the IAAEE scientists to the courtroom to overthrow *Brown v. Board of Education.*[36]

Stell v. Savannah

For the courtroom battle, the centerpiece of the scientific case for school segregation was the IQ argument. One thing that all IAAEE members agreed upon was that psychological tests had proven African Americans simply were not as innately intelligent as white Americans were. For the most part, this argument was based not on original research but on surveys of the results of IQ tests, especially the work of Audrey Shuey. The sheer mass of studies, IAAEE scientists argued, must prove that the gap in IQ between whites and blacks could not be due to environmental differences.

In a court of law, the IQ argument attempted to establish that race was a "reasonable" classification under the law for the purposes of educational policy. That is to say, given the wide differences in intelligence between the two races, it was a reasonable use of state power to require segregated schooling, because the curriculum of each school system could be adjusted to the level needed for each race.

The IQ argument, however, was not enough to clinch the cases for the IAAEE. The problem lay within the overlap between white and black test scores. A large overlap existed between the two populations, even granting that the mean of the scores of the black population was equivalent to the value of one standard deviation below the mean of the scores of the white population. IAAEE knew the NAACP would argue, as it did during the *Brown* case, that while the differences in IQ scores might justify educational tracking by test scores, they did not justify segregation by race. The NAACP would simply argue that the court should group the smart children, regardless of race, and the slower children, regardless of race. What was needed was some argument to add to the IQ argument that would guarantee race would be *the* relevant factor for the courts.

Pittman had two possible paths: first, to follow George and Putnam and argue that there were physiological differences between the races that made racial integration biologically dangerous; second, to follow Gregor and argue that racial separation was psychologically beneficial to Negro schoolchildren. As we will see, the problem faced by the segregationists was that these two arguments stood in direct contradiction to each other.

A case in Savannah, Georgia, provided Pittman with an opportunity to bring social science to the courtroom.[37] The first step of the litigation process was to prepare the legal brief that put forth the scientific case for segregation. Pittman circulated drafts of the brief to his scientific associates, asking for comments. Pittman's brief followed the path laid down by Gregor. First, it pointed to literally hundreds of IQ tests that found African Americans scored significantly lower than white Americans. Pittman argued that this difference in intelligence was a rational basis for the state to maintain segregated schools. Pittman explicitly sidestepped the biological argument and held that, regardless of the ultimate cause (genetics or environment), the IQ gap did exist. Further, since "Negroes" were socially conspicuous, integration would be psychologically harmful to Negro students by forcing them out of their natural and preferred segregated environment and into a hostile integrated environment where they could not possibly compete academically.[38]

When he read the brief, Carleton Putnam was aghast that the miscegenation argument was completely missing. In February 1963, he wrote to Pittman that he had read the entire brief where he saw "references to intelligence tests and sociology. I find no references to the gross morphology or the histology . . . of White and Negro brains." Putnam argued that this was terrible mistake for the legal case against integration:

> No matter how cumulative their impact or convincing their controls, the finding of intelligence tests and sociological studies leave in the mind of the layman a faint whisper of possibility that they may be the result of environment. . . . The only data which cannot be attacked on this ground is gross morphology and microscopic structure—these cannot be the result of environment . . . they must be inherent and hereditary.[39]

For Putnam, the results of IQ tests and sociological studies that pointed out the high crime rates and other problems in African American society were too susceptible to the environmentalist response. He maintained, "The Supreme Court and the American people do not need to be told about the limitations and misbehavior of the Negro. They are fully prepared to concede all that. *What you have to answer is the charge that the White man made him that way.*"[40]

Putnam was convinced that the brief's emphasis on the natural inclination toward segregation would not be persuasive. "These left wingers,"
he wrote to Pittman, "are not interested in what has happened among
races in the way of self segregation . . . or the inclination of birds to flock
together. They want a brave new world—an integrated world."[41]

In response, Gregor argued that the biological argument that Putnam
favored was, at best, tangential to the issues before the court. Putnam's
concerns about the "Negro brain" were dependent on racial intermarriage and miscegenation, which were not the issues before the court. "The
problems of interracial marriage can be faced when court cases are
mounted turning on this issue," Gregor wrote to Putnam. "Then perhaps
the biological arguments will be crucial. But in the *school segregation*
case they are of peripheral importance." Pittman was right to base his
case on the psychological damage that integration would cause. Gregor
wrote, "Group differences can justify separation as a convenience . . . *that
such separation causes no harm is the central issue* and is the issue on
which *Brown* turned."[42] Gregor explained that "all the available evidence indicates that *forced* congregation leads *to a greater sense of rejection*" than segregation. "The Whites reject the Negro irrespective of the
prescriptive and proscriptive laws to the contrary."[43]

For Gregor, Putnam's concerned with miscegenation was not just a tac-
tical error, but it was empirically denied by all available evidence. Gregor's belief that the races naturally self-segregated made the danger of
racial intermarriage a slight one. "Intermarriage between two diverse
races marked by high social visibility has never been the consequence of
'integration,'" Gregor wrote to Putnam. "Free interracial marriage will
never be the case in the United States." For Putnam, of course, having
read Grant and Cox on how race mixing caused the downfall of both the
great civilizations of the past as well as of Latin America, such a claim
must have been absurd.[44]

Gregor clinched his case by arguing that his approach guaranteed that
race would be the basis of the court's decision. "Even if Negro performance is proved to be the consequence of genetic inferiority," he wrote,
the court could still order educational tracking by ability rather than continued racial segregation. However, "high social visibility" was a trait
that was "uniformly distributed among all Negroes," and therefore, by
using it, "*race, in and of itself*" would be "*made a relevant fact*" for the
court. "We can show," Gregor concluded, "that Negroes, even the most

highly qualified, suffer psychodynamic impairments by protracted contact with Whites at critical phases of their personality development."[45]

Gregor's position that his argument, rather than George's, was the one that made race the key issue for the court was buttressed by an attack on the veracity of George's claims from the only member of IAAEE's inner circle who had any experience in brain anatomy: Robert E. Kuttner. At the time of the litigation in *Stell,* Kuttner had taken a position at Creighton Medical School in Omaha, Nebraska, which was ironic given that the *Truth Seeker* was nearly as anti-Catholic as it was anti-Semitic.

The controversy arose during a planning session in April 1963, when the attorneys met with the scientists to plan trial strategy. In a series of letters after this session. Kuttner pointed out the paucity of studies that George had quoted in his report, and that many of the studies were of questionable utility since modern methods of electrophysiology and experimental neurophysiology became standard. These methods had thrown serious doubt on George's claims that the particular parts of the brain had the functions he assigned to them. Kuttner pointed out that the last studies that had made the claims George was making appeared two decades before George's report.

Of particular importance was George's reliance on Vint's assessment that the supragranular layer of the Negro brain was 14 percent less than of the white brain. Kuttner argued that the sort of neuroanatomy represented by Vint's study was tremendously specialized, and he doubted that Vint, working in Kenya, "had the training or the facilities to undertake" such delicate measurements. At any rate, Kuttner pointed out, despite Putnam's and George's repeated claims that Vint had undertaken a comparative study, he had not. Vint had taken his samples from the Kenyan natives and compared them to estimates of Caucasian samples given in other people's studies. "There is no getting around the fact," Kuttner wrote to George, "that comparisons require physical comparisons in the same laboratory."[46]

After dissecting the flaws in George's material, Kuttner hastened to point out that he did not disagree with George's conclusions regarding white supremacy, but "that does not mean that I am blind to the canons of scientific proof. . . . Frankly," Kuttner concluded, "I do not need anatomic evidence to convince me of anything regarding the ability of the Negro to build civilizations. I have said and wrote for ten years that the history of the world provides all the proof we need that some races have flunked the evolutionary IQ test."[47]

IAAEE in Court: The Brief

In the end, Pittman fashioned an argument that included all the possible arguments against the court, eliding the possible contradictions among them, although clearly preferring Gregor's approach. Pittman argued in the brief he filed on January 31, 1963, that *Brown* turned on a finding of fact. The factual finding in *Brown* was that race was not a rational basis for school assignments because there were no significant differences between the races in learning ability and that school segregation therefore results in psychological damage to Negro children. This finding, Pittman argued, was completely contradicted by the state of psychological knowledge in 1963. Pittman argued that racial segregation in schools was a reasonable exercise of state power because there were different "socio-moral and behavioral" standards for white and Negro children. There were also significant differences in intelligence, at least as measured by IQ scores. In a key passage lifted directly from Gregor, Pittman argued, "Whatever the causes of the above mentioned ethnic group differences, the fact remains that these differences exist now and will continue to exist for the remaining term of petitioners' attendance upon the schools of Savannah-Chatham County. Thus petitioners are justified in requesting protection by the court of their educational opportunities." Mention of genetic or physiological differences was confined to a few paragraphs, and there was no mention of the slippery slope toward miscegenation and the racial basis of civilization.[48]

The studies that Pittman entered into evidence clearly favored the psychological studies of intelligence, including works by Garrett, McGurk, Shuey, and Robert Osborne, an IAAEE member from the local University of Georgia who would also appear as a witness. Pittman also introduced a work by Gregor, later published in the *Western Law Review,* that criticized *Brown* and argued that the available scientific evidence indicated segregation was psychologically beneficial for school-age children.

The scientists themselves wrote a separate brief that was submitted to the court, aping the actions of Kenneth Clark and his associates in the *Brown* litigation. The exact authorship of the brief is difficult to determine, but it is clear that it was written by some combination of the three individuals who were the organizational heart of the IAAEE: Donald Swan, Robert Kuttner, and A. James Gregor. One reason that authorship of the brief is not clear is that it was unsigned. Pittman wrote to Kuttner that "these great studies will be more impressive if they bear the names and affiliations of those who have made contributions to them or who have studied and approved the contents of the paper." Failing to find people, or at least some critical mass of people, to sign the brief, Pittman bowed to the authors' wishes to remain anonymous.[49]

The scientific brief itself was not always clear in the positions it took, further evidence that it was perhaps the work of a committee. It opened by a subtle claim that the fact that it was unsigned should be a merit rather than a fault. The IAAEE brief noted that while the social-scientific appendix submitted in *Brown* was written by some of the foremost authorities in race relations, "[s]ince the Appendix is a scientific document, its validity must be judged separately from the status and reputation of its signers."[50]

Having made the claim that scientific arguments had to be judged entirely on their merits rather than on the identity of those who wrote them, however, the IAAEE brief was unable to sustain that viewpoint, repeating Kuttner's familiar arguments that the Genetics Manifesto of 1939 was not to be trusted because it "was framed by an extremely partisan group of American and British liberals." The danger was that science could indeed be perverted by the ideology of the scientists, because "[a] strong figure in the academic world can build a personal following out of students and colleagues who would reject his prejudices as well as his truths. This appears to have happened in anthropology."[51]

Thus, when a court was confronted with expert opinions, the court should always hear opposing experts in order to provide a check on ideological wishes wearing a scientific mask. In the *Brown* case, the IAAEE brief argued, the problem was that no experts appeared on behalf of segregation because "it is well known that the need for opposing witnesses was unanticipated."[52] While this statement echoed Pittman's writings on the subject of how science was sneaked into the *Brown* litigation, it is inconceivable that the authors of the IAAEE brief believed it, given Henry Garrett's appearance on behalf of segregation in the *Brown* litigation and his role in the IAAEE. In fact, southern attorneys tended to ignore the social science during *Brown* simply because they thought it unimportant.[53]

The IAAEE brief also argued that the central argument made in the appendix in *Brown* was unscientific. The appendix defined *a priori* that a healthy personality was "one innocent of prejudice and insulated from discrimination." However, "[i]t is generally recognized that prejudice, discrimination and segregation are widely prevalent practices or attitudes in all cosmopolitan civilizations" and Arthur Keith had gone as far as to argue that it was the driving force behind evolutionary change. In a descriptive sense therefore, *normal* had to mean *prejudiced*, since to be prejudiced was the normal state of affairs, and to define normal as "free of prejudice" meant that value assumptions were being smuggled into science and "condemn the great majority of the world's population to the abnormal category."[54] A similar argument in the medical sciences might be that because most of the population at some time suffers tooth decay, tooth decay should go untreated, since it is the "normal" state of affairs.

Unlike the "normality of prejudice" argument, which was free of documentation, the IAAEE brief made some more telling points regarding the appendix's failure to isolate legally mandated segregation as *the* causal variable in causing psychological damage in schoolchildren. The brief argued, "The Appendix merely offers segregation as the responsible agent; the complexity of the final effect, however, argues for a constellation of causes."[55] In the decades that followed 1963, this would become the most common charge against the social scientists. The IAAEE here was correct: there were no studies that social scientists could use to prove that school segregation was the cause of psychological damage. First, the social scientist had to prove that damage flowed from segregated *education*. Because social scientists had no studies that proved that segregated education—as opposed to segregated housing, or segregated parks, or segregated churches, or segregated transportation facilities—was responsible for psychological damage, they had nothing on which to base their opinions. Second, social scientists had to show that damage from segregation flowed from *legally imposed* segregation. Since it was impossible to isolate the effects of *de jure* segregation from *de facto* segregation, the evidence in the appendix was irrelevant to the proceedings, since it was legally imposed segregation that was at issue.[56]

All the issues in the IAAEE brief were fleshed out in subsequent trial testimony by IAAEE expert witnesses. In the *Stell* trial, and in a later trial that followed the *Stell* model; *Evers v. Jackson* in Mississippi, IAAEE expert witnesses came forth to undercut *Brown* and uncover the equalitarian conspiracy.

Galileo's Heirs: The IAAEE Witnesses

The witnesses in the trials were presented to make a series of interlocking arguments. First the psychometricians would appear—Garrett, McGurk, and Robert Osborne—armed with the IQ tests that demonstrated the gap in performance between whites and Negroes. Then the social theorist would come forth—Ernest van den Haag—to argue that segregation would be more psychologically beneficial for children, even if their IQs happened to be the same, because of their natural inclination to group with the same race. Finally, the biological scientists would come forward —George and Kuttner—to testify about the genetic basis for behavior and the anatomical differences between the races that could not be ameliorated by environmental changes. As Pittman told the court in Jackson, "We are not jumping from one area to another; we are moving logically and gradually, we hope, from one area into the other. We have been dealing with educational and psychological factors, and now we will go into the anatomy, biology and genetics."[57]

Despite the absence of his favorite miscegenation argument, Carleton Putnam was thrilled at the trials. At last, he wrote,

> [i]t would be possible to expose the fallacies and supply the deficiencies in *Brown*. The proponents of the environmental sociology, the cultural anthropologists, the Montagues, the Klinebergs, and the Clarks could be cross-examined under oath on the witness stand. So could the Garretts and the Georges. Finally, adequate press coverage would permit a beginning in the education of the public about the facts.[58]

It was not to be, however. The law now favored the NAACP, and they relied on the rule of the law. With each scientific witness, the NAACP moved to strike the testimony as immaterial to the case, relying on the simple constitutional mandate of *Brown*. NAACP attorneys did not subject the witnesses to cross-examination, nor call witnesses of their own. The reliance on the rule of law fit perfectly with the strategy of the NAACP. In his masterful analysis of the career of Thurgood Marshall, Mark Tushnet noted that the overarching goal of the NAACP in the desegregation campaign was the transformation of unfavorable case precedent into favorable case precedent, "through a careful litigation strategy pointing out anomalies in doctrine and identifying the inevitable failure of society's efforts to explain why unjust doctrines nonetheless were acceptable." However, once the victories were won—that is, once the first *Brown* decision was won—the situation changed dramatically for the NAACP, and they would rely on the legal rule of *Brown* in subsequent desegregation litigation. Tushnet concluded, "Once law became favorable, the rule of law was an advantage," and the NAACP would argue against introducing social-scientific evidence.[59]

In their testimony, the IAAEE scientists pointed to the scientific truth of their positions, even though they represented the minority in scientific opinion on these subjects. On the witness stand, McGurk captured all the nuances of the conspiracy charges in the following colloquy with the segregationist attorney regarding his *U.S. News* article:

> *Attorney*: Was any reply made to your [*U.S. News*] article?
> *McGurk*: To this article, yes.
> *Attorney*: Have you written a rebuttal?
> *McGurk*: No, I was forbidden to.
> *Attorney*: By whom?
> *McGurk*: By the college [Villanova University] at which I was teaching.
> *Attorney*: For what reason?
> *McGurk*: I don't really know. The reason given was that they didn't want to get into controversial issues.
> *Attorney*: Well, if what you have told us is correct, Dr. McGurk, if all of the studies and all of the tests that have been made show the same conclusion, could it hardly be a controversial issue?
> *McGurk*: Well, I didn't feel it was controversial either, but college administrators have different ideas, I suppose.
> *Attorney*: In any event, you did not publish a rebuttal, at the specific request of your university?
> *McGurk*: Yes, because certain organizations had visited them in an attempt to have me discharged.[60]

Here, all the elements of conspiracy rhetoric come through: the scientific truth being smothered by a group of shadowy figures who are motivated by unscientific ends. Nor did the scientists miss an opportunity to invoke their persecuted status. Wesley Critz George declared on the stand that a scientist would be "handicapped if he doesn't accept the equalitarian view," although that point of view "has not basis in fact. It is widely promoted as an ideology." He was then asked by Pittman, "Are there no Galileos?" to which he responded, "I am sure that there are some around who are willing to be harried by . . . other members of the academic profession, but they don't relish the role."[61]

On the stand in the *Stell* trial, Ernest van den Haag, while obviously mistaking Galileo's discoveries for those of Copernicus, claimed, "When

Galileo decided that the earth moves around the sun the majority opinion at that time decided or insisted that the sun moves around the earth, but Galileo was right, though he was a minority of one, and so should I find myself in this minority of one I would not regret it."[62]

Besides declaring that they were bravely defending the scientific truth in the face of the equalitarian hordes, the scientists added little to their published accounts about the scientific basis for white supremacy. Garrett went through the familiar battery of IQ tests and concluded that "the difference between the mud huts of the Congo and the cathedrals of Europe show [the difference in abstract intelligence] in a concrete way." McGurk rehearsed the same six studies that he relied on for his *U.S. News and World Report* article, declaring that they were the only studies that had any bearing on the issue and concluding, "This I can say without any qualification: there is absolutely no evidence anywhere from anybody that the cultural hypothesis [for differences in intelligence test scores between the races] has any validity. . . . All the studies that are extant show exactly the opposite. All the studies."[63]

At the *Stell* trial, George made part of the record the central argument of *The Biology of the Race Problem,* including prominent mentions of Robert Bean, Carleton Coon, and Arthur Keith. In the subsequent trial in Mississippi, however, George had to attend to an illness in his family, and the burden of the biological argument fell to Robert Kuttner. Kuttner professed his allegiance to the views of Keith and Coon but also declared himself in fundamental agreement with the views of Vint, whose work he had criticized so strongly in his letters to George. All his concerns over the validity of Vint's methods and findings were erased from his public presentation of Vint's work and the conclusions that he made from his findings.[64] By publicly declaring his allegiance to Vint's work while privately declaring it scientifically worthless, Kuttner made clear that he would sacrifice his scientific integrity when racial purity was on the line.

In the decades that would follow, the notion that IQ tests and alleged morphological differences in brain structures justified school segregation would lose its appeal. The same cannot be said for the third prong of the IAAEE's attack. The idea that racial separation was psychologically beneficial would gain currency in social-scientific opinion, concomitant with the belief that the social scientists in *Brown* were not acting as scientists but as political reformers. This was the central argument that Gregor had laid at the feet of Kenneth Clark in his criticisms of *Brown.* In an article he wrote that was submitted as evidence in the *Stell* trial, later published as a law review article, Gregor argued that the social science "material introduced [to the Supreme Court] did not meet the most elementary formal requirements of a scientific account," and "it is evident that in critical periods of personality formation, racial separation may materially enhance the formation of a coherent self-system on the part of the Negro by reducing the psychological pressure to which the child is subjected."[65] The problem with the social science statement, according to Gregor, was

> [it] never succeeds in isolating the critical variable. No argument is offered to indicate that the "self-hatred" and "in-group rejection" evinced by Negroes was the consequence of school segregation *per se*—the issue before the Court. If anything, such personality impairments are the result of a multiplicity of variously weighted variables: segregation, prejudices, discrimination as well as their "social concomitants."[66]

By the time of the trials, however, Gregor had a post at the University of Hawaii and was not in a position to come serve as an expert witness. His argument would be carried by another social philosopher, Ernest van den Haag. Because this argument proved to be longer lasting in its effects than those of the psychometricians and biologists, it is worth seeing exactly how van den Haag presented it for the court.

Ernest van den Haag

Ernest van den Haag was born in the Netherlands and had come to the United States after being imprisoned in Fascist Italy in the 1930s. He burst onto the New York intellectual scene in 1950 by taking on Sidney Hook in an exchange on the role of religion in culture as well as the merits of mass versus popular culture, displaying both a formidable intellect and a willingness to confront those who disagreed with his beliefs. He was a practicing psychoanalyst as well as a Ph.D. in economics from New York University. In the 1950s he taught as an adjunct at the New School for Social Research in New York City and became associated with William F. Buckley Jr. and the *National Review*.[67]

van den Haag was also one of the first social scientists from outside the racist Right to offer a critique of the social science in *Brown*. In 1956, van den Haag argued that the obvious solution to the desegregation crisis was to replace the two segregated school systems not with a single school system but with a tripartite system:

> The desire for the maximization of liberty leads to the contention that there should be schools for whites, schools for Negroes, and schools which both can attend, just as there are colleges for males, females, and coeducational ones. . . . Neither the legal enforcement of segregation nor compulsory congregation—the outlawing of segregation—are consistent with freedom.[68]

van den Haag also had no patience for the argument that segregation inflicts psychological damage on minority children. Kenneth and Mamie Clark's doll tests, in particular, drew his fire. In fact, in his critique van den Haag wrote about almost nothing else. van den Haag's position marks the origin of one of the most important features of the postdecision arguments against *Brown*'s social science—reducing all the social science testimony to the doll tests. By making the doll tests a synecdoche for all the social science testimony in *Brown,* van den Haag was able to focus attention on what he thought was the weakest part of the social science testimony.

The doll tests were a series of projective tests originally conducted by Kenneth Clark with his wife, Dr. Mamie Clark, in the late 1930s and early 1940s. In these tests, the Clarks presented African American children with identical black and white dolls. They then asked the children a series of questions such as "Show me the doll that is like you" and "Show me the good doll." At two of the school segregation trials, Kenneth Clark conducted the doll tests with the plaintiffs' children, to show that his results pertained in the school districts that were under adjudication. Clark argued that his tests demonstrated that minority group children were psychologically damaged because they rejected the black doll and refused to identify it as the good doll.[69]

In his critique, van den Haag pointed out that, in their original papers, the Clarks had found that northern children rejected the black dolls at a greater rate than southern children, proving that "Professor Clark's findings then can be explained without any reference to injury by segregation or by prejudice."[70] In contrast to the criticisms of his work that emanated from southern segregationists or from the racist Right, Clark actually responded to van den Haag. In his response, Clark argued that southern children's identifications indicated that they had accepted their inferior status and that this acceptance was unhealthy and, itself, evidence of damage. Moreover, Clark argued that van den Haag was mistaken in thinking that the doll tests were the pivotal piece of evidence he claimed them to be. "Dr. van den Haag's criticism of the 'flimsy' nature of the scientific evidence would have to be taken more seriously," Clark wrote, "if he had examined the nearly sixty references which were used as the basis for the social science brief which was submitted to the United States Supreme Court."[71]

Not to be outdone, van den Haag argued in a particularly vituperative article, published in the same issue of *Villanova Law Review* in which Frank McGurk had made his plea for academic freedom, that Clark was either incompetent or guilty of perjury regarding the inconsistency between his trial testimony and his 1947 article.[72] In his 1966 testimony before the International Court of Justice on behalf of apartheid, van den Haag was even more strident in his accusations against Clark, leading to this exchange with one of the World Court judges:

> *Mr. van den Haag:* . . . not only is there no evidence for [Negro feelings of inferiority resulting from segregation] but whatever evidence appears in the body of [the Social Science Statement in *Brown*] has been largely faked.
> *Mr. Gross:* Has been largely what, sir?
> *Mr. van den Haag:* Faked.
> *Mr. Gross:* Faked? F.A.K.E.D.?
> *Mr. van den Haag:* Yes, sir.
> *Mr. Gross:* By whom, sir?
> *Mr. van den Haag:* By Professor Kenneth Clark.[73]

Although later in his testimony van den Haag withdrew the word *faked* in favor of *misleading,* one cannot help but suspect that the above interchange captured his feelings about Clark more accurately.

van den Haag's critique of Clark's differing interpretations of his doll tests was not original; it had been pointed out by Edmond Cahn, professor of jurisprudence at New York University, as early as 1955.[74] What was original with van den Haag, however, was his insistence that, of all the social science testimony in *Brown,* the only important studies were Clark's projective tests.

In the *Stell* and *Evers* case, van den Haag apparently abandoned his earlier claim that legal segregation was inconsistent with freedom and stepped forward to testify on behalf of the states of Georgia and Mississippi. In these cases, van den Haag focused his testimony on his critique of Clark's doll studies. While admitting that in the "Social Science Statement" submitted to the Supreme Court in *Brown*, "there are nearly a dozen works quoted," he maintained that "the type of evidence is pretty much the same in all, very largely based on several works of Kenneth B. Clark. . . . Professor Clark undertook a number of experiments [the doll tests] and submitted them to the Court."[75] By reducing all the social science testimony in *Brown* to Clark's doll experiments, van den Haag could then critique all that social scientists did in *Brown* by critiquing Clark's doll tests. As such, he was fitted perfectly for Carter Pittman, who was anxious for someone to testify as to "the fraud perpetrated by the witness Clark."[76]

Given the specific task of undercutting Clark's testimony, van den Haag showed that he was not a careful reader of the object of his study: the testimony of Kenneth B. Clark in the *Brown* litigation. For example, van den Haag testified correctly that Clark had used the dolls to test sixteen children in South Carolina as part of the *Briggs* trial that was later joined with *Brown*. The segregationist attorney George Leonard asked with mock incredulousness, "Do you mean to tell me that the doll test which went before the Supreme Court was based on the testimony of sixteen children? Only sixteen?" van den Haag replied:

> Well, that was in the South Carolina case. Mr. Clark testified in two more cases and undertook essentially the same test with essentially the same result, also with extremely small groups of children, 10 or 15 and 20, I believe. . . . He said that [the result in these cases] was consistent with the larger studies [he had previously published]. And I thereupon looked up the larger study. . . . Somewhat to my surprise I found that, contrary to his testimony, this larger study seemed to indicate the very opposite of what his testimony tended to show.[77]

In this brief argument, van den Haag was attacking a straw man rather than Clark. First, Clark had never claimed that his examination of the children under litigation was a true scientific experiment with an adequate sample size, only that it was an attempt to show that the sorts of damage experienced by other children generally also applied to the plaintiffs' children. Second, Clark did not use the doll tests in the other two trials in which he had given testimony; he used them in one but interviewed the plaintiffs' children in the other. Third, van den Haag declared himself surprised to find out Clark's results in the previously published studies, but Clark had been asked about the conflict between the two results in his testimony and had admitted that segregation was only one of many causal variables and that it was impossible to single it out as *the* cause of psychological damage. van den Haag's "discovery" of Clark's methods had been an open record for nearly ten years, as Clark had addressed all of van den Haag's objections in his testimony.[78]

Beyond attacking Clark's testimony, van den Haag introduced a study by Gregor that attempted to duplicate Clark's experiments. A few months before the trial, Gregor and an associate had conducted the doll tests, presumably so they could be introduced in a trial defending segregation. van den Haag reported that Gregor had found that "[n]inety five percent of the Negro children in the segregated schools of Jackson . . . when asked, 'Give me the doll that looks like you,' correctly designated the dark Negro doll." This, he concluded, was a sign of mental health, since they correctly self-identified themselves with the appropriate doll. The problem with van den Haag's argument was that Clark had never claimed that mistaking one's self-identity was a sign of psychological damage; it was claiming that the white doll was *preferable* to the Negro doll that was a sign of damage. Since van den Haag did not introduce how many of the children had given a racial *preference*, his testimony regarding Gregor's test was not germane to the point he wished to make.[79]

Regardless of how strongly argued it was, the point of van den Haag's testimony was to close off the "overlap" problem Gregor had raised before the litigation had begun. The psychometricians could not argue that every Negro child was below every white child; hence the IQ argument could not, in and of itself, seal the case for racial segregation. What van den Haag had added to the mix was the idea that even the bright Negro children should not mix with white children, as they would be happier among their own kind, where they were accepted as members of their own group. As William Tucker concluded in his history of the trials, "Taken as a whole, the testimony of the . . . expert witnesses precluded any possible method for placing a black child and a white child into the same classroom."[80]

A Short-Lived Victory

NAACP attorney Jack Greenberg believed that the presiding judge in the *Stell* trial was "adamantly hostile to blacks."[81] In his opinion in *Stell*, Frank M. Scarlett made this hostility quite evident, as it could have been written by Pittman. Scarlett found that *Brown* turned on a finding of fact about the harms of segregated education. Scarlett declared that it was up to him to determine whether the facts of the case before him agreed with those presented in *Brown*. He found that they did not and that it was a reasonable exercise of state power to assign pupils to separate schools on the basis of race, given the differences in their ability to learn and the need to identify with members of their own group.[82]

The NAACP, which had undoubtedly expected such a ruling from the notorious Judge Scarlett, immediately appealed the decision to the Fifth Circuit Court of Appeals, which wasted no time in overturning Scarlett's ruling. Pointing to *Brown*'s mandate that separate schools were unconstitutional, the Fifth Circuit informed Scarlett that the only question that remained for him to determine was if the schools were segregated, and if so, he was to order desegregation. This had been the position of the NAACP throughout the trial. "It is . . . clear that on the day of the entry by the trial court of its order it was a clear abuse of its discretion for the trial court to deny appellants' motion for a preliminary injunction requiring the defendant School Board to make a prompt and reasonable start towards desegregating the Savannah–Chatham County schools."[83]

The *Evers* decision read much like the Scarlett's *Stell* decision, but Judge Sidney Mize reluctantly followed the Fifth Circuit Court of Appeals and ruled against continuing segregation. However, Mize did set the stage for an appeal by concluding that "the facts in this case point up a most serious situation and, indeed, 'cry out' for a reappraisal and complete reconsideration of the findings and conclusions of the United States Supreme Court in the *Brown* decision."[84]

The entire series of events left Putnam bewildered. "In reading the opinion of the Fifth Circuit Court of Appeals," he wrote, "I had to pinch myself to believe I was not dreaming. I seemed to be wandering in some sort of Alice in Wonderland." When the Supreme Court refused to take the appeal of the Fifth Circuit's decision, Putnam realized, "*Stell* had dropped into a deeper chasm than any well of silence. The appeal to truth, the levy upon honor, had failed."[85]

George Leonard, who was Pittman's assistant during the trials, noted that with Fifth Circuit's ruling, "the equalitarian doctrine . . . gained such a degree of judicial acceptance as to make a future challenge in the courts dependent on a prior change in the climate of public opinion."[86] Carleton Putnam had always envisioned the attack on *Brown* as coming in two prongs: a change in public and scientific opinion on race differences and a legal challenge based on the scientific truth of white supremacy. It was obvious after the setbacks of *Stell* and *Evers* that the scientific mind-set would have to be changed before the courts could be. And Carleton Putnam, the man who had built an airline in the midst of the Great Depression, was not to be beaten so easily. For him, the failure of the court cases was only a temporary setback to what he was sure would be his ultimate victory. He redoubled his efforts to re-educate the American public about the scientific truth of white supremacy. Unfortunately for him, the scientific establishment had begun to react to his activities, and he would have to confront them directly.

7

The Scientists React

While the IAAEE scientists were deep into the fight to preserve racial segregation in the American South, they were also involved in a battle on a different front. They had launched their own journal, *Mankind Quarterly,* which purported to be dedicated to an open discussion of the scientific study of racial issues. The similarity between the doctrines presented in *Mankind Quarterly* and the eugenic/racialist arguments of the first half of the twentieth century were evident, causing many anthropologists to criticize the new journal for propagating dangerous and unscientific points of view.

For many American anthropologists, the resemblance between the kind of articles published in the *Mankind Quarterly* (*MQ*) and the scientific-political articles written and publicized by Carleton Putnam leaped out. Many noticed how often Putnam as well as Garrett and George, who were well known as scientific defenders of southern racial segregation, called upon Carleton Coon as an authority. Many suspected that he was involved in their project, as indeed he was. In the United States, then, and very much against his wishes, many of the debates over the activities of the IAAEE were filtered through interpretations of Coon's work and what his responsibility for his work should be. The first attacks on the IAAEE were in Great Britain, however, and they appeared nearly as soon as the *Mankind Quarterly* appeared.

Man *and the* Mankind Quarterly

In the 1960s, when inviting Wesley Critz George to join the executive committee of the IAAEE, Donald Swan explained, "The IAAEE is closely associated with the publication and distribution of the new scientific journal, *The Mankind Quarterly.*" George was naturally very excited about the prospect of a journal that respected the science of white supremacy but was concerned that his political activities on behalf of segregation might disqualify him from being an seen as an objective scientific investigator should he publish anything in the new journal. Robert Gayre, *Mankind Quarterly*'s editor, was quick to dispel such a notion, telling George that his "partisan activities" would not "be a particular disability" should George choose to be a member of the Honorary Advisory Board. Thus relieved, George joined the board of *MQ*. When he received his copies of the journal, it was through the offices of Alistair Harper, the Northern League's organizing secretary in Great Britain.[1]

Mankind Quarterly was edited by Scotsman Robert Gayre, who, like Roger Pearson and the Northern League, was a follower of the Nazi *Rassenhygienist* Hans F. K. Guenther and had extensive ties to the neo-Nazi movement throughout Europe, including the Northern League. Like those in the Northern League, Gayre believed that World War II was fratricidal, pitting Nordic against Nordic and leading to a lessening of the genetic quality of Europe. He was also a heraldist who loved to sport a long list of baronial titles after his name. When he founded *Mankind Quarterly*, he was aided by Henry Garrett, R. Ruggles Gates, and Corrado Gini, and they soon began publishing a journal of race science that suited their beliefs about white superiority.[2]

Mankind Quarterly created a stir within anthropology, not for the startling new studies it published about race but rather because evidence of what many suspected was its dedication to anything but an open discussion on race. One member of the *Mankind Quarterly*'s editorial board, Božo Škerlj announced his resignation from his position on the board rather noisily in the pages of the British anthropological journal *Man*. He noted that if he was to be listed as a member of the board, he felt partly responsible for the journal's contents. After the first issue, however, it was evident that the journal was completely lacking in scholarly purpose and dedicated to perpetuating one particular point of view. He wrote that he declined Gayre's offer to print a response to the objectionable pieces because it was clear that "anything critical which I might write on the subject would be wholly unacceptable to the Editor."[3]

In a review of the *Mankind Quarterly*, also published in *Man*, G. Ainsworth Harrison noted that "few of the contributions [to *Mankind Quarterly*] have any merit whatsoever, and many are no more than incompetent attempts to rationalize irrational opinions." Harrison proceeded to criticize specific articles by Gayre, who did not seem to understand the difference between polymorphism and polytypism; Gini, for ignoring entire bodies of evidence on heritability and IQ in his review of Shuey's *Testing of Negro Intelligence*; and Garrett, for using a review of Klineberg's work to state that Egypt's great civilization of the past declined due to racial intermingling, a statement that could not possibly be supported by any understanding of IQ tests, the purported subject of Garrett's review.[4]

Despite the fact that Harrison's review was very specific in the scientific flaws he had found in the journal, Gates attempted no real refutation of the charges. In response, he merely claimed that "[t]he attacks on the *Mankind Quarterly* . . . are not based on science at all, but have a political basis, having been made mainly by Communists or their fellow travelers." The *Mankind Quarterly*'s response to Škerlj's resignation was even more extreme: a libel suit against Škerlj and *Man* for publishing his views. The specific cause of action was Gayre and Garrett's claim that Škerlj had called them sympathetic to Nazi views. Of course, given both men's involvement with the Northern League and other such organizations, there would have been some merit in the Nazi charge; but in fact, Škerlj had not called either man a Nazi. The case was eventually settled out of court, but the fact that the lawsuit was brought at all tends to prove what Škerlj had said about the editorial policies of the *Mankind Quarterly*: that dissent from the views of Gayre and Garrett was not going to be tolerated. Indeed, in the controversies that would arise over the next several years about the IAAEE and the *Mankind Quarterly*, it would not be accused equalitarians who would attempt to stifle free and open debate, but the IAAEE who would seek to shut down all those who opposed their views. In the United States, libel laws were considerably different from those in Great Britain, where *Man* was published; however, that did not stop IAAEE members from threatening opponents with libel for daring to speak out against the IAAEE's views on science and white supremacy.

Juan Comas

The dispute in *Man* was just the opening salvo in mainstream anthropology's attack on *Mankind Quarterly*. Mexican anthropologist Juan Comas published a scathing review of the new journal in *Current Anthropology* in 1961, in which he linked the *Mankind Quarterly* with its historical antecedents: the writings of Gobineau, Houston Stewart Chamberlain, Vacher de Lapouge, Hans F. K. Guenther, and Madison Grant. Comas pointed out that the scientific battle had apparently been won by the close of World War II, as evidenced by the UN Statements on Race, which declared the scientific consensus. Comas argued, however, that scientific racism had returned with the *Mankind Quarterly*. He examined an article by Henry Garrett that criticized Klineberg's work. Comas pointed out that Garrett's arguments had been given a full hearing some decades before. "Such arguments," Comas argued, "Have been used for 25 years against . . . psychologists and anthropologists who for more than a quarter century have been gathering evidence that there is no mental inferiority of a racial character among non-White groups. It is useless, therefore, to engage in a discussion which would only repeat what has been said many times."[5] Comas pointed to the obvious racism in Garrett's comments regarding the decline of the Egyptian civilization owing to racial degradation, as well as those regarding modern Haiti as proof of the Negro's incapacity for self-governance, noting that these could hardly be considered scientific claims but were excellent evidence of Garrett's underlying racism.

Current Anthropology published Comas's critique with a number of comments appended. *Mankind Quarterly*'s editors, Garrett, Gates, and Gayre, leaped to the defense of their journal. IAAEE members Clarence P. Oliver and Stanley Porteus were more muted in the criticisms of Comas and defense of *Mankind Quarterly*. There were fourteen comments that declared their allegiance to Comas, including one member of *Mankind Quarterly*'s Advisory Board, Gutorm Gjessing, who wrote that he could "almost entirely agree with Comas's article."[6] Others who wrote against *Mankind Quarterly* included J. B. S. Haldane, Julian Huxley, Ashley Montagu, and Theodosius Dobzhansky. When Carleton Putnam totted up the count in the exchange in *Current Anthropology*, he arrived at a different tally. In his "Race and Reason Day" speech, which was widely distributed to American anthropologists, Putnam argued that six of the supporters of Comas "voted from behind the Iron Curtain . . . where the party line required strict conformity. Eliminate those six names and . . . it becomes eight to seven [against the *Mankind Quarterly*]. And you started with a list of voters selected by an equalitarian."[7]

Two things are notable about Putnam's comments. First, despite the continued claims from the IAAEE scientists about the equalitarian conspiracy to silence open discussion, even the hardliner Putnam was forced to admit that their views were published in a mainstream anthropology journal. Indeed, one anthropologist wrote to praise the publication of the exchange because, while Garrett and Gayre's "intemperate, hackneyed, and inconsequential arguments will sway few critical readers," nonetheless "these men should not be denied the opportunity to defend themselves."[8] By contrast, *Mankind Quarterly* would extend no such courtesy to opponents of its racial position. Anthropologist U. R. Ehrenfels criticized the journal for deleting paragraphs of an article he published there that were critical of South African apartheid because they were of a "political" nature, according to Gayre.[9] Garrett's arguments about Haiti and Egypt were of a similar "political" nature, and Gayre did publish those. Others who did not share the racist orientation of *Mankind Quarterly*'s editors were given similar treatment.

The second revealing aspect of Putnam's comments was that, despite continued claims that scientific truths were not decided by majority vote, and despite the continued claim that they were modern-day Galileos, most members of the IAAEE could not stop themselves from claiming that their views were more widely respected in the scientific community than at first appeared. Despite the continued claims that scientific facts needed to speak for themselves, a common IAAEE strategy was to enlist as many authorities as possible to support their position. This became apparent in the subsequent IAAEE attack on Juan Comas.

After Comas's article, Garrett wrote to George about the need to respond to the "Communist." Garrett was not particularly interested in an open exchange of ideas. "Instead of parrying blows," he told George, "I think we must hit these people hard: ridicule is always a good weapon."[10] The *Mankind Quarterly* would subsequently publish a number of attacks on Comas. Donald Swan came out from behind his "Thor Swenson" pseudonym and published the first thing under his own name since his 1954 letter where he declared his dedication to American fascism. Both Garrett and George vetted the young scholar's article before it was published in the *Mankind Quarterly*. Garrett published an attack on Comas as well.[11]

The one leading the charge against Comas, however, was A. James Gregor, who opened a protracted attack with a review of one of Comas's publications that was part of the UN volume *The Race Question in Modern Science*. Comas's book was originally published in 1950, and most of the book was a treatment of the Aryan myth and the view that the Jews should be considered a separate biological race.[12]

Something that never became apparent in the subsequent exchanges between Comas and Gregor was that Comas's views were very close to those of Gregor in his articles critiquing Nordicism. One reason this never became apparent was that Gregor's review was dedicated to minutiae rather than to the overall argument presented. Further, Gregor's review was written in an uncharitable tone that he would adopt for the remainder of his career—one wherein his scholarly opponent was so devoid of logic, learning, and intelligence that he or she was simply incoherent. Most of the Gregor review was an examination of typographical errors and the misspelling of names. These, he argued, were signs that Comas was "attempting to impart an air of scholarship to a work whose defects, to the initiated, are painfully obvious." The thrust of Gregor's review was that Comas had relied on secondary sources rather than reading the original sources, concluding that "Professor Comas has violated almost every canon of scientific procedure, detachment and good taste."[13]

Comas's reply, published in *Current Anthropology*, noted that Gregor's review was little more than a list of typographical errors, and it was not terribly unusual for a document meant for public consumption to rely on secondary sources. Comas also argued that it was probably not a coincidence that a personal attack on him appeared in *Mankind Quarterly* just as his article criticizing the editors appeared.[14] Gregor, proving that he was nothing if not contentious, wrote three more articles criticizing Comas, all written in the same intemperate tone that characterized the first. For example, in response to a sentence wherein Comas claims that the 1950 UNESCO statement represented the findings of modern scientific consensus regarding racial difference, Gregor claimed, "The history of Western Science contains, perhaps, no single statement more manifestly presumptuous." Nor could Gregor resist his own counting of noses in response to the UN consensus, arguing that, among other IAAEE stalwarts, G. Gedda, A. H. Sturtevant, C. D. Darlington, H. E. Garrett, C. Gini, and S. D. Porteus, as well as Nazi eugenicists F. Lenz and E. Fischer, "took violent objection" to the statement.[15] In yet another article, on the same page where Gregor accused Comas of leveling *ad hominem* arguments, Gregor concluded, "Charity would suggest that a man who systematically brings discredit upon himself, his colleagues and the international institution through which he works [as Comas has], is working under a serious emotional handicap."[16] One would hate to see what Gregor would have said had he not been in the mood to be charitable.

The equalitarian journal *Current Anthropology* allowed Gregor and Gates to have the last word in the ugly dispute, closing off the controversy in 1963.[17] Gayre was delighted with the attacks on Comas. He heard rumors that as a result of the concerted attack "Comas has been arraigned before his University":

> I think we have to do to Ashley Montagu now what we have done to Comas. Give him a thorough going over. . . . The more we spell it out to these birds that we have teeth and claws the better. We are too strong a group to be knocked on our backs, and they will begin to realize this— and that may be the beginning of honest anthropological thinking again![18]

Whether or not Comas was actually "arraigned by his university" is not as important as the fact that Gayre believed he *should have* been censured in some way for his remarks during a supposed academic exchange of ideas. Gayre's belief that those who opposed "honest anthropology" had no real right to their views was shared by others gathered around *Mankind Quarterly.* Those whose views did not recognize the scientific truth of white supremacy simply were not welcome in its pages, despite its purported call for an open exchange of ideas on race.

Carleton Putnam and the Anthropologists

In the United States, most exchanges around the IAAEE's agenda centered on the question of racial segregation in southern schools. The lightning rod was Carleton Putnam. Previous chapters have shown the enthusiastic reception of *Race and Reason* in the American South. Unsurprisingly, Putnam's book fared less well in the scholarly presses. Almost universally ignored, it garnered few reviews, and those reviewers who did notice it often treated it as curiosity rather than a serious book. Sociologist Louis Schneider wrote that "Mr. Putnam is unequivocally a racist" but also that "his polemic against Boas (as well as others) . . . reveals a certain sureness of touch. . . . One can only envy Putnam the precision of his knowledge." Sociologists Robert P. Stuckert and Irwin D. Rinder argued, "Social scientists can take this work seriously only as a symptom or datum showing the state of mind of one spokesman of an embattled social movement."[19]

Several reviewers noted that the driving force behind Putnam's argument was the conspiracy claim. Clark Knowlton, who found the book "a sad commentary on the intellectual bankruptcy of the defenders of segregation," pointed to the centrality of the claim that a "small number of anthropologists" were "Communists from whose ideas flow the doctrines of social and biological equalitarianism." Historian Barton Bernstein was closer to the mark when he noted that Putnam's central claim was that Boas hatched a "Jewish plot," which was transformed into a "Jewish-Communist conspiracy," to deny racial differences.[20]

Most negative reviews brought a sharp response from Putnam, raising his visibility even more. In the midst of the Comas controversy, anthropologist Manning Nash reviewed Putnam's book by linking it to common tropes of the proslavery argument of the previous century in order to "show the bone structure of racial ideology." Putnam retorted in an angry letter that Nash's "equalitarian gang" was "concocting a mess of half-truths and slanted evidence" that "deceived the Supreme Court and the American people. Worse than this, they lied to the Negro about himself and thus persuaded him that he had a grudge against the White man whereas . . . the Negro owes the White man every decent thing he has."[21]

When faced with Putnam's wrath, anthropologist Donald Simmons took a slightly different tack than most. Unknowingly following Henry Garrett's advice, he chose to ridicule Putnam in the *New Republic*. Noting that Putnam's writings were often mailed out to members of the American Anthropological Association "in an endeavor to locate apostate anthropologists," Simmons argued that "to delineate and rectify Putnam's many errors and half-truths would be a task equivalent to cleansing the Augean Stables."[22] Nonetheless, Simmons, who was an expert in African folktales, took Putnam to task for his ignorance of cultural diffusion and took aim at Putnam's claim that Africans never developed a system of writing, "an argument beloved by racists." Simmons pointed out that it was simply untrue.[23]

Simmons's charge that Negroes had indeed invented a system of writing sent Putnam scurrying to his reliable resources, Gayre, Swan, and Coon, to verify if one of his favorite claims was indeed out of date. In his subsequent exchange of letters with Simmons, the anthropologist refused to do the one thing that Putnam desperately wanted: take the segregationist seriously. While gently parrying all Putnam's claims about African writing systems with more recent studies, Simmons consistently made jokes about race, which to Putnam was no laughing matter, since it was the basis of all civilization. "Please overlook the skipping of my type-writer," Simmons ended one letter, "it was just repaired by Anglo Saxons and you know how they are." The final insult came when Simmons made up a flyer he claimed was from the "International Anti-Putnam Letters Committee" that contained a number of genuine scientific arguments but ended with "I would not like my sister to marry either Dr. George or Mr. Putnam."[24]

The most prestigious scientist to review *Race and Reason* was Theodosius Dobzhansky. One of the world's leading geneticists, Dobzhansky had long written on the social impact of genetics on society. Writing for a popular audience immediately after World War II with his colleague, geneticist L. C. Dunn, Dobzhansky argued that scientists should abandon attempts to classify races on the basis of phenotypic features. However, Dobzhansky and Dunn rejected the notion that race was "just a myth" and maintained that race was still a useful scientific concept if understood on the genetic level. "Race," they argued, "can be defined as populations which differ in the frequencies of some gene or genes." In his writing on race, Dobzhansky would maintain that race was a viable scientific concept, if understood at the level of the genotype rather than the phenotype, and that genetic variation was necessary for the health of the species. To maximize the benefits of genetic variation, one must maximize the opportunities available for all members of human society. In his soon-to-be published book, *Mankind Evolving,* Dobzhansky argued that "denial of equality of opportunity stultifies the genetic diversity with which mankind became equipped in the course of its evolutionary development. Inequality conceals and stifles some people's abilities and dissembles the lack of abilities in others. Conversely, equality permits . . . an optimal utilization of the wealth of the gene pool of the human species."[25]

Dobzhansky's review of *Race and Reason* was titled "A Bogus 'Science' of Race Prejudice." "[W]ritings giving vent to passions do not belong on the pages of the *Journal of Heredity*. . . . The situation changes . . . when such writings purport to be dealing with scientifically established facts, particularly facts of genetics and human biology. Silence should not be carried to point of aiding and abetting misrepresentation." Dobzhansky critiqued the book by merely quoting large passages with a minimum of commentary and concluded that the "pseudo-science" of race prejudice "fell temporarily into desuetude in most of the world"; however, "[i]t was to be expected that the murky tide will stage a come-back, and this is what we are actually observing."[26]

Dobzhansky's review established that he believed it was his responsibility to counteract what he saw as a dangerous misuse of science—this would emerge as a major point of contention between Dobzhansky and Carleton Coon the following year. But the issues were framed earlier by Putnam and *Race and Reason*: Dobzhansky believed that scientists needed to react to Putnam's work and was willing to lead by example by publicly criticizing Putnam's book.

One other aspect of Dobzhansky's review should be noted. In an addendum as the review went to press, Dobzhansky explained that, since he had written the review, he had received another pamphlet by Putnam in the mail. Noting the widespread circulation of Putnam's writings, Dobzhansky urged, "Geneticists and anthropologists may well give their immediate attention to the danger of misuse of their sciences for propagandistic ends."[27]

By this time, the National Putnam Letters Committee was making frequent mass mailings of segregationist pamphlets, such as that received by Dobzhansky. It is not clear which Putnam pamphlet Dobzhansky received as his review went to press. Perhaps it was a printed version of one of Putnam's many public speeches; his address on "Race and Reason Day" in Mississippi was mailed out to ten thousand people. Or it might have been an advance selection from Wesley Critz George's soon-to-be-published *Biology of the Race Problem*; before publishing the book itself, Putnam distributed the chapter "The Influence of Franz Boas," which illustrated the "influence that flows from a clever and forceful man when supported by other men trained by him."[28] By the end of 1961, many in the scientific community had noticed Putnam's activities and those of his IAAEE colleagues, and many agreed with Dobzhansky that scientists should take action.

Resolutions on Race

In November 1961 meeting of the American Anthropological Association, President Gordon Willey made the following statement:

> The concern which I wish to lay before you is I think a grave one. . . . It arises from recent press statements and certain publications on race and racial differences as a basis for social and political action. Many of you have seen such statements. Some of you have called these to our atten-

tion. The Board deliberated this matter which concerns use of the name "anthropology" and "anthropological science" in a way we believe to be false and misrepresentative of our profession by persons who are not recognized by the American Anthropological Association as professional anthropologists.

Willey called for the following resolution, which subsequently passed by a vote of 192–0:

The American Anthropological Association repudiates statements now appearing in the United States that Negroes are biologically and in innate mental ability inferior to whites, and reaffirms the fact that there is no scientifically established evidence to justify the exclusion of any race from the rights guaranteed by the Constitution of the United States. The basic principles of equality of opportunity and equality before the law are compatible with all that is known about human biology. All races possess the abilities needed to participate fully in the democratic way of life and in modern technological civilization.[29]

The AAA resolution was the first official attempt by anthropologists to respond to Carleton Putnam. Like all responses to his work, it did not escape Putnam's attention. His response was a press conference called two weeks later, where he warned "that organizations like the American Anthropological Association and certain groups of social psychologists were riddled with politically motivated propagandists and that truth oriented scientists were . . . persecuted." Concluded Putnam, "The integrity of our civilization in the Southern United States . . . is at stake . . . and the disease of equalitarianism must be cured where it started—in the scientific cloister." The AAA resolution and portions of Putnam's response were both reported in *Science,* bringing the issues to the larger scientific community.[30]

Putnam also fired off a letter to AAA president Willey. "I am informed" Putnam charged, "that the total attendance at the Philadelphia meeting was 1500. In view of the climate of suppression and persecution existing in this field, I write to inquire whether it would be fair to say that the actual vote was 1308 to 192 against the resolution." Putnam's letter was not answered by Willey, the outgoing president of AAA, but by the incoming president, Sherwood Washburn. "After reading your book," wrote Washburn to Putnam, "I believe you greatly exaggerate the role of

Boas in American anthropology in social science." Noting that sociologists and psychologists reached the same conclusions as did anthropologists regarding racial differences, Washburn concluded, "If there had
been no anthropologists at all, the findings . . . would be the same." In response, Putnam noted, "You cannot deceive a child of ten with that sort
of nonsense, so I wonder what your motives are. . . . It is not sociologists,
nor cultural anthropologists, who are best qualified to speak on this subject, but physical anthropologists and geneticists." Putnam held forth
against the "equalitarians" who were "hiding behind smoke screens of
ballots or other similar evasions."[31]

In the year after this exchange, controversy would break out regarding
Carleton Coon's work and its use by segregationists. The two most outspoken critics of Coon's *Origins of the Races,* Washburn and Dobzhansky, were engaged with Carleton Putnam a year before the release of
Coon's book. As we will see, Coon would paint his critics as sentimental
and unscientific writers who were introducing civil matters into what
should have been a scientific debate. But Coon's position was untenable,
given that Putnam had already transformed the scientific debate into a
political matter and had belligerently pushed the debate onto scientific societies and their leaders.

The AAA resolution on race was one of two that the scientific community passed in response to Putnam. In May 1962, the American Association of Physical Anthropologists (AAPA), obviously concerned that
Race and Reason was being used as a text in Louisiana classrooms,
passed the following resolution:

> We, the members of the American Association of Physical Anthropolo-
> gists professionally concerned with differences in man, deplore the mis-
> use of science to advocate racism. We condemn such writings as *Race
> and Reason* that urge the denial of basic rights to human beings. We
> sympathize with those of our fellow teachers who have been forced by
> misguided officials to teach race concepts that have no scientific founda-
> tion, and we affirm, as we have in the past, that there is nothing in sci-
> ence that justifies the denial of opportunities or rights to any group by
> virtue of race.[32]

Stanley Garn, one of Coon's coauthors on a 1950 book on race, introduced the resolution, and Carleton Coon was the presiding officer for the
meeting where this resolution was offered. Twenty years later, in his au-

tobiography, Coon recollected that when he asked how many of the assembled anthropologists had read Putnam's book, only one raised his hand. Coon claimed, "There they were, some of them old and trusted friends, apparently as brainwashed as Pavlov's puppies, or as most of the social anthropologists. As Khrushchev had boasted, beating his shoe upon a table in the United Nations, the Communists did not need to fight us. They could rot us from within. I could see it all in a horrid dream. . . . I told my fellow members that I would no longer preside over such a craven lot, and resigned from the presidency."[33]

Coon's account of the AAPA proceedings contains all themes made familiar by Putnam: that social or cultural anthropology was a "brainwashing" conspiracy; that left-wing politics, not objective scientific interest, drove scientific resolutions proclaiming the equality of the races; and the ever-present threat of Communists. The parallels are not accidental, as the men had remained in contact. Coon wrote to Putnam that when he wrote about the AAPA meeting's "show of hands," Putnam should "make it clear that it is NOT from me."[34]

When the AAPA resolution became publicized, Coon decried the motion, as it interfered with "freedom of the press," and claimed that "scientists should keep out of the integration issue."[35] What was hidden by Coon's public stand, however, was that he had already involved himself in the integration issue through his involvement with Putnam. Moreover, Coon's failure to mention that the AAPA resolution was prompted by *Race and Reason* being used as a text in high school classrooms makes it appear that physical anthropologists were eager to make scientific pronouncements about civil affairs, rather than that they were *responding* to the appropriation of science by the segregationist Louisiana legislature.

The resolutions, however, had only spurred Putnam on to further attacks. A few weeks after his press conference, Putnam mailed a pamphlet to the entire membership of the AAA. This was a copy of a speech he had given in New Orleans in which he attacked the organization because they were "social and cultural, rather than, physical anthropologists." That the physical anthropologists, as well as one of the world's leading geneticists, also were critical of his position was something that Putnam was trying to respond to at this time. When he made his mailing, Putnam had asked Coon if he could use Coon's name when requesting the addresses of the AAA membership.[36]

By this time, anthropologists noticed Putnam's ability to keep abreast of their activities—it was obvious that Putnam was getting information

from someone, and suspicions were high that it was Coon. Physical anthropologist Gabriel Lasker recalled later that "it was clear that [Putnam]
must have had help from someone who was in on all the rumors that
wend around physical anthropologists. . . . It must have been Coon, because he was given to broad offhand statements and, if phoned in the
middle of the night might have said those things."[37]

Anthropologists were not the only ones noticing the work of Putnam
and his associates. In the weeks that followed the announcement of the
AAA resolution on race, the Southern Education Reporting Service, a
news service dedicated to impartial reporting about school integration in
the South, asked the AAA to make "an objective, factual statement of the
Boas Theory," which was "under attack by Wesley C. George." As AAA
executive secretary Steve Boggs noted, it was now incumbent upon the
AAA to "draw up a fuller, scientific statement," for "if we do not come
up with something good for them, they will be hurt and so will we." During the first months of 1962, it fell to Washburn, as AAA president organize a committee to issue "a long statement on race," which he hoped to
have ready for the next AAA meeting.[38]

Drafting such a statement was not an easy task, however, as the minutes of a summer meeting of the governing board attest. The question of
the day was: What to do about Carleton Putnam? On suggestion was a
detailed "review of Putnam's book emphasizing his lack of qualifications
and suggesting that students taught from his book might face difficulty in
gaining admission to college." But Washburn argued that "it was preferable to clarify the general racial issue, rather than attack Putnam or his
followers." Unfortunately, Washburn believed that "there was no one
person today who could make a comprehensive and accurate statement
of the biological concept [of race]." The race concept, Washburn believed, was in a state of flux, and while race was still useful as a biological concept, "it is not relevant to what the racists talk about." According
to the minutes of the meeting, Washburn was asked if he would "consider
airing the whole topic in his Presidential Address. Washburn immediately
agreed to do so."[39]

By May, the governing board of the AAA had decided on two-pronged
attack. First, they would approach the American Association for the
Advancement of Science (AAAS) to appoint a small commission, headed
by one physical and one cultural anthropologist, to draft a position on
race. The second prong would be Washburn's presidential address that
fall.[40]

However, events soon overtook the AAA. On Monday, October 15, 1962, Carleton Coon's *The Origin of Races* would appear. The book contained Coon's provocative thesis that humans had broken into their racial groupings during the stage of *Homo erectus* and that each racial group had evolved into *Homo sapiens* at different times, with the white race evolving two hundred thousand years before the black race. It was this argument that Putnam and George had already adopted for the continuance of southern racial segregation. As Boggs wrote to Mead, "You know what it contains. . . . We *could* have a new political issue on our hands by Monday." The day of the release, Boggs was worried. "The book will certainly have come to everyone's attention by the time of the Council meeting." He wrote to Mead, "There is a good chance that we will have a movement from the floor to do something drastic, aimed specifically at Coon. The resolution passed last year will not serve as an answer. We cannot . . . possibly pass any censure of Coon's views and ever claim to be a body representing scientists."[41]

Just as *The Origin of Races* was released, anthropologists were attempting to deal with the place of their science in American political culture. Carleton Putnam and others were waging a very public campaign against anthropology, charging that anthropologists were responsible for "brainwashing" the American public into thinking that all races were equal. Moreover, Putnam sounded much like Carleton Coon trumpeting the virtues of physical over cultural anthropology in matters racial. He issued segregationist tracts that were dedicated to linking Coon's research to the segregationist cause, and these tracts would show up in the mailbox of any anthropologist of repute. In October 1962, this is the light by which many read *The Origin of Races*.

Dobzhansky on The Origin of Races

Ten days before the official release of *The Origin of Races,* the Charleston *News and Courier,* edited by T. R. Waring, who had written the preface to *Race and Reason,* editorialized that Coon's new book showed that "the Negro race is junior to the white race in the evolutionary calendar." The *News and Courier* claimed that Coon had documented "obvious physical differences among the races that make total integration impractical, unsound, and immoral." An acquaintance of Coon sent him the editorial, asking his opinion. His response would serve as a model for every subsequent inquiry into the use segregationists had for his book. Coon noted that he had been barraged with queries about his book, when all he really wanted to do was be left alone to write his next book. "I have no personal involvement in the tragic events of the South," Coon replied. "Were I to make a public statement of any kind my life would become even less tolerable. All I ask is that before people quote me pro or con on any national issue they read what I have said, carefully and in full, and then draw their own conclusions."[42] Coon would maintain this "neutral" stance as his book became a political rallying point for segregationists everywhere. How well it served to shield him from the public criticism he professed to dislike is questionable. Moreover, few reviewers of his book found it possible, as Coon did, to let the segregationists claim Coon's book as their own; indeed, many rushed defend Coon for what they viewed as the misuse of the central thesis of his book.

Even viewed in strictly scientific terms Coon's thesis would have been controversial, as it cut against most thinking about human evolution. Nonetheless, Coon's painstaking analysis of the existing fossil evidence and his ability to create a coherent story from that evidence won widespread admiration from reviewers. Ernst Mayr, while noting that Coon's "conclusions throughout are based on inference rather than being established by incontrovertible proof," admitted that "the basic framework of Coon's thesis is as well, or better, substantiated than various possible alternatives."[43]

Mayr's review was unusual in that it was one of the very few that contained no reference to the social implications of Coon's work. Margaret Mead perceptively noted the dilemma faced by reviewers of the book: "This repeated appeal to Coon, in a propagandistic literature that attacks both the integrity of anthropologists and the capabilities of all members of the human race . . . [means that] the reviews and discussion of *The Origin of Races* have been compromised, not only by the legitimate doubts of biologists about the sufficiency of Coon's data and the adequacy of his theory, but also by the fact that his book has been made the symbolic target for direct and indirect repudiations of the segregationist argument itself."[44]

The result is that, favorable or unfavorable, nearly every review felt it necessary to discuss the social implications as well as the scientific of the book under review. Coon's former coauthor, Joseph Birdsell, noted the problem faced by the scientific reviewers of Coon's new book: "The volume is difficult to review with complete fairness since the reviewer is obliged to deal evenhandedly both with the author and with some 2 billion nonwhites who certainly will suffer social and, consequently physical disabilities as a result of the construction which Coon places upon the Pleistocene evidences of human evolution." In a favorable review, George Gaylord Simpson noted that "Coon does not say that Congoids, now *Homo Sapiens* like everyone else, are biologically inferior in any way and it has nothing whatever to do with political and social equality of the races." Harvard's William W. Howells noted that the book had "already been pounced on with delight by the present cohort of racists and segregationists." The less-forgiving John Maddocks in the *New York Review of Books* wrote that "Professor Coon may become kind of a Herman Kahn of anthropology, remembered for a great thick book distinguished mostly by its tactlessness. . . . The uses that would be made of it were, after all, entirely predictable."[45]

In the last few months of 1962 and the first few months of 1963, many in the scientific community were concerned about the appropriation of Coon's book for segregationist ends. In December 1962, Cornell anthropologist Morris Opler wrote that "in July of this year this reviewer and many of his friends received a leaflet from a 'Committee' which has been encouraging resistance to the integration of the South" that relied on Coon's previous work. Given the present volume, Opler claimed that "it is easy to see why Coon's theories should make him the darling of segregationist 'Committees' and racists everywhere. He holds that common human ancestry is very remote and that the present racial lines have been distinct and adaptive for half a million years." In November 1962, writing to a concerned reader, Margaret Mead explained the anthropologists' current predicament. "The use that is being made of Carleton Coon's book by racists is very disturbing to all of us," wrote Mead. "In dealing with this new development, especially the campaign waged by Putnam, author of *Race and Reason,* in which he makes heavy use of Coon's speculations, we have tried to steer a course between adding to the publicity by attacking the racists, and yet making quite clear where anthropologists stand."[46]

Theodosius Dobzhansky's review of Coon highlights the controversy that surrounded the book. Dobzhansky's standing was equal to Coon's, and the particularly vituperative exchange between the men came to exemplify the debates surrounding Coon's book. In his autobiography, Coon claims that Dobzhansky "would give me no peace, not even a truce," and that Dobzhansky went as far as physically avoiding Coon at academic conferences.[47]

There was a genuine scientific dispute between the Coon and Dobzhansky. Much of the technical debate between two men would center on the role of peripheral gene flow between different races. Coon would argue that small exchanges of genetic material between *Home sapiens* and *Homo erectus* could account for pulling different groups of *erectus* through the *sapiens* threshold, hence making the possibility that *erectus* evolved five separate times into *sapiens* a likely scenario. Dobzhansky argued that in order for Coon's hypothesis to make sense, the races of *erectus* would have to be genetically isolated from each other, while the genetic isolation would disappear to allow what was essentially interspecies breeding. For Dobzhansky, such a scenario was impossible unless Coon maintained that geographical and social barriers that allowed for *erectus* evolving into races somehow disappeared to allow the exchange of genetic material when *erectus* evolved into *sapiens*. But the acrimony between the two men did not start because of a disagreement over the amount of genetic material needed for transforming one species into another or how that material was exchanged. Rather, it involved their fundamental view of the scientist's social responsibility.

The bitter dispute between Coon and Dobzhansky began when Dobzhansky was commissioned to write a review of *The Origin of Races* for the literary journal *Saturday Review*. In six double-spaced pages, Dobzhansky outlined his scientific disagreement with Coon's findings. For Dobzhansky, it was a genetic impossibility for *erectus* to transmute itself into *sapiens* by "parallel but independent development." Dobzhansky argued this could not happen without some "mystical inner drive that propels evolution." Evolution simply did not work this way, according to Dobzhansky; even granting that race was a real biological entity, "it is the whole species that evolves."

As befitting the audience for *Saturday Review*, who probably were not interested in a technical scientific debate, Dobzhansky did not dwell on the scientific aspects of Coon's work but on the scientist's responsibility in society. The main point of Dobzhansky's critique was found in its opening sentences: "Scientists living in ivory towers are now quaint relics of a bygone age. Nowadays, men of science must take note of outsiders peering at them and their work; more than ever before, their work and their writings are made of use of." Recalling the title of his review of *Race and Reason,* Dobzhansky argued that "race prejudice has time and again sought to shore itself with bogus 'science.' It appears that about 100,000 copies of a racist tract claiming to be 'scientific' have recently been distributed in this country." This was relevant for Coon's work, Dobzhansky argued, because Coon wrote bluntly and overstated his case, getting himself into "semantic mischief," because by arguing that "Congoids" evolved so much later than "Cacasoids the implication that they are also socially and culturally inferior can easily be read into the text." Dobzhansky concluded his review noting that *The Origin of Races* was the first of two books on the subject Coon was planning. Dobzhansky hoped in the second volume Coon would "clear up ambiguities and inconsistencies of the present volume, which unfortunately, lend themselves to such grievous misuse for the purpose of racist propaganda."[48]

As a matter of professional courtesy, Dobzhansky sent a prepublication copy of his review to Coon with an apologetic cover letter that "it grieves me tremendously that I have to contradict your way of describing your findings. For I feel that it is indeed the unfortunate language which you are using that creates a semantic predicament of a dangerous sort." Coon was not appeased. In response, Coon wrote that "it is incomprehensible to me that a man of your integrity and stature should misrepresent what I said so utterly, turn what was supposed to be a review into an anti-racist tract, and accuse me of 'mischievously' furnishing ammunition to racists." In a subsequent exchange of letters in the last week of October 1962, Coon wrote that "you accused me of 'mischievously' altering my style so as to provide easy quotes for political people. This is libel." Dobzhansky denied that he made such a claim, noting only that he argued that Coon got himself into "semantic mischief" with his style. If Coon doubted that his work was easily appropriated by racists, Coon should "see the letter of Garrett and George in the *New York Times.*"[49]

Henry Garrett and Wesley C. George, by now very familiar to the scientific community as outspoken white supremacists, had published a letter in the *New York Times* on October 24, 1962, in the middle of Coon and Dobzhansky's exchange of letters. In the letter, they repeated their often-heard complaints about the "cult" of Boas and its "socialistic ideology" but also called forth a paragraph in the introduction to Coon's new book where he wrote, "It is a fair inference . . . that the subspecies which crossed the evolutionary threshold into the category of Homo sapiens the earliest have evolved the most." Two Columbia anthropologists would answer Garrett and George's letter, charging them with misrepresenting Coon's book and arguing that "its misuse for political ends is only to be deplored." Coon himself had drafted, but apparently never sent, a letter to the *Times* in response to Garrett and George. In this letter, Coon directed no animus toward the segregationists who had appropriated his work but rather expressed that he felt "discouraged that a work of substance which took me five years to write and which covers the racial history of all mankind should be dismissed as a mere prop for domestic, partisan argument." This claim is particularly interesting when viewed in relationship with Coon's dispute with Dobzhansky, which was, after all, beginning that very week. Coon criticized not Garrett and George but Dobzhansky, who was guilty of "dismissing" Coon's work because it was being used by Garrett and George.[50]

Coon's response to Dobzhansky was extreme perhaps because Dobzhansky did more than merely decry the uses to which Coon's work had been put. Nearly every reviewer had commented that Coon's work had been misused by the segregationists. Dobzhansky went one step further and argued that Coon had a responsibility to speak out against this misuse, and this is what apparently raised Coon's ire. Writing to his editor at Knopf, Harold Strauss, Coon noted, "I have felt for sometime that Dobzhansky has passed his peak. I was also dimly aware that he, simpleton that he is, was well under the hairy thumb of Ashley Montagu, and now I am pretty sure of it." By invoking Montagu, Coon recast the dispute with the geneticist Dobzhansky as another aspect of the attack cultural anthropologists were waging against the use of the race concept. Although in his writings on race as well as his review of Coon, Dobzhansky rejected Montagu's claim that race was a "myth," apparently his view that scientists should take an active stance against racism tainted him in Coon's eyes.

For reasons that are not entirely clear, *Saturday Review* declined to print Dobzhansky's review.[51] By January 1963, Sol Tax, editor of *Current Anthropology*, had agreed to publish Dobzhansky's review with a response from Coon. Now writing for a strictly scientific audience, Dobzhansky emphasized his scientific differences with Coon; his social critique of Coon's irresponsible use of language remained, though it was de-emphasized. Coon saw Dobzhansky's revised review as a victory of sorts, since it focused more on the scientific questions. However, Ashley Montagu now joined the fray with a sarcastic review of Coon. As editor Tax explained, Montagu was "not always impersonal." Coon urged that Montagu's review not be revised for tone, "to show the world what kind of creature Montagu is. I certainly hope that you will not give him the chance to crawl and tone down now that Dobzhansky, whom Montagu has exploited for years, has turned in the job he has."[52]

The exchange between Coon, Montagu, and Dobzhansky would eventually appear in the October 1963 issue of *Current Anthropology*. Before it appeared, however, Coon took further steps against Dobzhansky. In February 1963, *Science* reported the remarks of Dobzhansky at the previous meeting of the American Association for the Advancement of Science (AAAS). In a brief paragraph, Dobzhansky repeated his belief that scientists "can no longer live in ivory towers" and "it is naïve and irresponsible for them to pretend they can."[53]

Coon once again was livid. He fired off a letter to *Science,* complaining about Dobzhansky's brief remarks. But Coon also sent a lengthy letter to Dobzhansky "on the advice of an eminent jurist whom I consulted on this matter" in order to get Dobzhansky to "end your campaign of defamation." Coon pointed to the other denunciations of his work, claiming that at the AAAS meeting Dobzhansky had "denounced me once more, without my knowledge." Coon claimed that the other critics of his work had taken their cue from Dobzhansky. "You are a man of great influence and many social anthropologists take your word as gospel. You have started an avalanche which you cannot stem but at least you can stop pushing it along." Coon also sent a copy of the letter to the president of Rockefeller University, Dobzhansky's home institution, calling on Detlev Bronk to get Dobzhansky to silence "his repeated accusation that I have slanted my writing to be quoted by racists." Dobzhansky sent a terse reply to Coon and repeated that he did not accuse Coon of "slanting" his style to be quoted by racists.[54]

By April, Coon's letter had an unexpected consequence when Columbia anthropologist Morton Fried publicized it in the anthropological community. Fried had long taken a public stand against Putnam and what he saw as a misuse of anthropological science. As most scientists who spoke out against racism did, Fried found himself on the receiving end of Putnam's wrath. The previous year, Putnam had written to Fried, "Your gang has had it pretty much as you wanted from the old Boas years. You've warped the minds of two generations of American youth. . . . But your games about up Fried. The American people are awakening to the laughable nonsense you've taught them."[55]

In April 1963, Fried sent a letter out to eighty-four anthropologists. He explained the events surrounding Dobzhansky's review and Coon's threat of "a slander suit." "Dobzhansky continues to receive mail," Fried explained, "from Carleton Coon and Carleton Putnam. The former still complains that Dobzhansky is persecuting him and the latter asserts that Dobzhansky knows nothing about human genetics." Fried called for anthropologists to stand together against the racists who were "gaining ground through sophisticated use of science-like arguments." According to Fried, many anthropologists refused to get involved because they felt that "this problem is old hat and that it does not require our efforts. While this is probably true scientifically, it is certainly not true in terms of race as a social issue." Unity was the key, Fried argued, because "the Putnamites and their ilk will spill their filth on anybody and any institution that becomes involved, but the more people and the more places the weaker and sillier will be his position."[56]

Coon received copies of the letter through Conrad Arensberg, the chair of the Columbia Department of Anthropology, and Anthony Wallace, chair of the Anthropology Department at the University of Pennsylvania. Both men advised Coon to forget the matter because, as Arensberg noted, Fried's "polemic is against Putnam, as you'll see, not you." Nonetheless, Coon claimed in his autobiography that he called Arensberg, who then summoned Fried and Margaret Mead to his office for a dressing down for their "conspiratorial" actions. Coon also called Columbia president Lawrence H. Chamberlain and demanded some sort of action. Chamberlain explained that Fried "wrote as an individual" and that the letter contained no "charges or intimations inimical to your interests."[57]

Coon's responses to his critics did little to distance him from the public controversy over the role of anthropology in the segregation issue. His threatened legal action and his attempts to apply administrative pressure to his critics could hardly be viewed sympathetically by his scientific colleagues. Coon's steadfast refusal to disavow Putnam's use of his book suggested that Coon was sympathetic to Putnam's aims. Coon seemed unable to distinguish an attack on Putnam from an attack on Coon. In the case of Fried's letter, for example, even Coon's allies advised him that the matter was directed at Putnam and did not directly concern him. Therefore, Coon's response to the letter could easily have been interpreted as a defense of Putnam. Indeed, given what we now know about Coon's close association with Putnam, it may have been such a defense.

Given the extensive "behind the scenes" maneuvering, there was little new information in actual reviews by Dobzhansky and Montagu that appeared in October 1963. As was to be expected, Montagu and Coon exchanged pointed remarks on matters that were far from central to the main scientific disputes. Coon maintained that "irresponsible and doctrinaire effusions, such as the one printed here . . . do much to spread a poor impression among exact scientists of the competence and responsibility and dignity of anthropologists."[58] Coon's claim that it was Dobzhansky and Montagu, rather than Putnam and George, who were tarnishing the image of anthropology must have been frustrating for many scientists who were looking for ways to respond to the segregationists. Perhaps nothing illustrates this better than Coon's response to Sherwood Washburn's 1962 AAA presidential address.

Sherwood Washburn and the Anti-Defamation League

In November 1962, Sherwood Washburn delivered his presidential address to the American Anthropological Association. It was intended to be a summary of the most current thinking regarding race, to provide a method to counter Putnam's invocation of science to support racial segregation.

Like Coon, Washburn had been trained as a physical anthropologist under Earnest Hooton. Unlike Coon, however, Washburn had gone to great pains to distance himself from his training. In his address, Washburn took aim at the sort of anthropology Coon exemplified by belittling his own, and by extension Coon's, training. "If we look back at the time when I was educated, races were regarded as types. We were taught to go to a population and divide it into a series of types and to re-create history out of this artificial arrangement. . . . This kind of anthropology is still alive, amazingly. . . . Genetics shows us that typology must be completely removed from our thinking if we are to progress."[59]

Washburn claimed that the physical anthropologists were so concerned with the subdivisions of humankind that they forgot evolution works on a species level, not on the level of races. He asserted that modern scientific thinking on race must draw from genetics to explain local variations in the species. According to Washburn, the use of genetics in anthropology "affirms the relation of culture and biology in a far firmer and more important way than ever in our history before. Selection is for reproductive success, and in man reproductive success is primarily determined by the social system and by culture."[60]

In the final portion of his address, Washburn argued against racism as "a relic supported by no phase of modern science." Recounting the toll discrimination took on "education, medical care, and economic progress," he proclaimed that "[a] ghetto of hatred kills more surely than a concentration camp, because it kills by accepted custom, and kills every day in the year."[61]

Coon was not too disturbed by Washburn's remarks. Although he had not attended the AAA address, he was convinced that the version printed in the *American Anthropologist* was, as he wrote to Putnam, "a much watered down version," containing "nothing that I needed to answer."[62] However, the AAA had planned Washburn's address to be used by public agencies seeking an authoritative statement on race. When it was used in this way, reprinted as an answer to Putnam, Coon's attitude toward what Washburn had to say about race would change.

In the summer of 1963 the Anti-Defamation League (ADL) of B'nai B'rith issued a pamphlet, *Race and Intelligence: An Evaluation,* designed to be an answer to Carleton Putnam, Henry Garrett, and Wesley C. George. Washburn was one of four scientists asked a series of questions about the segregationists' charge of a scientific cover-up regarding the worth of the races. In the ensuing "question and answer" section of the pamphlet, Washburn and the others responded to a series of questions concerned with the relationship between race and IQ levels. The short pamphlet concluded by reprinting Washburn's presidential address to the AAA. *The Origin of Races* was mentioned only twice: once in Washburn's address and once when the editor of the volume noted that "Dr. George leans rather heavily" on Coon's book.[63]

Putnam immediately sprang into action, writing off to Harry Weyher suggesting a "symposium of replies from Garrett, George, Coon, and my-self, all of whom are attacked" in the ADL booklet. Putnam noted that "if Coon did not care to write anything specifically for the symposium he might be willing to apply material he has already written and published elsewhere in answer to Dobzhansky and Washburn."[64]

Like Putnam, Coon took action when confronted with the ADL booklet. Immediately after hearing of its existence, he fired off a letter to the ADL about the work. Harry Schwarzchild, ADL director of publications, forwarded Coon's letter to Washburn and Princeton anthropologist Melvin Tumin, the volume's editor. But Schwarzchild also noted that Coon "could not have been unaware of the (perhaps unintended or even

unsanctioned) uses that would be made of your theses" by those who believed in the "essential bestiality of the American Negro" and wondered
why Coon did not "disclaim it in your book or at least to disavow it
firmly in the public debate that ensued after its publication."[65]

In his reply to Coon, Tumin took issue with Coon's charge that he and
the ADL had "dragged" Coon into the "civil rights controversy"; rather
it was "a group of Southern racists about whose plaudits of your work
and misuses of it you must certainly have been aware." Tumin argued, "If
you had chosen to speak out openly about their misconstructions of your
work, this might have put an end to it all. However, in the face of your silence . . . it was quite reasonable to infer either that you approved of what
they were doing or that you did not care." Tumin urged Coon that he "inform such gentlemen as Carleton Putnam and Wesley Critz George . . . regarding your own views of the legitimacy of their use of your book."
Coon replied that he did not "approve of the concept that I have to approve or disapprove of anything" regarding the use of his book. Moreover, Coon wrote that he did "not like to be told what to do or say, particularly in the face of pressure or intimidation."[66]

Of course, Coon was well aware of Putnam's use of his book; indeed,
he had guided Putnam in how to build a careful argument against cultural
anthropology. But, as before, Coon declined to join Putnam in public. He
helped Putnam with technical questions about the relationship of brain
size to intelligence but would not write any specific material for Putnam's
response to the ADL. Coon also toyed with the idea of bringing a defamation suit against the ADL for their booklet.[67]

The final answer to the ADL was written by Garrett, George, and Putnam, published by Putnam's National Letters Committee, funded by
Draper, and distributed by the IAAEE. Although he was pleased with
their final effort, Garrett expressed little hope that it would convince anyone in the scientific community; rather, he believed that "the rank-and-file
intelligent white is our best bet for reversing the tide. . . . The ordinary
white man who is called to eat and live with the Bantu is the one who
balks: he knows personally what 'integration' means."[68]

American Association for the Advancement of Science

As the controversy with the AAA was beginning to show signs of slow-
ing, the segregationist scientists received another blow from the American

Association for the Advancement of Science (AAAS). The AAAS committee, formed at the same time the AAA resolution condemning the segregationist scientists was passed, issued a report in November 1963. There were two main issues the report attempted to address. First was the concern that science was being used to deny Negroes their constitutional rights. The committee report pointed specifically to George and Putnam as two well-known advocates of the position that science had decided the question in favor of segregation. The second issue was the contention that "a group of scientists has conspired to mislead the public about scientific evidence regarding racial differences." The committee report pointed out that the segregationist scientists

> have been far from silent. If these scientists have assiduously expressed what they know and what they believe about racial difference, then their duty toward the truth has been performed. If their ideas have spread and attracted the attention and support of other scientists, then it should be clear that they have in fact successfully withstood scrutiny and criticism.[69]

The obverse proposition, that the segregationist scientists' views had been heard and failed to withstand critical examination, was not explicitly stated but clearly implied. The committee pointed to the controversies in the 1950s over the UNESCO statements on race as evidence that free discussion on racial issues took place within the mainstream scientific community. They quite pointedly contrasted this discussion with George's *Biology of the Race Problem*, which had been prepared for the segregationist Alabama governor's office rather than for a peer-reviewed journal.

In their response, the segregationists demonstrated that they really did not understand the nature of free and open exchange of ideas. George flatly rejected the idea that "I should have submitted my paper for review by (and veto by equalitarian) scientists." Unable to distinguish a criticism from censorship, he wrote to a friend that "the AAAS has embarked upon an extensive campaign to suppress me and Carleton Putnam." If the AAAS were trying to suppress George, they did a poor job of it, for *Science* published a response written by Garrett and submitted over Garrett's and George's signatures that was nearly as long as the original committee report, as well as a lengthy letter by Putnam.[70]

Nathaniel Weyl, a regular contributor to *Mankind Quarterly* and close friend of Putnam, suggested "a slander suit (or perhaps a criminal action for malicious slander) by you or Professor George against the members of the Committee individually and the AAAS for publishing their findings. This is a calculated effort to destroy your and George's reputation with the scientific community." Putnam quickly contacted his lawyer on this possibility, only to be told by him that it was "clear . . . that there are no direct defamatory words used either as to Dr. George or yourself." The attorney tried to make clear to Putnam what obviously was not: that the open exchange of ideas required that writers lay themselves open to criticism of their writing, or "there could be no critical book reviews."[71] Putnam, however, seemed to see any deviation from his views as a hanging offense, which made him both a tireless promoter of the segregationist scientists' cause and, ultimately, the cause's undoing. For even potential allies were becoming alienated by Putnam.

Debate with Ingle

On February 12, 1963, in celebration of Lincoln's birthday Carleton Putnam gave one of his many lectures defending segregation. He claimed that "all of the evidence" one needed to prove that integration would be disastrous "is contained in a short, concise little book, *The Biology of the Race Problem.*" Putnam laid out all of George's evidence for morphological differences between white and black brains and concluded, "The differences in question are physical and hereditary. That they account for differences in temperament, behavior, and intelligence between the two races is beyond doubt. That these differences make the amalgamation of the races undesirable is just as clear."[72]

As for all of Putnam's writing, the National Putnam Letters Committee sent a transcript of Putnam's lecture to "thought leaders" around the nation. One of the recipients was Dwight J. Ingle, a physiologist at the University of Chicago. Ingle was the editor of the prestigious journal *Perspectives in Biology and Medicine* and was a potential ally for the segregationist scientists. Two years earlier, in 1961, Ingle had published Henry Garrett's essay "The Equalitarian Dogma," wherein Garrett called the work of Boas and his followers "the most potent assault upon native racial differences" yet made, although the conclusions of cultural anthropologists "are often subjective and unconvincing." Garrett published the same piece in *Mankind Quarterly* except that he added "Jews" to the list of those responsible for the equalitarian dogma.[73]

Garrett's piece brought a spirited response from Melville Herskovits, who may have noticed the similarity between Garrett's thesis and Carleton Putnam's letters. The subsequent debate on Garrett's thesis spilled over into several issues of the journal.[74] Ingle defended his decision to publish Garrett's diatribe because "the polemic can stimulate thought, debate, and research." Ingle believed that more research was needed, for "the evidence for and against the proposition [of racial equality] is unsatisfactory."[75] Here was a possible ally for the segregationist cause, and one who was the editor of a prestigious biomedical journal that mainstream scientists could not ignore the way they could the *Mankind Quarterly*.

In February 1962, just after Ingle published Garrett's article, Ingle and Putnam began carrying out a vigorous correspondence on the merits of the evidence for racial inferiority, particularly the evidence that had become Putnam's favorite weapon against the equalitarians: the morphological differences in brain structure between whites and African Americans.

In his letters, Ingle attempted to lay out the shortcomings of the evidence George had presented in *Biology of the Race Problem*. Ingle noted that the studies of Bean and Mall were a half-century old and noted the same shortcoming in Vint's study of the Kenyan natives that Kuttner would note in his correspondence preparing for the *Stell* trial. Ingle argued that while these studies indicated there was a probability of significant differences between the brains of the two races, they certainly could not be taken as definitive. In his response, Putnam was almost brutal. He argued, "When it comes to social integration with its inevitable ultimate sequel in intermarriage, which is the better plan, to base public policy on what you call a probability, or to base it on improbability, as the United States is presently doing?"[76] Ingle's argument that more research was needed on racial differences drove Putnam to apoplexy:

You are a timid little academician with the intellectual conformity of sheep. You know full well that the overwhelming weight of evidence is enough to sink the American and British navies, yet you talk about waiting for more. You don't want more evidence, Ingle. You just want to hide behind a tree while white men are being gassed at Oxford, dispossessed and murdered in Kenya and slugged in Washington. They are being gassed and slugged and murdered because men in your sciences have spent thirty years lying to the Negro about himself and betraying the civilization that gave you suck. You have stood idly and silently while a hard core of Marxist subversives in your midst lied not only to the Negro but to the Supreme Court and the American people.[77]

In 1963, a few months after Ingle received the above letter from Putnam, Ingle took the dispute public in the pages *Perspectives in Biology and Medicine*. He laid out what he considered the requirements for adequate scientific proof for claiming significant differences in the brains of the white and black races:

> It would be necessary to gather representative samples of brains from different races in which environment, including prenatal and postnatal nutrition, was equivalent. The factors of age and health would have to be controlled. The brains would have to be removed from skulls at the same time after death; fixed, processed, and measured by identical methods; and then studied as "unknowns" by not one but several experts. If it were possible to establish significant average differences in brains among races, it still would remain to be shown that any difference is a mark of superiority or inferiority or a physical measure of intellect or other quality of mind. Claims to knowledge must withstand replication of the experiments which supply the evidence as well as debate and criticism of the design of the study, the technical details, and the interpretation of data.

Ingle explained the views of Putnam and George on the racial differences in brain structure and then noted that these men relied on just three studies for their position, those of Bean, Mall, and Connolly. Ingle concluded, "There was not one relevant variable controlled in any of the three studies, and the samples of each were highly selected."[78]

But Ingle went further. After his piece criticizing the studies on which Putnam and George relied for their comparative claims, he printed letters he had solicited from the authors of the studies on the importance of frontal lobes in the "maintenance of higher civilization." Wilder Penfield, Theodore Rasmussen, and Ward C. Halstead all categorically rejected the claims of George and Putnam. Penfield wrote, "I know of no good evidence of superiority in structure or function of the brain of white or black, either way." Halstead wanted to repudiate the "views on racism set forth by George and Putnam."[79] The letters printed by Ingle would open the dam to a flood of repudiations by authors quoted in *Biology of the Race Problem*. Within six months, eighteen of the thirty-one authorities quoted by George would repudiate the uses to which their work had been put. Such a state of affairs had been predicted by the IAAEE board member, geneticist Clarence P. Oliver, who had warned both Garrett and George that he was "certain" George would be accused of quoting authorities out of context.[80]

The dispute with Ingle came to a conclusion of sorts in the pages of the *Mankind Quarterly* when Ingle published a longer critique of the methodology of the studies relied upon by Putnam and George and argued that, given the enormous difficulties involved in neuroanatomical research, conclusive proof of racial differences in brain structure was an impossibility. Once again, however, deviations from the viewpoints of the editors was not be tolerated by *Mankind Quarterly*. Throughout Ingle's piece, any claim he made that did not follow the segregationist stance was given an "editorial footnote" in which an editor, undoubtedly Gayre or Garrett, pointed out Ingle's error. Segregationist scientists were allowed to publish their responses to attacks on their views in *Man, Science, Current Anthropology,* and *Perspectives in Biology and Medicine* without such editorial impertinence. Yet *Mankind Quarterly,* supposedly dedicated to an open discussion on race, could not allow even a somewhat sympathetic author access to its pages without editorial insertions making it clear where he was straying from racist orthodoxy.[81]

In his response, Putnam maintained his previous position, that the evidence indicated a probability that there were racial differences. Putnam then argued that the reason the evidence was not better was that the equalitarian scientific establishment refused to investigate the matter further. "Ingle suggests that in the nature of things this is impossible, but here he is wrong," Putnam wrote. "With the hundreds of millions of dollars available to them through leftist American foundations, these scientists could easily finance a project controlled to the most exacting taste. However, they have not conducted such tests and will not conduct any. For obvious reasons, they do not dare."[82] In other words, the equalitarian conspiracy had prevented the final proof of Negro inferiority. Even the lack of proof, Putnam argued, proved his point.

Soon after his exchange with Ingle, things began unraveling for Putnam. His dream of overturning *Brown* had met with failure. Anthropologists, even physical anthropologists, and geneticists criticized or ignored his arguments for white supremacy. The final blow was the passage of the Civil Rights Act in 1964. Putnam, with Draper's largesse, had been part of the Coordinating Committee for Fundamental American Freedoms (CCFAF), a Mississippi organization dedicated to defeating the proposed Civil Rights Act.[83]

He was not the only member of the IAAEE to fight the Civil Rights Act. Robert Kuttner testified in opposition to the act as a representative of the Liberty Lobby, Willis Carto's successor group to Liberty and Property. "In the area of scientific opinion," Kuttner told the congressional committee, "there has been Communist activity" promoting their ideology in the guise of science. The committee members, not understanding who they were dealing with, spent some time trying to link the Liberty Lobby with the John Birch Society, obviously unaware that Willis Carto was asked by John Welch, the Birch Society founder, to leave the society because of his extreme anti-Semitism.[84]

When it passed in 1964, the Civil Rights Act finally put federal teeth in the *Brown* decision, and many southern politicians ran for the cover of states' rights, denying that their opposition to *Brown* or the Civil Rights Act ever had anything to do with white supremacy. Putnam, who had always scolded southern politicians for not taking a firm stand on Negro inferiority, was increasingly isolated from his political allies. He would never again grace the stage in Jackson, holding forth on the equalitarian conspiracy to foist miscegenation on a naive American public. Yet the fight was not quite out of him. He would find new allies, and in most unlikely places.

8

Back to the Underground?

The views of the segregationist scientists fell into increasing disrepute after 1964. George, slightly older than the others and with fading eyesight, would contribute little to the cause after 1964. Garrett would continue writing and publishing (with Draper's money), warning the public on the dangers of desegregation until his death in 1972. For, the New York branch of the IAAEE—Gregor, Swan, and Kuttner—their career paths would take markedly different turns. Putnam would continue his attacks on the scientific establishment, though his public presence would never be as great as it was before 1964. His fervor and his certainty that his own position was the only acceptable one began to hurt his cause, though he did not seem to notice it.

Buckley and Putnam

In the years after World War II, conservatives of many stripes criticized what they perceived as the leftist drift of university education.[1] William F. Buckley Jr. sounded the opening salvo with his first, 1951 book, *God and Man at Yale,* where he charged Yale with indoctrinating "collectivism" rather than "individualism." This, Buckley charged, was part of Karl Marx's subtle plan "to destroy the bourgeoisie . . . through extended social services, taxation, and regulation, to a point where a smooth transition could be effected from an individualist to a collectivist society."[2] Other conservatives soon followed Buckley's lead and charged the universities with inculcating communism among unsuspecting college students.[3]

In this atmosphere, the notion that anthropological science had been co-opted by a leftist political agenda bent on weakening the nation would certainly have been appealing to the respectable Right represented

179

by *National Review.* Indeed, two IAAEE stalwarts, Ernest van den Haag and Nathaniel Weyl, were both closely associated with Buckley's magazine. When mainstream conservatives such as Buckley's colleague E. Merrill Root proclaimed that "a small minority of communists have been able to 'condition' the large majority of non-Communists" into collectivist thinking, such a stand could have given credibility to charges that a small clique of leftist, Boasian coconspirators had inculcated false doctrines of racial equality.[4]

Any hope of an alliance between Buckley and the IAAEE, however, was dashed as soon as Putnam came in contact with Buckley in 1965. Putnam sent Buckley a copy of one of his publications with a note that Buckley should stop concentrating on the dangers of communism because "all the talk in the world about Communism will do no good until you unmask the fraud that makes our people sympathetic to Communist ideals." After receiving a polite response from Buckley that made it clear he was unconvinced by Putnam's materials, Putnam became more forthright. He pointed out that if conservatives like Buckley had publicized the *Stell* case, "it could have blown the roof off public opinion as to the whole rotten foundation under *Brown v. Board of Education.*"[5]

Buckley refused to rise to Putnam's bait. He explained that any objections he had to integration were not based on race but on coercion: he rejected coerced segregation as well as coerced integration, echoing the position that van den Haag had taken in his published writings, which considered all integration to be "coerced" or "forced." Buckley argued that Christianity recognized all people were equal before the Lord. If modern science had different findings, it was irrelevant to the issue. "My observation," concluded Buckley, "which appears to go beyond your grasp, is that religion goes beyond the grasp of the little scientists who are always asseverating their latest little discoveries and constructing theologies around them." Buckley told Putnam that "I would send my son only to the best school I could afford to send him to. If it had Negroes in it, I would not the least mind."[6]

The question that faced the mainstream anthropological establishment at the opening of the preceding chapter now faced the *Mankind Quarterly* crowd: What to do about Carleton Putnam? Many were recognizing that he was the proverbial bull in the china shop. The situation was discussed openly by a friend of both Putnam and Buckley, Nathaniel Weyl, who was a reliable writer for both *Mankind Quarterly* and *National Review.*

In comparison to many writers for *Mankind Quarterly*, Weyl was fairly moderate, even daring to admit in private that he could see some circumstances under which miscegenation might be permissible. That being said, these differences in opinion between Weyl and other *Mankind Quarterly* writers were not readily apparent in works such as *The Negro in American Civilization*, which sported an approving introduction from Frank C. J. McGurk and presaged much of Putnam's *Race and Reason*, or Weyl's book coauthored with Stephan Possney, *The Geography of American Intellect*, which was so much a retelling of Galton's *Hereditary Genius* that Robert Gayre dubbed him "the modern exponent of Galtonism."[7]

Besides his racial writings, however, Weyl was a staunch anti-Communist. He had been a Communist in the 1930s and had, in fact, belonged to the same Communist cell to which Alger Hiss was reputed to have belonged. In the 1950s, Weyl had come forward to testify before Congress as to his former life and began a series of anti-Communist writings. It was this writing that made him valuable for Buckley and *National Review*.[8]

After the Buckley–Putnam exchange of letters, Weyl wrote to Gayre that he was concerned about Putnam's recent behavior. "To say that Carleton's letters [to Buckley] were overaggressive would be putting the matter mildly," Weyl confided. In fairly short order, Weyl complained, Putnam had alienated two potential allies to the cause: Buckley and Ingle. Gayre was sympathetic that Putnam had crossed the line with the two men. "I would have thought," wrote Gayre, "to win [them] over should be our policy, not to punch [them] in the nose." He suggested a plan to "bring Ingle, Putnam, and Buckley together, and then begin to run them in harness. If we could do that we would bring a considerable strength to the intellectual exposition of the conservative side." Weyl explained to Gayre that the chances of getting Buckley, who had his own magazine, newspaper column, and extensive television coverage of his views, to write for the *Mankind Quarterly* was not possible.[9]

Gayre's comments on "the conservative side" were also revealing, since *Mankind Quarterly*'s avowed purpose was apolitical. However, even the journal's allies, such as Weyl, were beginning to suspect it was not truly a scientific periodical. In 1964, writing to his coauthor Stefan Possony, Weyl complained that

Mankind Quarterly has recently been devoting a great deal of space to articles which are primarily agitational and argumentative, which are

concerned with the Negro problem specifically and not with ethnic issues generally, which contribute nothing of scientific value and which
are the grist for the organized Southern segregationists. The thought oc-
curred to me that Gayre must be getting his financing from the Citizens'
Councils either through such people as Col. Draper or directly and that
the quid pro quo is to change the character of the review.[10]

When Weyl asked Gayre directly about this very issue, Gayre responded
that "the *MQ* is not to serve the ends of the segregationist philosophy
[but] there are merits in the segregationist case which do not readily get
published, and so I am willing to publish these papers." However, Gayre
concluded, "I would rather have much more ethnological material: but I
can only work with the material I am receiving."[11] *Mankind Quarterly*
may not have started with the aim of being an arm of the segregationist
movement, yet it nonetheless functioned as one within a few years of its
existence, and as such, scholars were avoiding the journal. The conspiracy charges of the segregationist scientists might have sunk into obscurity
had they not found new champions for the larger public.

William B. Shockley, Arthur Jensen, and Carleton Putnam

In 1965, Nobel laureate William B. Shockley announced to the world that
the most serious problem facing human society was the genetic deterio-
ration of the human species. Shockley called for a new eugenics aimed at
limiting the propagation of the unfit in order to ensure the future of humankind. Shockley bemoaned that sterilization laws enacted in the 1920s
and 1930s were still on the books but not enforced, and he noted that "although census bureau studies have shown poverty and lack of education
are passed on from generation to generation within families, research on
genetic versus environmental aspects is apparently lacking."[12] Shockley's
remarks came during the increased student activism of the 1960s and the
nation's War on Poverty. He seemed to welcome the controversy that his
views caused, and his frequent public appearances were often sites of vigorous protests and outcry, themselves then regularly claimed as proof of
the conspiracy to silence scientific truths. "To the segregationists,"
William Tucker wrote, "Shockley's emergence was a godsend, as if they
had won the lottery without even having bought a ticket." Immediately

Shockley became the beneficiary of Draper's largesse, as the latter rerouted his money to the Nobel laureate.[13]

In 1966, Dwight Ingle established contact with Shockley, but he came with warnings. "Beware of Carleton Putnam," Ingle wrote, "he is a racist." In a later letter Ingle explained that "if our efforts ever become identified or even slightly associated with those of Carleton Putnam, we will fail to gain support." Ingle explained that Putnam, who was constantly complaining about stifling of freedom of speech, had threatened Ingle with a lawsuit should Ingle publish Putnam's letters to him. Ingle warned that Shockley should also steer clear of *Mankind Quarterly*, which was a "miserable journal."[14]

Despite these warnings, Shockley entered into a cautious relationship with Putnam. What is revealing about their relationship is that Shockley was not calling for segregation, usually a minimum requirement for Putnam's respect. While his increasingly bizarre writings on race made it obvious that he thought scientific studies would reveal black inferiority to white, his main call was for more scientific research into the area. A few years earlier, when Dwight Ingle had made a similar call for more research, Putnam's response had been to call for Ingle's head on a platter. Yet, when Shockley made the same call for more scientific research, Putnam's response was enthusiastically to second the motion. Perhaps Putnam was cowed by the Nobel laureate, or more likely he realized that Shockley, like Coon, was too valuable a resource for him to insult.

When Shockley called to the National Academy of Sciences (NAS) for more racial research, Putnam followed it with a letter of his own, supporting Shockley's proposal. "There is no credible evidence whatever on the side of the equalitarian theory," he wrote to NAS president Frederick Seitz, yet "our state and federal legislatures, executive departments and higher courts are committed to policies founded on the equalitarian dogma. . . . Our highest court cannot even bring itself to look at the record of the trial courts."[15]

It was undoubtedly the conspiracy claim that drew Shockley to Putnam, rather than any devotion to segregation. Early in his eugenics crusade, Shockley wrote to Carleton Coon to inquire about the political opposition to Coon's racial writings. "The movement against me seems to be dying down," Coon answered. "I prefer not be quoted on the suppression of my publications."[16] In his subsequent writings, a central point Shockley put forth in his eugenics speeches and writing was that there was a "taboo" against scientific research into the hereditary aspects of intelligence. Despite Ingle's warnings, Shockley pointed to Putnam's claims in *Race and Reason* and stated, "I found it straightforward to confirm Putnam's reporting of how these taboos block the seeking of enlightenment about our human-quality problems, especially as they may have racial aspects."[17]

William Shockley was soon joined by a quieter and more sophisticated voice, Berkeley psychologist Arthur Jensen, whose 1969 article in the *Harvard Educational Review* claimed that white and black differences in IQ scores were genetic in nature and impervious to environmental modification. Even before his 1969 article Putnam was writing to Jensen, offering his services as a liaison between Jensen and high-level governmental officials. In 1968, Putnam noted how important it was for Jensen's findings to be "rapidly disseminated and implemented as quickly as possible."[18] Jensen, however, maintained that nothing in his work lent any support to the racial segregation of schools. A few years after Jensen's 1969 article was published, in long lunch meeting, Putnam "took pains to explain our view of the inconsistency of [Jensen's] position on the existence of innate race differences when compared with his stand on school integration." Jensen, however, was unmoved and continued to insist that his work did not lend support to the segregationist cause.[19]

However, Jensen did continue the conspiratorial claim of the segregationists. In the subsequent controversy that swirled around Jensen, he consistently lamented that "a block [on scientific research into racial differences] has been raised because of obvious implications for the understanding of racial differences in ability and achievement. Serious consideration of whether genetic as well as environmental factors are involved has been taboo in academic circles." Jensen trotted out the classic cases of politicized science as well: "In the bizarre racist theories of the Nazis and in the disastrous Lysenkoism of the Soviet Union under Stalin, we have seen clear examples of what happens when science is corrupted by servitude to political dogma."[20] The conspiracy claim worked well for Shockley and Jensen. Throughout the late 1960s and early 1970s, the press's coverage of their controversial work was often agnostic on the racial aspect of their beliefs while fervently supporting their freedom of inquiry.[21]

Kuttner and Shockley

Perhaps because he was a new assistant professor, perhaps because his political work had occupied so much of his time, Kuttner had published only the occasional professional paper in the scientific literature. Beginning in 1964, first at Creighton and then at a University of Chicago hospital, Kuttner published a number of articles on the social distress experienced by Sioux Indians. These articles, underwritten by the Human Genetics Fund, a branch of Wickliffe Draper's Pioneer Fund, appeared in mainstream medical and psychological journals and detailed the health effects of slum living on urbanized American Indian populations, expounding on the stresses associated with the social position of this minority group.[22]

Kuttner brought his research to the attention of Shockley, telling the physicist that he was welcome to Kuttner's data on American Indians and could "use this argument and all related considerations in any way you can, and I hope you get a forum which reaches enough people of influence who can urge a re-evaluation of the role of genes in social performance."[23] Knowing Kuttner's racial views, and knowing that Draper certainly was not interested in funding any research aimed at the uplift of any of the colored races, Kuttner's research seems anomalous. It wasn't until 1968 that Kuttner explained the reasoning behind this particular line of research, in a paper presented at the National Academy of Sciences, sponsored by William Shockley, and later reprinted in the *Mankind Quarterly*. Kuttner wanted to use his research on the American Indians not as a way to help the Indian but as a way to prove the genetic inferiority of African Americans. In his NAS paper, Kuttner outlined the social history of American Indians under European domination. Kuttner argued the Indian's treatment by whites was worse than that of African Americans:

> While the Negro was a subservient but functional part of American civilization, the Indian had barely emerged from a Neolithic culture and was waging guerrilla warfare against intrusive frontier elements. The same regiments that emancipated the Negro were dispatched to exterminate the Indians. The same legislative bodies that debated with unprecedented candor the morality of genocidal attacks on peaceful Indians. The same founding declaration which expresses a belief in the quality of men refers to the Indian as a merciless savage.[24]

By most measures, American Indians continued to live under social circumstances worse than those experienced by African Americans, yet Indians consistently outscored African Americans on IQ tests. Thus, concluded Kuttner,

> [t]he results of comparisons of Indian and Negro school children indicate that the former record distinctly superior performance despite a generally inferior socio-economic position in society. This serves to demonstrate that the factors commonly regarded as exerting a decisive formative influence on test performance are strongly modified by the inherent capacities of the groups involved.[25]

Only hinted at in his NAS presentation was Kuttner's belief that African Americans had ever experienced significant oppression at the hands of white society. Writing in *American Mercury,* one of Willis Carto's publications, Kuttner explained that when Europeans were enslaved by the Turks, "instead of collapsing in the face of such a challenge, they overcame all obstacles till freedom was attained." Concluded Kuttner, "Comparing the record of the Negro, with his easier slavery, with his emancipation by outside forces, with his opportunities to learn and work for himself, we would expect that if he matched the white man in energy and spirit," he would have excelled. "This did not happen, and perhaps the White man is at fault for making the road too easy for the emancipated Negro."[26]

In 1971, Shockley brought Kuttner onto his staff, paid with Draper's money. Although both Shockley and Kuttner issued frequent calls for more research, neither man conducted research on race or anything else. Instead, Kuttner used his position to circulate his own writings from *Truth Seeker* and *Right,* believing that this would be the key to an open dialogue on race.[27] But it was probably too late for the segregationist cause. Indeed, the alliance represented by the IAAEE was almost fully unraveled by 1971. In many ways the IAAEE came to an effective end in 1967, when three key works were published that significantly changed the dynamics of the movement. Carleton Putnam published a second book on the *Stell* trials, *Race and Reality*; the IAAEE at long last published their answer to the UNESCO statements on race, *Race and Modern Science*; and historian I. A. Newby published a study of the *Stell* case, *Challenge to the Court.* Each of these books marked a change in the dynamics of the IAAEE.

Race and Reality

Carleton Putnam's sequel to *Race and Reason* was an attempt to resusci-
tate the brief victory of the *Stell* case. He recounted the events that led to
the case, as well what he found to be the incredible refusal of the case to
reverse *Brown*. The book contained the now well rehearsed tirades
against Boasian anthropology. Once again, Theodosius Dobzhansky reviewed Putnam for the *Journal of Heredity*. Dobzhansky asked why it
was that "the vast majority of scientifically informed people the world
over have rejected racist arguments" like those of Putnam. "Why," asked
Dobzhansky, "is almost everybody except Putnam and his followers so
blind?" Dobzhansky argued that Putnam's "explanation is so ridiculous
that one wonders if even many racists can believe it: a conspiracy hatched
by Franz Boas and his students!" He noted that Putnam was not always
careful about who was in the conspiracy. "This reviewer," Dobzhansky
stated, "is undeservedly honored by being listed among students of Boas,
is alleged to be now retired, and is justly accused of having been born in
Russia."[28]

Dobzhansky argued that more serious example of Putnam's twisting of
facts was his use of Coon's work as a defense of segregation. Dobzhansky repeated his scientific criticism of Coon's work and wrote, "Regret-
tably, Dr. Coon has not seen fit to state whether he approves or disap-
proves of his scientific hypothesis being used by Mr. Putnam for the latter's very unscientific ends. . . . It is a duty of a scientist to prevent misuse
and prostitution of his findings."[29]

Putnam sent a copy of Dobzhansky's review to Coon, who told him,
"It is clear [Dobzhansky] does not understand the mechanisms of evolution," but the journal "is read by a small number of specialists. . . . I can't
see that his review is of any great importance." Despite his soothing tone
to Putnam, however, Coon sent a heated letter off to the journal that disagreed with Dobzhansky about the duty of scientists. Coon claimed he
had no duty to prevent the misuse of his findings; "it is the duty of a scientist to do his work conscientiously and to the best of his ability . . . and
to reject publicly only the writings of those persons who, influenced by
one cause or another, have misquoted him." Concluded Coon, "Had Mr.
Putnam misquoted me I would have said so long ago."[30]

The exchange in *Journal of Heredity* was the last public dispute among
Coon, Dobzhansky, and Putnam, and *Race and Reality* was Putnam's last
public broadside against anthropology. Putnam saw that he had lost the

battle to preserve "white civilization" in the South. Though he would live another thirty years, he never spoke out publicly on racial issues again, though he continued to be very active privately.

Coon never forgot the "pontifications of that stuffed jackass Dobzhansky." For Coon, Dobzhansky's criticisms were only part of the ongoing feud cultural anthropologists had with his work and were political, not scientific, in nature. "I don't think that there is any question," he wrote to a friend, "about the socio-political influence of the Boasinine school at Columbia or its source. They have been trying to suppress me ever since Boas tried to suppress my *Races of Europe* in the 1930s." The criticisms of *The Origin of Races* came from "the doctrinaires. . . . The social anthropologists, almost to a man, fell in line behind the Boas dogma." For Coon, then, the reception afforded his work was merely another chapter in a long war with his chief scientific rival, the Columbia school of anthropology.[31]

What Coon seemed not to understand, however, is the extent that his war with cultural anthropology had been transformed into a political battle for scientific authority. Carleton Putnam and his associates had adopted Coon's rhetoric and proclaimed cultural anthropology as responsible for "brainwashing" the American public about race. Far from being a curious sidebar to the reception of *The Origin of Races,* Putnam is central to the story. Anthropologists did not suddenly develop a social conscience in the early 1960s and unjustifiably criticize Coon for not following their path. Rather, Putnam had forced them to explain the role their science should play in society.

The scientific community, exemplified by Theodosius Dobzhansky and Sherwood Washburn, recognized that they could not avoid the social implications of their science. Putnam had issued a direct challenge to their scientific authority, both in his public writings and his private letters. Concerned citizens and official agencies (such as the Southern Educational Reporting Service) were coming to them, asking for a response to Putnam's charges. Throughout the early 1960s, anthropologists were attempting to come to grips with an appropriate response to this situation.

Yet anthropologists were constrained by what they could accomplish as scientists. While they had an evolving sensibility about their social responsibility, they were unsure what actions they could take, *as scientists,* to remedy the situation. The scientific resolution was seen as one possible response. These resolutions, it should be noted, were reactive devices. For example, it was only *after* the state of Louisiana required science students to read *Race and Reason* that the American Association of Physical Anthropologists could justify issuing its statement condemning the book.

Direct responses to Putnam were debated and often rejected. It was felt that scientists should not dignify the polemicist by engaging him. Therefore, the scientific community needed to find a way to attack Putnam within the accepted discourse of the scientist. A review of *The Origin of Races,* clearly a scientific work, provided an acceptable scientific forum that could be used to condemn Putnam, because Putnam relied so heavily on Coon's work.

Finally, what of Carleton Coon himself? Coon's continued public claim that his critics were attempting to politicize his work was disingenuous at best. Putnam, with Coon's blessing and assistance, had transformed Coon's work into a political weapon. Moreover, despite Coon's and Putnam's continued claims that the Boasians had stifled open debate about the races, it was Coon who called for administrative action against his critics, who threatened Dobzhansky with a libel suit, and who considered a second suit against the ADL. Coon repeatedly and publicly proclaimed that the duty of a scientist was merely to report the truth, regardless of the consequences, but his actions violated his own standards for honesty and objectivity.

Beyond the last encounter between Coon and Dobzhansky, *Race and Reality* marked a subtle shift in Putnam's writing. For the first time, he argued that science dictated not just that school segregation was justified but also that it meant that most Negroes should be disenfranchised: "It may be essential as a practical matter to establish a more rigorous procedure for selection of voters, both white and black, in communities with a heavy Negro concentrations." Putnam pointed to the white government of Rhodesia, which argued that the franchise was properly limited only to those who were rational and could be trusted to make thoughtful decisions at the polls. Putnam agreed wholeheartedly, noting that such a limitation might prevent the occasional lower-class white from voting but would have the benefit of keeping the vast majority of Negroes from voting. "The unlimited suffrage concept is marginal when applied to a homogeneous electorate consisting of an advanced and experienced race like the Anglo-American. To apply to states or communities with high percentages of a retarded race is suicidal."[32]

The second change in Putnam's second book was his treatment of Jews. In his 1961 book, he treated Boas's Jewishness obliquely by referring to "white minority groups" and such. In his 1967 book, Putnam argued that when asked if "the Zionists and the international bankers [were] really at the bottom of this brotherhood movement," his answer was that it should not really matter who was "at the bottom of it," since the real problem was "the world-wide hypnosis on the subject of human equality." The task was "awakening the public from their trance" rather than uncovering Jewish involvement. However, he further argued, "[a]s to Hitler, the perversion of truth by evil men is no reason for abandoning truth."[33] In essence, Putnam was arguing that it was wrong to focus on Jewish involvement not because they were not responsible but simply because it was not productive to do so. As he moved into the 1970s, he would begin to focus more and more on the Jewish question.

Race and Modern Science

One of the tasks the IAAEE had set for itself when it formed in 1960 was a publication to answer the UNESCO viewpoints on race. For a number of years the project limped along, never coming to fruition. The first problem was the death of the book's first editor, R. Ruggles Gates. Another possible editor was Donald Swan, but his editorship came to an abrupt end in 1966 when he was arrested for mail fraud for ordering approximately $100,000 worth of books under a variety of assumed names. The arrest created a minor stir in New York City as police found not only stolen books but a variety of Nazi paraphernalia in Swan's apartment, including many copies of anti-Semitic and racist books. Anthony O'Keefe, Swan's successor as IAAEE secretary, quickly issued a press release trying to explain away the embarrassing press reports by portraying Swan as a scholar who had books on a range of subjects and was unfairly portrayed as having Nazi sympathies. O'Keefe admitted that the police had found books by American Nazi Party leader George Lincoln Rockwell, as well as Adolf Hitler's *Mein Kampf*, but they had also found *Das Kapital* and *The Wealth of Nations*.[34]

This was not the first time Swan's connections with the racist Right had caused problems to the group. One reason that the Association for the Preservation for the Freedom of Choice (APFC) in New York City had such limited resources in the fight to preserve racially pure neighborhoods was that its resources were dedicated to a series of libel suits when the papers began reporting on the APFC and included Donald Swan's publicly declared fascist sympathies in their accounts.[35] Moreover, it was tendentious for O'Keefe to claim that Swan was interested in Nazi racial ideology only as an intellectual exercise, given his association with *Truth Seeker,* his writings praising Hans F. K. Guenther, and his close connections with H. Keith Thompson and the Northern League. When Swan died in 1981, Draper's Pioneer Fund awarded Northern League founder Roger Pearson a grant to buy Swan's library. Presumably it was not for Swan's copy of *The Wealth of Nations* but rather for Swan's library on race, which self-declared Nazi H. Keith Thompson called "one of the best on the subject."[36]

In the 1960s, Swan's arrest meant yet another delay in the IAAEE's answer to UNESCO. An additional problem was finding a publisher. In 1964, Nathaniel Weyl warned the IAAEE that the book had to appear scientific rather than a segregationist tract. O'Keefe was sympathetic. "[W]e try to take every precaution against IAAEE's being linked up in the public mind as a segregationist organization," although "the hatchet men of the totalitarian liberal press have an easy enough time" doing so. Eventually, Draper's money invented an entirely new press called the Social Science Press, which would publish IAAEE's works exclusively. It published the IAAEE answer to UNESCO and the second edition of Audrey Shuey's *Testing of Negro Intelligence.*[37]

The IAAEE book, *Race and Modern Science,* was edited by Kuttner and contained essays by the usual IAAEE stable: Kuttner, Gregor, C. D. Darlington, Stanley Porteus, Corrado Gini, and Frank C. J. McGurk, among others. It failed to transform the scientific view of race. One reviewer, while assuring his readers that the authors in the book were undoubtedly writing from the purest of motives, pointed out that "it is too easy for this big and instructive book to be read as a racist document." A reviewer more knowledgeable of the authors represented, geneticist L. C. Dunn, noted that the "bibliographies . . . are formidable," and yet, despite the fact that all of the contributors were listed as "eminent authorities," they had not referred to each other's work in their own essays; "out of hundreds of citations only a dozen referred to other contributors. Apparently the authors had been chosen because of their known views rather than because of their original work." Willis Carto, by contrast, writing as "E. L. Anderson" and reviewing a book edited by his old friend Robert Kuttner, was full of praise: "If this is not the first of series of honest books on race, then it will be the last, and the Dark Age of Equalitarianism is on us all."[38] Since the Social Science Press did not issue any further books, Carto's worst fears were confirmed.

Challenge to the Court

In 1967 historian I. A. Newby published an account of the scientific efforts to overthrow *Brown*. Newby's book was, with a few minor errors such as Robert Kuttner's birthday, by and large an accurate portrait of the activities of the segregationist scientists. Throughout the book, Newby consistently applied the term *racist* to all those involved in the scientific defense of segregation. The "field marshals" were Garrett and George, ably assisted by McGurk, Shuey, Kuttner, and others. Putnam was the "popularizer" of scientific racism.

A major gap in the book, in retrospect, is that Newby did not uncover the connections of Kuttner to the *Truth Seeker* and the American neo-Nazi movement, which were extensive. However, what would become most controversial was Newby's treatment of A. James Gregor. Newby discovered Gregor's publication on "National Socialism and Race" in Fascist Oswald Mosley's *The European*. Newby wrote, "The most striking fact about Gregor's racism is its admitted kinship with the ideas of fascist race theories." He gave an accurate portrayal of Gregor's views in that article, noting with alarm that Gregor could so calmly describe the ideology that led to genocide.[39]

R. Carter Pittman, the attorney for the *Stell* trial, alerted the segregationist scientists to Newby's book, casting it as part of a conspiracy to scuttle the *Stell* appeal to the Supreme Court. "His book came out as planned by his employers so that unfounded assumptions triumphed over truth," Pittman concluded darkly. Despite this call to Newby's mysterious "employers," most of those attacked were not unduly disturbed by Newby. Charles Josey, Alfred Avins, and Kuttner thought the book would be good publicity for the cause, as did William Simmons of the Citizens' Councils. After all, this is when a lot of life had gone out of the movement, and many followed old dictum: "Publicity is good. Good publicity is even better." According to O'Keefe, however, Gregor was "really disturbed" by Newby's insinuation that Gregor had fascist sympathies and had "obtained an injunction from a California court banning the sale of the book in that state pending the outcome of a libel suit."[40]

Gregor was not the only one disturbed by the revelation that he had published in Mosley's journal. Nathaniel Weyl, who had been worried earlier about Gregor publishing in the Marxist *Science and Society*, noted with alarm, "If Gregor was mixed up with British Nazi as well as American Communist publications, then I think he would be the last person on earth conservatives on the racial issue would wish as their defender." He urged Gayre not to sponsor a response from Gregor, arguing that Newby charged "Gregor with pro-Nazism not merely on the basis of having published in that organ, but on having apparently attempted a partial defense of Nazi race doctrines as scientific."[41] One wonders what Weyl's reaction would have been had he known that he was addressing his letter to an admirer of Hans F. K. Guenther.

Eventually, the Louisiana State University Press editor responded to Gregor's complaint by offering a revised edition of *Challenge to the Court* in which those criticized would get "equal time" to respond to Newby's charges.[42] The responses by George, Putnam, Garrett, and most of the others were nothing they had not said dozens of times before in other venues. Gregor's response, which would be his last public statement on his activities of the 1950s and 1960s, was revealing. Like most of the responses to his critics, Gregor claimed that his intellectual opponent was incoherent. Newby was, according to Gregor, guilty of "a catalogue of harrowing intellectual and academic abuses," a purveyor of "falsehoods and half-truths calculated to defame" all held together by "a string of feckless and indifferent logic." While Gregor claimed that he hesitated to commit these charges to print, he did so only because of "the decision by my attorneys and the attorneys of the Louisiana State University Press that Newby's libels are not legally 'actionable.'"[43]

Gregor's defense of his actions, although sometimes obscured by venom, was that Newby mischaracterized Gregor as a "segregationist." Gregor argued that the term was so emotionally loaded "that to so identify an academician is to seriously impair his credibility." He charged that in his writing he had claimed only that the social-scientific research *tended* to support racial separation in schools, whereas Newby claimed that Gregor had *positively asserted* that segregated schools were psychologically more beneficial to children. "A tendency statement is *not* a positive assertion," Gregor exclaimed.[44] In his response, Gregor appended yet another social-scientific paper that showed that racial amalgamation "increased social tension" and was "a grievous imposition on the forbearance of Negro Americans." He concluded, "That such an assessment should be conceived of as . . . a brief for 'segregation' is a sad commentary on the state of free and responsible discussion."[45]

Perhaps one reason his assessment was given that reading is that Gregor had written the exact argument in 1963 for the *Western Law Review,* and it had been filed in a court of law, with his blessing, as a *brief for seg-*

regation in Savannah, Georgia. What was obscured by Gregor's extended parsing of "positive assertions" versus "tendency statements" was that Gregor *acted* as if "tendency statements" were enough to continue racial segregation in the American South. He had toured the American South with Donald Swan, meeting southern educational officials to discuss the race issue. Gregor wrote his *Western Law Review* article as a defense of racial segregation, and it had been submitted in the *Stell* case as such. He had worked with segregationist R. Carter Pittman to ensure in the *Stell* case that *race* would be the deciding factor to maintain segregation, with the end of preventing any bright African American children from sneaking into white classrooms simply by virtue of their high IQ scores.

Gregor's furious response to Newby, in which he portrayed himself as an academician unfairly tarred with the epithet "segregationist," hid what he himself had privately proclaimed as his hard work to preserve Jim Crow. Four years earlier, writing to Carleton Putnam, Gregor proclaimed that it had been a "privilege" to work with Henry Garrett and Charles Josey. "I have dedicated my time and energy to what I believe to be a just cause. [The *Stell* case]—to which I have devoted no little time and effort—is part of that just cause."[46] Gregor's response to Newby was disingenuous because, for all the careful caveats he pointed out, he believed there was enough evidence for him to act in support of segregation. What he apparently did not believe is that he should admit his role in the maintenance of segregation in print when confronted with his own writings. In the early 1960s, Gregor had criticized those social scientists in *Brown* for twisting the scientific data to suit their political ends. Yet at least they were publicly declaring their allegiance to their social agenda, which, of course, made such charges against them possible. By contrast, Gregor obscured his own political activities in support of segregation and pretended that he was a disinterested scientist completely distanced from the segregationist cause.

Gregor's other argument in his response to Newby was that he could not be a fascist since he had also published in Marxist journals such as *Science and Society* and *Studies on the Left*. It was these associations that had concerned Nathaniel Weyl some years before. In 1963, he had asked Gregor about his association with *Science and Society*. "Is it still under the ideological direction and control of the international communist movement?" Weyl asked Gregor anxiously. Gregor reassured Weyl that he was no Communist, merely publishing there to "undermine our Marxists!" As far as ideological purity was concerned, Gregor explained that the leftists had never asked him to modify anything he wrote for them, and indeed, many welcomed him challenging their preconceived notions. By contrast, "[t]here have been occasions," Gregor wrote to Weyl, "when Gayre of *Mankind Quarterly* has asked me to alter a manuscript. I have simply withdrawn the ms. and published it elsewhere."[47] Gregor never wrote on the "equalitarian conspiracy" to control the free discussion of race, perhaps because he found the Communists open to his ideas and encountered attempts to control his ideas only when he published in the journal dedicated to a "free and open" discussion of race.

His response to Newby was Gregor's last writing on race. In the Department of Political Science at the University of California–Berkeley, he built a distinguished career for himself as a sophisticated interpreter of fascism. Newby was the first, but not the last, to note the similarities between Gregor's ideas and those of the fascists. Pointing to his sympathetic portrayal of fascism, one reviewer noted in 1970, "If an American neo-fascist needs ideological material to support his cause, he will find it here." Reviewing two of Gregor's books in 1981, Roland Sari noted, "Anyone familiar with Fascist propaganda will immediately recognize a strange affinity between Gregor's interpretation and the image of their achievements that the Fascists wished to project."[48]

The 1970s

The older generation of scientists involved with the IAAEE did not continue into the 1970s. Garrett and George, the quintessential Southerners in the fight, were quite elderly by the time the 1970s arrived. Gregor abandoned race to study fascism. van den Haag abandoned his defense of segregation and began a long career of defending capital punishment. The hard core, Kuttner, Swan, and Putnam, continued to fight, although in somewhat different ways.

University of Southern Mississippi

The Northern League remained an important organizing tool for the racist Right in the 1970s. Many segregationist scientists still contributed to Carto's publications in the 1960s. For example, Northern League founders Roger Pearson and Willis Carto edited a new journal, *Western*

Destiny, and its masthead boasted Henry Garrett, Robert Kuttner, and other academics, along with proto–Holocaust denier Austin J. App and ex–Waffen S.S. officer Arthur Ehrart.[49] In the late 1960s, Carto abandoned *Western Destiny* to edit *American Mercury* and give a forum to his old comrades in arms such as Frank C. J. McGurk, who continued his claim that "[t]here seems to be a conspiracy on the part of all branches of news agencies to give exposure only to the Culture Hypothesis [for racial differences in intelligence] in spite of the prevailing evidence that it is not factual."[50] The League also provided important employment opportunities for the scientists in its ranks.

William D. McCain, the president of the University of Southern Mississippi (USM), was long active in the Citizens' Councils. He had introduced Carleton Putnam to the readers of *The Citizen* in the special issue that commemorated "Race and Reason Day."[51] A segregationist bastion, USM had reorganized three departments in 1973, merging the Departments of Religion, Philosophy, and Anthropology. The chair of the new department was Roger Pearson, founder of the Northern League and a freshly minted Ph.D. in anthropology from the University of London. Pearson quickly brought in Kuttner and Swan to teach anthropology at USM.[52]

The arguments put forth by Swan and Kuttner in the 1970s were essentially the same arguments they had offered since the 1950s, stripped of their overt racism. Kuttner and Swan argued that anthropologists should abandon their hesitation in "applying biological laws to the subjects of their discipline," for "anthropology suffers from theoretical stagnation when it separates itself from biology."[53] Culture, they argued, was a result of Darwinian natural selection based on intense group competition, just as Arthur Keith argued. Those anthropologists who refused to recognize that group competition explained social relations were "too influenced by twentieth century notions on the cofraternity of man and the collective impulse behind social institutions to be objective biologists."[54] Kuttner and Swan argued that when two races came into contact, there were three possible outcomes: genocide, interbreeding to produce a hybrid race, or "the two populations will begin to diverge so that their original biological differences become magnified." It was this last option that explained racial stratification and the inferiority of African Americans:

> [A]dvanced civilizations have utilized African slaves for menial agricul-
> tural labor which was accompanied by a selective process encouraging

psychological traits such as passivity and docility. Personality facets which were incompatible with a slave status were increasingly screened out by extreme punitive measures. As is becoming increasingly clear from modern research, both intelligence and personality have a genetic basis and can be varied by prolonged selective force.[55]

Kuttner became chair of the department in 1974, when Pearson left the University of Southern Mississippi. After a year as chair, he moved to a research position at Louisiana State University, starting a new research program into the effect of circulatory shock. He continued to write for Willis Carto's newspaper *The Spotlight* until 1977. Although he lived another decade, he didn't publish more political writings after 1977.

In 1978, the year after Kuttner withdrew from political life, his two closest associates entered new phases of their careers. Roger Pearson took over the editorship of *Mankind Quarterly,* where he remains today. *Mankind Quarterly* remains an important outlet for those scientists who share many of Kuttner's racial views, such as Glayde Whitney. Also in 1978, Willis Carto established the Institute for Historical Review, dedicated to proving that the "myth" that the Nazis committed genocide during World War II is part of a Jewish conspiracy to distort the past and, as Glayde Whitney told the assembled IHR conference in 2000, to distort the scientific truth about racial differences.[56]

The Last True Believer: Carleton Putnam's Last Years

Race and Reality would be Carleton Putnam's last published work. However, one reason he ceased writing may be that he found writers that he thought were doing the job properly: John Baker and Wilmot Robertson.

John Baker was the British biologist who, along with C. D. Darlington and Michael Polyani, spoke out against Lysenkoism and argued for an unfettered science. In 1974 he published *Race,* which proclaimed that nothing truly objective had been published on race since the 1920s because of revulsion toward Nazi Germany. Baker clearly saw his work as carrying on the tradition that had been lost as those who believed in racial differences were stifled while "those who believed in the equality of the races were free to write what they liked, without fear of contradiction."[57] For many reviewers, Baker's book could have been produced in the 1920s, as he ignored recent findings of population genetics and presented arguments on the reality of race based on a typology of skull shape and brain size. Baker came down on the side of Garrett, Shuey, and McGurk in the controversy regarding the relationship of race and IQ.[58]

Baker's book was everything Carleton Putnam had been writing for years: black people were not the intellectual equal of white people, these differences were biological in nature and not environmental, and the failure of Africans to develop their own civilization was the ultimate proof of the unsuitability of Negroes to advanced civilization. In 1974, Putnam visited Baker at his home, where he told Baker of his attempts to "act as a liaison between those studying the *biology,* and those working on the *politics* of race." Baker was a sympathetic audience for Putnam, later writing that everything Putnam had told him "was strongly reinforced by Dr. Roger Pearson, who visited us afterwards and spoke with emphasis of the constant pushing forward of Negroes into academic posts for which they are unfitted, while suitable Europid applicants are prevented *by law* from filling them."[59] Both Putnam, the unrepentant segregationist, and Pearson, the neo-Nazi ideologue, were therefore working to keep the scientific racists of the 1970s together against the equalitarian hordes.

With Baker providing the scientific backing, Putnam could promote the second author he thought was vital to read: Wilmot Robertson. A pseudonym, "Robertson" and Putnam had been in contact as early as 1968. In the early 1970s, Robertson began publishing *Instautaration,* a journal filled with racial invective and anti-Semitic articles. By 1972, Putnam was actively promoting Robertson's manifesto, *The Dispossessed Majority,* a book that had been financed by Draper. Robertson's position was a return to the roots of Nordicism: civilization was racial in nature, and liberals were mistaken in thinking that white civilization could be grafted onto inferior races. The only true solution was racial separation, including the deportation of blacks back to Africa—a solution opposed by liberals because of the political gains they get from the black vote.[60]

First published in 1972, Robertson's book quickly became the new bible for the racist right wing of American politics. It went through a number of printings, sporting recommendations that had obviously been arranged by Putnam, since most of them were his close friends, including Carleton S. Coon, Allan Ochsner, and Hart Fessenden. Indeed, Robertson dedicated later editions to "[m]y co-author. No other title adequately describes your inestimable assistance," which could have been a veiled reference to Putnam.[61]

Putnam tirelessly promoted *The Dispossessed Majority.* Upon hearing that his friend Albert Wedemeyer had attempted to bring the book to the attention of various notable conservatives, Putnam advised him to forget William F. Buckley because he was "so wrapped up in his Catholic point of view" that it would be a useless gesture. But "Ronald Reagan must somehow be brought to read *The Dispossessed Majority.*"[62]

However, despite the occasional glimmer of hope, Putnam grew increasingly dispirited about possibility of success through persuasion and the democratic process. The problem was the Jews:

> More than any other single element in our population, the Jew has been responsible for our current Negro problem. The incitement of the Negro to insurrection against our White culture resulting from the propagation of the innate-equality fallacy (teaching the Negro to believe his status in our society is primarily due to social injustice) has wrought irreparable harm. From Boas on, the movement has been led by Jews, and their control over the media has assured the dissemination of the underlying deceit like a scourge throughout the society.[63]

Such pessimism about breaking the Jewish control over the democratic process led Putnam to question the "republican ideal." Visiting Baker and C. D. Darlington in Great Britain made him appreciate the virtues of a hereditary monarchy. "The idea of looking up, and having something worth looking up to, however symbolically, has its value, especially in eras of waning religious faith. Certainly it is an antidote to the leveling impulse which inevitably ensues for the equalitarian ideology, leaving nothing 'upward.'"[64]

After 1974 or so, Putnam sank further and further from the public light. His views, which had not changed from his first public pronouncement on race in 1958, had marked him as extreme even by such as Shockley and Jensen, who shared many of his beliefs about white supremacy. Putnam had remained convinced that the equalitarian conspiracy, which he was increasingly willing to identify as a Jewish conspiracy, was a threat to white civilization. In 1961, such views made him the darling of the segregationist establishment in the American South. By the mid-1970s he still had an audience, but it was confined to those on the far right of American politics.

In 1980 a recent college graduate named Keith Stimely came to the East Coast to begin researching a biography of Francis Parker Yockey, a hero of the neo-Nazi underground who had committed suicide after his capture by the FBI in 1960. Yockey, who had written extensively on the "culture distortion" of the Jews in Western culture, was a particular hero of Willis Carto, who had been the last visitor to Yockey's jail cell. Stimely was an aspiring neo-Nazi and follower of Yockey who flew from his Oregon home and made the rounds of the racist right wing—meeting with Willis Carto as well as Edward Fields, the founder of the paramilitary National States Rights Party; William Pierce, the organizer of the National Alliance; and Anthony O'Keefe and Mark Weber, who were important figures at the Institute for Historical Review. Stimely's closest friend was Bob Lenski, who was staying at the home of a wealthy patron. One evening, while swimming in the pool, Stimely recalled that he and Lenski

> [f]antasized about who would get what personal fiefdoms after the Revolution. There is no doubt Bob [Lenski] should be minister of Race and Eugenics. Mark [Weber] would be the perfect Minister of Foreign Affairs . . . I would like to be Minister of Culture. My act would be descend on Hollywood with my retinue in a huge fleet of planes, and there administer the "Hollywood Holocaust"—final solution to the question of culture distortion in the greatest of art forms, film. Next . . . films of Wagner's operas, other Western epics, and documentaries for the Party! When do we take over?[65]

Stimely and his friends planned their revolution in the pool of Carleton Putnam, who was Bob Lenksi's patron. From the sharing the stage with governors and U.S. representatives to playing host for a party attended by American neo-Nazis was a short trip for Putnam, which he made by remaining absolutely sure of his beliefs and never budging from his defense of white civilization.

Conclusion

A. James Gregor always claimed that he was acting to defend segregation not because of white fears, but because segregation was in the best interests of Negro children. In the planning sessions for the *Stell* case, he urged that Pittman recruit a Negro plaintiff. "*Appropriate tactics would require that some Negroes (a Negro) petition for intervention against integration in order to protect his child from the impairments which result from con-*

tact with majority children in the school situation," Gregor wrote; for "even minimal contact with majority children in the school situation."[66] Whether or not Pittman took Gregor's suggestion seriously, the reality was that he did not represent Negroes in *Stell*, but white parents who were concerned about the effects of having their children intermingle with an inferior race.

By 1963, when the IAAEE mounted its attack on *Brown*, it took a particular blindness to think, as Gregor did, that legalized segregation served to protect African Americans. The *Stell* case was after the Montgomery bus boycott, when African Americans walked miles every day for a year rather than ride a segregated bus system. It was after Little Rock where the children that Gregor was professing to protect braved angry mobs of whites in order to attend Central High School. It was after the sit-in movement, when young African Americans were harassed and spat upon as they calmly sat at lunch counters waiting to be served. It was after James Meredith's admission to Ole Miss caused a riot. It was after the children Gregor professed to speak for faced Bull Connor's police dogs and fire hoses and willingly filled Birmingham's jails. It was after the murders of Emmett Till and Schwermer, Goodman, and Cheney. In the face of the massive uprising against legalized segregation that swept the nation for the decade between *Brown* and the Civil Rights Act of 1964, the notion that a handful of scientists could somehow hold back African American demands for their civil rights was absurd. It required a willful blindness on the part of Carleton Putnam, Henry Garrett, Wesley Critz George, Robert Kuttner, and the rest to believe that the activity that surrounded the segregation protests of that decade were somehow not genuine demands for equal rights but part of a conspiracy to destroy the white race.

In part, the IAAEE scientists *simply did not see* African American demands for civil rights. To see them, they would have had to realize that African Americans had agency of their own: that they knew what they wanted, that they understood the promise of freedom held in the U.S. Constitution, that they had the strength to demand that freedom in the face of brutal violence and oppression. Such recognition was impossible for men who were convinced that "the Negro" was incapable of civilization, that African Americans did not understand the white man's government, that they were too stupid, ignorant, and lazy to comprehend that they were capable of participating in modern society. Because Negroes could not speak for themselves, their demands for equal rights must have originated elsewhere: from the equalitarian Jews and liberals who were bent on destroying the Nordic civilization of the United States. That Carleton Putnam, this view's most vocal proponent, was marginalized by the mid-1970s signaled that at least part of the message was no longer politically acceptable—legalized segregation was no longer a viable political option in the United States. However, claims about the equalitarian conspiracy have continued to be issued by isolated members of the scientific community.

For the past three decades, Arthur Jensen has been the leading voice for the case for racial differences in IQ. In a recent celebration of his work in the psychological journal *Intelligence,* several authors echoed Pioneer Fund recipient Linda Gottfredson, who praised Jensen as "a masterful scientist whose work broke a social taboo."[67] While he eschewed the grandstanding that characterized Shockley's career, and he professed that nothing in his research supported racial segregation, Jensen consistently maintained that his views were being stifled for unscientific reasons. His most recent book, published in the late 1990s, argues that the "concept of human races [as] a fiction" has several "main sources, none of them scientific." Jensen maintained that one source is "Neo-Marxist philosophy," which "excludes consideration of genetic or biological factors from any part in explaining behavioral differences among humans."[68] Since the end of the Cold War, little rhetorical ground has been gained by invoking the Communist conspiracy; however, conservatives maintained their beliefs about "tenured radicals" inculcating a leftist "illiberal education," just as Buckley maintained in 1952.[69] In this climate, race/IQ researchers can continue their charges of scientific conspiracy.

Jensen's rhetoric was muted and avoided any of the florid charges of his predecessors. The same cannot be said of other authors when they wrote on the taboo surrounding scientific racial research. Psychologist J. Philippe Rushton even exhumed the ghost of Henry Garrett by revisiting Garrett's most famous charges in an article Rushton titled "The Equalitarian Dogma Revisited" in the mainstream psychological journal *Intelligence.*[70] According to Rushton, the control over racial research is nearly absolute. "There is no parallel to [the taboo on racial research] in the history of science: not the inquisition, not Stalin, not Hitler."[71] Like Garrett, George, and Putnam, Rushton argues that the "political left" in the 1930s had "come to believe that the concept of 'survival of the fittest' was incompatible with the notion of equality. Powerful ideologues, such as anthropologist Franz Boas and his student Margaret Mead, fought against the idea of biological universals." However, once determining that racial research fell under this complete control, Rushton is quick to seize back presumption by arguing that racial research is the scientific status quo when he concludes, "Evolutionary studies of human nature are inherently mainstream. Radical environmentalism and cultural determinism are the anomalous conditions in need of justification."[72]

Kevin MacDonald, a professor of psychology at California State University at Long Beach, is not content to blame amorphous "leftists," as Rushton is. MacDonald points squarely to the Jews, who have seized control of the academy. Like Arthur Keith, MacDonald argues that evolution in humans depends on the creation of social barriers to ensure reproductive isolation. Jews have historically cut themselves off from mingling with others, while encouraging commingling on the part of outsiders as part of a strategy to maximize their reproductive success. This was the underpinning of the Boasian revolution in anthropology, MacDonald explains, which was a "highly authoritarian political movement centered around a charismatic leader." After Boas conquered anthropology, MacDonald writes, "research on racial differences ceased, and the profession completely excluded eugenicists and racial theorists like Madison Grant and Charles Davenport." MacDonald seems unaware or unwilling to concede that Grant and his coterie were willing to expunge Boas and his followers because they were racially unacceptable. The quality of MacDonald's historical scholarship can perhaps be illustrated by the fact that he, like Glayde Whitney, has ties to the Holocaust denial movement. MacDonald was the only scholar who testified on behalf of Holocaust denier David Irving in his libel trial in London in 2000.[73]

The continuation of the conspiracy argument that originated with Madison Grant is important because it allows the continuation of scientific racism, even in an age when such racism is no longer respectable. Casting racist sentiments in a scientific voice allows speakers to say the otherwise unsayable. Kevin MacDonald perpetuates old stereotypes about Jewish cliquishness in a scientific vein and is thus published by an academic press that would, no doubt, never allow such arguments in a book that purported to be about politics rather than about science. The implication is that scholars allow racism in a scientific guise because they simply do not recognize that politics are as embedded in science as anywhere else. Morton Hunt, a writer on the history of psychology, criticized many in the Behavioral Genetics Association for their actions regarding Whitney's presidential address, recounted at the beginning of this book.

None of the responses, according to Hunt, "involved scientific rebuttal; it was all a purely political response to politically repellent research data. Whether or not Whitney's data and suggestions have any scientific merit is beside the point"; once the data were seen to conflict with "the nurturist position on race," the BGA declared Whitney's data "unacceptable and requiring condemnation and ostracism."[74] Hunt portrays Jensen, Rushton, and the other recent race researchers as simply searching for scientific truth and set upon by leftist ideologues. He is undoubtedly correct in his claim that political ideology informed much of the critique of racial research in the postwar United States. However, Hunt fails to raise the question that race researchers themselves are engaging in a political quest and just happen to be using the language of science in the process. Indeed, Hunt's book was underwritten by the Pioneer Fund, which funded most of the figures I have recounted in this book and which is hardly an apolitical institution. Harry Weyher, the administrator of the Pioneer Fund, and its current director, Philippe Rushton, were always quick to threaten legal action against the Fund's critics, hardly the sign of a disinterested search for scientific truth in the open market of ideas.[75]

The great philosopher of science Karl Popper was also a political philosopher who argued that "the open society" must listen to all voices, an idea that certainly underpins the democratic ideal. Many interpreters of scientific practice have viewed science as an open system that discovers truth when purged of politics. I would argue that Popper's ideal can be better upheld by recognizing that there is no line of demarcation between science and politics, that we should look for how science and power align themselves. In the postwar United States, the scientific battle over race was, and continues to be, a political one. That racism speaks in a scientific voice should be no reason for not naming it as racism. As Robert Nye asked, "Could it not be argued that the twin demons of race and eugenics were politically but not scientifically exorcised in the wake of World War II, and that the ideal of genetic engineering based on assessments of biological worthiness is ticking along like a time bomb ready to explode again when the political conditions are ripe?"[76] If it does explode, the fuse that has kept burning since Grant has been the claim that racial science was smothered by a conspiracy.

Notes

NOTES TO CHAPTER 1

1. Mission statement of the Behavioral Genetics Association from their Web site: http://www.bga.org/ (viewed 23 July 2003).

2. For a recent statement on this wedding of science to political power in the USSR, see Kirill O. Rossianov, "Editing Nature: Joseph Stalin and the 'New' Soviet Biology," *Isis* 84 (1993): 728–754.

3. Glayde Whitney, "Ideology and Censorship in Behavior Genetics," *Mankind Quarterly* 35 (1995): 330, 336, 339. For an analysis of Whitney's claims about the racial basis of crime, see Andrew S. Winston and Michael Peters, "On the Presentation and Interpretation of International Homicide Data," *Psychological Reports* 86 (2000): 865–871.

4. Daniel Kevles, *In the Name of Eugenics: Genetics and the Uses of Human Heredity* (New York: Knopf, 1985), 192. Martin was quoted in "Specter at the Feast," *Science* 269 (7 July 1995): 35.

5. Andrew C. Heath, "Secretary's Report on the 25th Annual Meeting of the Behavior Genetics Association, Richmond, Virginia," *Behavior Genetics* 25 (1995): 589. On the resignations, see Declan Butler, "Geneticist Quits in Protest at 'Genes and Violence' Claim," *Nature* 378 (16 November 1995): 224. On the compromise see "Behavior Geneticists Shun Colleague" *Science* 270 (17 November 1995): 1125.

6. Glayde Whitney, "Foreword," in David Duke, *My Awakening: A Path to Racial Understanding* (Covington, LA: Free Speech Press, 1998), n.p.

7. Quoted in Alison Schneider, "Florida State Professor Criticized for His Laudatory Foreword to David Duke's Book," *Chronicle of Higher Education* 45, no. 33 (23 April 1999): A24.

8. Glayde Whitney, "Subversion of Science: How Psychology Lost Darwin," *Journal of Historical Review* 21 (March/April 2002): 29. Whitney developed his argument in a number of other articles, including "Raymond B. Cattell and the Fourth Inquisition," *Mankind Quarterly* 38 (1997): 99–125; "On the Races of Man," *Mankind Quarterly* 39 (1999): 319–335; "Races Do Not Exist—So Study Them!" *Mankind Quarterly* 41 (2000): 119–127; "Ideology Contra-Sci-

ence," *Occidental Quarterly* 1, no. 2 (2001) (viewed online at http://theocciden-talquarterly.com/ on 23 July 2003).

9. Whitney, "Subversion of Science," 20. For another IHR article on Boas, see Ted O'Keefe, "Mead, Freeman, Boas: Jewish Anthropology Comes of Age in America," *National Vanguard* (June 1983): 5–10. On the history of Holocaust denial, see Deborah Lipstadt, *Denying the Holocaust: The Growing Assault on Truth and Memory* (New York: Plume, 1994); Michael Shermer and Alex Grobman, *Denying History: Who Says the Holocaust Never Happened and Why Do They Say It?* (Berkeley: University of California Press, 2000).

10. Glayde Whitney, "A Contextual History of Behavior Genetics," in *Developmental Behavior Genetics: Neural, Biometrical, and Evolutionary Approaches,* ed. Martin E. Hahn et al. (New York: Oxford University Press, 1990), 15; "Genetics and Human Behavior," in *Encyclopedia of Bioethics,* ed. Warren T. Reich (New York: Simon and Schuster, 1995), vol. 2, 953; and "On Possible Genetic Bases of Race Differences in Criminality," in *Crime in Biological, Social, and Moral Contexts,* ed. Lee Ellis and Harry Hoffman (New York: Praeger, 1990), 145.

11. George M. Fredrickson, *Racism: A Short History* (Princeton: Princeton University Press, 2002), 99.

12. David L. Chappell, "Religious Ideas of the Segregationists," *Journal of American Studies* 32 (1998): 237–238. The first extended treatment of the proslavery argument was William Sumner Jenkins, *Proslavery Thought in the Old South* (Chapel Hill: University of North Carolina Press, 1935). For more recent treatments, see David Donald, "The Proslavery Argument Reconsidered," *Journal of Southern History* 37 (1971): 3–18; David F. Ericson, *The Debate over Slavery: Antislavery and Proslavery Liberalism in Antebellum America* (New York: New York University Press, 2000); Drew Gilpin Faust, "A Southern Stewardship: The Intellectual and the Proslavery Argument," *American Quarterly* 31 (1979): 63–80; Gary S. Selby, "Mocking the Sacred: Frederick Douglass's 'Slaveholder's Sermon' and the Antebellum Debate over Religion and Slavery," *Quarterly Journal of Speech* 88 (2002): 326–341; John David Smith, *An Old Creed for the New South: Proslavery Ideology and Historiography, 1865–1918* (Westport, CT: Greenwood Press, 1985); Michael Wayne, "An Old South Morality Play: Reconsidering the Social Underpinnings of the Proslavery Ideology," *Journal of American History* 77 (1990): 838–863.

13. David Chappell, "The Divided Mind of Southern Segregationists," *Georgia Historical Quarterly* 82 (1998): 53.

14. Carleton Putnam, "This Is the Problem!" *The Citizen* 6 (November 1961): 28, emphasis in original.

15. Audrey Smedley, *Race in North America: Origin and Evolution of a Worldview,* 2d ed. (Boulder, CO: Westview Press, 1999), 28. Other writers who emphasize that racism is a recent ideology include Fredrickson, *Racism*; Ivan

Hannaford, *Race: The History of an Idea in the West* (Baltimore: Johns Hopkins University Press, 1996); George L. Mosse, *Toward the Final Solution: A History of European Racism* (New York: Howard Fertig, 1985); Dante A. Puzzo, "Racism and the Western Tradition," *Journal of the History of Ideas* 25 (1964): 579–586.

16. For a nice statement of the central puzzle regarding racialized slavery without racial concepts, see Naomi Zack, *Bachelors of Science: Seventeenth-Century Identity, Then and Now* (Philadelphia: Temple University Press, 1996), 168–181.

17. George M. Fredrickson, *The Comparative Imagination: On the History of Racism, Nationalism, and Social Movements* (Berkeley: University of California Press, 1997), 81–82; *Racism*, 8.

18. Gordon R. Mitchell, "Did Habermas Cede Nature to the Positivists?" *Philosophy and Rhetoric* 36 (2003), 3.

19. Thomas Nagel, *The View from Nowhere* (New York: Oxford University Press, 1986); Donna Haraway, *Simians, Cyborgs, and Women* (New York: Routledge, 1991), 193.

20. David Hollinger, "The Knower and the Artificer," *American Quarterly* 39 (1987): 37–55.

21. Lorraine Daston, "Objectivity and the Escape from Perspective," *Social Studies of Science* 22 (1992): 599.

22. Alan G. Gross, Joseph E. Harmon, and Michael Reidy, *Communicating Science: The Scientific Article from the Seventeenth Century to the Present* (New York: Oxford University Press, 2002), 215.

23. Michael L. Blakely, "Passing the Buck: Naturalism and Individualism as Anthropological Expressions of Euro-American Denial," in *Race*, ed. Steven Gregory and Roger Sanjek (New Brunswick: Rutgers University Press, 1994), 272.

24. Immaculada de Melo-Martin, "Biological Explanations and Social Responsibility," *Studies in the History and Philosophy of the Biological and Biomedical Sciences* 34 (2003): 346.

25. Robert N. Proctor, *Racial Hygiene: Medicine under the Nazis* (Cambridge: Harvard University Press, 1988), 36.

26. The phrase "liberal orthodoxy" is from Walter A. Jackson, *Gunnar Myrdal and America's Conscience* (Chapel Hill: University of North Carolina Press, 1990). On social scientists' work in *Brown*, see John P. Jackson Jr. *Social Scientists for Social Justice: Making the Case against Segregation* (New York: New York University Press, 2001).

27. The collapse of scientific racism is well documented. Major monographs include: Elazar Barkan, *The Retreat of Scientific Racism* (Cambridge: Cambridge University Press, 1992); Hamilton Cravens, *The Triumph of Evolution* (Baltimore: Johns Hopkins University Press, 1988); Carl N. Degler, *In Search of*

Human Nature (New York: Oxford University Press, 1991), 59–104; Stephen J. Gould, *The Mismeasure of Man* (New York: Norton, 1981); Joseph L. Graves Jr., *The Emperor's New Clothes: Biological Theories of Race at the Millennium* (New Brunswick: Rutgers University Press, 2001); and Jonathan Marks, *Human Biodiversity: Genes, Race, and History* (New York: Aldine de Gruyter, 1995). On the return of scientific arguments for racial differences in intelligence, see Arthur R. Jensen, "How Much Can We Boost IQ and Scholastic Achievement?" *Harvard Educational Review* 39 (1969): 1–123; Richard Herrnstein and Charles Murray, *The Bell Curve* (New York: Free Press, 1994). For authoritative critiques of the scientific case for racial differences in IQ, see the articles collected in *The IQ Controversy*, ed. N. J. Block and Gerald Dworkin (New York: Pantheon, 1976); and in *Race and Intelligence: Separating Science from Myth,* ed. Jefferson M. Fish (Mahwah, NJ: Lawrence Erlbaum, 2002).

28. Graham Richards, *"Race," Racism and Psychology* (London: Routledge, 1997), 265.

29. J. Philippe Rushton, "Review Essay," *Society* 34 (March/April 1997): 82.

30. Thomas M. Lessl, "The Galileo Legend as Scientific Folklore," *Quarterly Journal of Speech* 85 (1999): 146–168.

31. Peter Weingart, "Science Abused? Challenging a Legend," *Science in Context* 6 (1993): 557.

32. The best treatment of the social network of race/IQ researchers is William H. Tucker, *The Science and Politics of Racial Research* (Urbana: University of Illinois Press, 1994). On the Pioneer Fund, see William H. Tucker, *The Funding of Scientific Racism: Wickliffe Draper and the Pioneer Fund* (Urbana: University of Illinois Press, 2002). The centrality of *Mankind Quarterly* in the scientific case for racial differences is evidenced by the use of its articles in *The Bell Curve,* even though Richard Herrnstein was never a part of the *Mankind Quarterly* crowd. See Charles Lane, "Tainted Sources," in *The Bell Curve Debate,* ed. Russell Jacoby and Naomi Glauberman (New York: Times Books, 1995), 125–139.

33. Uskali Maki, "Science as a Free Market: A Reflexivity Test in an Economics of Economics," *Perspectives on Science* 7 (1999): 487.

34. Vannevar Bush, *Science the Endless Frontier* (Washington, DC: National Science Foundation, 1960 [1950]).

35. David A. Hollinger, *Science, Jews, and Secular Culture: Studies in Mid-Twentieth-Century American Intellectual History* (Princeton: Princeton University Press, 1996), 102–103.

36. Ibid., 155–174.

37. Thomas F. Gieryn, *Cultural Boundaries of Science: Credibility on the Line* (Chicago: University of Chicago Press, 1999), 4–5. Also see Charles Alan Taylor, *Defining Science: A Rhetoric of Demarcation* (Madison: University of Wisconsin Press, 1996).

38. Gieryn, *Cultural Boundaries*, 4.

39. Hollinger, "Knower and Artificer," 42.

40. Steve Fuller, *Thomas Kuhn: A Philosophical History of Our Times* (Chicago: University of Chicago Press, 2000), 151.

41. On argument by disassociation, see Chaim Perelman and L. Olbrechts-Tyteca, *The New Rhetoric: A Treatise on Argumentation* (South Bend, IN: University of Notre Dame Press, 1969), 436–450.

42. Gieryn, *Cultural Boundaries*, 15–16.

43. On the use of conspiracy rhetoric to define social reality, see Mark Fenster, *Conspiracy Theories: Secrecy and Power in American Culture* (Minneapolis: University of Minnesota Press, 1999); G. Thomas Goodnight and John Poulakos, "Conspiracy Rhetoric: From Pragmatism to Fantasy in Public Discourse," *Western Journal of Speech Communication* 45 (1981): 299–316; Peter Knight, "'A Plague of Paranoia': Theories of Conspiracy Theory since the 1960s," in *Fear Itself: Enemies, Real and Imagined in American Culture,* ed. Nancy Lusignan Schultz (West Lafayette, IN: Purdue University Press, 1999), 23–50.

44. David Zarefsky, "Conspiracy Arguments in the Lincoln-Douglas Debates," *Journal of the American Forensic Association* 21 (1984): 72.

45. Goodnight and Poulakos, "Conspiracy Rhetoric," 310.

46. Zarefsky, "Conspiracy Arguments," 73.

47. Henry E. Garrett, "The Equalitarian Dogma," *Perspectives in Biology and Medicine* 4 (1961): 484.

48. Jill G. Morawski and Gail A. Hornstein, "Quandary of the Quacks: The Struggle for Expert Knowledge in American Psychology, 1890–1940," in *The Estate of Social Knowledge,* ed. J. Brown and D. K. van Keuren (Baltimore: Johns Hopkins University Press, 1991); Peggy Pascoe, "Miscegenation Law, Court Cases, and Ideologies of 'Race' in Twentieth-Century America," *Journal of American History* 83 (1996): 44–69; Ian F. Haney Lopez, *White by Law: Legal Construction of Race* (New York: New York University Press, 1996).

49. Neil R. McMillen, *The Citizens' Council: Organized Resistance to the Second Reconstruction, 1954–64* (Urbana: University of Illinois Press, 1971).

NOTES TO CHAPTER 2

1. Rayford W. Logan, *The Betrayal of the Negro* (New York: Macmillan, 1965).

2. John S. Haller, *Outcasts from Evolution: Scientific Attitudes of Racial Inferiority, 1859–1900* (Urbana: University of Illinois Press, 1971), 210; Eric Foner, *Reconstruction: America's Unfinished Revolution, 1863–1877* (New York: Harper and Row, 1988), 604.

3. David W. Bishop, "*Plessy v. Ferguson*: A Reinterpretation," *Journal of*

Negro History 62 (1977): 131. Such a view is echoed in the most extensive treatment of the case: Charles A. Lofgren, *The Plessy Case: A Legal-Historical Interpretation* (New York: Oxford University Press, 1987).

4. Edward J. Larson, *Sex, Race, and Science: Eugenics in the Deep South* (Baltimore: Johns Hopkins University Press, 1995), 154.

5. Frank Dikötter, "Race Culture: Recent Perspectives on the History of Eugenics," *American Historical Review* 103 (1998): 467. Two earlier reviews that captured the exciting and sometimes confusing character of eugenics scholarship were Robert A. Nye, "The Rise and Fall of the Eugenics Empire: Recent Perspectives on the Impact of Biomedical Thought in Modern Society," *Historical Journal* 36 (1993): 687–700; and Philip J. Pauly, "Eugenics Industry: Growth or Restructuring?" *Journal of the History of Biology* 26 (1993): 131–145.

6. On the comparative approach to eugenics, see the collected essays in Mark B. Adams, ed., *The Wellborn Science: Eugenics in Germany, France, Brazil, and Russia* (New York: Oxford University Press, 1990).

7. On the eugenic thought of the political Left, see Diane B. Paul, *The Politics of Heredity: Essays on Eugenics, Biomedicine, and the Nature-Nurture Debate* (Albany: State University of New York Press, 1998).

8. Daniel J. Kevles, *In the Name of Eugenics: Genetics and the Uses of Human Heredity* (New York: Knopf, 1985).

9. Stefan Kühl, *The Nazi Connection: Eugenics, American Racism, and German National Socialism* (New York: Oxford University Press, 1994), 73–74.

10. Reginald Horsman, "Origins of Racial Anglo-Saxonism in Great Britain before 1850," *Journal of the History of Ideas* 37 (1976): 387–410.

11. Thomas R. Gossett, *Race: The History of an Idea in America* (Dallas: Southern Methodist University Press, 1963), 84–122. Freeman quotation on p. 109.

12. William Z. Ripley, *The Races of Europe: A Sociological Study* (New York: Appleton and Company, 1899), 52.

13. Arthur de Gobineau, *Inequality of the Human Races,* trans. Adrian Collins (New York: Putnam and Sons, 1915); Houston Stewart Chamberlain, *Foundations of the Nineteenth Century,* trans. John Lees (New York: John Lane Company, 1914). For discussions of these writers, see Ivan Hannaford, *Race: The History of an Idea in the West* (Baltimore: Johns Hopkins University Press, 1996), 264–275, 348–357.

14. The best biographical work on Madison Grant is Jonathan P. Spiro, "Patrician Racist: The Evolution of Madison Grant" (Ph.D. diss., University of California–Berkeley, 2000).

15. Madison Grant, *The Passing of the Great Race or the Racial Basis of European History* (New York: Scribner's, 1916), 82.

16. Ibid., 14.

17. Ibid., 15–16.

18. Ibid., 47, 49.

19. On Grant ignoring "the Negro question" in the 1920s, see Mathew Pratt Guterl, *The Color of Race in America, 1900–1940* (Cambridge: Harvard University Press, 2001), 35–37; and on Grant's role in the passage of the Immigration Restriction Act, see pp. 46–47.

20. Grant, *Passing of the Great Race,* 14.

21. For example, Frederick Adams Woods, "Review of *The Passing of the Great Race,*" *Science* 48 (1918): 419–420; A.B.S. "Review of *The Passing of the Great Race,*" *American Historical Review* 22 (1917): 842–844.

22. On Boas's views and influence in American anthropology, see John S. Allen, "Franz Boas's Physical Anthropology: The Critique of Racial Formalism Revisited," *Current Anthropology* 30 (1989): 79–84; Elazar Barkan, *The Retreat of Scientific Racism: Changing Concepts of Race in Britain and the United States between the World Wars* (Cambridge: Cambridge University Press, 1992), 76–95; Richard Handler, "Boasian Anthropology and the Critique of American Culture," *American Quarterly* 42 (1990): 252–273; Dwight W. Hoover, "A Paradigm Shift: The Concept of Race in the 1920s and 1930s," *Conspectus of History* 1 (1981): 82–100; George Stocking, *Race, Culture, and Evolution* (Chicago: University of Chicago Press, 1968); Vernon J. Williams, *Rethinking Race: Franz Boas and His Contemporaries* (Lexington: University of Kentucky Press, 1996).

23. Jonathan Spiro, "Nordic vs. Anti-Nordic: The Galton Society and the American Anthropological Association," *Patterns of Prejudice* 36 (2002): 38.

24. Barkan, *Retreat of Scientific Racism,* 108.

25. Quoted in Spiro, "Nordic vs. Anti-Nordic," 39.

26. On the founding of the Galton Society, see Spiro, "Nordic vs. Anti-Nordic"; Barkan, *Retreat of Scientific Racism,* 67–70; Brian Regal, *Henry Fairfield Osborn: Race and the Search for the Origins of Man* (Burlington, VT: Ashgate, 2002), 121–122.

27. Spiro, "Nordic vs. Anti-Nordic," 42.

28. Earnest Sevier Cox, *White America* (Richmond: White America Society, 1923), 357. On Vardaman, see Joel Williamson, *The Crucible of Race* (New York: Oxford University Press, 1984), 379.

29. Williamson, *Crucible of Race,* 460, 461.

30. J. Douglas Smith, "The Campaign for Racial Purity and the Erosion of Paternalism in Virginia, 1922–1930: 'Nominally White, Biologically Mixed, and Legally Negro,'" *Journal of Southern History* 68 (2002): 67.

31. Jonathan Spiro maintains that Grant's early treatment of the "Negro problem" was more extensive than usually understood, but even Spiro admits that Grant's concern was much greater in his later writings. See Spiro, "Patrician Racist," 562. This view is consistent with Guterl, *Color of Race in America,* 64.

32. Quoted in Williamson, *Crucible of Race,* 219.

33. Biographical details are from Ethel Wolfskill Hedlin, "Earnest Cox and Colonialization: A White Racist's Response to Black Repatriation, 1923–1966" (Ph.D. diss., Duke University, 1974).

34. On the move to self-publish, see Hedlin, "Earnest Cox and Colonialization," 47.

35. Spiro, "Patrician Racist," 572.

36. Cox, *White America*, 23.

37. Ibid., 26, 27.

38. Ibid., 231.

39. On Chamberlain's interest in history as social action, see Geoffrey G. Field, *Evangelist of Race: The Germanic Vision of Houston Stewart Chamberlain* (New York: Columbia University Press, 1981), 174.

40. Earnest Sevier Cox, *The South's Part in Mongrelizing the Nation* (Richmond: White America Society, 1926), 31.

41. Melville Herskovits, "Extremes and Means in Racial Interpretation," *Journal of Social Forces* 2 (1924): 551.

42. Guy Johnson, "Recent Literature on the Negro," *Journal of Social Forces* 3 (1925): 318.

43. Spiro, "Patrician Racist," 573–574.

44. On Powell, see Richard B. Sherman, "'The Last Stand': The Fight for Racial Integrity in Virginia in the 1920s," *Journal of Southern History* 54 (1988): 69–92. On Plecker, see Derryn E. Moten, "Racial Integrity or 'Race Suicide': Virginia's Eugenic Movement, W. E. B. Du Bois, and the Work of Walter A. Plecker," *Negro History Bulletin* 61 (April–September 1999): 6–17. On Burleigh, see Barbara Bair, "Remapping the Black/White Body: Sexuality, Nationalism, and the Biracial Antimiscegenation Activism in 1920s Virginia," in *Sex, Love, Race: Crossing Boundaries in North American History,* ed. Martha Hodes (New York: New York University Press, 1999), 399–419.

45. Cox, *South's Part in Mongrelizing the Nation,* 98. On ASCOA, see Bair, "Remapping the Black/White Body," 400–401; Sherman, "Last Stand," 74–77.

46. For Grant's views and inspiration for Cox and his allies, see Spiro, "Patrician Racist," 574–575. For the history of Virginia's efforts legally to define "colored person," see Judy Scales-Trent, "Racial Purity Laws in the United States and Nazi Germany: The Targeting Process," *Human Rights Quarterly* 23 (2001): 264–267. On the passage of the act, see Sherman, "Last Stand," 77–79. On the Supreme Court, see Paul A. Lombardo, "Miscegenation, Eugenics, and Racism: Historical Footnotes to *Loving v. Virginia,*" *University of California Davis Law Review* 21 (1988): 421–452.

47. Cox, *South's Part in Mongrelizing the Nation,* 98. On the burden of proof, see Scales-Trent, "Racial Purity Laws," 266.

48. Sherman, "Last Stand," 69. Others also claim that the act was the first to

be based on science rather than popular prejudice. See Bair, "Remapping the Black/White Body," 400–401; Moten, "Racial Integrity or 'Race Suicide.'"

49. Williamson, *Crucible of Race,* 116. On railways, see Barbara Y. Welke, "When All the Women Were White, and All the Blacks Were Men: Gender, Class, and Race, and the Road to *Plessy,* 1855–1914," *Law and History Review* 13 (1995): 261–316.

50. Cox, *South's Part in Mongrelizing the Nation,* 53.

51. Gary Nash, "The Hidden History of Mestizo America," in *Sex, Love, Race,* ed. Hodes, 22; Julie Novkov, "Racial Constructions: The Legal Regulation of Miscegenation in Alabama, 1890–1934," *Law and History Review* 20 (2002): 135 pars.; 1 Dec. 2003, http://historycooperative.org/journals/lhr/20.2/novkov.html.

52. Bair, "Remapping the Black/White Body," 410.

53. Quoted in Moten, "Racial Integrity or 'Race Suicide,'" 7.

54. Sherman, "Last Stand," 85; Cox, *South's Part in Mongrelizing the Nation,* 98–107.

55. Major biographies of Garvey include: David Cronon, *Black Moses: The Story of Marcus Garvey and the Universal Negro Improvement Association* (Madison: University of Wisconsin Press, 1969); Elton C. Fax, *Garvey: The Story of a Pioneer Black Nationalist* (New York: Dodd and Mead, 1972); and Judith Stein, *The World of Marcus Garvey: Race and Class in Modern Society* (Baton Rouge: Louisiana State University Press, 1986).

56. Bair, "Remapping the Black/White Body," 404–405; William A. Edwards, "Racial Purity in Black and White: The Case of Marcus Garvey and Earnest Cox," *Journal of Ethnic Studies* 15 (1987): 132–133.

57. Earnest Sevier Cox, *Let My People Go* (Richmond: White America Society, 1925). See the advertisement in *Philosophy and Opinions of Marcus Garvey,* ed. Amy Jacques Garvey (New York: Atheneum, 1969), 414.

58. Emory Tolbert, "Outpost Garveyism and the UNIA Rank and File," *Journal of Black Studies* 5 (1975): 238.

59. Molefi Asante characterizes systematic nationalism as being first and foremost about establishing common bonds among a given people. The achievement of a geographic separation "is merely the ultimate stage of nationalism." See "Systematic Nationalism: A Legitimate Strategy for National Selfhood," *Journal of Black Studies* 9 (1978): 124. In effect, Cox mistook the end of nationalism for the whole of the program.

60. On the relationship between Draper and Madison Grant and the other racial anthropologists, see Paul A. Lombardo, "'The American Breed': Nazi Eugenics and the Origins of the Pioneer Fund," *Albany Law Review* 65 (2002): 743–830.

61. Charles B. Davenport and Morris Steggerda, *Race Crossing in Jamaica*

(Washington, DC: Carnegie Institution, 1929). On Draper's background and funding of Davenport, see William H. Tucker, *The Funding of Scientific Racism: Wickliffe Draper and the Pioneer Fund* (Urbana: University of Illinois Press, 2002), 30–32. On the poor reception of the study, see Barkan, *Retreat of Scientific Racism,* 162–168.

62. Tucker, *Funding of Scientific Racism,* 33–39.

63. Michael W. Fitzgerald, "'We Have Found a Moses': Theodore Bilbo, Black Nationalism, and the Greater Liberia Bill of 1939," *Journal of Southern History* 63 (1997): 293–320.

64. Lombardo, "American Breed," 768–774.

65. There is a large literature on the subject of the origins and use of the army tests. A good place to start is John Carson, "Army Alpha, Army Brass, and the Search for Army Intelligence," *Isis* 84 (1993): 278–309.

66. Graham Richards, *"Race," Racism, and Psychology* (London: Routledge, 1997), 91.

67. W. B. Thomas, "Black Intellectuals, Intelligence Testing in the 1930s, and the Sociology of Knowledge," *Teachers College Record* 85 (1984): 478. Also see V. P. Franklin, "Black Social Scientists and the Mental Testing Movement, 1920–1940," in *Black Psychology,* ed. R. L. Jones, 2d ed. (New York: Harper and Row, 1980), 201–215; Robert V. Guthrie, *Even the Rat Was White: A Historical View of Psychology* (Boston: Allyn and Bacon, 1998); Carl Jorgensen, "The African American Critique of White Supremacist Science," *Journal of Negro Education* 64 (1995): 232–242; C. M. Taylor, "W. E. B. Du Bois's Challenge to Scientific Racism," *Journal of Black Studies* 11 (1981): 449–460.

68. Biographical details from M. Fultz, "A 'Quintessential American': Horace Mann Bond, 1924–1939," *Harvard Educational Review* 55 (1985): 416–442; Wayne J. Urban, *Black Scholar: Horace Mann Bond, 1904–1972* (Athens: University of Georgia Press, 1992).

69. Horace M. Bond, "Intelligence Tests and Propaganda," *The Crisis* 28 (1924): 63.

70. Horace M. Bond, "What the Army 'Intelligence' Tests Measured," *Opportunity* 2 (1924): 198, 200.

71. See, for example, Thomas R. Garth, *Race Psychology: A Study of Racial Mental Differences* (New York: McGraw-Hill, 1931); Otto Klineberg, *Race Differences* (New York: Harper and Brothers, 1935).

72. Graham Richards, "Reconceptualizing the History of Race Psychology: Thomas Russell Garth (1872–1939) and How He Changed His Mind," *Journal of the History of the Behavioral Sciences* 34 (1998): 25–26.

73. Carl N. Degler, *In Search of Human Nature: The Decline and Revival of Darwinism in American Social Thought* (New York: Oxford University Press, 1991); Richards, *"Race," Racism, and Psychology;* Franz Samelson, "From 'Race Psychology' to 'Studies in Prejudice': Some Observations on the Thematic

Reversal in Social Psychology," *Journal of the History of the Behavioral Sciences* 14 (1978): 265–278.

74. Quoted in Spiro, "Nordic vs. Anti-Nordic," 46. Spiro argues that the Galton Society was not intended to spark new research but to provide a friendly environment for hereditarian scientists to share their ideas in a friendly environment. The alternative view is provided by Barkan, *Retreat of Scientific Racism,* 68.

75. Both Grant and Osborn quoted in Spiro, "Nordic vs. Anti-Nordic," 47.

76. William McDonald, "Mr. Grant's Plea for a Nordic, Protestant America," *New York Times,* 5 November 1933, 16.

77. Guterl, *Color of Race in America,* 67.

78. On the white South's attack on the Nazis and blindness toward southern racial injustice, see Johnpeter Horst Grill and Robert L. Jenkins, "The Nazis and the American South in the 1930s: A Mirror Image?" *Journal of Southern History* 58 (1992): 667–693. On scientific mobilization against racism, see James Capshew, *Psychologists on the March: Science, Practice, and Professional Identity in America, 1929–1969* (Cambridge: Cambridge University Press, 1999), 116–127; Ellen Herman, *The Romance of American Psychology: Political Culture in the Age of Experts* (Berkeley: University of California Press, 1995), 48–81; John P. Jackson Jr., *Social Scientists for Social Justice: Making the Case against Segregation* (New York: New York University Press, 2001), 43–59.

79. Ruth Benedict and Gene Weltfish, *Races of Mankind,* reprinted in Ruth Benedict, ed., *Race, Science and Politics* (New York: Viking Press, 1947), 170.

80. Ibid., 185.

81. May quoted in "Army Drops Race Equality Book: Denies May's Stand Was Reason," *New York Times,* 6 March 1944, 1, 11. On the USO, see "Ban by USO Criticized," *New York Times,* 16 March 1944, 17; Sloan quoted in "Plans New Edition of Race Pamphlet," *New York Times,* 8 March 1944, 11.

82. David H. Price, *Threatening Anthropology: McCarthyism and the FBI's Surveillance of Activist Anthropologists* (Durham: Duke University Press, 2004), 108–134; Ellen W. Schrecker, *No Ivory Tower: McCarthyism and the Universities* (New York: Oxford University Press, 1986), 255–257; Will Lissner, "Columbia Is Dropping Dr. Weltfish, Leftist," *New York Times,* 1 April 1953, 1, 19; E. R. Shipp, "Prof. Gene Weltfish Dead at 78; Was Target of Anti-Red Drives," *New York Times,* 5 August 1980, B10. On *Races of Mankind* in State Department libraries, see "Replies Refused by Dr. Weltfish," *New York Times,* 2 April 1953, 16.

83. Earnest Sevier Cox, *The Races of Mankind: A Review* (Jellico, TN: Arthur Daugherty, 1951), 5–6.

84. Ibid., 7.

85. Ibid., 15.

86. Ibid., 17–18.

87. From the online edition of Theodore G. Bilbo, *Take Your Choice: Separation or Mongrelization,* at http://www.solargeneral.com/library/TakeYour-Choice.pdf (viewed 30 September 2003). It is hardly a coincidence that Bilbo's views are being preserved online by a neo-Nazi Web site. Originally published as Theodore G. Bilbo, *Take Your Choice: Separation or Mongrelization* (Poplarville, MS: Dream House, 1947).

88. Tucker, *Funding of Scientific Racism,* 39–41.

NOTES TO CHAPTER 3

1. Earnest Sevier Cox, *Teutonic Unity* (Richmond: Earnest Sevier Cox, 1951), 10.

2. Johann von Leers to Earnest Sevier Cox, Earnest Sevier Cox Papers (hereafter ESC papers), Box 10, Folder "1955, Apr–May."

3. Kurt P. Tauber, *Beyond Eagle and Swastika: German Nationalism since 1945,* vol. 1 (Middletown, CT: Wesleyan University Press, 1967), 243. Additional biographical information on von Leers can be found in Martin A. Lee, *The Beast Reawakens* (New York: Routledge, 2000), 128–129.

4. Cox, *Teutonic Unity,* 174.

5. Ibid., 73.

6. Ibid., 139. On von Leers's affinity for both an alliance with the Soviets and rejection of Christianity, see Kevin Coogan, *Dreamer of the Day: Francis Parker Yockey and the Postwar Fascist International* (New York: Automedia, 1999), 274–278.

7. Ethel Wolfskill Hedlin, "Earnest Cox and Colonialization: A White Racist's Response to Black Repatriation, 1923–1966" (Ph.D. diss., Duke University, 1974), 171–213.

8. Accounts of the Northern League include Michael Billig, *Psychology, Racism and Fascism* (London: Searchlight, 1979). I have relied on the online version provided by Andrew Winston at http://www.psychology.uoguelph.ca/papers/winston/billig/billigframe.html (viewed 11 November 2003). Also see Coogan, *Dreamer of the Day,* 468–477; William H. Tucker, *The Science and Politics of Racial Research* (Urbana: University of Illinois Press, 1994), 174; William H. Tucker, *The Funding of Scientific Racism: Wickliffe Draper and the Pioneer Fund* (Urbana: University of Illinois Press, 2002), 161–164; Andrew S. Winston, "Science in the Service of the Far Right: Henry E. Garrett, the IAAEE, and the Liberty Lobby," *Journal of Social Issues* 54 (1998): 195–198.

9. For descriptions of Keith's career, see Elazar Barkan, *The Retreat of Scientific Racism: Changing Concepts of Race in Britain and the United States between the World Wars* (Cambridge: Cambridge University Press, 1992), 43–53; C. Loring Brace, "The Roots of the Race Concept in American Physical Anthropology," in *A History of American Physical Anthropology, 1930–1980,* ed.

Frank Spencer (New York: Academic Press, 1982), 13–15; Nancy Leys Stepan, *The Idea of Race in Science: Great Britain, 1800–1960* (Hamden: Archon, 1982), 108–110; Milford Wolpoff and Rachel Caspari, *Race and Human Evolution: A Fatal Attraction* (New York: Simon and Schuster, 1997), 144–147. On Montagu's relationship with Keith, see Leonard Lieberman, Andrew Lyons, and Harriet Lyons, "An Interview with Ashley Montagu," *Current Anthropology* 36 (1995): 836–837.

10. Arthur Keith, *An Autobiography* (London: Watts, 1950), 395–396. For Keith's writings on race, see Arthur Keith, *Nationality and Race from an Anthropologist's Point of View* (London: Oxford University Press, 1919); Arthur Keith, *Ethnos: The Problem of Race Considered from a New Point of View* (London: Kegan, Paul, Trench, Trubner, 1931); Arthur Keith, *The Place of Prejudice in Modern Civilization* (London: Williams and Norgate, 1931).

11. Arthur Keith, *Essays on Human Evolution* (London: Watts, 1946), 210, 215–216. On the role of World War I in forming Keith's ideas about race and evolution, see Nancy Leys Stepan, "'Nature's Pruning Hook': War, Race, and Evolution," in *The Political Culture of Modern Britain,* ed. J. M. W. Bean (London: Hamish Hamilton, 1987), 129–148.

12. Roger Pearson, "Evolution and the Modern State," *The European* 8 (April 1958), 21, 22, 24. On *The European*'s contributors and readership, see Robert Skidelsky, *Oswald Mosely* (New York: Holt, Rhinehart, and Winston, 1975), 493–494. One of the first publications of the Northern League was a pamphlet detailing Keith's views. See "Formation of the Northern League: At Last! A World Group," *The Northlander* 1 no. 1 (April 1985): 1, in ESC Papers, Box 13, Folder "1958 April–March."

13. On Guenther, see "New Studies of Greek and Roman History," *The Northlander* 1, no. 1 (April 1985): 3, in ESC Papers, Box 13, Folder "1958 April–March." Quotation on Pan-Nordicism from Roger Pearson, "Pan-Nordicism as a Modern Policy," *Northern World* 3, no. 5 (1959): 12. On Chamberlain, see Edward Langford, "Profile: Authors of Human Science, Houston Stewart Chamberlain," *The Northlander* 1, no. 3 (June 1958): 3, in ESC Papers, Box 29, Folder "Northern League." Quotations on League aims are in "League Policy Outlined: Ethnic Heritage Must Be Preserved!" *The Northlander* 1, no. 3 (June 1958): 2, in ESC Papers, Box 29, Folder "Northern League." On Keith, see Roger Pearson, "Sir Arthur Keith and Evolution," *Northern World* 2, no. 1 (1957): 4–7.

14. Roger Pearson to Earnest Sevier Cox, 2 April 1958, ESC Papers, Box 13, Folder "1958 April–May"; Cox to Williams, 20 December 1957, ESC Papers Box 12, Folder "1957 Oct.–Dec." Pearson's enthusiasm for Cox's idea is evident in his letter of 8 February 1958, ESC Papers, Box 13, Folder "1958 Jan.–March."

15. On Guenther, see Earnest Sevier Cox to Roger Pearson, 10 July 1958,

and Pearson to Cox, 15 July 1958, both letters in ESC Papers, Box 13, Folder "1958, June–Sept"; and William Stephenson to Cox, 30 June 1959, ESC Papers, Box 13, Folder "June–Dec. 1959."

16. An announcement of the Northern League was in Carto's newspaper: "Northern League Office Opened," *Right*, no. 38 (November 1958): 1–2.

17. Willis Carto to Earnest Sevier Cox, 29 March 1954, ESC Papers, Box 9, Folder "Corr. 1954, Jan.–Apr."

18. "Important Letter to the Regents of California," 1 October 1955, in H. Keith Thompson Papers, Hoover Institution Archives, Stanford University, Palo Alto, California, Box 10 (hereafter HKT Papers). An abbreviated version of this letter was reprinted as E. L. Anderson, "The Testimony of History," *Truth Seeker* 84 (April 1957): 62.

19. For biographical information on Carto, see Coogan, *Dreamer of the Day*, 468–470; Sara Diamond, *Roads to Dominion: Right Wing Movements and Political Power in the United States* (New York: Guilford, 1995), 85; Frank Mintz, *The Liberty Lobby and the American Right: Race, Conspiracy and Culture* (Westport, CT: Greenwood Press, 1985), 40–41.

20. On Klan violence in Oklahoma and the colorful career of J. C. Walton, see David Chalmers, *Hooded Americanism: The History of the Ku Klux Klan* (Chicago: Quadrangle, 1968), 49–55; Brad L. Duren, "'Klanspiracy' or Despotism? The Rise and Fall of Governor Jack Walton, Featuring W. D. McBee," *Chronicles of Oklahoma* 80 (2002): 468–485. On Blake's role fighting Klan actions in Tulsa, see "Order Martial Law in Tulsa, Oklahoma," *New York Times*, 14 August 1923, 5; "Bares Terrorism of Tulsa Floggers," *New York Times*, 7 September 1923, 17.

21. "Tear Bombs Scatter Detroit Mob of 5,000 Which Masses before Anti-Klan Meeting," *New York Times*, 22 October 1924, 1.

22. Aldrich Blake, *The Ku Klux Kraze: A Trip through the Klavern* (Oklahoma City: Aldrich Blake, 1924), 14.

23. Ibid., 16–17.

24. Thomas J. Sugrue, "Crabgrass-Roots Politics: Race, Rights, and the Reaction against Liberalism in the Urban North, 1940–1964," *Journal of American History* 82 (1995): 554. On "freedom of choice," see Eric Foner, *The Story of American Freedom* (New York: Norton, 1998), p. 315.

25. Aldrich Blake, *My Kind! My Country!* (Philadelphia: Dorrance, 1950), 35.

26. Ibid., 51.

27. Ibid., 81.

28. Ibid., 337.

29. Ibid., 227.

30. Ibid., 248.

31. Ibid., 146.

32. Ibid., 181.

33. Ibid., 358–359.

34. Ibid., vi. Emphasis in original.

35. Ibid., 334.

36. Aldrich Blake, *Civil Rights or Civil Wrongs* (Laguna Beach, CA: Aldrich Blake, 1953), 3, 50.

37. Ted Oster, "America Plus—Democracy Minus," *New Republic* 127 (11 August 1952): 16–17.

38. Letter to "Dear Friend" from Willis Carto, 20 August 1954, ESC Papers, Box 10, Folder "1954, May–Dec." On the Second Bill of Rights, see the Prospectus of Liberty and Property, ESC Papers, Box 28, Folder "Le–Liberty A." Carto describes Blake's role in Liberty and Property in a letter to Cox on 9 June 1954, ESC Papers, Box 10, Folder "1954 May–Dec."

39. See Liberty and Property Progress Report, 7 January 1955, ESC Papers, Box 28, Folder "Le–Liberty A."

40. Carto to Cox, 2 February 1955, ESC Papers, Box 10, Folder "1955 Jan.–Mar."

41. Carto to Blake, 5 August 1955, ESC Papers, Box 10, Folder "1955 Sept.–Oct."

42. *Right,* no. 2 (November 1955): 3; E. L. Anderson, "The Reality of Race," *Right,* no. 20 (May 1957): 3.

43. Carto to Cox, 29 September 1956, ESC Papers, Box 11, Folder "Sept.–Dec. 1956"; and Carto to Cox, 26 January 1957, ESC Papers, Box 12, Folder "1957, Jan.–Feb."

44. Mintz, *Liberty Lobby and the American Right,* 67; Carto to Cox, 5 December 1956, ESC Papers, Box 11, Folder "1956 Sept.–Dec."

45. For the history of *Truth Seeker,* see Coogan, *Dreamer of the Day,* 478–489; George E. MacDonald, *Fifty Years of Freethought: Being the Story of the Truth Seeker, with the Natural History of Its Third Editor,* 2 vols. (New York: Truth Seeker, 1929–31); Mintz, *Liberty Lobby and the American Right,* 66–67; and the *Truth Seeker* Web site, http://www.truthseeker.com (viewed 11 November 2003). On evangelical atheism, see Jennifer Michael Hecht, *Doubt: A History* (San Francisco: HarperSanFrancisco, 2003), 370–427.

46. MacDonald, *Fifty Years of Freethought,* vol. 2, 621. Biographical details on Smith are from Gordon Stein, "Charles Lee Smith (1887–1964)," *American Rationalist* 29 (1984): 11–13. For Smith's clashes with religious leaders in New York, see "Atheists in Clash with Dr. Straton," *New York Times,* 18 October 1926, 39; "Atheist Is Cleared of Straton Attack," *New York Times,* 20 December 1927, 22. On Arkansas, see "New York Atheist Enters Jail in Arkansas; Won't Pay Fine for Fighting Anti-Evolution Law," *New York Times,* 18 October 1928, 1.

47. On Vacher de Lapouge, see Jennifer Michael Hecht, "The Solvency of Metaphysics: The Debate over Racial Science and Moral Philosophy in France,

1890–1919," *Isis* 90 (1999): 1–24; Jennifer Michael Hecht, "Vacher de Lapouge and the Rise of Nazi Science," *Journal of the History of Ideas* 61 (2000): 285–304; Jennifer Michael Hecht, *The End of the Soul: Scientific Modernity, Atheism, and Anthropology in France* (New York: Columbia University Press, 2003), 168–210. On Haeckel, see Daniel Gasman, *The Scientific Origins of National Socialism* (New York: Elsevier, 1971); and Daniel Gasman, *Haeckel's Monism and the Birth of Fascist Ideology* (New York: Peter Lang, 1998). On Haeckel's association with *Truth Seeker* at the beginning of the twentieth century, see Coogan, *Dreamer of the Day,* 485.

48. Coogan, *Dreamer of the Day,* 478. Smith recounted his experiences in the forest in "Northmen Meet at Detmold," *Truth Seeker* 86 (September 1959): 134–135.

49. Charles Smith, *Sensism: The Philosophy of the West,* 2 vols. (New York: Truth Seeker, 1956).

50. See the summary in Mintz, *Liberty Lobby and the American Right,* 67.

51. Smith, *Sensism,* 961.

52. Ibid., 977–978.

53. Ibid., 1442–1443.

54. Ibid., 1427.

55. Charles Smith, "The Stars Battle the White Race," *Truth Seeker* 84 (1957): 36.

56. Charles Smith, "Love Mongers and Love Sheets," *Truth Seeker* 86 (March 1959): 40; Charles Smith, "A Misdirected Letter," *Truth Seeker* 84 (April 1957): 62; Charles Smith, "Eugenics: Sterilization of Defectives and Discrimination in Immigration," *Truth Seeker* 84 (November 1957): 173.

57. On the Weiss's role in the NRP, see Coogan, *Dreamer of the Day,* 252–255, 418–421.

58. George Lincoln Rockwell, "The U.S. Right Wing Picture," *Rockwell Report,* no. 7 (15 January 1962): 5. On the printing of the *Bulletin* and the close association of Madole and the *Truth Seeker,* see Coogan, *Dreamer of the Day,* 486. A nearly complete run of the *National Renaissance Bulletin* is available in *The Right Wing Collections of the University of Iowa Libraries, 1918–1977,* Reel 84 (Glen Rock, NJ: Microfilming Corporation of America, 1977), at N23. The *Bulletin* included some of the earliest examples of Holocaust denial. On the NRP and Holocaust denial, see Deborah Lipstadt, *Denying the Holocaust: The Growing Assault on Truth and Memory* (New York: Plume, 1993), 66; and James H. Madole, "Did Nazi Germany Destroy Six Million Jews?" *National Renaissance Bulletin* 11, no. 3 (March 1960): 2–5.

59. *Preliminary Report on Neo-Fascist and Hate Groups,* Committee on Un-American Activities, U.S. House of Representatives, 17 December 1954, 5.

60. James H. Madole, "The Scientific and Historical Basis for Racial Segregation," *National Renaissance Bulletin* 7, no. 4 (April 1956): 2, 3, 4.

61. Charles Lee Smith, "Jews Block Racist Forum," *Truth Seeker* 86 (1959): 31; Robert Kuttner, "Jewish Slanders and Democratic Forums," *Truth Seeker* 86 (1959): 3.

62. Northern League quotation from "The Alphafest" ESC Papers, Box 29, Folder "Northern League." This document is attributed to the "Organizing Secretary of the Northern League" for North America, who was undoubtedly Carto.

63. Byram Campbell, *American Race Theorists: A Critique of Their Thoughts and Methods* (Boston: Chapman and Grimes, 1952), 123.

64. Ibid., 100–101.

65. Ibid., 48, 50.

66. Ibid., 137. Also Byram Campbell, "Jewized Textbook Sociology: Broom and Selznick," *Truth Seeker* 88 (1961): 49–51.

67. Campbell, *American Race Theorists*, 139, 140.

68. Byram Campbell, "The Nordic as an Ideal," *Northern World* 3, no. 3 (1959): 7.

69. Byram Campbell, *The World of Oneness* (New York: Vantage, 1956), 111.

70. Robert Kuttner, "The Nordic as the Natural Leader of the White Race," *Truth Seeker* 85 (1958): 114.

71. Theodore Lothrop Stoddard, "The French Revolution in San Domingo" (Ph.D. diss., Harvard University, 1914). On the Haitian revolt as a standard appeal in racist thought, see George M. Fredrickson, *The Black Image in the White Mind* (Hanover: Wesleyan University Press, 1971), 53–54; Winthrop D. Jordan, *White over Black* (New York: Norton, 1968), 396.

72. Robert Kuttner, "The Unequal Races of Man," *Truth Seeker* 83 (December 1956): 186.

73. Robert Kuttner, "The North European in Homeric Greece," *Northern World* 3 (1958): 8–15; Robert Kuttner, "The Early History of the Celt," *Northern World* 3 (1958): 12–18; Robert Kuttner, "The Early History of the Teuton," *Northern World* 3 (1959): 12–20.

74. Robert Kuttner, "On Strike against Science," *Truth Seeker* 86 (1959): 19.

75. Robert Kuttner, "The Status of Scientific Racism I," *Truth Seeker* 84 (1957): 75.

76. Ashley Montagu, *Statement on Race* (New York: Oxford University Press, 1972), 12. For a good account of the history of the UNESCO statements, see Elazar Barkan, "The Politics of the Science of Race: Ashley Montagu and UNESCO's Anti-Racist Declarations," in *Race and Other Misadventures: Essays in Honor of Ashley Montagu in His Ninetieth Year,* ed. Larry T. Reynolds and Leonard Lieberman (Dix Hills, NJ: General Hall, 1996), 96–105.

77. Kuttner, "Status of Scientific Racism I," 75.

78. Ibid., 75.

79. Robert Kuttner, "Manifestoes and Resolutions on Race," *Truth Seeker* 84 (August 1957). 118.

80. Kuttner, "Status of Scientific Racism I," 76.

81. Kuttner, "Manifestoes and Resolutions on Race," 118.

82. Kuttner, "Status of Scientific Racism I," 75.

83. Robert Kuttner, "The Status of Scientific Racism II," *Truth Seeker* 84 (June 1957): 87.

84. Eustace Mullins, "Adolph Hitler: An Appreciation," *National Renaissance Bulletin* (October 1952): 4, reprinted in *Preliminary Report on Neo-Fascist and Hate Groups,* 27. For other biographical details on Mullins see the Nizkor Web site, http://nizkor.org/ftp.cgi/people/m/ftp.py?people/m//mullins.eustace; and a biographical sketch prepared by Julie Gutmanis at http://slisweb.lis.wisc.edu/~jcherney/gutmanis.html (both Web sites viewed 8 November 2003). Also Martin A. Lee, *The Beast Reawakens* (New York: Routledge, 2000), 91; Marc H. Caplan and Lori Linzer, *Uncommon Ground: The Black African Holocaust Denial Council and Other Links between Black and White Extremists* (New York: Anti-Defamation League, 1994), 16.

85. Eustace Mullins, "Writer Charges Oil Lobby with Breach of Contract," 28 February 1956, HKT Papers, Box 10. On the Federal Reserve, see Eustace Mullins, *The Federal Reserve Conspiracy* (Union, NJ: Common Sense, 1954).

86. Keith, *Autobiography,* 425. Keith also furnished the introduction to Morley Roberts, *Warfare in the Human Body: Essays on Method, Malignity, Repair, and Allied Subjects* (London: Eveleigh Nash, 1920). On the close association between Keith and Roberts, see Rhodri Hayward, "The Biopolitics of Arthur Keith and Morley Roberts," *Clio Medica* 60 (August 2000), 251–274. On Morley Roberts and the origin of the term *biopolitics,* see Robert H. Blank and Samuel H. Hines Jr., *Biology and Political Science* (New York: Routledge, 2001), 6.

87. Morley Roberts, *Biopolitics: An Essay in the Physiology, Pathology, and Politics of the Social and Somatic Organism* (London: Dent, 1937), 51.

88. *The Biopolitics of Organic Materialism,* in *The Right Wing Collections of the University of Iowa Libraries, 1918–1977,* Reel 89 (Glen Rock, NJ: Microfilming Corporation of America, 1977), at N86; the reprints of Roberts are on p. 29, reprinted from *Biopolitics,* 165–166. Rhodri Hayward argued that Roberts's *Biopolitics* appears to support a reactionary form of government but that a close reading makes apparent Robert's anarchist tendencies and concerns. See Hayward, "Biopolitics of Arthur Keith and Morley Roberts," 264–265. Hayward is undoubtedly correct, but Kuttner and Mullins were happy with the reactionary reading.

89. The first announcement of the Institute of Biopolitics was Eustace Mullins and M. Nelson, "Christianity, Communism, and Biopolitics," *Truth Seeker* 85 (August 1958): 122–123.

90. First three quotations in Eustace Mullins, "The New Man in Our Image," *Truth Seeker* 85 (November 1958): 170, 171, 172. The original article was in *Biopolitics of Organic Materialism*, 20–25. Final quotation in Eustace Mullins, "The Role of America," in *Biopolitics of Organic Materialism*, 28.

91. Robert Kuttner, "Biopolitics: The Theory of Racial Nationalism," *Truth Seeker* 86 (1959): 42.

92. Ibid.

93. Robert Kuttner, "Biopolitics: The Validity of Racial Nationalism," *Truth Seeker* 86 (1959): 129.

94. Ibid., 131.

95. Charles G. Bennett, "Ban on Housing Bias Voted by City Board," *New York Times*, 24 December 1957, 1; Charles G. Bennett, "Housing Bill Signed by Mayor," *New York Times*, 31 December 1957, 9.

96. A. James Gregor, "Emergency City-Wide Citizen's Committee for the Preservation of Freedom of Choice," 28 February 1958, 2, in Wesley Critz George Papers, Box 6, Folder 38, Southern Historical Collection, University of North Carolina, Chapel Hill, North Carolina. (hereafter WCG Papers). On the formation of the APFC, see Tucker, *Funding of Scientific Racism*, 88–90.

97. Press release titled "Memorandum to All Persons Interested in Joining the Association for the Preservation of Freedom of Choice," HKT Papers, Box 16.

98. Eric Foner, *The Story of American Freedom* (New York: Norton, 1998), 314.

99. Alfred Avins, "Anti-Discrimination Legislation as an Infringement on Freedom of Choice," *New York Law Forum* 6 (1960): 23.

100. Ibid., 25.

101. Ibid., 28.

102. *Application of Association for Preservation of Freedom of Choice, Inc.*, 187 N.Y.S. 2d 706 (1959), at 707.

103. *Association for the Preservation for the Freedom of Choice v. Shapiro*, 214 N.Y.S. 2d 388 (1961).

104. Leo Egan, "Liberals Back Republican for Bronx Borough Chief," *New York Times*, 11 August 1961, 11.

105. *Association for the Preservation for the Freedom of Choice v. Dudley*, 29 Misc. 2d 710 (1961).

106. Ben A. Franklin, "New Voting Law Attacked in Suit," *New York Times*, 7 August 1965, 1; "Professor Loses Publication Suit," *New York Times*, 12 November 1967, 63; Sophy Burnham, "Twelve Rebels of the Student Right," *New York Times*, 9 March 1969, SM32. Biographical details of Avins can be found in "Legal Scholar Alfred Avins Dies at Age 64," *Washington Post*, 11 June 1999, B6.

107. Gregor, "Emergency City-Wide Citizen's Committee," 4.

108. Alfred Avins, "Anti-Miscegenation Laws and the Fourteenth Amendment. The Original Intent," *Virginia Law Review* 52 (1966): 1224–1255; Alfred Avins, "De Facto and De Jure School Segregation: Some Reflected Light on the Fourteenth Amendment from the Civil Rights Act of 1875," *Mississippi Law Journal* 38 (1967): 179–253. On Avins's association with Thurmond, see his letter to the editor in the *Washington Post*, 22 June 1994, A20.

NOTES TO CHAPTER 4

1. Stuart Omer Landry, *The Cult of Equality: A Study of the Race Problem* (New Orleans: Pelican Publishing Co., 1945). On his earlier concerns about race suicide, see Stuart Omer Landry, "Why Race Suicide with Advancing Civilization?" *The Arena* 41 (1909): 569.

2. Landry, *Cult of Equality*, 13, 42.

3. Ibid., 54–55.

4. Ibid., 2.

5. E. B. Reuter, "Southern Scholars and Race Relations," *Phylon* 7 (1946): 222; E. B. Reuter, "Review of *Cult of Equality*," *American Journal of Sociology* 51 (1946): 348–349; Landry, *Cult of Equality*, vii.

6. David Zarofsky, "Conspiracy Arguments in the Lincoln-Douglas Debates," *Journal of the American Forensic Association* 21 (1984): 73.

7. Stuart Omer Landry, *Facts to Fight Communism* (New Orleans: Pelican Publishing Co., 1948), 32.

8. *Brown v. Board of Education*, 347 U.S. 483 (1954).

9. Michael J. Klarman, "How *Brown* Changed Race Relations: The Backlash Thesis," *Journal of American History* 81 (1994): 82. Also see Klarman's more extended presentation of his argument in Michael J. Klarman, *"Brown,* Racial Change, and the Civil Rights Movement," *Virginia Law Review* 80 (1994): 7–150. Other standard sources on the political reaction to *Brown* are Numan V. Bartley, *The Rise of Massive Resistance and the Politics of the South during the 1950s* (Baton Rouge: Louisiana State University Press, 1969); Francis M. Wilhoit, *The Politics of Massive Resistance* (New York: George Braziller, 1973).

10. "Southern Manifesto" (1956), reprinted in *The Burden of Race: A Documentary History of Negro-White Relations in America*, ed. Gilbert Osofsky (New York: Harper and Row, 1967), 493. On the origins of the Southern Manifesto, see Robert Mann, *The Walls of Jericho: Lyndon Johnson, Hubert Humphrey, Richard Russell, and the Struggle for Civil Rights* (New York: Harcourt, Brace and Company, 1996), 161–166.

11. David R. Goldfield, *Black, White, and Southern: Race Relations and Southern Culture 1940 to the Present* (Baton Rouge: Louisiana State University Press, 1990), 79.

12. The best treatment of the Citizens' Councils remains Neil R. McMillen, *The Citizens' Council: Organized Resistance to the Second Reconstruction, 1954–64* (Urbana: University of Illinois Press, 1971; reprint, 1994).

13. *Brown v. Board of Education,* 347 U.S. 483 (1954), at 494.

14. Mark V. Tushnet, *Making Civil Rights Law* (New York: Oxford University Press, 1994), 314–315. On the origins of the specific studies cited and the collaboration between social scientists and attorneys in the *Brown* litigation, see John P. Jackson Jr. *Social Scientists for Social Justice: Making the Case against Segregation* (New York: New York University Press, 2001).

15. Edmond Cahn, "Jurisprudence." *New York University Law Review* 30 (1955): 157–158. Also Jackson, *Social Scientists for Social Justice,* 175–181.

16. Klarman, "*Brown,* Racial Change, and the Civil Rights Movement," 109.

17. Charles Bloch, *States' Rights: The Law of the Land* (Atlanta: Harrison Company, 1958), 207. On Bloch's career, see Clive Webb, "Charles Bloch: Jewish White Supremacist," *Georgia Historical Quarterly* 83 (1999): 267–292.

18. See his speech in the *Congressional Record,* 84th Cong., 1st sess. (26 May 1955), 7120–7124. The reprint on which I have relied is James Eastland, "The Supreme Court's 'Modern Scientific Authorities' in the Segregation Cases," in Elizabeth Churchill Brown Papers, Box 22, Folder 13, Hoover Institution Archives, Stanford University, Palo Alto, California.

19. James Byrnes, *The Supreme Court Must Be Curbed* (Winona: Association of Citizens' Councils of Mississippi, 1956), 9.

20. Leander Perez, "Civil Rights—1959," Committee on the Judiciary, 86th Cong., 1st sess., part 1 (15 May 1959), 807.

21. George D. Strayer, *Report of a Survey of the Public Schools of the District of Columbia Conducted under the Auspices of the Chairmen of the Subcommittees on District of Columbia Appropriations of the Respective Appropriations Committees of the Senate and House of Representatives* (Washington, DC: Government Printing Office, 1949), 497; Kenesaw M. Landis, *Segregation in Washington: A Report of the National Committee on Segregation in the Nation's Capital* (Chicago: National Committee on Segregation in the Nation's Capital, 1948), 76.

22. Quoted in T. K. Page, "A Study of the District of Columbia Public Schools Desegregation Policies, 1954–1967" (Ph.D. diss., Virginia Polytechnic Institute, 1978), 140.

23. John C. Davis, *Investigation of Public School Conditions,* Committee on the District of Columbia, House of Representatives, 84th Cong., 2nd sess. (19 September 1956), 1.

24. Ibid., 51.

25. Ibid., 135.

26. Floyd Fleming, "Integration means Degeneration" (undated), in *The*

Right Wing Collection of the University of Iowa Libraries, 1918–1977, Reel R9 (Glen Rock, NJ: Microfilming Corporation of America, 1977), at A64.

27. *Congressional Committee Report on What Happened When Schools Were Integrated in Washington DC* (Greenwood, MS: Citizens' Councils, undated), 11, in ESC Papers, Box 26, Folder "Association of Citizen Councils."

28. Richard Kluger, *Simple Justice: The History of Brown v. Board of Education and Black America's Struggle for Equality* (New York: Vintage Books, 1975), 621–623.

29. Horace Mann Bond to Clarence Mitchell, 1 October 1956, Horace Mann Bond Papers, Box 65, Folder 270D, W. E. B. Du Bois Library, University of Massachusetts, Amherst, Massachusetts (hereafter HMB Papers).

30. G. W. Lee to Bond, undated, HMB Papers, Box 64, Folder 270D.

31. Horace Mann Bond, "Speech to the Hungry Club," 1962, HMB Papers, Box 172, Folder 13.

32. Horace Mann Bond, "A Study of the Intelligence of Congressmen Who Signed the Southern Manifesto as Measured by I.Q. Tests Administered by the Army to Them and to Their Constituents, and by the American Council on Education Psychological Examinations as Administered to, and Reported by, Their Colleges" (1956), 2, Papers of the National Association for the Advancement of Colored People, Box A172, Manuscript Division, Library of Congress, Washington, D.C. (hereafter NAACP Papers).

33. Ibid., 13.

34. Ibid., 14.

35. Ibid., 13.

36. Ibid., 15.

37. "Southerners Branded 'Moron' by NAACP," press clipping, HMB Papers, Box 64, Folder 270D; Bond to Lee, 21 December 1956, HMB Papers, Box 64, Folder 270D.

38. Bond to Mitchell, 28 December 1956, HMB Papers, Box 64, Folder 270D.

39. Frank C. J. McGurk, "Comparative Test Scores of Negro and White School Children in Richmond, VA," *Journal of Educational Psychology* 34 (1943): 480.

40. Ibid., 480, 482.

41. Frank C. J. McGurk, "Socio-economic Status and Culturally-Weighted Test Scores of Negro Subjects," *Journal of Applied Psychology* 37 (1953): 277. See also Frank C. J. McGurk, "On White and Negro Test Performance and Socioeconomic Factors," *Journal of Abnormal and Social Psychology* 48 (1953), 448–450. Both articles were taken from his dissertation: Frank C. J. McGurk, "Comparison of the Performance of Negro and White High School Seniors on Cultural and Non-Cultural Psychological Test Questions" (Ph.D. diss., Catholic University of America, 1951).

42. McGurk to Wesley Critz George, 12 July 1955, in Wesley C. George Papers, Box 2, Folder 15, Southern Historical Collection, University of North Carolina, Chapel Hill (hereafter WCG Papers).

43. The central argument of McGurk's *U.S. News and World Report* piece can be found in "A Psychological Phenotype for Race," an unpublished paper in WCG Papers, Box 2, Folder 15.

44. Frank C. J. McGurk, "A Scientist's Report on Race Differences," *U.S. News and World Report* 41 (21 September 1956): 92.

45. Ibid., 93, 96. Emphasis in original.

46. Ibid., 96.

47. "From Here, There, and Most Everywhere," *Right,* no. 13 (October 1956): 4; Bernard Hennessy, "Race, Intelligence, and Equality," *New Republic* 135 (24 December 1956): 10.

48. Otto Klineberg et al., "Does Race Really Make a Difference in Intelligence?" *U.S. News and World Report* 41 (26 October 1956): 74–75; Ashley Montagu, "Negro Intelligence Capacity—A Scientist's View," *Harvard Law Record* (18 October 1956): 3–4, 6.

49. Kenneth Green, "Memorandum to Executive Director," in *A Chicago Urban League Report on "A Scientist's Report on Racial Differences,"* ed. Kenneth Green (Chicago: Urban League, 1957), 1.

50. Willard A. Kerr, "Psychological Test Results Do Not Support the Idea of Inherent Differences between the Intelligence Levels of Various Racial Groups," in *A Chicago Urban League Report on "A Scientist's Report on Racial Differences,"* 15.

51. Ibid., 14; Peter Jacobsohn, "A Scientist's Unscientific Report," in *A Chicago Urban League Report on "A Scientist's Report on Racial Differences,"* 33.

52. Howard Hale Long, "The Relative Learning Capacities of Negroes and Whites," *Journal of Negro Education* 26 (1957): 129.

53. William M. McCord and Nicholas J. Demerath III, "Negro versus White Intelligence: A Continuing Controversy," *Harvard Educational Review* 28 (1958): 122.

54. Frank C. J. McGurk, "Negro vs. White Intelligence—An Answer," *Harvard Educational Review* 29 (1959): 56.

55. Ibid., 60.

56. McGurk to Wesley Critz George, 31 July 1959, WCG Papers, Box 7, Folder 44.

57. Carole Polsgrove, *Divided Minds: Intellectuals and the Civil Rights Movement* (New York: Norton, 2001), 103–123.

58. Emma Harrison, "Professor's Right to Views Upheld: Psychologist Says Villanova Resisted Calls for Ouster after Article on Negro," *New York Times,* 8 September 1959, 39.

59. Frank C. J. McGurk, "The Law, Social Science, and Academic Freedom A Psychologist's View," *Villanova Law Review* 5 (1959 60): 253, 251.

60. Wesley Critz George to Frank Graham, 30 September 1933, WCG Papers, Box 1, Folder 5.

61. Background on Odum is from David Southern, *Gunnar Myrdal and Black-White Relations: The Use and Abuse of* An American Dilemma, *1944–1969* (Baton Rouge: Louisiana State University Press, 1987), 17–19, 157–160; Walter A. Jackson, *Gunnar Myrdal and America's Conscience: Social Engineering and Racial Liberalism, 1938–1987* (Chapel Hill: University of North Carolina Press, 1990), 96–97; Daryl Michael Scott, *Contempt and Pity: Social Policy and the Image of the Damaged Black Psyche, 1880–1996* (Chapel Hill: University of North Carolina Press, 1997), 126.

62. George to Howard Odum, 24 May 1944, WCG Papers, Box 1, Folder 5.

63. Wesley Critz George, "Lecture to Dr. Odum's Class, April 24, 1946," WCG Papers, Box 13, Folder 103. On agriculture and eugenics, see Phillip Thurtle, "Harnessing Heredity in Gilded Age America: Middle Class Mores and Industrial Breeding in a Cultural Context," *Journal of the History of Biology* 35 (2002): 43–78. On the prevalence of agricultural metaphors in eugenicist discourse, see Celeste Michelle Condit, *The Meanings of the Gene: Public Debates about Human Heredity* (Madison: University of Wisconsin Press, 1999); Edward J. Larson, *Sex, Race, and Science: Eugenics in the Deep South* (Baltimore: Johns Hopkins University Press, 1995).

64. Wesley Critz George, "The Responsibility of Scientists in This Era," *School and Society* 76 (13 December 1952): 371.

65. Ibid., 372–373.

66. George to William B. Umstead, May 20, 1954, WCG Papers, Box 1, Folder 9.

67. McMillen, *Citizen Councils,* 111–114; John N. Popham, "Organized Resistance to Racial Laws Grows," *New York Times,* 2 December 1956, E9. On George's involvement, see Steven Niven, "Wesley Critz George: Scientist and Segregationist," *North Carolina Literary Review,* no. 7 (1998): 39–41.

68. Wilhoit, *Politics of Massive Resistance,* 118. Also see his discussion of the Patriots on 116–117.

69. It was published as Wesley Critz George, *The Race Problem from the Standpoint of One Who Is Concerned about the Evils of Miscegenation* (Shreveport: American States Rights Association, 1955).

70. Wesley Critz George, *Race, Heredity, and Civilization and Human Progress and the Race Problem* (London: Britons, 1961), 42.

71. James Eastland to J. A. Henry, 5 July 1955, Box 7, Folder 15; Eugene Cook to George, 27 March 1957, Box 6, Folder 34; Frederick H. McDonald to George, 19 November 1954, Box 2, Folder 10, all in WCG Papers.

72. George to Wickliffe Draper, 19 August 1955, WCG Papers, Box 3,

Folder 16; William H. Tucker, *The Funding of Scientific Racism: Wickliffe Draper and the Pioneer Fund* (Urbana: University of Illinois Press, 2002), 69–70.

NOTES TO CHAPTER 5

1. Taylor Branch, *Parting the Waters: America in the King Years, 1954–1963* (New York: Simon and Schuster, 1988), 222–224.

2. Michael Klarman, "*Brown,* Racial Change, and the Civil Rights Movement," *Virginia Law Review* 80 (1994): 119. For other treatments of how Little Rock transformed the massive resistance movement, see Numan Bartley, *The Rise of Massive Resistance and the Politics of the South during the 1950s* (Baton Rouge: Louisiana State University Press, 1969), 251–269; and Francis M. Wilhoit, *The Politics of Massive Resistance* (New York: George Braziller, 1973), 176–182.

3. Byram Campbell, "Open Letter to President Dwight D. Eisenhower," in *The Right Wing Collection of the University of Iowa Libraries, 1918–1977,* Reel R35, (Glen Rock, NJ: Microfilming Corporation of America, 1977), at C71; "An American Tragedy: School Children under the Gun," *The Virginian* 3, no. 10 (October 1957): 1. There is a nearly complete run of *The Virginian* in *The Right Wing Collection of the University of Iowa Libraries, 1918–1977,* Reel R138 (Glen Rock, NJ: Microfilming Corporation of America, 1977), at V5. On *The Virginian* and the Northern League, see Kevin Coogan, *Dreamer of the Day: Francis Parker Yockey and the Postwar Fascist International* (New York: Automedia, 1999), 479–480.

4. Adam Nossiter, *Of Long Memory: Mississippi and the Murder of Medgar Evers* (Reading: Addison Wesley, 1994), 94; David W. Southern, *Gunnar Myrdal and Black-White Relations: The Use and Abuse of* An American Dilemma, *1944–1969* (Baton Rouge: Louisiana State University Press, 1987), 183.

5. Putnam named these writers as his inspiration in a letter to Carleton S. Coon, 12 June 1960, Carleton Stevens Coon Papers, Box 10, Folder "L–Sl, 1960" (hereafter CSC Papers).

6. Biographical details of Carleton Putnam can be found in "Carleton Putnam Dies at 96; Led Delta and Wrote on Race," *New York Times,* 16 March 1998, 7; "Carleton Putnam," *Washington Post,* 9 March 1998, C6. On his business career, see David W. Lewis and Wesley Phillips Newton, *Delta: The History of an Airline* (Athens: University of Georgia Press, 1979); Carleton Putnam, *High Journey: A Decade in the Pilgrimage of an Air Line Pioneer* (New York: Scribner's, 1945). The Roosevelt biography was Carleton Putnam, *Theodore Roosevelt: The Formative Years, 1858–1886* (New York: Scribner's, 1958).

7. "A Northerner on the Race Issue," *Richmond Times-Dispatch,* 16 October 1958, 14.

8. "Supreme Court's 'Arrogance' Viewed by Distinguished Northerner," *Richmond Times-Dispatch,* 16 October 1958, 14.

9. Putnam's letter appeared as "My Dear Mr. President," *New York Times,* 5 January 1959, 19. A copy of the Citizens' Councils' pamphlet is in ESC Papers, Box 26, Folder "Association of Citizens' Councils." Putnam also reprinted the letter in his *Race and Reason: A Yankee View* (Washington, DC: Public Affairs Press, 1961), 5–9.

10. Alfred Baker Lewis, "To Equalize Education," *New York Times,* 10 January 1959, 16; Fawn M. Brodie, "A Lincoln Who Never Was," *The Reporter* 20 (25 June 1959): 25–27. On Cox's views on Abraham Lincoln, see Earnest Sevier Cox, *Lincoln's Negro Policy* (Los Angeles: Noontide Press, 1968).

11. Carleton Putnam to William Rogers, 16 March 1959, Box 919, Folder "GF 124A, School Decision–Con," Eisenhower Papers, Eisenhower Presidential Library, Abilene, Kansas (hereafter DDE Papers). The letter was also reprinted in Putnam, *Race and Reason,* 21–29.

12. Carleton Putnam to Carleton Coon, 10 October 1959, CSC Papers, Box 9, Folder "Corrsp. L–R 1959."

13. Handwritten note on Putnam's letter in Box 919, Folder "GF 124A, School Decision–Con," DDE Papers.

14. Felix Frankfurter to Putnam, 24 May 1960, MS 18,868, Microfilm Reel 55, Container 91, Manuscript Division, Library of Congress, Washington, D.C. I would like to thank Kevin Yelvington for calling my attention to this correspondence.

15. Roy Wilkins to P. L. Prattis, 11 March 1959, NAACP Papers, Series III, Box A257, Folder "Putnam, Carleton," Manuscript Division, Library of Congress, Washington, D.C. (hereafter NAACP Papers). This folder contains numerous letters asking the NAACP to answer Putnam's letters.

16. John A. Morsell to Putnam, 28 April 1959, NAACP Papers, Series III, Box A257, Folder "Putnam, Carleton."

17. Putnam to Morsell, 10 April 1959, NAACP Papers, Series III, Box A257, Folder "Putnam, Carleton." For his acknowledgment of this correspondence in his published writings, see Putnam, *Race and Reason,* 30–31.

18. Putnam to Morsell, 13 May 1959, NAACP Papers, Series III, Box A257, Folder "Putnam, Carleton."

19. Putnam to Clyde Kluckhohn, 5 January 1959, Clyde Kluckhohn Papers, HUG 4490.6, Harvard University Archives, Cambridge, Massachusetts.

20. Putnam to Dwight D. Eisenhower, 29 July 1959, and "Preliminary Draft, Questions from Readers," 7, Box 99, Folder "GF 124-A-1, School Decision–Con (8)," DDE Papers.

21. Milford Wolpoff and Rachel Caspari, *Race and Human Evolution: A Fatal Attraction* (New York: Simon and Schuster, 1997), 140. On the tension between Harvard and Columbia during the 1920s, see Elazar Barkan, *The Retreat*

of Scientific Racism (Cambridge: Cambridge University Press, 1992), 66–119; Rachel Silverman, "The Blood Group 'Fad' in Post-War Racial Anthropology," *Kroeber Anthropological Society Papers* 84 (2000): 11–27.

22. Carleton S. Coon, *The Story of Man* (New York: Knopf, 1954), 187–188.

23. Bella V. Dodd, *School of Darkness* (New York: Kenedy, 1954). For biographical details on Dodd and her importance to the anti-Communist cause, see Ellen W. Schrecker, *No Ivory Tower: McCarthyism and the Universities* (New York: Oxford University Press, 1986), 167–169.

24. Carleton Coon to Harry Turney-High, 14 June 1960, Box 11, Folder Unsorted, 1962–64, CSC Papers.

25. Putnam to Coon, 10 October 1959; Coon to Putnam, 25 October 1959, both in Box 9, Folder "L–R, 1959," CSC Papers.

26. Coon to Putnam, 10 July 1969, Box 10, Folder "L–Sl, 1960," CSC Papers.

27. Carleton Coon, *Races of Europe* (New York: Macmillan, 1939), 677; Coon to Putnam, 17 June 1960, Box 10, Folder "L–Sl, 1960," CSC Papers. See also Putnam, *Race and Reason,* 51–52.

28. Putnam to Coon, 1 August 1960; Coon to Putnam, 4 August 1960, both in Box 10, Folder "L–Sl, 1960," CSC Papers.

29. Putnam to Coon, 1 September 1960, Box 10, Folder "L–Sl, 1960," CSC Papers. The quotation was in Putnam, *Race and Reason,* 50.

30. Putnam, *Race and Reason,* 37.

31. Ibid., 18.

32. Ibid., 47.

33. Ibid., 18–19.

34. Ibid., 32.

35. First quotation from "National Putnam Letters Committee," 16 August 1962, Box 14, Folder "1962–Jan.–Aug.," ESC Papers. Second quotation from Mark German to L. Fields, 12 October 1961, NAACP Papers, Series III, Box A257, Folder "Putnam, Carleton."

36. Putnam, *Race and Reason,* viii.

37. Donald Swan to Wesley Critz George, 12 December 1960, Box 8, Folder 52, WCG Papers.

38. A good account of the founding of the IAAEE is William H. Tucker, *The Science and Politics of Racial Research* (Urbana: University of Illinois Press, 1994), 170–174. The attendance of the first meeting of the IAAEE is from "Announcement of the First General Meeting of the International Society for the Advancement of Ethnology and Eugenics and the Association for the Preservation of Freedom of Choice," in Herbert Sanborn Papers, Vanderbilt University, Nashville, Tennessee. I thank Andrew S. Winston for making this document available to me.

39. Charles C. Tansill, *Back Door to War* (Chicago: Henry Regnery, 1952). Tansill is cited as a founder of Holocaust denial at http://www.vho.org/GB/Journals/JHR/# (viewed 10 December 2003). See also Deborah Lipstadt, *Denying the Holocaust: The Growing Assault on Truth and Memory* (New York: Plume, 1993), 40.

40. Charles Tansill to Albertis Harrison, 29 September 1962, Charles Callan Tansill Papers, Box 1, Folder H 1919–1964, Herbert Hoover Presidential Library, West Branch, Iowa (hereafter CCT Papers).

41. Biographical details on Thompson can be found in Coogan, *Dreamer of the Day*, 255–257; and Martin A. Lee, *The Beast Reawakens* (New York: Routledge, 2000), 85–91. On his relationship with Tansill, see Coogan, *Dreamer of the Day*, 472; on the printing for the IAAEE, see 481. Anthony O'Keefe, who became the secretary of the IAAEE in the mid-1960s, was another figure who counted both Tansill and Thompson as friends. See O'Keefe to Tansill, 10 March 1964, CCT Papers, Box 2, Folder O 1933–1970.

42. Tucker, *Funding of Scientific Racism*, 205.

43. Donald A. Swan, "Likes Fascism," *Expose*, no. 34 (September 1954): 4. Biographical details are from Tucker, *Funding of Scientific Racism*, 85–86.

44. Thompson to Cox, 15 October 1956, ESC Papers, Box 11, Folder "F Sept.–Dec. 1956."

45. Donald Swan to Karl Doenitz, 25 December 1956, H. Keith Thompson Papers, Box 16, Hoover Institute, Stanford University, Palo Alto, California (hereafter HKT Papers). Kuttner to Thompson, 23 November 1956, HKT Papers, Box 16. Thompson eventually published a volume of letters, though it did not include those of Kuttner and Swan. H. Keith Thompson Jr. and Henry Strutz, eds., *Doenitz at Nuremburg: A Reappraisal, War Crimes and the Military Professional* (New York: Amber Publishing, 1976).

46. Thor Swenson, "The Inherited Natures of Negroes and Whites Compared," *Truth Seeker* 86 (1959): 119–120; Thor Swenson, "The Inherited Natures of Negroes and Whites Compared II," *Truth Seeker* 86 (1959): 137–139; Thor Swenson, "The Inherited Natures of Negroes and Whites Compared III," *Truth Seeker* 86 (1959): 172–175; Thor Swenson, "The Inherited Natures of Negroes and Whites Compared IV," *Truth Seeker* 86 (1959): 188–189; Thor Swenson, "The Inherited Natures of Negroes and Whites Compared V," *Truth Seeker* 86 (1959): 91–92. On Swan's use of the "Thor Swenson" pseudonym, see Coogan, *Dreamer of the Day*, 481.

47. Thor Swenson, "Professor Hans F.K. Günther: Eminent European Raciologist," *Truth Seeker* 86 (1959): 167; Thor Swenson, "The Works of Professor Hans F.K. Günther," *Northern World* 5, no. 2 (1961): 7–10.

48. Gregor's speech at the Racist Forum, "Some Racial Theories," was announced in *Truth Seeker* 85 (1958): 191. Gregor published exclusively in *The European* until 1958. See the following by A. James Gregor: "Eisenhoover: A

Study in American Economy," *The European,* no. 17 (July 1954): 7–13; "An American Considers European Socialism," *The European,* no. 33 (November 1955): 17–24; "Syndicalism: A Critical History," *The European,* no. 38 (April 1956): 10–20; "Marxism as Philosophy," *The European* 7 (August 1956): 11–26; and "Marxism as a Theory of History," *The European* 8 (November 1956): 146–162.

49. Anthony James Gimigliano, "The Ethical and Political Thought of Giovanni Gentile" (Ph.D. diss., Columbia University, 1961).

50. Paul Weindling, "Fascism and Population in Comparative European Perspective," *Population and Development Review* 14 (1988): 109.

51. Corrado Gini, "The Scientific Basis of Fascism," *Political Science Quarterly* 42 (1927): 102–103. On the organism metaphor in Nazi Germany, see Paul Weindling, "Dissecting German Social Darwinism: Historicizing the Biology of the Organic State," *Science in Context* 11 (1998): 619–637.

52. Franklin Giddings, *Principles of Sociology* (New York: Macmillan, 1896), 17. On Gumplowicz's racial views, see Ivan Hannaford, *Race: The History of an Idea in the West* (Baltimore: Johns Hopkins University Press, 1996), 298–302.

53. A. James Gregor, "Some Problems of Race," *The European,* no. 24 (1955): 21.

54. A. James Gregor, "National Socialism and Race," *The European* 11 (1958): 281, 286. A. James Gregor, "Nordicism Revisited," *Phylon* 22 (1961): 351–360.

55. John P. Jackson Jr., *Social Scientists for Social Justice: Making the Case against Segregation* (New York: New York University Press, 2001).

56. A. James Gregor, "On the Nature of Prejudice," *Eugenics Review* 52 (1961): 217.

57. Gordon W. Allport, *The Nature of Prejudice* (Reading, MA: Addison-Wesley, 1979 [1954]), 17–28.

58. Gustav Ichheiser, "Sociopsychological and Cultural Factors in Race Relations," *American Journal of Sociology* 54 (1949): 395–399; Louis Wirth, "Comment," *American Journal of Sociology* 54 (1949): 399–400, quotation on 399.

59. A. James Gregor, "The Dynamics of Prejudice," *Mankind Quarterly* 3 (1962): 79.

60. A. James Gregor, "Review of *Darwinism and the Study of Society,*" *Mankind Quarterly* 2 (1961): 139.

61. Gregor, "On the Nature of Prejudice," 222.

62. Jackson, *Social Scientists for Social Justice,* 63–78, 122–123, 171–173.

63. Quotations from the reprint: Charles Conant Josey, *The Philosophy of Nationalism* (Washington, DC: Cliveden, 1983), 223–224. The original was published as *Race and National Solidarity* (New York: Scribner's, 1923). Cliveden Press was operated by Roger Pearson, founder of the Northern League.

64. Malcolm M. Willey, "Review of *Race and National Solidarity,*" *American Journal of Sociology* 30 (1924): 97; A. B. Wolfe, "Review of *Race and National Solidarity,*" *Journal of Philosophy* 21 (1924): 444.

65. Robert Kuttner, "Race Evolution: Competitive or Cooperative?" *Truth Seeker* 84 (1957): 163. A sample of Josey's work for IAAEE was Charles C. Josey, *An Inquiry concerning Race Prejudice* (New York: International Association for the Advancement of Ethnology and Eugenics, 1965).

66. Biographical details can be found in Andrew S. Winston, "Science in the Service of the Far Right: Henry E. Garrett, the IAAEE, and the Liberty Lobby," *Journal of Social Issues* 54 (1998): 179–210.

67. John Morsell to Putnam, 28 April 1959, NAACP Papers, Series III, Box A257, Folder "Putnam, Carleton"; "Rightist Intellectuals Take Offensive," *Right,* no. 15 (December 1956): 3. On Garrett's testimony in *Brown,* see Jackson, *Social Scientists for Social Justice,* 147–150.

68. Winston, "Science in the Service of the Far Right," 182–183.

69. FBI Report NY 123-7671. Copy in possession of the author. I thank Benjamin Harris for making this document available to me.

70. R. Ruggles Gates, *Heredity and Eugenics* (New York: Macmillan, 1923), 233.

71. Gates, *Heredity and Eugenics,* 224; R. Ruggles Gates, *Human Ancestry: From a Genetical Point of View* (Cambridge: Harvard University Press, 1948), 366–367. On Gates's continued adherence to his racial views, see Barkan, *Retreat of Scientific Racism,* 168–176.

72. Oren Solomon Harman, "C.D. Darlington and the British and American Reaction to Lysenko and the Soviet Conception of Science," *Journal of the History of Biology* 36 (2003): 309–352.

73. Gates to Coon, 17 March 1962, Box 11, Folder "A–G, 1962"; Gini to Coon, 26 December 1959, Box 9, Folder "F–K, 1960," and Box 12, Folder "L–Z, 1963"; Coon to Edith Roosevelt, 21 August 1961, Box 11, Folder "N–Z, 1961," all in CSC Papers.

74. Coon to Robert Gayre, 6 November 1962, Box 11, Folder "A–G, 1962," CSC Papers. Coon's invitations to join the board are Gayre to Coon, 13 January 1960, Box 9, Folder "E–K, 1960," and Gayre to Coon, 29 October 1962, Box 11, Folder "A–G, 1962," CSC Papers.

75. Donald Swan to Carleton Coon, 23 April 1960, Box 10, Folder "Si–Z, 1960"; Coon to A. James Gregor, 12 December 1961, Box 10, Folder "G–M, 1961," both in CSC Papers.

76. Swan to George, 12 December 1960, WCG Papers, Box 8, Folder 52.

77. Swan to George, 15 July 1962, WCG Papers, Box 9, Folder 61.

78. Tucker, *Funding of Scientific Racism,* 56.

79. Ibid., 65–130.

80. Audrey Shuey, *The Testing of Negro Intelligence* (Lynchburg, VA: J. P. Bell, 1958), 318.

81. Ibid., 207.

82. "New Book Tells the Truth about Negro Intelligence," *The Virginian* 4 (May–June 1958): 14; Putnam, *Race and Reason,* 26; "Science and Equality," *Right,* no. 33 (June 1958): 1.

83. Horace Mann Bond to Paul Clifford, 21 March 1960, HMB Papers, Box 13, Folder 38B. Also see Tucker, *Funding of Scientific Racism,* 74.

84. Horace Mann Bond, "Cat on a Hot Tin Roof," *Journal of Negro Education* 27 (1958): 519, 520, 523.

85. Ibid., 523. For a further critique of Shuey's methods, see Graham Richards, *"Race," Racism, and Psychology: Towards a Reflexive History* (London: Routledge, 1997), 245–248.

NOTES TO CHAPTER 6

1. Earnest Sevier Cox to Carleton Putnam, 5 September 1962, ESC Papers, Box 14, Folder "1962 Sept.–Dec."

2. David Duke, *My Awakening: A Path to Racial Understanding* (Covington, LA: Free Speech Press, 1998), 33, 36; Stuart B. Campbell, "Books for Lawyers," *ABA Journal* 48 (1962): 567.

3. Corey T. Lesseig, "Roast Beef and Racial Integrity: Mississippi's 'Race and Reason Day,' October 26, 1962 [*sic*]" *Journal of Mississippi History* 56 (1994): 1–15.

4. Carleton Putnam, "This Is the Problem!" *The Citizen* 6 (November 1961): 16, 32.

5. "The Turning Point," *The Citizen* 6 (November 1961): 2; "Race and Reason to Be Studied in Louisiana's Schools," *The Citizen* 6 (November 1961): 34. On Virginia, see Joseph A. Loftus, "Virginia Debates Negro Abilities," *New York Times,* 18 February 1962, 62.

6. Carleton Putnam to Harry Weyher, 9 October 1962, WCGH Papers, Box 9, Folder 63.

7. Dan T. Carter, *The Politics of Rage: George Wallace, the Origins of the New Conservatism, and the Transformation of American Politics* (New York: Simon and Schuster, 1995), 91–96.

8. Wesley Critz George to Henry E. Garrett, 18 February 1961, WCG Papers, Box 8, Folder 54.

9. Garrett to George, 1 March 1961, WCG Papers, Box 8, Folder 54.

10. George to Ralph Smith, 18 February 1961, WCG Papers, Box 8, Folder 54.

11. Smith and Wilkins quoted in "Alabama Orders a Study of Races," *New*

York Times, 3 November 1961, 45; "The Color Line," *Newsweek* 58 (27 November 1961). 87.

12. Wesley Critz George, "Integration, Christianity, and the Law of the Land," *The Cross and the Flag* 19, no. 11 (February 1961): 3, 27–29. On Gerald L. K. Smith's fondness for George's segregationist views, see Glen Jeansonne, *Gerald L.K. Smith: Minister of Hate* (New Haven: Yale University Press, 1988), 138.

13. For the argument that intelligence tests replaced craniometry for scientific racists, see Allan Chase, *The Legacy of Malthus: The Social Costs of the New Scientific Racism* (Urbana: University of Illinois Press, 1980), 180; Stephen Jay Gould, *The Mismeasure of Man* (New York: Norton, 1981).

14. Wesley Critz George, *The Biology of the Race Problem* (Richmond: Patrick Henry Press, 1962), 84–85.

15. Ibid., 27.

16. Ibid., 28–32.

17. On Bean, Mall, and Wilder, see Edward Beardsley, "The American Scientist as Social Activist: Franz Boas, Burg G. Wilder, and the Cause of Racial Justice" (1973), reprinted in *Science, Race, and Ethnicity: Readings from Isis and Osiris,* ed. John P. Jackson Jr. (Chicago: University of Chicago Press, 2002), 155–172; Chase, *Legacy of Malthus,* 178–181; Gould, *Mismeasure of Man,* 77–82.

18. George, *Biology of the Race Problem,* 30; emphasis in original.

19. On Vint's work, see Saul Dubow, *Scientific Racism in Modern South Africa* (Cambridge: Cambridge University Press, 1995), 201–202; Graham Richards, *"Race," Racism, and Psychology: Towards a Reflexive History* (London: Routledge, 1997), 202–204.

20. Richards, *"Race," Racism, and Psychology,* 248.

21. Carleton S. Coon, *Origin of Races* (New York: Knopf, 1962), 657.

22. George, *Biology of the Race Problem,* 64.

23. Carleton Putnam, "Evolution and Race: New Evidence," *The Citizen* 6 (1962): 7; Putnam to Lee C. White, 2 June 1962, White House Name File, Box 2256, Kennedy Papers.

24. Putnam to George, 21 May 1962, WCG Papers, Box 9, Folder 61. On Weyher's heavy hand on the writing of the document, see William H. Tucker, *The Funding of Scientific Racism: Wickliffe Draper and the Pioneer Fund* (Urbana: University of Illinois Press, 2002), 75–76. On Putnam arranging with Weyher and Simmons for publicity and distribution, see Putnam to George, 12 July 1962, WCG Papers, Box 9, Folder 61.

25. William J. Simmons, "The Truth about Racial Differences," *The Citizen* 7 (October 1962): 7.

26. Byron M. Wilkinson, Fusion of the Races for a Mongrel Tomorrow," Elizabeth Churchill Brown Papers, Box 22, Folder 13, Hoover Institution, Stanford University, Palo Alto, California (hereafter ECB Papers).

27. Eugene Cook, testimony before Committee on the Judiciary, 85th Cong., 1st sess. (10 April 1957), 814.

28. A. James Gregor, "The Law, Social Science, and School Segregation: An Assessment," *Western Reserve Law Review* 14 (1963): 635–636.

29. Clairette P. Armstrong, Ralph W. Erickson, Henry E. Garrett, and A. James Gregor, "Interracial Housing and the Law: A Social Science Assessment," in *Open Occupancy vs. Forced Housing under the Fourteenth Amendment,* ed. Alfred Avins (New York: The Bookmailer, 1963), 147.

30. Donald A. Swan to George, 7 June 1961, WCG Papers, Box 8, Folder 55. On Louisiana's purchasing board, see Swan to George, 26 July 1961, WCG Papers, Box 8, Folder 55.

31. Carleton Putnam, *The Road to Reversal* (New York: National Putnam Letters Committee, 1962), 5.

32. Charles J. Bloch, "Civil Rights—or Civil Wrongs?" *Georgia Bar Journal* 22 (1959): 138.

33. John D. Graves to Putnam, 5 March 1962, WCG Papers, Box 9, Folder 60; Herbert Sanborn to George, undated, WCG Papers, Box 9, Folder 67.

34. R. Carter Pittman, "Liberty or Equality, Americanism or Marxism, Which Shall It Be?" *Alabama Lawyer* 15 (1954): 352, 355, 356. On Pittman and the States' Rights Council, see Neil R. McMillen, *The Citizens' Councils: Organized Resistance to the Second Reconstruction* (Urbana: University of Illinois Press, [1971] 1994), 83–91; Francis M. Wilhoit, *The Politics of Massive Resistance* (New York: George Braziller, 1973), 115.

35. R. Carter Pittman, "All Men Are Not Equal," *Alabama Lawyer* 17 (1956): 253. Also see R. Carter Pittman, "Equality versus Liberty: The Eternal Conflict," *ABA Journal* 46 (1960): 873–880. The latter piece, which is slightly more muted than the former, was widely distributed by the segregationist Virginia Commission on Constitutional Government; see "Equality versus Liberty: The Eternal Conflict," in *The Right Wing Collections of the University of Iowa Libraries, 1918–1977,* Reel 134 (Glen Rock, NJ: Microfilming Corporation of America, 1977), at V3.

36. On the formation of the Liberty Lobby, see Frank P. Mintz, *The Liberty Lobby and the American Right: Race, Conspiracy, and Culture* (Westport, CT: Greenwood Press, 1985), 85–105. On Pittman and the Liberty Lobby, and his role with the IAAEE scientists, see Tucker, *Funding of Scientific Racism,* 111–117. Pittman was listed on the Liberty Lobby's letterhead as a member of the Board of Policy by 1961; see "A Report from the Treasurer," April 1961, ESC Papers, Box 28, Folder "Liberty Lobby."

37. On the origins of the case, see Tucker, *Funding of Scientific Racism,* 112–113.

38. See *Petitioner's Brief, Stell v. Savannah,* available from the Federal District Court in Savannah, Georgia. Copy in possession of the author.

39. Putnam to Pittman, 8 February 1963, WCG Papers, Box 10, Folder 69.

40. Putnam to Pittman, 25 February 1963, WCG Papers, Box 10, Folder 69; emphasis in original.

41. Putnam to Pittman, 25 February 1963, WCG Papers, Box 10, Folder 69.

42. Gregor to Putnam, 10 April 1963, WCG Papers, Box 10, Folder 71; emphasis in original.

43. Gregor to Nathaniel Weyl, 4 April 1963, Nathaniel Weyl Papers, Box 3, Hoover Institution, Stanford University, Palo Alto, California (hereafter NW Papers); emphases in original.

44. Gregor to Putnam, 10 April 1963, WCG Papers, Box 10, Folder 71.

45. Gregor to Weyl, 28 March 1963, NW Papers, Box 3; emphasis in original.

46. Kuttner to George, 15 May 1963, WCG Papers, Box 10, Folder 72; Kuttner to George, 8 June 1963, WCG Papers, Box 10, Folder 73.

47. Kuttner to George, 8 June 1963, WCG Papers, Box 10, Folder 73.

48. "Pleas and Answers of Intervenors," *Stell v. Savannah,* 6. Copy in possession of the author. The full briefs for the case are available only from the Federal District Court in Savannah, Georgia, although portions are reprinted in I. A. Newby, *The Development of Segregationist Thought* (Homewood, IL: Dorsey Press, 1968), 146–153.

49. Pittman to Kuttner, 13 March 1963, WCG Papers, Box 10, Folder 70; Tucker, *Funding of Scientific Research,* 113, 246n.146. Tucker argues that the rough draft was prepared by Swan.

50. "General Comments on the Scientific Appendix to the Appellants' Briefs," *Stell v. Savannah,* 1, Federal District Court in Savannah, Georgia. Copy in possession of the author.

51. Ibid., 11, 13.

52. Ibid., 13.

53. John P. Jackson Jr., *Social Scientists for Social Justice: Making the Case against Segregation* (New York: New York University Press, 2001), 145–150.

54. "General Comments on the Scientific Appendix to the Appellants' Briefs," 14.

55. Ibid., 20.

56. I have argued elsewhere that this charge misunderstands how Clark and his colleagues framed the issues in *Brown.* See Jackson, *Social Scientists for Social Justice,* 1–6, 125–145.

57. Trial transcript, *Evers v. Jackson,* 232 F.Supp. 241 (1964), at 413.

58. Carleton Putnam, *Race and Reality* (Washington, DC: Public Affairs Press, 1967), 74.

59. Mark V. Tushnet, *Making Civil Rights Law* (New York: Oxford University Press, 1994), 314–315.

60. Trial transcript, *Evers v. Jackson.* See also Frank C. J. McGurk, "The

Law, Social Science, and Academic Freedom—A Psychologist's View," *Villanova Law Review* 5 (1959–60): 247–254.

61. Trial transcript of *Stell v. Savannah*, 215.

62. Trial testimony of Ernest van den Haag, *Stell v. Savannah*, 251.

63. Trial transcript of *Evers v. Jackson*, 301 (Garrett), 328 (McGurk).

64. Trial transcript of *Evers v. Jackson*, 481–484.

65. A. James Gregor, "The Law, Social Science, and School Segregation: An Assessment," *Western Reserve Law Review* 14 (1963): 626, 628.

66. Ibid., 625.

67. Biographical details from "Ernest van den Haag, 87. Educator and Backer of the Death Penalty," *New York Times*, 27 March 2002, 21. On his clashes with Sidney Hook, see Ernest van den Haag, "An Open Letter to Sidney Hook," *Partisan Review* 17 (1950): 607–616; Neil Jumonville, *Critical Crossings: The New York Intellectuals in Postwar America* (Berkeley: University of California Press, 1991), 171.

68. Ernest van den Haag, *Education as an Industry* (New York: Augustus M. Kelley, 1956), 147, 148, 151.

69. William E. Cross Jr., *Shades of Black: Diversity in African-American Identity* (Philadelphia: Temple University Press, 1991), 16–38; Jackson, *Social Scientists for Social Justice*, 30–34.

70. Ralph Ross and Ernest van den Haag, *The Fabric of Society* (New York: Harcourt, Brace, and Company, 1957), 165–166. Also Ernest van den Haag, *Passion and Constraint* (New York: Stein and Day, 1963), 279–285.

71. Kenneth B. Clark, *Prejudice and Your Child*, 2d ed. (Boston: Beacon Press, 1963), 202.

72. Ernest van den Haag, "Social Science Testimony in the Desegregation Cases—A Reply to Professor Kenneth Clark," *Villanova Law Review* 6 (1960): 69–79.

73. Testimony of Ernest van den Haag, *I.C.J. Pleadings, South West Africa* 10 (1966): 462.

74. Edmond Cahn, "Jurisprudence," *New York University Law Review* 30 (1955): 150–169.

75. Trial testimony of Ernst van den Haag, *Stell v. Savannah–Chatham County Board of Education*, Civil Action No. 1316, 232. The transcript of the *Stell* trial is available only from the Federal District Court in Savannah, Georgia.

76. Pittman to Kuttner, 13 March 1963, WCG Papers, Box 10, Folder 70.

77. Trial testimony of Ernest van den Haag, *Evers v. Jackson*, 342.

78. Jackson, *Social Scientists for Social Justice*, 135–145.

79. Trial testimony of Ernest van den Haag, *Evers v. Jackson*, 251. The mistake is a curious one, since the subsequently published results of the study showed that very few Negro children chose the white doll as the "good" doll. See A. James Gregor and D. Angus McPherson, "Racial Attitudes among White

and Negro Children in a Deep-South Standard Metropolitan Area," *Journal of Social Psychology* 68 (1966): 95–106.

80. Tucker, *Funding of Scientific Racism*, 115.

81. Jack Greenberg, *Crusaders in the Courts* (New York: Basic Books, 1994), 257.

82. *Stell v. Savannah–Chatham County Board of Education*, 220 F.Supp. 667 (1963).

83. *Stell v. Savannah–Chatham County Board of Education*, 318 F.2d 425 (1963), at 427. Also see *Stell v. Savannah–Chatham County Board of Education*, 333 F.2d 55 (1964).

84. *Evers v. Jackson Municipal Separate School District*, 232 F.Supp. 241 (1964).

85. Putnam, *Race and Reality*, 93, 94.

86. George Leonard, "Ethnic Differentiation in the United States School Desegregation Cases," *Mankind Quarterly* 6 (1966): 148.

NOTES TO CHAPTER 7

1. Donald Swan to Wesley Critz George, 12 December 1960; Robert Gayre to George, 19 November 1960; George to Alistair Harper, 20 September 1960, all in WCG Papers, Box 8, Folder 52. On Harper's role in the Northern League, see Kevin Coogan, *Dreamer of the Day: Francis Parker Yockey and the Postwar Fascist International* (New York: Automedia, 1999), 470.

2. Biographical information on Gayre is from Coogan, *Dreamer of the Day*, 480; Magnus Linklater, "The Curious Laird of Nigg," in *The Bell Curve Debate: History, Documents, Opinions*, ed. Russell Jacoby and Naomi Glauberman (New York: Times Books, 1995), 140–143; William H. Tucker, *The Funding of Scientific Racism: Wickliffe Draper and the Pioneer Fund* (Urbana: University of Illinois Press, 2002), 91–92.

3. Božo Škerlj, "The Mankind Quarterly," *Man* 60 (1960): 172.

4. G. Ainsworth Harrison, "The Mankind Quarterly," *Man* 61 (1961): 163.

5. Juan Comas, " 'Scientific' Racism Again?" *Current Anthropology* 2 (1961): 309.

6. Gutorm Gjessing, "Comments," *Current Anthropology* 2 (1961): 322.

7. Carleton Putnam, "This Is the Problem!" *The Citizen* 6 (November 1961): 20.

8. James F. Downs, "More on Scientific Racism," *Current Anthropology* 3 (1962): 298.

9. U. R. Ehrenfels, "Critical Paragraphs Deleted," *Current Anthropology* 3 (1962): 154–155.

10. Henry E. Garrett to George, 2 January 1962, WCG Papers, Box 9, Folder 60.

11. Donald W. Swan, "Juan Comas on 'Scientific Racism Again?': A Scientific Analysis," *Mankind Quarterly* 2 (1962): 231–245; Henry E. Garrett, "The Scientific Racism of Juan Comas," *Mankind Quarterly* 2 (1962): 100–106. On Garrett and George's help with Swan, see Garrett to George, 7 March 1962, WCG Papers, Box 9, Folder 60.

12. Juan Comas, *Racial Myths* (Paris: UNESCO, 1951).

13. A. James Gregor, "Comas' Chapter on Racial Myths: A Review," *Mankind Quarterly* 2 (1961): 31, 34.

14. Juan Comas, "A McCarthyan Attack," *Current Anthropology* 3 (1962): 155–158.

15. A. James Gregor, "Notes on a 'Scientific' Controversy," *Mankind Quarterly* 2 (1962): 169.

16. A. James Gregor, "Juan Comas: Critic and Scholar," *Mankind Quarterly* 3 (1962): 47.

17. R. Ruggles Gates and A. James Gregor, "Mankind Quarterly: Gates and Gregor Respond to Critics," *Current Anthropology* 4 (1963): 119–121.

18. Robert Gayre to Nathaniel Weyl, 1 March 1965, NW Papers, Box 12.

19. Louis Schneider, "Race, Reason, and Rubbish Again," *Phylon* 23 (1962): 149, 150; Robert P. Stuckert and Irwin D. Rinder, "The Negro in the Social Science Literature," *Phylon* 23 (1962): 112.

20. Clark S. Knowlton, "Review of *Race and Reason*," *Western Political Quarterly* 15 (1962): 570; Barton J. Bernstein, "Review of *Race and Reason*," *Journal of Negro History* 48 (1963): 49.

21. Manning Nash, "Race and Ideology of Race," *Current Anthropology* 3 (1962): 285; Putnam to Nash, 2 January 1963, WCG Papers, Box 10, Folder 68.

22. Donald C. Simmons, "A Yankee Looks at the Races," *New Republic* 147 (10 September 1962): 23.

23. Donald C. Simmons, " 'Scientific' Racism," *New Republic* 148 (5 January 1963): 10. See also Putnam's published reply: Carleton Putnam, " 'Scientific' Racism: A Reply," *New Republic* 148 (23 February 1963): 29–31.

24. On Gayre, Swan, and Coon's help, see Putnam's handwritten note at the top of Donald C. Simmons to Carleton Putnam, 29 March 1963, WCG Papers, Box 10, Folder 70. On Anglo-Saxon typewriter repair, see Simmons to Putnam, 19 April 1963, WCG Papers, Box 10, Folder 71. The flyer is "A Reply to Carleton Putnam," WCG Papers, Box 10, Folder 72.

25. L. C. Dunn and Theodosius Dobzhansky, *Heredity, Race, and Society* (New York: New American Library, 1952), 118; Theodosius Dobzhansky, *Mankind Evolving: The Evolution of the Human Species* (New Haven: Yale University Press, 1962), 285. On Dobzhansky's life and work, see Diane Paul, "Dobzhansky in the Nature Nurture Debate," in *The Evolutions of Theodosius Dobzhansky*, ed. Mark B. Adams (Princeton: Princeton University Press, 1994), 219–232. On Dobzhansky's belief in the desirability of genetic variation, see

John Beatty, "Weighing the Risks: Stalemate in the Classical/Balance Controversy," *Journal of the History of Biology* 20 (1987): 289–319.

26. Theodosius Dobzhansky, "A Bogus 'Science' of Race Prejudice," *Journal of Heredity* 52 (1961): 189–190.

27. Ibid., 190.

28. On mailing Putnam's speeches, see "Race and Reason," WCG Papers, Box 9, Folder 60. For the mailing of George's work, see "The Influence of Franz Boas" in White House Name File, B2256, John F. Kennedy Papers, Box 2256, Boston, Massachusetts.

29. Press release on the Sixtieth Annual Meeting of the American Anthropological Association, Box E7, Folder "AAA, 1962, #2," Margaret Mead Papers, Manuscript Division, Library of Congress, Washington, D.C. (hereafter MM Papers).

30. Press conference, Friday, December 1, Box 8, Folder 58, WCG Papers; "Science and the News," *Science* 134 (8 December 1961): 1868–1869.

31. Putnam to Gordon Willey, 24 November 1961, Box 11, Folder, "N–Z, 1961," CSC Papers; Sherwood Washburn to Putnam, 5 December 1961, and Putnam to Washburn, 12 December 1961, both in WCG Papers, Box 8, Folder 58.

32. "Proceedings of the Thirty-first Annual Meeting of the American Association of Physical Anthropologists, 1963," *American Journal of Physical Anthropology* 21 (1963): 402.

33. Carleton S. Coon, *Adventures and Discoveries* (Englewood Cliffs, NJ: Prentice-Hall, 1981), 335.

34. Coon to Putnam, 22 January 1963, WCG Papers, Box 10, Folder 18.

35. Coon to Eric Goldman, 6 November 1962, Box 11, Folder "A–G, 1962," Carleton S. Coon Papers, National Anthropological Archives, Smithsonian Institution, Washington, D.C. (hereafter CSC Papers).

36. Carleton Putnam, *The Road to Reversal* (Washington, DC: National Putnam Letters Committee, 1962), 9. Putnam to Coon, 25 February 1962, Box 11, Folder "O–Z, 1962," CSC Papers.

37. Gabriel Lasker, *Happenings and Hearsay: Experiences of a Biological Anthropologist* (Detroit: Savoyard, 1999), 148.

38. Steve Boggs to Margaret Mead, 22 December 1961, Box E23, Folder "AAAS, 1962, 3#"; and Washburn to Mead, 28 February 1962, Box E7, Folder "AAA, 1962, #2," both in MM Papers.

39. Minutes of Board Meeting, Box E23, Folder "AAAS, 1962, #3," MM Papers.

40. Boggs to Mead, 8 May 1962, Box E7, Folder "AAA, 1962 #2," MM Papers.

41. Boggs to Mead, 11 October 1962, Box E24, Folder "AAA Commission

on Science in Promotion of Human Welfare"; and Boggs to Mead, 15 October 1962, Box E7, Folder "AAA, 1962, #2," both in MM Papers.

42. "A Plea for Moderation," *Charleston News and Courier,* 5 October 1962, A8; Coon to Margaretta Childs, 16 October 1962, WCG Papers, Box 9, Folder 64.

43. Ernst Mayr, "Origin of the Human Races," *Science* 138 (1962): 421.

44. Margaret Mead, "Clocking the Timetable of Man," *Saturday Review* 46 (22 June 1963): 41.

45. Joseph Birdsell, "The Origin of Races," *Quarterly Review of Biology* 28 (1963): 178; George Gaylord Simpson, "The Origins of Races," *Perspectives in Biology and Medicine* 6 (1963): 271–272; William W. Howells, "Our Family Tree," *New York Times,* 9 December 1962, 171.

46. Morris E. Opler, "Did the Races Come from Different Ancestors?" *New York Herald Tribune,* 9 December 1962, 22. Mead to Mrs. D. E. Andrews, 21 November 1962, Box E24, Folder "AAAS, 1962 #4," MM Papers.

47. Coon, *Adventures and Discoveries,* 355–356. Coon's account of the events surrounding the reception of his book should not be accepted without question. In several instances, Coon's contemporaneous letters contradict the account he gives in his autobiography.

48. Dobzhansky review, Box 72, Folder "Dobzhansky Review," CSC Papers.

49. Dobzhansky to Coon, 17 October 1961; Coon to Dobzhansky, 20 October 1962; Coon to Dobzhansky, 29 October 1962; and Dobzhansky to Coon, 29 October 1962, all in Box 72, Folder "Dobzhansky Review," CSC Papers. To the last, Coon believed that Dobzhansky's review was defamatory; see his *Adventures and Discoveries,* 353.

50. Henry E. Garrett and Wesley Critz George, "Letter to the Editor," *New York Times,* 24 October 1962, 38; Barbara J. Price and Edith R. Sanders, "Letter to the Editor," *New York Times,* 30 October 1962, 34; Coon to *New York Times,* 29 October 1962, Box 71, Folder "Letter to the Editor, NYT," CSC Papers. Unknown to the disputants at the time, the Garrett and George letter was actually written by Carleton Putnam and Garrett and submitted over the signature of Garrett and George. Putnam sent a draft of the letter to Garrett and George. George was informed to "do nothing yourself" and that Garrett would be sending the final draft. See the copy of the letter, Box 9, Folder 64, WCG Papers.

51. Coon claims in his autobiography that the journal decided not to publish it after he contacted them. See Coon, *Adventures and Discoveries,* 353. But his contemporaneous letters do not necessarily support this interpretation; see Coon to Harold Strauss, 25 October 1962, Box 72, Folder "Dobzhansky Review," CSC Papers. There is no evidence to claim, as Pat Shipman has, that the *Saturday Review* declined to publish the review because Dobzhansky's comments were

"so highly critical, even scathing." See Pat Shipman, *The Evolution of Racism* (New York: Simon and Schuster, 1994), 207. Dobzhansky's tone in the original review (which Shipman apparently had not read) was relatively mild. A far more likely explanation, offered by Margaret Mead, was that Dobzhansky had unknowingly violated the protocols for a literary journal. Mead argued that, unlike scientific reviewers, literary reviewers should not share prepublication copies of their reviews with the authors of the books under review. See Mead to editor of *Science,* Box 72, Folder "Reviews of *Origin of Races,*" CSC Papers.

52. Sol Tax to Coon, 15 January 1963, and Coon to Tax, 20 January 1963, both in Box 72, Folder "Dobzhansky Review," CSC Papers. Dobzhansky's revised review also appeared as Theodosius Dobzhansky, "A Debatable Account of the Origin of Races," *Scientific American* 208 (1963): 169–172.

53. Eleanor Leacock, "Anthropology (H)," *Science,* 15 (February 1963): 638.

54. Coon to Dobzhansky, 25 February 1963; Coon to Detlev Bronk, 25 February 1963; and Dobzhansky to Coon, 28 February 1963, all in Box 72, Folder "Dobzhansky Review," CSC Papers. Coon's letter to *Science* was "Letter to the Editor," *Science* 140 (12 April 1963): 208.

55. Putnam to Morton Fried, 13 March 1962, WCG Papers, Box 9, Folder 60. On Fried's public stand against Putnam, see Fried's letter to the *New York Times,* 10 October 1962, 46.

56. Fried to Colleagues, 5 April 1963, Box G1, Folder "1963, Fl–Fn," MM Papers.

57. "Connie" [Conrad Arensberg] to Coon, undated; Lawrence Chamberlain to Coon, 15 May 1963; Anthony Wallace to Coon, 16 May 1963, all in Box 71, Folder "Letters, 1962–66," CSC Papers. On Coon's call to Arensberg, see Coon, *Adventures and Discoveries,* 354.

58. Carleton S. Coon, "Comments," *Current Anthropology* 4 (1963): 363. See also Theodosius Dobzhansky, "Possibility That Homo Sapiens Evolved Independently 5 Times Is Vanishingly Small," *Current Anthropology* 4 (1963): 360, 364–366; Ashley Montagu, "What Is Remarkable about Varieties of Man Is Likeness, Not Differences," *Current Anthropology* 4 (1963): 361–363.

59. Sherwood Washburn, "The Study of Race," *American Anthropologist* 65 (1963): 522–523.

60. Ibid., 522.

61. Ibid., 532, 531.

62. Coon to Putnam, 14 September 1963, Box 11, Folder "Unsorted, 1962–64," CSC Papers.

63. Melvin Tumin, *Race and Intelligence: An Evaluation* (New York: Anti-Defamation League of B'nai B'rith, 1963), 6.

64. Putnam to Harry Weyher, 31 August 1963, WCG Papers, Box 10, Folder 75.

65. Schwarzchild to Coon, 24 September 1963, Box 71, Folder "B'nai B'rith," CSC Papers.

66. Melvin Tumin to Coon, 30 September 1963, and Coon to Tumin, 4 October 1963, both in Box 71, Folder "B'nai B'rith," CSC Papers.

67. On Coon's assistance and threatened lawsuit, see Coon to Putnam, 14 September 1963, Box 11, Folder "Unsorted, 1962–64," CSC Papers.

68. Garrett to George, 12 November 1964, WCG Papers, Box 11, Folder 84. The reply was Henry E. Garrett, Wesley Critz George, and Carleton Putnam, *Race: A Reply to Race and Intelligence: A Scientific Evaluation by the Anti-Defamation League of B'nai B'rith* (Washington, DC: National Putnam Letters Committee, 1964). On the publication, funding, and distribution, see Garrett to George, 24 September 1963, WCG Papers, Box 10, Folder 76; Tucker, *Funding of Scientific Racism,* 73.

69. Committee on Science in the Promotion of Human Welfare, "Science and the Race Problem," *Science* 142 (1 November 1963): 559.

70. George to William Gardella, 12 December 1963, WCG Papers, Box 11, Folder 79; George to F. H. E. Weil, 8 November 1963, WCG Papers, Box 11, Folder 78; Henry E. Garrett and Wesley Critz George, "Science and the Race Problem," *Science* 143 (1964): 913–915; Carleton Putnam, "Letter to the Editor," *Science* 142 (1963): 1419.

71. Nathaniel Weyl to Putnam, 6 November 1963, WCG Papers, Box 11, Folder 78; George Leonard to Putnam, 2 December 1963, WCG Papers, Box 11, Folder 79.

72. Carleton Putnam, "These Are the Guilty," *The Citizen* 7 (March 1963): 38, 39.

73. Henry E. Garrett, "The Equalitarian Dogma," *Perspectives in Biology and Medicine* 4 (1961): 481; Henry E. Garrett, "The Equalitarian Dogma," *Mankind Quarterly* 1 (1961): 253–257. On the differences between these two versions, see Andrew S. Winston, "Science in the Service of the Far Right," *Journal of Social Issues* 54 (1998): 184–186.

74. William H. Tucker, *The Science and Politics of Racial Research* (Urbana: University of Illinois Press, 1994), provides valuable insight into Ingle's racial beliefs and his decision to publish Garrett's piece; see 155–157. On the response to Garrett's piece, see Melville Herskovits, "Rearguard Action," *Perspectives in Biology and Medicine* 5 (1961): 122–128.

75. Dwight Ingle, "Letter from the Editor," *Perspectives in Biology and Medicine* 5 (1961): 130.

76. Putnam to Dwight Ingle, 14 February 1962, WCG Papers, Box 9, Folder 60.

77. Putnam to Ingle, 26 December 1962, WCG Papers, Box 9, Folder 66.

78. Dwight Ingle, "Letter to the Reader," *Perspectives in Biology and Medicine* 6 (1963): 539.

79. Letters to the Editor, *Perspectives in Biology and Medicine* 6 (1963): 540, 541. Putnam, of course, responded to these charges; see Carleton Putnam, *Three New Letters on Science and Race* (Washington, DC: National Putnam Letters Committee, 1964).

80. Clarence P. Oliver to Henry Garrett, 11 December 1962, WCG Papers, Box 9, Folder 66; for the remaining authorities, see John C. Fuller, Letter to Editor of *Science*, 18 February 1964, WCG Papers, Box 11, Folder 18.

81. Dwight Ingle, "Comments on the Teachings of Carleton Putnam," *Mankind Quarterly* 4 (1963): 28–42. Tucker, *Funding of Scientific Racism*, 73, calls the editorial comments "cranky editorial insertions."

82. Carleton Putnam, "A Reply to Dwight Ingle," *Mankind Quarterly* 4 (1963): 44.

83. On Putnam, Draper, and the CCFAF, see Tucker, *Funding of Scientific Racism*, 122–126. On the CCFAF generally, see Yasuhiro Katagiri, *The Mississippi State Sovereignty Commission: Civil Rights and States' Rights* (Jackson: University of Mississippi Press, 2001), 150–152.

84. Testimony of Robert Kuttner before the Committee on the Judiciary, House of Representatives, 88th Cong., 1st sess., (Friday, July 19, 1963), p. 1977. On Carto's relationship with the John Birch Society, see Frank P. Mintz, *The Liberty Lobby and the American Right: Race, Conspiracy, and Culture* (Westport, CT: Greenwood Press, 1985), 141–162.

NOTES TO CHAPTER 8

1. For a brief overview, see George H. Nash, *The Conservative Intellectual Movement in America since 1945* (New York: Basic Books, 1976), 140–143, 296–305.

2. William F. Buckley Jr., *God and Man at Yale* (Chicago: Regnery, 1951), 46.

3. See, for example, E. Merrill Root, *Collectivism on the Campus: The Battle for the Mind in American Colleges* (New York: Devin-Adair, 1955); Felix Wittmer, *Conquest of the American Mind: Comments on Collectivism in Education* (Boston: Meador, 1956).

4. Root, *Collectivism on Campus*, 21.

5. Carleton Putnam to William F. Buckley, 15 March 1965, and Putnam to Buckley, 7 May 1965, both in William F. Buckley, Jr. Papers, Box 136, Yale University Library, New Haven, Connecticut (hereafter WFB Papers).

6. Buckley to Putnam, 10 June 1965, WFB Papers, Box 136.

7. Robert Gayre to Nathaniel Weyl, 29 October 1963, NW Papers, Box 12. On miscegenation, see Weyl to Gayre, 8 August 1961, Box 12, NW Papers. See also Nathaniel Weyl, *The Negro in American Civilization* (Washington, DC:

Public Affairs Press, 1960); Nathaniel Weyl and Stefan Possony, *The Geography of Intellect* (Chicago: Regnery, 1963).

8. An example of Weyl's anti-Communist writing was *Treason: The Story of Disloyalty and Betrayal in American History* (Washington, DC: Public Affairs Press, 1960). On his Communist Party membership, see Sam Tannenhaus, *Whittaker Chambers: A Biography* (New York: Modern Library, 1998), 517–518.

9. Weyl to Gayre, 25 June 1965; Gayre to Weyl, 28 June 1965; and Weyl to Gayre, 8 July 1965, all in NW Papers, Box 12. Soon after this, the respectable Right and the racist Right would have a serious falling out, as Carto launched a series of attacks on the *National Review* from the pages of his publications. See Frank P. Mintz, *The Liberty Lobby and the American Right: Race, Conspiracy, and Culture* (Westport, CT: Greenwood Press, 1985), 131–135.

10. Weyl to Stefan Possony, 10 March 1964, NW Papers, Box 23.

11. Gayre to Weyl, 23 March 1964, NW Papers, Box 12.

12. William B. Shockley, "Population Control or Eugenics" (1965), reprinted in *Shockley on Eugenics and Race,* ed. Roger Pearson (Washington, DC: Scott Townsend, 1992), 81.

13. William H. Tucker, *The Funding of Scientific Racism* (Urbana: University of Illinois Press, 2002), 140; see also 140–156, which documents Draper's involvement and the assistance of the segregationists to Shockley's cause. Also valuable is William H. Tucker, *The Science and Politics of Racial Research* (Urbana: University of Illinois Press, 1994), 182–195.

14. Dwight Ingle to William Shockley, 1 September 1955, Series II, Box 21, Folder 1C; Ingle to Shockley, 22 September 1966, Series II, Box 21, Folder 1C; Ingle to Shockley, 10 January 1967, 86-050, Box 13, Folder 2A, all in William Shockley Papers, Stanford University Library, Palo Alto, California (hereafter WS Papers).

15. Putnam to Frederick Seitz, 30 November 1967, WS Papers, Series II, Box 2, Folder 5B.

16. Carleton Coon to Shockley, 25 August 1966, WS Papers, Series II, Box 1, Folder 1C.

17. William B. Shockley, "Human Quality Problems and Research Taboos" (1969), reprinted in *Shockley on Eugenics and Race,* 131.

18. Putnam to Arthur Jensen, 28 February 1968, WS Papers, Series II, Box 2, Folder 8.

19. Putnam to Wilmot Robertson, 23 September 1974, Albert Wedemeyer Papers, Box 57, Folder 2, Hoover Institute, Stanford University, Palo Alto, California (hereafter AW Papers). I am very grateful to Kevin Yelvington for calling the Putnam material in the Wedemeyer collection to my attention.

20. Arthur R. Jensen, *Genetics and Education* (New York: Harper and Row, 1972), 328.

21. Celeste Michelle Condit, *The Meanings of the Gene: Public Debates about Human Heredity* (Madison: University of Wisconsin Press, 1999), 141–142.

22. Robert E. Kuttner, "Serum Pepsinogen in Urbanized Sioux Indians," *Journal of the National Medical Association* 56 (1964): 471–473; Robert E. Kuttner, "Serum Pepsinogen in Migrant Mexicans and Stressed Caucasians," *Journal of the National Medical Association* 57 (1965): 109–111; Robert E. Kuttner and Albert B. Lorincz, "Alcoholism and Addiction in Urbanized Sioux Indians," *Mental Hygiene* 51 (1967): 530–542.

23. Robert Kuttner to Shockley, 9 November 1967, WS Papers, Series II, Box 2, Folder 5B.

24. Robert E. Kuttner, "Use of Accentuated Environmental Inequalities in Research on Racial Differences," *Mankind Quarterly* 8 (1968): 148.

25. Ibid., 160.

26. Robert Kuttner, "What Do We Owe the Negroes?" *American Mercury* 103 (1967): 9. Also see Robert E. Kuttner, "Why Aren't Indians 'Disadvantaged'?" *American Mercury* 105 (1969): 8–9.

27. Tucker, *Funding of Scientific Racism,* 146.

28. Theodosius Dobzhansky, "More Bogus 'Science' of Race Prejudice," *Journal of Heredity* 59 (1968): 102, 103. Putnam's second book on race was Carleton Putnam, *Race and Reality: A Search for Solutions* (Washington, DC: Public Affairs Press, 1967).

29. Dobzhansky, "More Bogus 'Science' of Race Prejudice," 104.

30. Coon to Putnam, 3 October 1968, Box 72, Folder "Dobzhansky Review," CSC Papers.

31. Coon to Mrs. Winner, 28 February 1963, Box 72, Folder "Dobzhansky Review"; Coon to Clyde E. Noble, Box 71, Folder "Operation Pollyanna"; Coon to Mr. Gordon, 1 August 1969, Box 71, Folder "Letters, 1962–66," all in CSC Papers. On Boas's "suppression" of Coon's *Races of Europe,* see Carleton S. Coon, *Adventures and Discoveries* (Englewood Cliffs, NJ: Prentice-Hall, 1981), 137–138.

32. Putnam, *Race and Reality,* 130, 132.

33. Ibid., 173.

34. Anthony O'Keefe, "IAAEE Memorandum," 14 April 1966, H. Keith Thompson Papers, Box 16, Hoover Institute, Stanford University, Palo Alto, California.

35. *Association for the Preservation for the Freedom of Choice v. New York Post Corporation,* 228 N.Y.S. 2d 767 (1962); *Association for the Preservation for the Freedom of Choice v. The Nation Company,* 228 N.Y.S. 2d 628 (1962); *Association for the Preservation for the Freedom of Choice v. Emergency Civil Liberties Committee,* 236 N.Y.S. 2d 216 (1962).

36. Quoted in Kevin Coogan, *Dreamer of the Day: Francis Parker Yockey*

and the Postwar Fascist International (New York: Automedia, 1999), 481. Also see Tucker, *Funding of Scientific Racism,* 205–206.

37. Anthony O'Keefe to Weyl, 9 March 1964; and, on the creation of the press, see O'Keefe to Weyl, 26 November 1966, both in NW Papers, Box 8, Folder "Anthony O'Keefe." Also see Tucker, *Funding of Scientific Racism,* 98–99, 157–158.

38. Edward Joseph Shoben, "Review of *Race and Modern Science,*" *Personnel and Guidance Journal* 47 (1969): 488; L. C. Dunn, "Review of *Race and Modern Science,*" *Eugenics Quarterly* 15 (1969): 301; E. L. Anderson, "Racial Revolutions," *American Mercury* 104 (1968): 64.

39. I. A. Newby, *Challenge to the Court* (Baton Rouge: Louisiana State University Press, 1969), 125.

40. O'Keefe to Gayre, 10 February 1968, NW Papers, Box 3.

41. Weyl to O'Keefe, 7 March 1968, Box 8, Folder "Anthony O'Keefe"; and Weyl to Gayre, 7 March 1968, Box 3, both in NW Papers.

42. Richard Wentworth to George, 17 April 1968, WCG Papers, Box 12, Folder 94.

43. A. James Gregor, "On Learned Ignorance: A Brief Inquiry into I.A. Newby's *Challenge to the Court,*" in *Challenge to the Court,* by I. A. Newby, rev. ed. (Baton Rouge: Louisiana State University Press, 1969), 238.

44. Ibid., 262.

45. Ibid., 283.

46. Gregor to Putnam, WCG Papers, 10 April 1963, Box 10, Folder 71.

47. Weyl to Gregor, 5 May 1963, and Gregor to Weyl, 8 May 1963, NW Papers, Box 3.

48. Howard L. Parsons, "Review of *Contemporary Radical Ideologies,*" *Philosophy and Phenomenological Research* 31 (1970): 307; Roland Sarti, "Review of *Italian Fascism and Developmental Dictatorship,*" *American Historical Review* 86 (1981): 169.

49. On *Western Destiny,* see Coogan, *Dreamer of the Day,* 515; Mintz, *Liberty Lobby and the American Right,* 77–78.

50. Frank McGurk, "Racial Differences Are Racial," *American Mercury* 115 (1979): 61.

51. W. D. McCain, "Who Is Carleton Putnam?" *The Citizen* 6 (November 1961): 9–11.

52. Monte Piliawsky, *Exit 13: Oppression and Racism in Academia* (Boston: South End Press, 1982), 73–74.

53. Robert Kuttner and Donald Swan, "Biological Aspects of Evolution," *Southern Quarterly* 12 (1974): 323, 324.

54. Ibid., 330.

55. Ibid., 333.

56. Deborah Lipstadt, *Denying the Holocaust: The Growing Assault on*

Truth and Memory (New York: Plume, 1994), 136–157; Michael Shermer and Alex Grobman, *Denying History. Who Says the Holocaust Never Happened and Why Do They Say It?* (Berkeley: University of California Press, 2000), 43–46.

57. John R. Baker, *Race* (New York: Oxford University Press, 1974), 61. On Baker's career, see Michael G. Kenny, "Racial Science in Social Context: John R. Baker on Eugenics, Race, and the Public Role of the Scientist," *Isis* 95 (2004): 394–419.

58. Reviewers who pointed to the anachronistic nature of Baker's work included Wolf Roder, "Race," *International Journal of African Historical Studies* 8 (1975): 518–522; Michael Banton, "Race," *British Journal of Sociology* 25 (1974): 514–515.

59. Putnam to Wilmot Robertson, 23 September 1974, and John Baker to Putnam, 14 September 1974, AW Papers.

60. On Draper and financing of Robertson, see Tucker, *Funding of Scientific Racism,* 136–139. On Robertson, see Mitch Berbrier, "Impression Management for the Thinking Racist: A Case Study of Intellectualization as Stigma Transformation in Contemporary White Supremacist Discourse," *Sociological Quarterly* 40 (1999): 411–433.

61. See the blurbs on the back of the third edition and dedication page: Wilmot Robertson, *The Dispossessed Majority* (Cape Canaveral: Howard Allen Press, 1981).

62. Putnam to Albert Wedemeyer, 22 February 1974, AW Papers, Box 57, Folder 2.

63. Putnam to William McCleery, 29 May 1974, AW Papers, Box 57, Folder 2.

64. Putnam to Robertson, 23 September 1974, AW Papers, Box 57, Folder 2.

65. Keith Stimely, "Capsule Report on My Trip to the East." A copy of this document was given to me by Kevin Coogan from the research papers he collected for his biography of Yockey, *Dreamer of the Day.* I would like to thank Kevin Coogan for making this document available to me.

66. Gregor to Weyl, 28 March 1963, NW Papers, Box 3; emphasis in original.

67. Linda Gottfredson, "Jensen, Jensenism, and the Sociology of Intelligence," *Intelligence* 26 (1998): 291.

68. Arthur R. Jensen, *The G Factor: The Science of Mental Ability* (Westport, CT: Praeger, 1998), 419, 420.

69. Roger Kimball, *Tenured Radicals: How Politics Corrupted Our Higher Education* (New York: Harper and Row, 1990); Dinesh D'souza, *Illiberal Education: The Politics of Race and Sex on Campus* (New York: Macmillan, 1991).

70. J. Philippe Rushton, "The Equalitarian Dogma Revisited," *Intelligence* 19 (1994): 263–280.

71. J. Philippe Rushton, "Political Correctness and the Study of Racial Dif-

ferences," *Journal of Social Distress and the Homeless* 5 (1996): 219. For an analysis of the specific charges made by Rushton regarding his research, see Andrew S. Winston, "The Context of Correctness: A Comment on Rushton," *Journal of Social Distress and the Homeless* 5 (1996): 231–249.

72. J. Philippe Rushton, *Race, Evolution, and Behavior: A Life History Perspective* (New Brunswick, NJ: Transaction, 1995), 13, 14. Rushton makes similar claims on his Web site at http://www.charlesdarwinresearch.org/ (viewed 27 July 2002).

73. Kevin MacDonald, *The Culture of Critique: An Evolutionary Analysis of Jewish Involvement in Twentieth-Century Intellectual and Political Movements* (Westport, CT: Praeger, 1998), 28. On MacDonald's testimony on behalf of Irving, see Richard J. Evans, *Lying about Hitler: History, Holocaust, and the David Irving Trial* (New York: Basic Books, 2002), 192–193. Irving has posted MacDonald's testimony at his Web site: http://www.fpp.co.uk/Legal/Penguin/experts/MacDonald/ (viewed 17 September 2004).

74. Morton Hunt, *The New Know-Nothings: The Political Foes of the Scientific Study of Human Nature* (New Brunswick, NJ: Transaction, 1999), 46.

75. William Tucker recounts that Rushton made vague but real legal threats against the publication of his history of the Pioneer Fund. See William H. Tucker, "A Closer Look at the Pioneer Fund: A Response to Rushton," *Albany Law Review* 66 (2003): 1145–1146.

76. Robert A. Nye, "The Rise and Fall of the Eugenics Empire: Recent Perspectives on the Impact of Biomedical Thought in Modern Society," *Historical Journal* 36 (1993): 699. For two recent studies that see "reform" eugenics as a stalking horse for mainline eugenics, see Molly Ladd-Taylor, "Eugenics, Sterilisation, and Modern Marriage in the USA: The Strange Career of Paul Popenoe," *Gender and History* 13 (2001): 298–237; and Paula M. Mazumdar, "'Reform' Eugenics and the Decline of Mendelism," *Trends in Genetics* 18 (2002): 48–52.

Bibliography

MANUSCRIPT SOURCES

Duke University Archives, Duke University, Durham, NC:
  Earnest Sevier Cox Papers
Eisenhower Presidential Library, Abilene, KS:
  Dwight D. Eisenhower Papers
Harvard University Archives, Cambridge, MA:
  Clyde Kluckhohn Papers
Herbert Hoover Presidential Library, West Branch, IA:
  Charles Callan Tansill Papers
Hoover Institution Archives, Stanford University, Palo Alto, CA:
  Albert Wedemeyer Papers
  Elizabeth Churchill Brown Papers
  Nathaniel Weyl Papers
  H. Keith Thompson Papers
  Right Wing Collection
Kennedy Presidential Library, Boston, MA
  John F. Kennedy Papers
Manuscript Division, Library of Congress, Washington, DC:
  Margaret Mead Papers
  NAACP Papers
National Anthropological Archives, Smithsonian Institution, Washington, DC:
  Carleton S. Coon Papers
Southern Historical Collection, University of North Carolina, Chapel Hill, NC:
  Wesley Critz George Papers
Stanford University Archives, Stanford University, Palo Alto, CA:
  William S. Shockley Papers

BOOKS AND ARTICLES

"Alabama Orders a Study of Races." *New York Times*, 3 November 1961, 45.
"An American Tragedy: School Children under the Gun." *The Virginian* 3, no. 10 (October 1957): 1.

"Army Drops Race Equality Book: Denies May's Stand Was Reason." *New York Times,* 6 March 1944, 1, 11.

"Atheist Is Cleared of Straton Attack." *New York Times,* 20 December 1927, 22.

"Atheists in Clash with Dr. Straton." *New York Times,* 18 October 1926, 39.

"Ban by USO Criticized." *New York Times,* 16 March 1944, 17.

"Bares Terrorism of Tulsa Floggers." *New York Times,* 7 September 1923, 17.

"Behavior Geneticists Shun Colleague." *Science* 270 (17 November 1995): 1125.

"Carleton Putnam." *Washington Post,* 9 March 1998, C6.

"Carleton Putnam Dies at 96; Led Delta and Wrote on Race." *New York Times,* 16 March 1998, 7.

"The Color Line." *Newsweek* 58 (27 November 1961): 87.

Congressional Committee Report on What Happened When Schools Were Integrated in Washington DC. Greenwood, MS: Citizens' Councils, undated.

"Ernest van den Haag, 87. Educator and Backer of the Death Penalty." *New York Times,* 27 March 2002, 21.

"From Here, There, and Most Everywhere." *Right,* no. 13 (October 1956): 4.

"Legal Scholar Alfred Avins Dies at Age 64." *Washington Post,* 11 June 1999, B6.

"New Book Tells the Truth about Negro Intelligence." *The Virginian* 4 (May–June 1958): 14.

"New York Atheist Enters Jail in Arkansas; Won't Pay Fine for Fighting Anti-Evolution Law." *New York Times,* 18 October 1928, 1.

"Northern League Office Opened." *Right,* no. 38 (November 1958): 1–2.

"A Northerner on the Race Issue." *Richmond Times-Dispatch,* 16 October 1958, 14.

"Order Martial Law in Tulsa, Oklahoma." *New York Times,* 14 August 1923, 5.

"Plans New Edition of Race Pamphlet." *New York Times,* 8 March 1944, 11.

"A Plea for Moderation." *Charleston News and Courier,* 5 October 1962, A8.

Preliminary Report on Neo-Fascist and Hate Groups. Committee on Un-American Activities, U.S. House of Representatives, 17 December 1954.

"Proceedings of the Thirty-first Annual Meeting of the American Association of Physical Anthropologists, 1963." *American Journal of Physical Anthropology* 21 (1963): 399–403.

"Professor Loses Publication Suit." *New York Times,* 12 November 1967, 63.

"Race and Reason to Be Studied in Louisiana Schools." *The Citizen* 6 (November 1961): 34.

"Replies Refused by Dr. Weltfish." *New York Times,* 2 April 1953, 16.

"Rightist Intellectuals Take Offensive." *Right,* no. 15 (December 1956): 3.

"Science and Equality." *Right,* no. 33 (June 1958): 1.

"Science and the News." *Science* 134 (8 December 1961): 1868–1869.

"Southern Manifesto." In *The Burden of Race: A Documentary History of Negro-White Relations in America,* edited by Gilbert Osofsky, 491–494. New York: Harper and Row, 1967.

"Specter at the Feast." *Science* 269 (1995): 35.

"Supreme Court's 'Arrogance' Viewed by Distinguished Northerner." *Richmond Times-Dispatch,* 16 October 1958, 14.

"Tear Bombs Scatter Detroit Mob of 5,000 Which Masses before Anti-Klan Meeting." *New York Times,* 22 October 1924, 1.

"The Turning Point." *The Citizen* 6 (November 1961): 2.

A.B.S. "Review of *The Passing of the Great Race.*" *American Historical Review* 22 (1917): 842–844.

Adams, Mark B., ed. *The Wellborn Science: Eugenics in Germany, France, Brazil, and Russia.* New York: Oxford University Press, 1990.

Allen, John S. "Franz Boas's Physical Anthropology: The Critique of Racial Formalism Revisited." *Current Anthropology* 30 (1989): 79–84.

Allport, Gordon W. *The Nature of Prejudice.* Reading, MA: Addison-Wesley, 1954. Reprint, 1979.

Anderson, E. L. [pseudonym]. "Racial Revolutions." *American Mercury* 104 (1968): 63–64.

———. "The Reality of Race." *Right,* no. 20 (May 1957): 1, 3.

———. "The Testimony of History." *Truth Seeker* 84 (April 1957): 62.

Armstrong, Clairette P., Ralph W. Erickson, Henry E. Garrett, and A. James Gregor. "Interracial Housing and the Law: A Social Science Assessment." In *Open Occupancy vs. Forced Housing under the Fourteenth Amendment,* edited by Alfred Avins. New York: Bookmailer, 1963.

Asante, Molefi. "Systematic Nationalism: A Legitimate Strategy for National Selfhood." *Journal of Black Studies* 9 (1978): 115–128.

Avins, Alfred. "Anti-Discrimination Legislation as an Infringement on Freedom of Choice." *New York Law Forum* 6 (1960): 13–37.

———. "Anti-Miscegenation Laws and the Fourteenth Amendment: The Original Intent." *Virginia Law Review* 52 (1966): 1224–1255.

———. "De Facto and De Jure School Segregation: Some Reflected Light on the Fourteenth Amendment from the Civil Rights Act of 1875." *Mississippi Law Journal* 38 (1967): 179–253.

———. "Letter to the Editor." *Washington Post,* 22 June 1994, A20.

Bair, Barbara. "Remapping the Black/White Body: Sexuality, Nationalism, and the Biracial Antimiscegenation Activism in 1920s Virginia." In *Sex, Love, Race: Crossing Boundaries in North American History,* edited by Martha Hodes, 399–419. New York: New York University Press, 1999.

Baker, John R. *Race.* New York: Oxford University Press, 1974.

Banton, Michael. "Race." *British Journal of Sociology* 25 (1974): 514–515.

Barkan, Elazar. "The Politics of the Science of Race: Ashley Montagu and UN-ESCO's Anti-Racist Declarations." In *Race and Other Misadventures: Essays in Honor of Ashley Montagu in His Ninetieth Year*, edited by Larry T. Reynolds and Leonard Lieberman, 96–105. Dix Hills, NJ: General Hall, 1996.

———. *The Retreat of Scientific Racism: Changing Concepts of Race in Britain and the United States between the World Wars*. Cambridge: Cambridge University Press, 1992.

Bartley, Numan V. *The Rise of Massive Resistance and the Politics of the South during the 1950s*. Baton Rouge: Louisiana State University Press, 1969.

Beardsley, Edward H. "The American Scientist as Social Activist: Franz Boas, Burg G. Wilder, and the Cause of Racial Justice" (1973). In *Science, Race, and Ethnicity: Readings from Isis and Osiris*, edited by John P. Jackson Jr., 155–172. Chicago: University of Chicago Press, 2002.

Beatty, John. "Weighing the Risks: Stalemate in the Classical/Balance Controversy." *Journal of the History of Biology* 20 (1987): 289–319.

Benedict, Ruth, and Gene Weltfish. *Races of Mankind*. Reprinted in *Race, Science, and Politics*, edited by Ruth Benedict. New York: Viking Press, 1947.

Bennett, Charles G. "Ban on Housing Bias Voted by City Board." *New York Times*, 24 December 1957, 1.

———. "Housing Bill Signed by Mayor." *New York Times*, 31 December 1957, 9.

Berbrier, Mitch. "Impression Management for the Thinking Racist: A Case Study of Intellectualization as Stigma Transformation in Contemporary White Supremacist Discourse." *Sociological Quarterly* 40 (1999): 411–433.

Bernstein, Barton J. "Review of *Race and Reason*." *Journal of Negro History* 48 (1963): 58–60.

Bilbo, Theodore G. *Take Your Choice: Separation or Mongrelization*. Poplarville, MS: Dream House, 1947.

Billig, Michael. *Psychology, Racism and Fascism*. London: Searchlight, 1979.

Birdsell, Joseph. "The Origin of Races." *Quarterly Review of Biology* 28 (1963): 178–185.

Bishop, David W. "*Plessy v. Ferguson*: A Reinterpretation." *Journal of Negro History* 62 (1977): 125–133.

Blake, Aldrich. *Civil Rights or Civil Wrongs*. Laguna Beach, CA: Aldrich Blake, 1953.

———. *The Ku Klux Kraze: A Trip through the Klavern*. Oklahoma City: Aldrich Blake, 1924.

———. *My Kind! My Country!* Philadelphia: Dorrance, 1950.

Blakely, Michael L. "Passing the Buck: Naturalism and Individualism as Anthropological Expressions of Euro-American Denial." In *Race*, edited by Steven

Gregory and Roger Sanjek, 270–284. New Brunswick: Rutgers University Press, 1994.

Blank, Robert H., and Samuel H. Hines Jr. *Biology and Political Science*. New York: Routledge, 2001.

Bloch, Charles. "Civil Rights—or Civil Wrongs?" *Georgia Bar Journal* 22 (1959): 127–139.

———. *States' Rights: The Law of the Land*. Atlanta: Harrison Company, 1958.

Block, N. J., and Gerald Dworkin, eds. *The IQ Controversy*. New York: Pantheon, 1976.

Bond, Horace Mann. "Cat on a Hot Tin Roof." *Journal of Negro Education* 27 (1958): 519–525.

———. "Intelligence Tests and Propaganda." *The Crisis* 28 (1924): 61–64.

———. "What the Army 'Intelligence' Tests Measured." *Opportunity* 2 (1924): 197–202.

Brace, C. Loring. "The Roots of the Race Concept in American Physical Anthropology." In *A History of American Physical Anthropology, 1930–1980*, edited by Frank Spencer, 11–29. New York: Academic Press, 1982.

Branch, Taylor. *Parting the Waters: America in the King Years, 1954–1963*. New York: Simon and Schuster, 1988.

Brodie, Fawn M. "A Lincoln Who Never Was." *The Reporter* 20 (25 June 1959): 25–27.

Buckley, William F., Jr. *God and Man at Yale*. Chicago: Regnery, 1951.

Burnham, Sophy. "Twelve Rebels of the Student Right." *New York Times*, 9 March 1969, SM32.

Bush, Vannevar. *Science the Endless Frontier*. Washington, DC: National Science Foundation, 1950. Reprint, 1960.

Butler, Declan. "Geneticist Quits in Protest at 'Genes and Violence' Claim." *Nature* 378 (16 November 1995): 224.

Byrnes, James F. *The Supreme Court Must Be Curbed*. Winona: Association of Citizens' Councils of Mississippi, 1956.

Cahn, Edmond. "Jurisprudence." *New York University Law Review* 30 (1955): 150–169.

Campbell, Byram. *American Race Theorists: A Critique of Their Thoughts and Methods*. Boston: Chapman and Grimes, 1952.

———. "Jewized Textbook Sociology: Broom and Selznick." *Truth Seeker* 88 (1961): 49–51.

———. "The Nordic as an Ideal." *Northern World* 3, no. 3 (1959): 4–7.

———. *The World of Oneness*. New York: Vantage, 1956.

Campbell, Stuart B. "Books for Lawyers." *ABA Journal* 48 (1962): 567.

Caplan, Marc H., and Lori Linzer. *Uncommon Ground: The Black African Holocaust Denial Council and Other Links between Black and White Extremists*. New York: Anti-Defamation League, 1994.

Capshew, James H. *Psychologists on the March: Science, Practice, and Professional Identity in America, 1929–1969*. Cambridge: Cambridge University Press, 1999.

Carson, John. "Army Alpha, Army Brass, and the Search for Army Intelligence." *Isis* 84 (1993): 278–309.

Carter, Dan T. *The Politics of Rage: George Wallace, the Origins of the New Conservatism, and the Transformation of American Politics*. New York: Simon and Schuster, 1995.

Chalmers, David. *Hooded Americanism: The History of the Ku Klux Klan*. Chicago: Quadrangle, 1968.

Chamberlain, Houston Stewart. *Foundations of the Nineteenth Century*. Translated by John Lees. New York: John Lane Company, 1914.

Chappell, David L. "The Divided Mind of Southern Segregationists." *Georgia Historical Quarterly* 82 (1998): 45–72.

———. "Religious Ideas of the Segregationists." *Journal of American Studies* 32 (1998): 237–262.

Chase, Allan. *The Legacy of Malthus: The Social Costs of the New Scientific Racism*. Urbana: University of Illinois Press, 1980.

Clark, Kenneth B. *Prejudice and Your Child*. 2d ed. Boston: Beacon Press, 1963.

Comas, Juan. "A McCarthyan Attack." *Current Anthropology* 3 (1962): 155–158.

———. *Racial Myths*. Paris: UNESCO, 1951.

———. "'Scientific' Racism Again?" *Current Anthropology* 2 (1961): 303–314.

Committee on Science in the Promotion of Human Welfare. "Science and the Race Problem." *Science* 142 (1 November 1963): 558–561.

Condit, Celeste Michelle. *The Meanings of the Gene: Public Debates about Human Heredity*. Madison: University of Wisconsin Press, 1999.

Coogan, Kevin. *Dreamer of the Day: Francis Parker Yockey and the Postwar Fascist International*. New York: Automedia, 1999.

Coon, Carleton S. *Adventures and Discoveries*. Englewood Cliffs, NJ: Prentice-Hall, 1981.

———. "Comments." *Current Anthropology* 4 (1963): 363.

———. "Letter to the Editor." *Science* 140 (12 April 1963): 208.

———. *The Origin of Races*. New York: Knopf, 1962.

———. *Races of Europe*. New York: Macmillan, 1939.

———. *The Story of Man*. New York: Knopf, 1954.

Cox, Earnest Sevier. *Let My People Go*. Richmond: White America Society, 1925.

———. *Lincoln's Negro Policy*. Los Angeles: Noontide Press, 1968.

———. *The Races of Mankind: A Review*. Jellico, TN: Arthur Daugherty, 1951.

———. *The South's Part in Mongrelizing the Nation*. Richmond: White America Society, 1926.

————. *Teutonic Unity.* Richmond: Earnest Sevier Cox, 1951.

————. *White America.* Richmond: White America Society, 1923.

Cravens, Hamilton. *Triumph of Evolution.* Baltimore: Johns Hopkins University Press, 1988.

Cronon, David. *Black Moses: The Story of Marcus Garvey and the Universal Negro Improvement Association.* Madison: University of Wisconsin Press, 1969.

Cross, William E., Jr. *Shades of Black: Diversity in African-American Identity.* Philadelphia: Temple University Press, 1991.

Daston, Lorraine. "Objectivity and the Escape from Perspective." *Social Studies of Science* 22 (1992): 597–618.

Davenport, Charles B., and Morris Steggerda. *Race Crossing in Jamaica.* Washington, DC: Carnegie Institution, 1929.

de Gobineau, Arthur. *Inequality of the Human Races.* Translated by Adrian Collins. New York: Putnam and Sons, 1915.

de Melo-Martin, Immaculada. "Biological Explanations and Social Responsibility." *Studies in History and Philosophy of the Biological and Biomedical Sciences* 34 (2003): 345–358.

Degler, Carl N. *In Search of Human Nature: The Decline and Revival of Darwinism in American Social Thought.* New York: Oxford University Press, 1991.

Diamond, Sara. *Roads to Dominion: Right Wing Movements and Political Power in the United States.* New York: Guilford, 1995.

Dikötter, Frank. "Race Culture: Recent Perspectives on the History of Eugenics." *American Historical Review* 103 (1998): 467–478.

Dobzhansky, Theodosius. "A Bogus 'Science' of Race Prejudice." *Journal of Heredity* 52 (1961): 189–190.

————. "A Debatable Account of the Origin of Races." *Scientific American* 208 (1963): 169–172.

————. *Mankind Evolving: The Evolution of the Human Species.* New Haven: Yale University Press, 1962.

————. "More Bogus 'Science' of Race Prejudice." *Journal of Heredity* 59 (1968): 102–104.

————. "Possibility That Homo Sapiens Evolved Independently 5 Times Is Vanishingly Small." *Current Anthropology* 4 (1963): 464–466.

Dodd, Bella V. *School of Darkness.* New York: Kenedy, 1954.

Donald, David. "The Proslavery Argument Reconsidered." *Journal of Southern History* 37 (1971): 3–18.

Downs, James F. "More on Scientific Racism." *Current Anthropology* 3 (1962): 298.

D'souza, Dinesh. *Illiberal Education: The Politics of Race and Sex on Campus.* New York: Macmillan, 1991.

Dubow, Saul. *Scientific Racism in Modern South Africa.* Cambridge: Cambridge University Press, 1995.

Duke, David. *My Awakening: A Path to Racial Understanding.* Covington, LA: Free Speech Press, 1998.

Dunn, L. C. "Review of *Race and Modern Science.*" *Eugenics Quarterly* 15 (1969): 298–301.

Dunn, L. C., and Theodosius Dobzhansky. *Heredity, Race, and Society.* New York: New American Library, 1952.

Duren, Brad L. "'Klanspiracy' or Despotism? The Rise and Fall of Governor Jack Walton, Featuring W. D. McBee." *Chronicles of Oklahoma* 80 (2002): 468–485.

Edwards, William A. "Racial Purity in Black and White: The Case of Marcus Garvey and Earnest Cox." *Journal of Ethnic Studies* 15 (1987): 117–142.

Egan, Leo. "Liberals Back Republican for Bronx Borough Chief." *New York Times,* 11 August 1961, 11.

Ehrenfels, U. R. "Critical Paragraphs Deleted." *Current Anthropology* 3 (1962): 154–155.

Ericson, David F. *The Debate over Slavery: Antislavery and Proslavery Liberalism in Antebellum America.* New York: New York University Press, 2000.

Evans, Richard J. *Lying about Hitler: History, Holocaust, and the David Irving Trial.* New York: Basic Books, 2002

Faust, Drew Gilpin. "A Southern Stewardship: The Intellectual and the Proslavery Argument." *American Quarterly* 31 (1979): 63–80.

Fax, Elton C. *Garvey: The Story of a Pioneer Black Nationalist.* New York: Dodd and Mead, 1972.

Fenster, Mark. *Conspiracy Theories: Secrecy and Power in American Culture.* Minneapolis: University of Minnesota Press, 1999.

Field, Geoffrey G. *Evangelist of Race: The Germanic Vision of Houston Stewart Chamberlain.* New York: Columbia University Press, 1981.

Fish, Jefferson M., ed. *Race and Intelligence: Separating Science from Myth.* Mahwah, NJ: Lawrence Erlbaum, 2002.

Fitzgerald, Michael W. "'We Have Found a Moses': Theodore Bilbo, Black Nationalism, and the Greater Liberia Bill of 1939." *Journal of Southern History* 63 (1997): 293–320.

Foner, Eric. *Reconstruction: America's Unfinished Revolution, 1863–1877.* New York: Harper and Row, 1988.

———. *The Story of American Freedom.* New York: Norton, 1998.

Franklin, Ben A. "New Voting Law Attacked in Suit." *New York Times,* 7 August 1965, 1.

Franklin, Vincent P. "Black Social Scientists and the Mental Testing Movement, 1920–1940." In *Black Psychology,* edited by Reginald L. Jones, 201–215. 2d ed. New York: Harper and Row, 1980.

Fredrickson, George M. *The Black Image in the White Mind: The Debate on Afro-American Destiny, 1817–1914.* Hanover: Wesleyan University Press, 1971.

———. *The Comparative Imagination: On the History of Racism, Nationalism, and Social Movements.* Berkeley: University of California Press, 1997.

———. *Racism: A Short History.* Princeton: Princeton University Press, 2002.

Fried, Morton. "Letter to the Editor." *New York Times,* 10 October 1962, 46.

Fuller, Steve. *Thomas Kuhn: A Philosophical History of Our Times.* Chicago: University of Chicago Press, 2000.

Fultz, Michael. "A 'Quintessential American': Horace Mann Bond, 1924–1939." *Harvard Educational Review* 55 (1985): 416–442.

Garrett, Henry E. "The Equalitarian Dogma." *Perspectives in Biology and Medicine* 4 (1961): 480–484.

———. "The Equalitarian Dogma." *Mankind Quarterly* 1 (1961): 253–257.

———. "The Scientific Racism of Juan Comas." *Mankind Quarterly* 2 (1962): 100–106.

Garrett, Henry E., and Wesley Critz George. "Letter to the Editor." *New York Times,* 24 October 1962, 38.

———. "Science and the Race Problem." *Science* 143 (1964): 913–915.

Garrett, Henry E., Wesley Critz George, and Carleton Putnam. *Race: A Reply to Race and Intelligence: A Scientific Evaluation by the Anti-Defamation League of B'nai B'rith.* Washington, DC: National Putnam Letters Committee, 1964.

Garth, Thomas. *Race Psychology: A Study of Racial Mental Differences.* New York: McGraw-Hill, 1931.

Garvey, Amy Jacques, ed. *Philosophy and Opinions of Marcus Garvey.* New York: Atheneum, 1969.

Gasman, Daniel. *Haeckel's Monism and the Birth of Fascist Ideology.* New York: Peter Lang, 1998.

———. *The Scientific Origins of National Socialism.* New York: Elsevier, 1971.

Gates, R. Ruggles. *Heredity and Eugenics.* New York: Macmillan, 1923.

———. *Human Ancestry: From a Genetical Point of View.* Cambridge: Harvard University Press, 1948.

Gates, R. Ruggles, and A. James Gregor. "Mankind Quarterly: Gates and Gregor Respond to Critics." *Current Anthropology* 4 (1963): 119–121.

George, Wesley Critz. *The Biology of the Race Problem.* Richmond: Patrick Henry Press, 1962.

———."Integration, Christianity, and the Law of the Land." *The Cross and the Flag* 19, no. 11 (February 1961): 3, 27–29.

———. *Race, Heredity, and Civilization and Human Progress and the Race Problem.* London: Britons, 1961.

———. *The Race Problem from the Standpoint of One Who Is Concerned about the Evils of Miscegenation.* Shreveport: American States Rights Association, 1955.

———. "The Responsibility of Scientists in This Era." *School and Society* 76 (13 December 1952): 369–374.

Giddings, Franklin H. *Principles of Sociology.* New York: Macmillan, 1896.

Gieryn, Thomas F. *Cultural Boundaries of Science: Credibility on the Line.* Chicago: University of Chicago Press, 1999.

Gimigliano, Anthony James. "The Ethical and Political Thought of Giovanni Gentile." Ph.D. diss., Columbia University, 1961.

Gini, Corrado. "The Scientific Basis of Fascism." *Political Science Quarterly* 42 (1927): 99–115.

Gjessing, Gutorm. "Comments." *Current Anthropology* 2 (1961): 321–322.

Goldfield, David R. *Black, White, and Southern: Race Relations and Southern Culture 1940 to the Present.* Baton Rouge: Louisiana State University Press, 1990.

Goodnight, G. Thomas, and John Poulakos. "Conspiracy Rhetoric: From Pragmatism to Fantasy in Public Discourse." *Western Journal of Speech Communication* 45 (1981): 299–316.

Gossett, Thomas F. *Race: The History of an Idea in America.* Dallas: Southern Methodist University Press, 1963.

Gottfredson, Linda. "Jensen, Jensenism, and the Sociology of Intelligence." *Intelligence* 26 (1998): 291–299.

Gould, Stephen Jay. *The Mismeasure of Man.* New York: Norton, 1981.

Grant, Madison. *The Passing of the Great Race or the Racial Basis of European History.* New York: Scribner's, 1916.

Graves, Joseph L., Jr. *The Emperor's New Clothes: Biological Theories of Race at the Millennium.* New Brunswick: Rutgers University Press, 2001.

Green, Kenneth. "Memorandum to Executive Director." In *A Chicago Urban League Report on "A Scientist's Report on Racial Differences,* edited by Kenneth Green, 1–2. Chicago: Urban League, 1957.

Greenberg, Jack. *Crusaders in the Courts.* New York: Basic Books, 1994.

Gregor, A. James. "An American Considers European Socialism." *The European,* no. 33 (November 1955): 17–24.

———. "Comas' Chapter on Racial Myths: A Review." *Mankind Quarterly* 2 (1961): 20–34.

———. "The Dynamics of Prejudice." *Mankind Quarterly* 3 (1962): 79–88.

———. "Eisenhoover: A Study in American Economy." *The European,* no. 17 (July 1954): 7–13.

———. "Juan Comas: Critic and Scholar." *Mankind Quarterly* 3 (1962): 37–47.

———. "The Law, Social Science, and School Segregation: An Assessment." *Western Reserve Law Review* 14 (1963): 621–636.

———. "Marxism as a Theory of History." *The European* 8 (November 1956): 146–162.

———. "Marxism as Philosophy." *The European* 7 (August 1956): 11–26.

———. "National Socialism and Race." *The European* 11 (1958): 273–291.

———. "Nordicism Revisited." *Phylon* 22 (1961): 351–360.

———. "Notes on a 'Scientific' Controversy." *Mankind Quarterly* 2 (1962): 166–177.

———. "On Learned Ignorance: A Brief Inquiry into I.A. Newby's *Challenge to the Court*." In *Challenge to the Court,* by I. A. Newby, 237–283. Rev. ed. Baton Rouge: Louisiana State University Press, 1969.

———. "On the Nature of Prejudice." *Eugenics Review* 52 (1961): 217–224.

———. "Review of *Darwinism and the Study of Society*." *Mankind Quarterly* 2 (1961): 139–140.

———. "Some Problems of Race." *The European,* no. 24 (1955): 19–25.

———. "Syndicalism: A Critical History." *The European,* no. 38 (April 1956): 10–20.

Gregor, A. James, and D. Angus McPherson. "Racial Attitudes among White and Negro Children in a Deep-South Standard Metropolitan Area." *Journal of Social Psychology* 68 (1966): 95–106.

Grill, Johnpeter Horst, and Robert L. Jenkins. "The Nazis and the American South in the 1930s: A Mirror Image?" *Journal of Southern History* 58 (1992): 667–693.

Gross, Alan G., Joseph E. Harmon, and Michael Reidy. *Communicating Science: The Scientific Article from the Seventeenth Century to the Present.* New York: Oxford University Press, 2002.

Guterl, Mathew Pratt. *The Color of Race in America, 1900–1940.* Cambridge: Harvard University Press, 2001.

Guthrie, Robert V. *Even the Rat Was White: A Historical View of Psychology.* Boston: Allyn and Bacon, 1998.

Haller, John S., Jr. *Outcasts from Evolution: Scientific Attitudes of Racial Inferiority, 1859–1900.* Urbana: University of Illinois Press, 1971.

Handler, Richard. "Boasian Anthropology and the Critique of American Culture." *American Quarterly* 42 (1990): 252–273.

Haney Lopez, Ian F. *White by Law: Legal Construction of Race.* New York: New York University Press, 1996.

Hannaford, Ivan. *Race: The History of an Idea in the West.* Baltimore: Johns Hopkins University Press, 1996.

Haraway, Donna. *Simians, Cyborgs, and Women.* New York: Routledge, 1991.

Harman, Oren Solomon. "C.D. Darlington and the British and American Reaction to Lysenko and the Soviet Conception of Science." *Journal of the History of Biology* 36 (2003): 309–352.

Harrison, Emma. "Professor's Right to Views Upheld: Psychologist Says Villanova Resisted Calls for Ouster after Article on Negro." *New York Times,* 8 September 1959, 39.

Harrison, G. Ainsworth. "The Mankind Quarterly." *Man* 61 (1961): 163–164.

Hayward, Rhodri. "The Biopolitics of Arthur Keith and Morley Roberts." *Clio Medica* 60 (August 2000): 251–264.

Heath, Andrew C. "Secretary's Report on the 25th Annual Meeting of the Behavior Genetics Association, Richmond, Virginia." *Behavior Genetics* 25 (1995): 589–590.

Hecht, Jennifer Michael. *Doubt: A History.* San Francisco: HarperSanFrancisco, 2003.

———. *The End of the Soul: Scientific Modernity, Atheism, and Anthropology in France.* New York: Columbia University Press, 2003

———. "The Solvency of Metaphysics: The Debate over Racial Science and Moral Philosophy in France, 1890–1919." *Isis* 90 (1999): 1–24.

———. "Vacher de Lapouge and the Rise of Nazi Science." *Journal of the History of Ideas* 61 (2000): 285–304.

Hedlin, Ethel Wolfskill. "Earnest Cox and Colonialization: A White Racist's Response to Black Repatriation, 1923–1966." Ph.D. diss., Duke University, 1974.

Hennessey, Bernard. "Race, Intelligence, and Equality." *New Republic* 135 (24 December 1956): 10.

Herman, Ellen. *The Romance of American Psychology: Political Culture in the Age of Experts.* Berkeley: University of California Press, 1995.

Herrnstein, Richard J., and Charles Murray. *The Bell Curve: Intelligence and Class Structure in American Life.* New York: Free Press, 1994.

Herskovits, Melville. "Extremes and Means in Racial Interpretation." *Journal of Social Forces* 2 (1924): 550–551.

———. "Rearguard Action." *Perspectives in Biology and Medicine* 5 (1961): 122–128.

Hollinger, David A. "The Knower and the Artificer." *American Quarterly* 39 (1987): 37–55.

———. *Science, Jews, and Secular Culture: Studies in Mid-Twentieth-Century American Intellectual History.* Princeton: Princeton University Press, 1996.

Hoover, Dwight W. "A Paradigm Shift: The Concept of Race in the 1920s and 1930s." *Conspectus of History* 1 (1981): 82–100.

Horsman, Reginald. "Origins of Racial Anglo-Saxonism in Great Britain before 1850." *Journal of the History of Ideas* 37 (1976): 387–410.

Howells, William W. "Our Family Tree." *New York Times,* 9 December 1962, 171.

Hunt, Morton. *The New Know-Nothings: The Political Foes of the Scientific Study of Human Nature.* New Brunswick, NJ: Transaction, 1999.

Ichheiser, Gustav. "Sociopsychological and Cultural Factors in Race Relations." *American Journal of Sociology* 54 (1949): 395–399.

Ingle, Dwight. "Comments on the Teachings of Carleton Putnam." *Mankind Quarterly* 4 (1963): 28–42.

———. "Letter from the Editor." *Perspectives in Biology and Medicine* 5 (1961): 130.

———. "Letter to the Reader." *Perspectives in Biology and Medicine* 6 (1963): 539–542.

Jackson, John P., Jr. *Social Scientists for Social Justice: Making the Case against Segregation.* New York: New York University Press, 2001.

Jackson, Walter A. *Gunnar Myrdal and America's Conscience: Social Engineering and Racial Liberalism, 1938–1987.* Chapel Hill: University of North Carolina Press, 1990.

Jacobsohn, Peter. "A Scientist's Unscientific Report." In *A Chicago Urban League Report on "A Scientist's Report on Racial Differences,* edited by Kenneth Green, 31–38. Chicago: Urban League, 1957.

Jeansonne, Glen. *Gerald L.K. Smith: Minister of Hate.* New Haven: Yale University Press, 1988.

Jenkins, Williams Sumner. *Proslavery Thought in the Old South.* Chapel Hill: University of North Carolina Press, 1935.

Jensen, Arthur R. *The G Factor: The Science of Mental Ability.* Westport, CT: Praeger, 1998.

———. *Genetics and Education.* New York: Harper and Row, 1972.

———. "How Much Can We Boost IQ and Scholastic Achievement?" *Harvard Educational Review* 39 (1969): 1–123.

Johnson, Guy. "Recent Literature on the Negro." *Journal of Social Forces* 3 (1925): 318.

Jordan, Winthrop D. *White over Black: American Attitudes toward the Negro, 1550–1812.* New York: Norton, 1969.

Jorgensen, Carl. "The African American Critique of White Supremacist Science." *Journal of Negro Education* 64 (1995): 232–242.

Josey, Charles C. *An Inquiry concerning Racial Prejudice.* New York: International Association for the Advancement of Ethnology and Eugenics, 1965.

———. *The Philosophy of Nationalism.* Washington, DC: Cliveden, 1983.

———. *Race and National Solidarity.* New York: Scribner's, 1923.

Jumonville, Neil. *Critical Crossings: The New York Intellectuals in Postwar America.* Berkeley: University of California Press, 1991.

Katagiri, Yasuhiro. *The Mississippi State Sovereignty Commission: Civil Rights and States' Rights.* Jackson: University of Mississippi Press, 2001.

Keith, Arthur. *An Autobiography.* London: Watts, 1950.

———. *Essays on Human Evolution.* London: Watts, 1946.

————. *Ethnos: The Problem of Race Considered from a New Point of View.* London: Kegan, Paul, Trench, Trubner, 1931.

————. *Nationality and Race from an Anthropologist's Point of View.* London: Oxford University Press, 1919.

————. *The Place of Prejudice in Modern Civilization.* London: Williams and Norgate, 1931.

Kenny, Michael G. "Racial Science in Social Context: John R. Baker on Eugenics, Race, and the Public Role of the Scientist." *Isis* 95 (2004): 394–419.

Kerr, Willard A. "Psychological Test Results Do Not Support the Idea of Inherent Differences between the Intelligence Levels of Various Racial Groups." In *A Chicago Urban League Report on "A Scientist's Report on Racial Differences,* edited by Kenneth Green, 13–16. Chicago: Urban League, 1957.

Kevles, Daniel J. *In the Name of Eugenics: Genetics and the Uses of Human Heredity.* New York: Knopf, 1985.

Kimball, Roger. *Tenured Radicals: How Politics Corrupted Our Higher Education.* New York: Harper and Row, 1990.

Klarman, Michael J. "*Brown,* Racial Change, and the Civil Rights Movement." *Virginia Law Review* 80 (1994): 7–150.

————. *From Jim Crow to Civil Rights: The Supreme Court and the Struggle for Racial Equality.* New York: Oxford University Press, 2004.

————. "How *Brown* Changed Race Relations: The Backlash Thesis." *Journal of American History* 81 (1994): 81–118.

Klineberg, Otto. *Race Differences.* New York: Harper and Brothers, 1935.

Klineberg, Otto, Theodore Newcomb, Gardner Murphy, Nevitt Sanford, Robin Williams, David Krech, Jerome Bruner, Allison Davis, Daniel Katz, Anne Anastasi, Stuart Cook, Isidor Chein, Marie Jahoda, Kenneth Clark, Bingham Dai, Irving Lorge, Solomon Asch, and David Rapaport. "Does Race Really Make a Difference in Intelligence?" *U.S. News and World Report* 41 (26 October 1956): 74–76.

Kluger, Richard. *Simple Justice: The History of Brown v. Board of Education and Black America's Struggle for Equality.* New York: Vintage, 1975.

Knight, Peter. "'A Plague of Paranoia': Theories of Conspiracy Theory Since the 1960s." In *Fear Itself: Enemies, Real and Imagined in American Culture,* edited by Nancy Lusignan Schultz, 23–50. West Lafayette, IN: Purdue University Press, 1999.

Knowlton, Clark S. "Review of *Race and Reason.*" *Western Political Quarterly* 15 (1962): 568–570.

Kühl, Stefan. *The Nazi Connection: Eugenics, American Racism, and German National Socialism.* New York: Oxford University Press, 1994.

Kuttner, Robert. "Biopolitics: The Theory of Racial Nationalism." *Truth Seeker* 86 (1959): 41–43.

———. "Biopolitics: The Validity of Racial Nationalism." *Truth Seeker* 86 (1959): 129–131.

———. "The Early History of the Celt." *Northern World* 3 (1958): 12–18.

———. "The Early History of the Teuton." *Northern World* 3 (1959): 12–20.

———. "Jewish Slanders and Democratic Forums." *Truth Seeker* 86 (1959): 3.

———. "Manifestoes and Resolutions on Race." *Truth Seeker* 84 (August 1957): 117–119.

———. "The Nordic as the Natural Leader of the White Race." *Truth Seeker* 85 (1958): 113–114.

———. "The North European in Homeric Greece." *Northern World* 3 (1958): 8–15.

———. "On Strike against Science." *Truth Seeker* 86 (1959): 19.

———. "Race Evolution: Competitive or Cooperative?" *Truth Seeker* 84 (1957): 161–163.

———. "The Status of Scientific Racism I." *Truth Seeker* 84 (1957): 75–76.

———. "The Status of Scientific Racism II." *Truth Seeker* 84 (June 1957): 85–87.

———. "The Unequal Races of Man." *Truth Seeker* 83 (December 1956): 177–178, 185–186.

Kuttner, Robert E. "Serum Pepsinogen in Migrant Mexicans and Stressed Caucasians." *Journal of the National Medical Association* 57 (1965): 109–111.

———. "Serum Pepsinogen in Urbanized Sioux Indians." *Journal of the National Medical Association* 56 (1964): 471–473.

———. "Use of Accentuated Environmental Inequalities in Research on Racial Differences." *Mankind Quarterly* 8 (1968): 147–160.

———. "What Do We Owe the Negroes?" *American Mercury* 103 (1967): 7–9.

———. "Why Aren't Indians 'Disadvantaged'?" *American Mercury* 105 (1969): 8–9.

Kuttner, Robert E., and Albert B. Lorincz. "Alcoholism and Addiction in Urbanized Sioux Indians." *Mental Hygiene* 51 (1967): 530–542.

Kuttner, Robert, and Donald Swan. "Biological Aspects of Evolution." *Southern Quarterly* 12 (1974): 323–333.

Ladd-Taylor, Molly. "Eugenics, Sterilisation, and Modern Marriage in the USA: The Strange Career of Paul Popenoe." *Gender and History* 13 (2001): 298–327.

Landis, Kenesaw M. *Segregation in Washington: A Report of the National Committee on Segregation in the Nation's Capital.* Chicago: National Committee on Segregation in the Nation's Capital, 1948.

Landry, Stuart Omer. *The Cult of Equality: A Study of the Race Problem.* New Orleans: Pelican Publishing Co., 1945.

———. *Facts to Fight Communism.* New Orleans: Pelican Publishing Co., 1948.

———. "Why Race Suicide with Advancing Civilization?" *Arena* 41 (1909): 569.

Lane, Charles. "Tainted Sources." In *The Bell Curve Debate,* edited by Russell Jacoby and Naomi Glauberman, 125–139. New York: Times Books, 1995.

Larson, Edward J. *Sex, Race, and Science: Eugenics in the Deep South.* Baltimore: Johns Hopkins University Press, 1995.

Lasker, Gabriel. *Happenings and Hearsay: Experiences of a Biological Anthropologist.* Detroit: Savoyard, 1999.

Leacock, Eleanor. "Anthropology (H)." *Science* 139 (February 1963): 638.

Lee, Martin A. *The Beast Reawakens.* New York: Routledge, 2000.

Leonard, George. "Ethnic Differentiation in the United States School Desegregation Cases." *Mankind Quarterly* 6 (1966): 139–148.

Lesseig, Corey T. "Roast Beef and Racial Integrity: Mississippi's 'Race and Reason Day,'" October 26, 1962 [*sic*]." *Journal of Mississippi History* 56 (1994): 1–15.

Lessl, Thomas M. "The Galileo Legend as Scientific Folklore." *Quarterly Journal of Speech* 85 (1999): 146–168.

Lewis, Alfred Baker. "To Equalize Education." *New York Times,* 10 January 1959, 16.

Lewis, David W., and Wesley Phillips Newton. *Delta: The History of an Airline.* Athens: University of Georgia Press, 1979.

Lieberman, Leonard, Andrew Lyons, and Harriet Lyons. "An Interview with Ashley Montagu." *Current Anthropology* 36 (1995): 835–844.

Linklater, Magnus. "The Curious Laird of Nigg." In *The Bell Curve Debate: History, Documents, Opinions,* edited by Russell Jacoby and Naomi Glauberman, 140–143. New York: Times Books, 1995.

Lipstadt, Deborah. *Denying the Holocaust: The Growing Assault on Truth and Memory.* New York: Plume, 1993.

Lissner, Will. "Columbia Is Dropping Dr. Weltfish, Leftist." *New York Times,* 1 April 1953, 1, 19.

Lofgren, Charles A. *The Plessy Case: A Legal-Historical Interpretation.* New York: Oxford University Press, 1987.

Loftus, Joseph. "Virginia Debates Negro Abilities." *New York Times,* 18 February 1962, 62.

Logan, Rayford W. *The Betrayal of the Negro.* New York: Macmillan, 1965.

Lombardo, Paul A. "'The American Breed': Nazi Eugenics and the Origins of the Pioneer Fund." *Albany Law Review* 65 (2002): 743–830.

———. "Miscegenation, Eugenics, and Racism: Historical Footnotes to *Loving v. Virginia*." *University of California Davis Law Review* 21 (1988): 421–452.

Long, Howard Hale. "The Relative Learning Capacities of Negroes and Whites." *Journal of Negro Education* 26 (1957): 121–134.

MacDonald, George E. *Fifty Years of Freethought: Being the Story of the Truth*

Seeker, with the Natural History of Its Third Editor. 2 vols. New York: Truth Seeker, 1929–31.

MacDonald, Kevin. *The Culture of Critique: An Evolutionary Analysis of Jewish Involvement in Twentieth-Century Intellectual and Political Movements.* Westport, CT: Praeger, 1998.

Madole, James H. "Did Nazi Germany Destroy Six Million Jews?" *National Renaissance Bulletin* 11, no. 3 (March 1960): 2–5.

———. "The Scientific and Historical Basis for Racial Segregation." *National Renaissance Bulletin* 7, no. 4 (April 1956): 2–4.

Maki, Uskali. "Science as a Free Market: A Reflexivity Test in an Economics of Economics." *Perspectives on Science* 7 (1999): 486–509.

Mann, Robert. *The Walls of Jericho: Lyndon Johnson, Hubert Humphrey, Richard Russell, and the Struggle for Civil Rights.* New York: Harcourt, Brace, and Company, 1996.

Marks, Jonathan. "Human Biodiversity as a Central Theme of Biological Anthropology: Then and Now." *Krober Anthropological Society Papers* 84 (2000): 1–10.

———. *Human Biodiversity: Genes, Race, and History.* New York: Aldine de Gruyter, 1995.

Mayr, Ernst. "Origin of the Human Races." *Science* 138 (1962): 420–422.

Mazumdar, Paula M. "'Reform' Eugenics and the Decline of Mendelism." *Trends in Genetics* 18 (2002): 48–52.

McCain, W. D. "Who Is Carleton Putnam?" *The Citizen* 6 (November 1961): 9–11.

McCord, William M., and Nicholas J. Demerath III. "Negro versus White Intelligence: A Continuing Controversy." *Harvard Educational Review* 28 (1958): 120–135.

McDonald, William. "Mr. Grant's Plea for a Nordic, Protestant America." *New York Times,* 5 November 1933, 16.

McGurk, Frank C. J. "Comparative Test Scores of Negro and White School Children in Richmond, VA." *Journal of Educational Psychology* 34 (1943): 427–484.

———. "Comparison of the Performance of Negro and White High School Seniors on Cultural and Non-Cultural Psychological Test Questions." Ph.D. diss., Catholic University of America, 1951.

———. "The Law, Social Science, and Academic Freedom—A Psychologist's View." *Villanova Law Review* 5 (1959–60): 247–254.

———. "Negro vs. White Intelligence—An Answer." *Harvard Educational Review* 29 (1959): 54–62.

———. "On White and Negro Test Performance and Socioeconomic Factors." *Journal of Abnormal and Social Psychology* 48 (1953): 448–450.

———. "Racial Differences Are Racial." *American Mercury* 115 (1979): 58–61.

———. "A Scientist's Report on Race Differences." *U.S. News and World Report* 41 (21 September 1956): 92–98.

———. "Socio-economic Status and Culturally-Weighted Test Scores of Negro Subjects." *Journal of Applied Psychology* 37 (1953): 276–277.

McMillen, Neil R. *The Citizens' Council: Organized Resistance to the Second Reconstruction, 1954–64.* Urbana: University of Illinois Press, 1971. Reprint, 1994.

Mead, Margaret. "Clocking the Timetable of Man." *Saturday Review* 46 (22 June 1963): 41.

Mintz, Frank P. *The Liberty Lobby and the American Right: Race, Conspiracy, and Culture.* Westport, CT: Greenwood Press, 1985.

Mitchell, Gordon R. "Did Habermas Cede Nature to the Positivists?" *Philosophy and Rhetoric* 36 (2003): 1–21.

Montagu, Ashley. "Negro Intelligence Capacity—A Scientist's View." *Harvard Law Record* (18 October 1956): 2–4, 6.

———. *Statement on Race.* New York: Oxford University Press, 1972.

———. "What Is Remarkable about Varieties of Man Is Likeness, Not Differences." *Current Anthropology* 4 (1963): 361–363.

Morawski, Jill G., and Gail A. Hornstein. "Quandary of the Quacks: The Struggle for Expert Knowledge in American Psychology, 1890–1940." In *Estate of Social Knowledge,* edited by David van Keuren and JoAnne Brown, 106–133. Baltimore: Johns Hopkins University Press, 1991.

Mosse, George L. *Toward the Final Solution: A History of European Racism.* New York: Howard Fertig, 1985.

Moten, Derryn E. "Racial Integrity or 'Race Suicide': Virginia's Eugenic Movement, W. E. B. Du Bois, and the Work of Walter A. Plecker." *Negro History Bulletin* 61 (April–September 1999): 6–17.

Mullins, Eustace. *The Federal Reserve Conspiracy.* Union, NJ: Common Sense, 1954.

———. "The New Man in Our Image." *Truth Seeker* 85 (November 1958): 170–172.

Mullins, Eustace, and M. Nelson. "Christianity, Communism, and Biopolitics." *Truth Seeker* 85 (August 1958): 122–123.

Nagel, Thomas. *The View from Nowhere.* New York: Oxford University Press, 1986.

Nash, Gary B. "The Hidden History of Mestizo America." In *Sex, Love, Race: Crossing Boundaries in North American History,* edited by Martha Hodes, 10–32. New York: New York University Press, 1999.

Nash, George H. *The Conservative Intellectual Movement in America since 1945.* New York: Basic Books, 1976.

Nash, Manning. "Race and Ideology of Race." *Current Anthropology* 3 (1962): 285–288.

Newby, I. A. *Challenge to the Court.* Baton Rouge: Louisiana State University Press, 1969.

———. *The Development of Segregationist Thought.* Homewood, IL: Dorsey Press, 1968.

Niven, Steven. "Wesley Critz George: Scientist and Segregationist." *North Carolina Literary Review,* no. 7 (1998): 39–41.

Nossiter, Adam. *Of Long Memory: Mississippi and the Murder of Medgar Evers.* Reading: Addison Wesley, 1994.

Novkov, Julie. "Racial Constructions: The Legal Regulation of Miscegenation in Alabama, 1890–1934." *Law and History Review* 20 (2002): 135 pars., 1 Dec. 2003, http://historycooperative.org/journals/lhr/20.2/novkov.html.

Nye, Robert A. "The Rise and Fall of the Eugenics Empire: Recent Perspectives on the Impact of Biomedical Thought in Modern Society." *Historical Journal* 36 (1993): 687–700.

O'Keefe, Ted. "Mead, Freeman, Boas: Jewish Anthropology Comes of Age in America." *National Vanguard* (June 1983): 5–10.

Opler, Morris E. "Did the Races Come from Different Ancestors?" *New York Herald Tribune,* 9 December 1962, 22.

Oster, Ted. "America Plus—Democracy Minus." *New Republic* 127 (11 August 1952): 16–17.

Page, Thornell Kenly. "A Study of the District of Columbia Public Schools Desegregation Policies, 1954–1967." Ph.D. diss., Virginia Polytechnic Institute, 1978.

Parsons, Howard L. "Review of *Contemporary Radical Ideologies.*" *Philosophy and Phenomenological Research* 31 (1970): 307.

Pascoe, Peggy. "Miscegenation Law, Court Cases, and Ideologies of 'Race' in Twentieth-Century America." *Journal of American History* 83 (1996): 44–69.

Paul, Diane B. "Dobzhansky in the Nature Nurture Debate." In *The Evolution of Theodosius Dobzhansky,* edited by Mark B. Adams, 219–232. Princeton: Princeton University Press, 1994.

———. *The Politics of Heredity: Essays on Eugenics, Biomedicine, and the Nature-Nurture Debate.* Albany: State University of New York Press, 1998.

Pauly, Philip J. "Eugenics Industry—Growth or Restructuring?" *Journal of the History of Biology* 26 (1993): 131–145.

Pearson, Roger. "Pan-Nordicism as a Modern Policy." *Northern World* 3, no. 5 (1959): 4–12.

———. "Evolution and the Modern State." *The European* 8 (April 1958): 21–24.

———. "Sir Arthur Keith and Evolution." *Northern World* 2, no. 1 (1957): 4–7.

Perelman, Chaim, and Lucie Olbrechts-Tyteca. *The New Rhetoric: A Treatise on Argumentation.* South Bend, IN: University of Notre Dame Press, 1969.

Perez, Leander H. "Civil Rights—1959." U.S. Senate, Committee on the Judiciary, Subcommittee on Constitutional Rights (1959), 783–809.

Piliawsky, Monte. *Exit 13: Oppression and Racism in Academia.* Boston: South End Press, 1982.

Pittman, R. Carter. "All Men Are Not Equal." *Alabama Lawyer* 17 (1956): 252–263.

———. "Equality versus Liberty: The Eternal Conflict." *ABA Journal* 46 (1960): 873–880.

———. "Liberty or Equality, Americanism or Marxism, Which Shall It Be?" *Alabama Lawyer* 15 (1954): 342–360.

Polsgrove, Carole. *Divided Minds: Intellectuals and the Civil Rights Movement.* New York: Norton, 2001.

Popham, John H. "Organized Resistance to Racial Laws Grows." *New York Times,* 2 December 1956, E9.

Price, Barbara J., and Edith R. Sanders. "Letter to the Editor." *New York Times,* 30 October 1962, 34.

Price, David H. *Threatening Anthropology: McCarthyism and the FBI's Surveillance of Activist Anthropologists.* Durham: Duke University Press, 2004.

Proctor, Robert N. *Racial Hygiene: Medicine under the Nazis.* Cambridge: Harvard University Press, 1988.

Putnam, Carleton. "Evolution and Race: New Evidence." *The Citizen* 6 (1962): 7–10.

———. *High Journey: A Decade in the Pilgrimage of an Air Line Pioneer.* New York: Scribner's, 1945.

———. "Letter to the Editor." *Science* 142 (1963): 1419.

———. *Race and Reality: A Search for Solutions.* Washington, DC: Public Affairs Press, 1967.

———. *Race and Reason: A Yankee View.* Washington, DC: Public Affairs Press, 1961.

———. "A Reply to Dwight Ingle." *Mankind Quarterly* 4 (1963): 43–48.

———. *The Road to Reversal.* New York: National Putnam Letters Committee, 1962.

———. "'Scientific' Racism—A Reply." *New Republic* 148 (23 February 1963): 29–31.

———. *Theodore Roosevelt: The Formative Years, 1858–1886.* New York: Scribner's, 1958.

———. "These Are the Guilty." *The Citizen* 7 (March 1963): 36–51.

———. "This Is the Problem!" *The Citizen* 6 (November 1961): 6–35.

———. *Three New Letters on Science and Race.* Washington, DC: National Putnam Letters Committee, 1964.

Puzzo, Dante A. "Racism and the Western Tradition." *Journal of the History of Ideas* 25 (1964): 579–586.

Regal, Brian. *Henry Fairfield Osborn: Race and the Search for the Origins of Man.* Burlington, VT: Ashgate, 2002.

Reuter, E. B. "Review of *Cult of Equality.*" *American Journal of Sociology* 51 (1946): 348–349.

———. "Southern Scholars and Race Relations." *Phylon* 7 (1946): 221–235.

Richards, Graham. *"Race," Racism, and Psychology: Towards a Reflexive History.* London: Routledge, 1997.

———. "Reconceptualizing the History of Race Psychology: Thomas Russell Garth (1872–1939) and How He Changed His Mind." *Journal of the History of the Behavioral Sciences* 34 (1998): 15–32.

Ripley, William Z. *The Races of Europe: A Sociological Study.* New York: Appleton and Company, 1899.

Roberts, Morley. *Biopolitics: An Essay in the Physiology, Pathology, and Politics of the Social and Somatic Organism.* London: Dent, 1937.

———. *Warfare in the Human Body: Essays on Method, Malignity, Repair, and Allied Subjects.* London: Eveleigh Nash, 1920.

Robertson, Wilmot. *The Dispossessed Majority.* Cape Canaveral: Howard Allen Press, 1981.

Rockwell, George Lincoln. "The U.S. Right Wing Picture." *Rockwell Report,* no. 7 (15 January 1962): 2–5.

Roder, Wolf. "Race." *International Journal of African Historical Studies* 8 (1975): 518–522.

Root, E. Merrill. *Collectivism on the Campus: The Battle for the Mind in American Colleges.* New York: Devin-Adair, 1955.

Ross, Ralph, and Ernest van den Haag. *The Fabric of Society.* New York: Harcourt, Brace, and Company, 1957.

Rossianov, Kirill O. "Editing Nature: Joseph Stalin and the 'New' Soviet Biology." *Isis* 84 (1993): 728–754

Rushton, J. Philippe. "The Equalitarian Dogma Revisited." *Intelligence* 19 (1994): 263–280.

———. "Political Correctness and the Study of Racial Differences." *Journal of Social Distress and the Homeless* 5 (1996): 213–229.

———. *Race, Evolution and Behavior: A Life History Perspective.* New Brunswick, NJ: Transaction, 1995.

———. "Review Essay." *Society* 34 (1997): 78–82.

Russell, Richard B. "Southern Manifesto." In *Burden of Race: A Documentary History of Negro-White Relations in America,* edited by Gilbert Osofsky, 491–494. New York: Harper and Row, 1967.

Samelson, Franz. "From 'Race Psychology' to 'Studies in Prejudice': Some Observations on the Thematic Reversal in Social Psychology." *Journal of the History of the Behavioral Sciences* 14 (1978): 265–278.

Sarti, Roland. "Review of *Italian Fascism and Developmental Dictatorship.*" *American Historical Review* 86 (1981): 169.

Scales-Trent, Judy. "Racial Purity Laws in the United States and Nazi Germany: The Targeting Process." *Human Rights Quarterly* 23 (2001): 259–307.

Schneider, Alison. "Florida State Professor Criticized for His Laudatory Foreword to David Duke's Book." *Chronicle of Higher Education* 45, no. 33 (23 April 1999): A24.

Schneider, Louis. "Race, Reason, and Rubbish Again." *Phylon* 29 (1962): 149–155.

Schrecker, Ellen W. *No Ivory Tower: McCarthyism and the Universities.* New York: Oxford University Press, 1986.

Scott, Daryl M. *Contempt and Pity: Social Policy and the Image of the Damaged Black Psyche, 1880–1996.* Chapel Hill: University of North Carolina Press, 1997.

Selby, Gary S. "Mocking the Sacred: Frederick Douglass's 'Slaveholder's Sermon' and the Antebellum Debate over Religion and Slavery." *Quarterly Journal of Speech* 88 (2002): 326–341.

Sherman, Richard B. "'The Last Stand': The Fight for Racial Integrity in Virginia in the 1920s." *Journal of Southern History* 54 (1988): 69–92.

Shermer, Michael, and Alex Grobman. *Denying History: Who Says the Holocaust Never Happened and Why Do They Say It?* Berkeley: University of California Press, 2000.

Shipman, Pat. *The Evolution of Racism.* New York: Simon and Schuster, 1994.

Shipp, E. R. "Prof. Gene Weltfish Dead at 78; Was Target of Anti-Red Drives." *New York Times,* 5 August 1980, B10.

Shoben, Edward Joseph. "Review of *Race and Modern Science.*" *Personnel and Guidance Journal* 47 (1969): 487–489.

Shockley, William B. "Human Quality Problems and Research Taboos" (1969). Reprinted in *Shockley on Eugenics and Race,* edited by Roger Pearson, 130–167. Washington, DC: Scott Townsend, 1992.

———. "Population Control or Eugenics" (1965). Reprinted in *Shockley on Eugenics and Race,* edited by Roger Pearson, 51–83. Washington, DC: Scott Townsend, 1992.

Shuey, Audrey. *The Testing of Negro Intelligence.* Lynchburg, VA: J. P. Bell, 1958.

Silverman, Rachel. "The Blood Group 'Fad' in Post-War Racial Anthropology." *Kroeber Anthropological Society Papers* 84 (2000): 11–27.

Simmons, Donald C. "'Scientific' Racism." *New Republic* 148 (5 January 1963): 9–10.

———. "A Yankee Looks at the Races." *New Republic* 147 (10 September 1962): 23–24.

Simmons, William J. "The Truth about Racial Differences." *The Citizen* 7 (October 1962): 7–8.

Simpson, George Gaylord. "The Origins of Races." *Perspectives in Biology and Medicine* 6 (1963): 268–272.

Škerlj, Božo "The Mankind Quarterly." *Man* 60 (1960): 172–173.

Skidelsky, Robert. *Oswald Mosely.* New York: Holt, Rhinehart, and Winston, 1975.

Smedley, Audrey. *Race in North America: Origin and Evolution of a Worldview.* 2d ed. Boulder, CO: Westview Press, 1999.

Smith, Charles. "Eugenics: Sterilization of Defectives and Discrimination in Immigration." *Truth Seeker* 84 (November 1957): 173.

———. "Jews Block Racist Forum." *Truth Seeker* 86 (1959): 31.

———. "Love Mongers and Love Sheets." *Truth Seeker* 86 (March 1959): 40.

———. "A Misdirected Letter." *Truth Seeker* 84 (April 1957): 62.

———. "Northmen Meet at Detmold." *Truth Seeker* 86 (September 1959): 134–135.

———. *Sensism: The Philosophy of the West.* 2 vols. New York: Truth Seeker, 1956.

———. "The Stars Battle the White Race." *Truth Seeker* 84 (1957): 36.

Smith, J. Douglas. "The Campaign for Racial Purity and the Erosion of Paternalism in Virginia, 1922–1930: 'Nominally White, Biologically Mixed, and Legally Negro.'" *Journal of Southern History* 68 (2002): 65–106.

Smith, John David. *An Old Creed for the New South: Proslavery Ideology and Historiography, 1865–1918.* Westport, CT: Greenwood Press, 1985.

Southern, David W. *Gunnar Myrdal and Black-White Relations: The Use and Abuse of* An American Dilemma, *1944–1969.* Baton Rouge: Louisiana State University Press, 1987.

Spiro, Jonathan P. "Nordic vs. Anti-Nordic: The Galton Society and the American Anthropological Association." *Patterns of Prejudice* 36 (2002): 35–48.

———. "Patrician Racist: The Evolution of Madison Grant." Ph.D. diss., University of California–Berkeley, 2000.

Stein, Gordon. "Charles Lee Smith (1887–1964)." *American Rationalist* 29 (1984): 11–13.

Stein, Judith. *The World of Marcus Garvey: Race and Class in Modern Society.* Baton Rouge: Louisiana State University Press, 1986.

Stepan, Nancy Leys. *The Idea of Race in Science: Great Britain, 1800–1960.* Hamden: Archon, 1982.

———. "'Nature's Pruning Hook': War, Race, and Evolution." In *The Political Culture of Modern Britain,* edited by J. M. W. Bean, 129–148. London: Hamish Hamilton, 1987.

Stocking, George W. *Race, Culture, and Evolution: Essays in the History of Anthropology.* Chicago: University of Chicago Press, 1968.

Stoddard, Theodore Lothrop. "The French Revolution in San Domingo." Ph.D. diss., Harvard University, 1914.

Strayer, George D. *Report of a Survey of the Public Schools of the District of Columbia Conducted under the Auspices of the Chairmen of the Subcommittees on District of Columbia Appropriations of the Respective Appropriations Committees of the Senate and House of Representatives.* Washington, DC: Government Printing Office, 1949.

Stuckert, Robert P., and Irwin D. Rinder. "The Negro in the Social Science Literature." *Phylon* 23 (1962): 111–127.

Sugrue, Thomas J. "Crabgrass-Roots Politics: Race, Rights, and the Reaction against Liberalism in the Urban North, 1940–1964." *Journal of American History* 82 (1995): 551–578.

Swan, Donald A. "Juan Comas on 'Scientific Racism Again?': A Scientific Analysis." *Mankind Quarterly* 2 (1962): 231–245.

———. "Likes Fascism." *Expose,* no. 34 (September 1954): 4.

Swenson, Thor [pseudonym]. "The Inherited Natures of Negroes and Whites Compared." *Truth Seeker* 86 (1959): 119–120.

———. "The Inherited Natures of Negroes and Whites Compared II." *Truth Seeker* 86 (1959): 137–139.

———. "The Inherited Natures of Negroes and Whites Compared III." *Truth Seeker* 86 (1959): 172–175.

———. "The Inherited Natures of Negroes and Whites Compared IV." *Truth Seeker* 86 (1959): 188–189.

———. "The Inherited Natures of Negroes and Whites Compared V." *Truth Seeker* 86 (1959): 91–92.

———. "Professor Hans F.K. Günther: Eminent European Raciologist." *Truth Seeker* 86 (1959): 167–169.

———. "The Works of Professor Hans F.K. Günther." *Northern World* 5, no. 2 (1961): 7–10.

Tannenhaus, Sam. *Whittaker Chambers: A Biography.* New York: Modern Library, 1998.

Tansill, Charles C. *Back Door to War.* Chicago: Henry Regnery, 1952.

Tauber, Kurt P. *Beyond Eagle and Swastika: German Nationalism since 1945.* Vol. 1. Middletown, CT: Wesleyan University Press, 1967.

Taylor, Carol M. "W. E. B. Du Bois's Challenge to Scientific Racism." *Journal of Black Studies* 11 (1981): 449–460.

Taylor, Charles Alan. *Defining Science: A Rhetoric of Demarcation.* Madison: University of Wisconsin Press, 1996.

Thomas, William B. "Black Intellectuals, Intelligence Testing in the 1930s, and the Sociology of Knowledge." *Teachers College Record* 85 (1984): 475–501.

Thompson, H. Keith, and Henry Strutz. *Doenitz at Nuremburg: A Reappraisal, War Crimes and the Military Professional.* New York: Amber Publishing, 1976.

Thurtle, Philip. "Harnessing Heredity in Gilded Age America: Middle Class Mores and Industrial Breeding in a Cultural Context." *Journal of the History of Biology* 35 (2002): 43–78.

Tolbert, Emory. "Outpost Garveyism and the UNIA Rank and File." *Journal of Black Studies* 5 (1975): 233–253.

Tucker, William H. "A Closer Look at the Pioneer Fund: A Response to Rushton." *Albany Law Review* 66 (2003): 1145–1159.

———. *The Funding of Scientific Racism: Wickliffe Draper and the Pioneer Fund.* Urbana: University of Illinois Press, 2002.

———. *The Science and Politics of Racial Research.* Urbana: University of Illinois Press, 1994.

Tumin, Melvin. *Race and Intelligence: An Evaluation.* New York: Anti-Defamation League of B'nai B'rith, 1963.

Tushnet, Mark V. *Making Civil Rights Law: Thurgood Marshall and the Supreme Court, 1936–1961.* New York: Oxford University Press, 1994.

Urban, Wayne J. "The Black Scholar and Intelligence Testing: The Case of Horace Mann Bond." *Journal of the History of the Behavioral Sciences* 25 (1989): 323–334.

———. *Black Scholar: Horace Mann Bond, 1904–1972.* Athens: University of Georgia Press, 1992.

van den Haag, Ernest. *Education as an Industry.* New York: Augustus M. Kelley, 1956.

———. "An Open Letter to Sidney Hook." *Partisan Review* 17 (1950): 225–232.

———. *Passion and Constraint.* New York: Stein and Day, 1963.

———. "Social Science Testimony in the Desegregation Cases—A Reply to Professor Kenneth Clark." *Villanova Law Review* 6 (1960): 69–70.

Washburn, Sherwood. "The Study of Race." *American Anthropologist* 65 (1963): 521–531.

Wayne, Michael. "An Old South Morality Play: Reconsidering the Social Underpinnings of the Proslavery Ideology." *Journal of American History* 77 (1990): 838–863.

Webb, Clive. "Charles Bloch: Jewish White Supremacist." *Georgia Historical Quarterly* 83 (1999): 267–292.

Weindling, Paul. "Dissecting German Social Darwinism: Historicizing the Biology of the Organic State." *Science in Context* 11 (1998): 619–637.

———. "Fascism and Population in European Perspective." *Population and Development Review* 14 (1988): 102–121.

Weingart, Peter. "Science Abused? Challenging a Legend." *Science in Context* 6 (1993): 555–567.

Welke, Barbara Y. "When All the Women Were White, and All the Blacks Were Men: Gender, Class, and Race, and the Road to *Plessy,* 1855–1914." *Law and History Review* 13 (1995): 261–316.

Weyl, Nathaniel. *The Negro in American Civilization.* Washington, DC: Public Affairs Press, 1960.

———. *Treason: The Story of Disloyalty and Betrayal in American History.* Washington, DC: Public Affairs Press, 1960.

Weyl, Nathaniel, and Stefan Possony. *The Geography of Intellect.* Chicago: Regnery, 1963.

Whitney, Glayde. "A Contextual History of Behavior Genetics." In *Developmental Behavior Genetics: Neural, Biometrical, and Evolutionary Approaches,* edited by Martin E. Hahn, John K. Hewitt, Norman D. Henderson, and Robert Benno, 7–24. New York: Oxford University Press, 1990.

———. "Foreword." In David Duke, *My Awakening: A Path to Racial Understanding.* Covington, LA: Free Speech Press, 1998.

———. "Genetics and Human Behavior." In *Encyclopedia of Bioethics,* edited by Warren T. Reich, vol. 2, 946–954. New York: Simon and Schuster, 1995.

———. "Ideology and Censorship in Behavior Genetics." *Mankind Quarterly* 35 (1995): 327–342.

———. "Ideology Contra-Science." *Occidental Quarterly* 1, no. 2 (2001).

———. "On Possible Genetic Bases of Race Differences in Criminality." *Crime in Biological, Social, and Moral Contexts,* edited by Lee Ellis and Harry Hoffman, 134–149. New York: Praeger, 1990.

———. "On the Races of Man." *Mankind Quarterly* 39 (1999): 319–335.

———. "Races Do Not Exist—So Study Them!" *Mankind Quarterly* 41 (2000): 119–127.

———. "Raymond B. Cattell and the Fourth Inquisition." *Mankind Quarterly* 38 (1997): 99–125.

———. "Subversion of Science: How Psychology Lost Darwin." *Journal of Historical Review* 21 (March/April 2002): 20–30.

Wilhoit, Francis M. *The Politics of Massive Resistance.* New York: George Braziller, 1973.

Willey, Malcolm M. "Review of *Race and National Solidarity.*" *American Journal of Sociology* 30 (1924): 97–98.

Williams, Vernon J. *Rethinking Race: Franz Boas and His Contemporaries.* Lexington: University of Kentucky Press, 1996.

Williamson, Joel. *The Crucible of Race: Black-White Relations in the American South since Emancipation.* New York: Oxford University Press, 1984.

Winston, Andrew S. "The Context of Correctness: A Comment on Rushton." *Journal of Social Distress and the Homeless* 5 (1996): 231–249.

————. "Science in the Service of the Far Right: Henry E. Garrett, the IAAEE, and the Liberty Lobby." *Journal of Social Issues* 54 (1998): 179–210.

Winston, Andrew S., and Michael Peters. "On the Presentation and Interpretation of International Homicide Data." *Psychological Reports* 86 (2000): 865–871.

Wirth, Louis. "Comment." *American Journal of Sociology* 54 (1949): 399–400.

Wittmer, Felix. *Conquest of the American Mind: Comments on Collectivism in Education*. Boston: Meador, 1956.

Wolfe, A. B. "Review of *Race and National Solidarity*." *Journal of Philosophy* 21 (1924): 444–445.

Wolpoff, Milford, and Rachel Caspari. *Race and Human Evolution: A Fatal Attraction*. New York: Simon and Schuster, 1997.

Woods, Frederick Adams. "Review of *The Passing of the Great Race*." *Science* 48 (1918): 419–420.

Zack, Naomi. *Bachelors of Science: Seventeenth-Century Identity, Then and Now*. Philadelphia: Temple University Press, 1996.

Zarefsky, David. "Conspiracy Arguments in the Lincoln-Douglas Debates." *Journal of the American Forensic Association* 21 (1984): 63–75.

Index

About the Author

John P. Jackson Jr. is Assistant Professor of Communication at the University of Colorado. He is also the author of *Social Scientists for Social Justice: Making the Case against Segregation* and editor of *Science, Race, and Ethnicity: Readings from Isis and Osiris.*